A REFERENCE GUIDE TO AMERICAN
Science Fiction Films

Printed in the United States of America

ISBN 0-89917-268-7

Reproduced by photo offset from typeset manuscript.
For information, write T.I.S. Publications Division, P.O. Box 1998,
Bloomington, Indiana 47402.

A REFERENCE GUIDE TO AMERICAN Science Fiction Films

Volume 1

A.W. STRICKLAND
FORREST J ACKERMAN

To Jane, with all my love,

Albert

TABLE OF CONTENTS

THE SCIENTIFILM STORY

FORREST J ACKERMAN

The first known list of science fiction films was compiled and published in 1932 in the first issue of The American Amateur Science Fiction magazine, THE TIME TRAVELLER.

Perhaps, had the titles been compiled by an older person, say someone 50 at the time who had been interested in science fiction films since age 20, the result would have resembled what you now hold in your hands, except the resumes of the plots would have resulted from the memories--and perhaps records-- of one single dedicated individual.

As it was, at age 15, with only 10 years of consciously remembered fantasy films behind me, I listed every such motion picture I had seen or heard of, making no distinction between a supernatural horror movie like DRACULA and a genuine futuristic film like METROPOLIS or a prehistoric picture like THE LOST WORLD.

En passant, an interesting historical note: at the First World Science Fiction Convention, New York, July 1939, the two films chosen for revival were Lang's vision of the future and Doyle's classic of the past. A hundred years ahead--a million years back!

The list of known films of the fantastic (worldwide) now totals in the neighborhood (and it's a pretty incredible neighborhood) of 25,000! Researchers such as Walter W. Lee, Jr., Eldon K. Everett, Luis Gasca of Spain, Jurgen Menningen of Germany, Hajime Ishida of Japan, Jean-Claude Romer of France, Hector Raul Pessina of Argentina and the scholar with whom I have collaborated on this book have added inestimably to the volume of international knowledge about "imagi-movies" since my primitive pioneering 50 years ago.

And the rate of production at the presentime! Often I pick up a daily paper, turn to the movie ads--and feel sorry for those unenlightened mundanes who want to go to a show to see a western or a detective story or a love story or a musical and all they see advertised is THE EMPIRE STRIKES BACK, WITHOUT WARNING, 2001 (revival), CE3K (new version), FINAL COUNTDOWN, BATTLE BEYOND THE STARS and maybe a month-long marathon of oldies-but-goodies from WOMAN IN THE MOON through CREATURE FROM THE BLACK LAGOON to DARK STAR.

I'm frank to confess I thought I knew a lot about the scientifilms prior to 1920, such few as I thought there were, but along comes Al Strickland with 20,000 concentrated hours of research to his credit during the 3 years preceeding the publication of the four volumes of which this is the first, and I realize I only was acquainted with the tip of the proverbial iceberg!

I didn't know about the silent scientifilm that was in 3-D!

I knew of Edison's TRIP TO MARS, but nothing of its plot!

I hadn't realized how many early silents had concerned themselves with artificial diamonds, super explosives, and arresting age.

I--but, if the old expert can be excited practically 60 years after seeing his first fantasy film (for the record: ONE GLORIOUS DAY) how much more interesting and revelatory the following pages must prove for YOU! To keep you from them any longer would be cruelty of DeSadean Proportions!

Besides . . . I'm anxious to go see the latest scientifilm, to add it to Volume 5: 1980-2000.

Forrest J Ackerman

Forrest J Ackerman

PREFACE

The creation of moving pictures appears to have been the coalescing of several unique and rather isolated scientific discoveries and inventions. This coalescence was catalyzed by the volatile personalities of the men who perfected the extraordinary devices. Even when the motion picture industry finally came into existence, few if any of the principles envisioned the phenomenal growth which has taken place during the past 96 years.

James Burke in his marvelous book, CONNECTIONS, provides a sterling account of the evolution of moving pictures, although at times it reads like a scenario from a first rate science fiction film. From 1824 to 1893 a series of events took place which resulted in the merging of efforts between George Eastman and Thomas Edison. Out of this came the birth of Edison's Kinetoscope: the American film industry was born on January 7, 1894 with his film KINETOSCOPIC RECORD OF A SNEEZE. Shortly afterward, on April 14, 1894, the first "movie theater" was created, The Holland Brothers' Kinetoscope Parlor.

At about the same time, France, England, and Germany were developing similar motion picture systems. Film makers sprang up almost overnight in these countries. One of the foremost of these was George Melies who prepared many early science fiction films. In fact, his A TRIP TO THE MOON (1902) set the criteria for future SF efforts, clearly identifying the necessary attributes for an excellent science fiction production--good story, creative special effects, precise cinematography, and, most important, a generous supply of imagination.

The next decade saw SF film develop into its own distinct genre as many of the noteworthy science fiction literary works began to appear on the silver screen. This same period also saw the emergence of the "serial," a film offering which became the rage of the time. This immense popularity resulted in making the early serial stars, such as Pearl White, almost immortal, and certainly very rich and famous.

Meanwhile, many of the producers who had helped establish the film industry began to fade as new conglomerates formed from their remnants. The lessons learned by these masters continued to be treasured, however, and the legacy they left contributed to the new pioneers' efforts, as each production resulted in a higher quality product for the audience.

As the 1920's arrived, a plethora of SF-A (science fiction-adventure) films and serials captured the interest of movie fans. In addition, since the end of World War I, many of the foreign films which had been unable to find their way into the American cinema during these troubled years began to have impacts on our industry. Their influence gave rise to a new dedication toward excellence and rekindled a sense of exploration as new film techniques were experimented.

By the end of this decade, color film productions and the addition of sound to films were heralding the beginning of a new era for SF films: the "talkies" had arrived!

LIST OF ILLUSTRATIONS

EXPLANATION KEY AND ABBREVIATIONS

In designing the format for this reference guide we considered features that would facilitate researchers and readers in locating detailed information on the films. The book is arranged in sections, each representing one decade (with the exception of the first section which contains only one film from the period prior to 1900). At the end of each decade there are two lists. The first summarizes the SF films of that period by classification; the second, provides a list of SF films arranged by the company releasing the film. Overall summary lists for the period 1897-1929 are located in the back of the book.

To aid in the interpretation of each film as listed in the book, the following example and explanations are given.

(A) 1917

(B) THE DINOSAUR AND THE MISSING LINK

(C) Release: 1917, Edison Film Company
(D) Description: Silent, 850 feet
(E) Classification: SF-C
(F) References: No. 1, p. 221; No. 14, p. 129; No. 46, p. 23; No. 50, p. 103; CNF, 1971, etc.

(A) 1917

This indicates the year in which the film was released. In some cases the film may have been completed in the late months of the previous year, but not released to the public until the next year. In an effort to be consistent, the year in which the film was first publicly shown is the date that determined its placement in the book.

(B) THE DINOSAUR AND THE MISSING LINK

The title of the film (in the cases of those movies released under multiple titles, the one recognized by the United States copyright records, or where the title had not been copyrighted, the one most used by the releasing company) is shown here.

(C) Release: 1917, Edison Film Company

This is the date released and the releasing company's name. This date was determined by the best data available, and the releasing company by the name used on the copyright information where available.

(D) Description: Silent, 850 feet

Whenever possible, the film's length in feet is listed. However, some features failed to record this data and had unfortunately been destroyed. In these cases, there was simply no way to provide this information. If the film appeared in color, this information would be listed here. Most movies from this period, 1897-1929, were black and white only; this was not noted since we felt only the exceptions, that is color, would be of interest.

(E) Classification: SF-C

In order for a film to be placed in the general classification schema of science fiction prior to being placed in a sub-classification (i.e., SF, SF-C, SF-A, SF-H, SF-F) the film must satisfy at least one of the following conditions:

1 attempt to employ the use of scientific laws, principles, or limits to explore the vast unknown areas of science, psychology, or sociology;
2 attempt to expand known technology either forward or backward in time, carefully extrapolating from the known to the unknown;
3 attempt to utilize technology in an entirely unique or unusual manner surrounded by a present-day setting.

Additionally, before a film may be placed in a sub-classification (i.e., SF, SF-A, SF-C, SF-F, SF-H) it must be examined for intent. Obviously, in attempting to place films in sub-classifications there are bound to be borderline cases. Care has been taken to be consistent in these borderline areas. In this way, the films with similar attributes remain in the same sub-class.

Science Fiction

Films within this category have satisfied at least one of the afore mentioned conditions. Moreover, the emphasis of films has been more than a mere attempt to employ (expand or utilize) one of the three criteria.

In the film TWENTY THOUSAND LEAGUES UNDER THE SEA (1916), there is a definite concern for scientific laws and limits, i.e., the submarine has finite propulsion power and a distinct limit to which it may submerge. It is this clear attempt to make the science as real as possible that differentiates films of this sub-class from other film classifications.

In the film DR. JEKYLL AND MR. HYDE (Paramount, 1920), John Barrymore scientifically explores the human mind and chemical processes to understand the mysterious creature within him.

In THE LOST WORLD (1925), the technology of man seems futile when pitted against the isolated prehistoric beasts of the film. The story by Sir Arthur Conan Doyle is treated as a careful scientific investigation into the prehistoric past of the earth.

Each of these films are examples of the characteristics needed in this sub-class. One common attribute is the exploration of science by scientific means coupled with a careful eye toward technological detail.

Science Fiction-Comedy

When the comedy aspect of the film becomes equal to or greater than the science fiction importance of the picture, the feature becomes a prime candidate for the sub-class of Science Fiction-Comedy (SF-C).

Many of the science fiction films from 1897 to 1929 are classified SF-C. The greatest percentage of these appeared prior to 1916, illustrating how the early film makers used comedy as a vehicle to transmit complex or futeristic views of science and technology.

A TRIP TO MARS (1910), produced by Thomas Edison, is the story of a professor who invents anti-gravity powers. These powers accidently combine and hurl the professor on a very humerous trip to the angry red planet. A TRIP TO MARS attempts to provide humerous entertainment for the viewer while exploring the realm of science through science fiction. Likewise, the feature THE MECHANICAL MAN (1915), released by Universal, produced an array of humerous predicaments through the creation of Professor Shultz's mechanical man.

An ultramodern house (for the early twenties) provides the setting for Buster Keaton's THE ELECTRIC HOUSE (1922). The film provides a witty view of one man's dilemmas in dealing with the technology of the future.

Each of the above films have clear science fiction and comedy elements. This set of attributes appear in each of the films contained in this sub-classification.

Science Fiction-Adventure

Films within this sub-classification emphasize the adventure or drama surrounding the principle players and is equal to, or greater than, the science fiction aspect of the story. Nevertheless, the SF emphasis, even though subdued, must be of significant importance to the film's continuity and realism.

Many of the features and serials released between 1914 and 1929 used the courageous scientific detective Craig Kennedy as the main character: THE EXPLOITS OF ELAINE (1914), THE NEW EXPLOITS OF ELAINE (1915), THE ROMANCE OF ELAINE (1915). These capitalized on Craig Kennedy's use of scientific devices to thrill audiences during each of their spine-tingling episodes.

The period from 1897 to 1929 is loaded with SF-A films which provided thousands of exciting viewing hours for cinema fans. Often the science and/or technologically advanced devices were used to provide an escape from certain perils, discarding the device afterwards until another precarious situation arose.

Science Fiction-Fantasy

There were few American science fiction-fantasy (SF-F) films between 1897 and 1929, but the ones which emerged were easily identifiable. THE GHOST OF SLUMBER MOUNTAIN (1919) is a clear example with the hero falling asleep and having a nightmare about a ghost who possesses a telescopic device allowing views of the past.

In the film YOUNG DIANA, Diana revisits her youth via the mysterious mystical powers of Dr. Demitrius. The doctor's powers appear to be without scientific basis and go unexplained throughout the entire movie.

These features serve only as examples of films possessing the attributes common to all the members of the SF-F category.

The members of the sub-classification science fiction-fantasy (SF-F) have attributes which illustrate an attempt toward scientific laws, principles and limits, but their efforts are inconsistent and often times lack detail. Moreover, the technology which is introduced seems to perform almost magical tasks which frequently go unexplained. Additionally, some SF-F films present scientific events through dreamlike sequences. Films containing any of the above attributes are classified as SF-F films.

Science Fiction-Horror

Films within this sub-class share attributes which are designed to scare or shock the viewer. These films share a relationship between the science fiction content and horror content producing a chilling effect. Therefore, the film's intent must be carefully examined: Was it the film's primary intent to scare or horrify members of the audience? An affirmative answer to this question would place the film among the other members of the classification of science fiction-horror (SF-H) films.

The first American science fiction-horror film did not appear until 1915, LIFE WITHOUT SOUL. It was an attempt to produce Mary Shelly's FRANKENSTEIN into a SF-H film. The screenplay differed considerably from the traditional FRANKENSTEIN story. This was clearly an attempt by the producers to terrify the audience. The monster--without a soul--begins to murder members of the Frankenstein household, and in the final scene Dr. Frankenstein kills his creature and vows never to experiment with the creation of life again.

In A BLIND BARGAIN (1922), Lon Chaney sends chills up the audience's spine as he portrays a hunchback (a role he would immortalize a year later as Quasimoto (?) in THE HUNCHBACK OF NOTRE DAME) created during a transplantation experiment to create greater longevity for man. The contrast between A BLIND BARGAIN and THE HUNCHBACK OF NOTRE DAME serves as a clear example of gender classification. A BLIND BARGAIN clearly involves a scientific experiment gone awry as the monster seeks vengeance on its creator, resulting in a distinct direction toward horror. On the other hand, THE HUNCHBACK OF NOTRE DAME involves a similar creature creating even more horrifying moments, but the creature and the film do not have any scientific basis. Therefore, it is classified as a horror film and not placed in the SF-H category.

(F) References: No. 1, p. 221; No. 14, p. 129; No. 46, etc...

There are two types of references, those with number designations (i.e., No. 1, No. 39, No. 52, etc., etc.) and those with a letter abbreviation (i.e., FAM, LC, MPN, etc., etc.). A list of the number references may be found in the reference section in the rear of this volume; the letter abbreviations key is found in the section entitled Bibliography.

ACKNOWLEDGEMENTS

To my wife, Jane, who has spent countless hours helping with research, typing, filing, and editing so that this effort could be published;

To my children, Mary Jane, Wes, Molly Anne, Kate, and Tom, each of whom has, in some way, contributed to this effort;

To Walt Lee for his superior reference work, A REFERENCE GUIDE TO FANTASTIC FILMS, which pioneered the way;

To Forrest J Ackerman for the use of his archives, still files, friendship, and vast knowledge and writing ability in co-authoring this reference material;

To Anthony Slide and Carol Cullens and the entire library staff of the Margaret Herrick Library at The Academy of Motion Picture Arts and Sciences for their invaluable aid in the research;

To Steve Sowards and Jan Mauritson of the Indiana University Microforms Department for their tireless efforts, which can never be measured;

To the other libraries--University of California, Los Angeles; University of Southern California; New York Public Library, Lincoln Center Branch; Monroe County Public Library; Indiana University Graduate Library; Lilly Library; The California Institute of Technology--that provided extensive research aid and reference materials;

And, to Shari Cook, Kathy O'Brien, and Debbie Roll, students at Indiana University who, over the years involved in this work, provided their assistance;

To all these people and institutions, as well as the authors of the fine literary works listed in the bibliography and reference list and the many studios and museums, among them Universal Studios, Twentieth Century, and the Metropolitan Museum of Modern Art, without whose guiding works this task would have been impossible, I formally acknowledge my gratitude and debt of thanks.

1897–1909

AN OVERVIEW OF 1897-1909

From the beginning of motion pictures it has generally been conceded that Thomas Alva Edison was the father of the industry and is credited with creating the first motion picture studio called Black Maria (1894) located in West Orange, New Jersey. These early film productions were never intended for public showing, but to be purchased for private home viewing. Many of the features produced by Edison were for educational and informational purposes and not for amusement.

Gradually, however, entertainment became the dominant force in Edison's film studio. By 1900 he had employed a young man, Edwin S. Porter, who, by 1909, was responsible for the entire New Jersey film production facility. Porter is responsible for two science fiction films during the period from 1897 to 1909: *Fun in the Butcher Shop* (1901) and *Dog Factory* (1904). The third science fiction effort produced by Edison's company was *The Wonderful Electro-Magnet* (1909). During this same period (1897-1909) the Thomas Edison Film Company produced in excess of 2175 movies. That is an average of nearly three films a week for 15 years . . . certainly a remarkable achievement.

While at the Edison studio, Edwin Porter produced an epic entitled *The Great Train Robbery* (1903). This is a classic film utilizing some camera techniques which have proved very valuable in some outstanding science fiction films. Porter also gave D. W. Griffith his first acting assignment, a career start that led Griffith toward becoming one of the most outstanding directors in movie history.

In 1897 a young energetic German named Sigmund "Pop" Lubin established Lubin Film Company which, despite its great financial troubles, proved to be as prolific as Edison in turning out films. During the time from 1897 to 1909 Lubin produced six science fiction films, most of which were comedies. All six occurred between 1908 and 1909 during a period when Lubin had assembled a large company of players to regularly perform in his features. The result was a film every two days, including weekends.

About the same time Lubin was getting started on a rooftop in Philadelphia, J. Stuart Blackton and Albert E. Smith were establishing a company called Vitagraph Film Company of America. Vitagraph became one of the most powerful film companies during the next two decades, and during a period from 1897 to 1909 contributed seven science fiction films—more than any other film company of the time. Additionally, they produced more films than the Edison Company even though they had started in the business several years later. Part of the reason for their great success was their quick establishment of a group of actors that far exceeded the quality and efforts of the rival film production studios. As Anthony Slide in his *Early American Cinema* (1970) stated, "The Vitagraph Company might justifiably be labeled the M-G-M of the early American cinema" (p. 26).

At the same time Vitagraph was getting their cameras rolling (1897), another company was being established, The American Mutoscope and Biograph Company. (They had absorbed the American Mutoscope Company which was established two years earlier.) This new company soon became the second leading producer of motion picture films in America.

Biograph gave us five features in the science fiction category from 1897 to 1909. Moreover, they contributed the first science fiction entry in this reference book, *The Sausage Machine* (1897).

George Kleine, Samuel Long, and Frank Marion, with a cash investment of $600, established the Kalem Film Company in 1905. This studio released only one science fiction film from 1897-1909, *Nature Fakirs* (1907). This was probably because they were busy producing epic masterpieces: "Of all early American films, some of the most beautiful to look at are those of the Kalem Company. Everything about them is so natural, so easy on the eye." (Slide, 1970, p. 47).

While Edison, Kalem and Vitagraph used the Edison kinescope, Biograph used a modified version called the mutoscope. The difference in projection devices meant that the films of these various groups were not interchangeable.

By 1907 other film companies had sprung into existence. And in 1908, the Gaumont Company, the Essanay Company, Pathe, and the Selig Polyscope Company, in addition to all the previously mentioned (excluding Biograph), went together and formed the Motion Picture Patents Company. Each of the member companies recognized Edison as the creator of motion pictures and agreed only to produce films under his authorization. They further agreed to pay a royalty fee to Edison for each film produced. They also distributed their films only through licensed theater exhibitors (those who had paid a fee to Edison). This made the lives of the independent motion picture producers most difficult. Even if they produced films, they could seldom find theaters willing to show them. A suit against the Motion Picture Patents Company on behalf of the independent producers was not resolved until 1917—a long period for outside creative genius to go unnoticed.

During the period from 1897 to 1909 two independently produced science fiction entries were made and are included in this book: *The Hair Restorer* (1907) and *The Earthquake Alarm* (1909).

While the movie industry had come a long way since the first copyrighted film, *Kinetoscopic Record of a Sneeze* (January 7, 1884), feature films and their daring producers were still in the embryonic stages of development. Nevertheless, enough had happened during the first few years that a vision of a *golden era* to come would not be denied. During the next decade the movie industry moved to the forefront of American financial circles, becoming a significant force as its popularity grew and captured the imagination of a large segment of the population.

1897

THE SAUSAGE MACHINE

Release: 1897, American Mutoscope & Biograph Co.
Description: Silent, 425 feet
Classification: SF-C
References: No. 2, p. 85, 122; No. 5, p. 5; No. 20, p. xii; No. 50, p. 419; LC, H23772

Credits

Producer .... American Mutoscope & Biograph Co.

As in many of the early science fiction (SF) movies the focus of this film is on an unusual mechanical device which converts dogs into sausages. The opening scene is of a large factory with an enormous sign reading "Sausage Factory." Upon entering the factory, the viewer sees a large machine with wheels, belts, gears, input and output tubes. Into this *sausage machine* the workers (all males wearing derby-type hats) are placing small dogs in the input tubes. The machine then transforms these dogs into sausages, which are extracted on the opposite side by the workers.

This comedic film's success led to many remakes using similar machines in which dogs and other animals were gobbled up and regurgitated as sausages. One of the first sequels, *Making Sausages* (alternate title, *The End of all Things*, British Film catalog number 00074), appeared in 1898 and was produced by George A. Smith. The film not only boasted of being much longer than its predecessor (1250 feet compared to the earlier 425 feet), but introduced cats as well as dogs in the manufacturing of sausages.

1901

FUN IN THE BUTCHER SHOP

Release: 1901, Edison Film Company
Description: Silent, 65 feet
Classification: SF-C
References: No. 2, p. 37, 119; No. 5, p. 9; No. 50, p. 154; LC, H4089

Credits

Producer .... Edison Film Co.
Director .... Edwin S. Porter

This film appears to be a remake of an earlier film entitled *The Sausage Machine* (1897). Edison added little to the previous film's premise. The sequence of events take place on a vaudeville stage; the setting that of a butcher shop with a large device labeled *sausage machine* as the focus of attention. The action commences when a young lab technician carries a small dog to the butcher, who places it in the *sausage machine* converting the animal into sausage links. Soon dogs of various sizes and breeds are brought to the butcher and placed in the machine, producing an endless string of sausages. The process continues to the end of the film.

The *sausage machine* concept is the prime reason for this film being classified in a science fiction category, but admittedly it is less convincing than its predecessor.

The film was one of Edwin S. Porter's first films for the Edison Film Company, and began a career which established him as a pioneer film director. During the next two years Porter directed two more films, *The Life of An American Fireman* and *The Great Train Robbery*. The latter was the more famous of his endeavors.

1904

DOG FACTORY

Release: 1904, Edison Film Company
Description: Silent, 245 feet
Classification: SF-C
References: No. 2, p. 28, 118, p. 9; No. 50, p. 109; LC, H44668

Credits

Producer .... Edison Film Co.
Director .... Edwin S. Porter

The Dog Factory, a sequel to the Edison film *Fun in the Butcher Shop*, intended to assure the audience that the conversion of dogs into sausages was reversible. The movie features a much larger (piano size) device than its predecessor. The new machine's purpose is that of transforming sausages into dogs of various breeds. The setting depicts a butcher shop with a machine labeled *dog transformer* and large quantities of sausages hanging on pegs distributed about the shop. A customer enters the shop and points to one of the signs that reads *bull pups, spaniels*. The butcher goes to the wall, removes a string of sausages, and places them into the *dog transformer*. Soon a cocker spaniel puppy leaps out of the machine's other side. The customer exits, obviously a satisfied patron.

The *Dog Factory* displays acting continuity that comes with experience in film making, resulting in an obvious improvement over its forerunner. Additionally, Porter's previous experience in direction made the film a much better project.

1907

DR. SKINUM

Release: 1907, American Mutoscope & Biograph Co.
Description: Silent, 592 feet
Classification: SF-C
References: No. 16, p. 324-25; No. 50, p. 108

Credits

Producer .... American Mutoscope & Biograph Co.

Cast

Dr. Skinum .... Robert Harron

Dr. Skinum, a learned professor of physiology, dermatology, biology, and assorted other professional interests, has invented a marvelous device *chambre mysterieux* which can perform unbelievable physical transformations. Subjects enter the chamber with some physical defect and exit the chamber with a new altered form—the antithesis of their former selves. Dr. Skinum, using his newly created machine, converts tiny women into medium height women; tall women into medium height, and performs cosmetic alterations on numerous other women. He encounters one mishap, however, in converting a gargantuan woman into a new shapely creature. The machine is left running unattended and the woman is reduced to infant size. But, she is conveniently recycled through the device and reappears as a beautiful normal sized woman.

FORM NO. 1283

BULLETIN No. 115, December 14, 1907

DR. SKINUM

A Scintillant Satire of the Physical Culture Fad

LENGTH, 592 FEET. PRICE, 12 CENTS PER FOOT.

Dr. Skinum (1907) perfects an instant beauty machine.

At 12 cents per foot, for a total cost of $71.04, this film would be a real bargain at today's prices. Even so, it was a rather expensive undertaking for the period in which it was made. It is interesting to note that this concept is the opposite of a later feature in which a chemical changed the character from good to evil—*Dr. Jekyll and Mr. Hyde*. In this film, Dr. Skinum uses his machine for the betterment of his subjects (all of whom were female).

> "The promulgation of this fact [invention] draws to his office a most startling variety of monstrosities, all anxious to submit to his esoteric powers whereby they hope to become utopian as to face and figure . . . unquestionably an assured laughing hit."
>
> *The Moving Picture World*, Vol. 1, p. 670

HAIR RESTORER

Release: 1907, Williams, Brown, & Earle
Description: Silent, 610 feet
Classification: SF-C
References: No. 50, p. 179; MPW, Vol. 1, p. 393

Credits

Producer .... Williams, Brown, & Earle

A wealthy man and his maid are caught by his wife in a compromising situation. She attacks her husband and the maid with a club. The maid manages to make a narrow escape, but the husband is thrown to the floor by his wife where she begins to pull the hair from his chest and head, rendering him nearly bald.

After escaping from her fury, the husband seeks to restore his lost hair by purchasing a special hair restoring formula from the local *hair restorer*. Upon returning home he quickly proceeds to the bathroom and generously applies the secret elixir, resulting in a fine new crop of hair. His wife, upon discovering her husband's restored hair, renews her attack on him. A struggle ensues, resulting in the woman falling into the bathtub-filled hair restoring solution. Almost immediately her entire body is covered with thick hair, giving her a bear-like appearance. The man has meanwhile escaped, locking the bathroom door after him. He leaves the house and returns later with a muzzle, a pole, and a number of men. The scene fades to a local fairground where a new animal attraction is shown. The film ends with the husband (now an animal trainer) and his assistant (formerly the maid) in a tight embrace—in the background a large furry bear angrily watches.

This film is a forerunner of many SF films which used chemical compounds to produce strange effects on human beings.

LIQUID ELECTRICITY

Release: 1907, Vitagraph Company of America
Description: Silent, 455 feet
Classification: SF-C
References: No. 14, p. 281; No. 50, p. 259; LC, H98946; MPW, Vol. 2, p. 103

Credits

Producer .... J. Stuart Blackton
Director .... J. Stuart Blackton

When first released, this film had the alternate title of *The Inventor's Galvanic Fluid.* Part of this title, *galvanic fluid*, was used in a sequel to the feature.

Professor Watt, the outstanding chemist, has recently invented a new chemical process, the byproduct of which is *liquid electricity*. The professor accidently discovers that liquid electricity possesses some unusual properties when the substance is sprayed on anyone; the person is suddenly able to move with lightning speed. The professor takes great delight in experimenting by spraying an array of people, and providing the levity of the film.

In the sequel, the professor refines the substance to allow people to fly. Both features show a great deal of imagination and creativity for the 1907 era.

THE LOVE MICROBE

Release: 1907, American Mutoscope & Biograph Co.
Description: Silent, 670 feet
Classification: SF-C
References: No. 2, p. 61; No. 8, p. 308, 309, 319; LC, H101443; MPW, Vol. 1, p. 526

Professor Cupido is seeking the secret of love—he hypothesizes that love is due to inoculation by a certain germ. The professor's quest leads him to an isolated corner of a nearby park where he encounters two young lovers. Hidden by the dense foliage, he cautiously approaches the pair. The professor then uses a syringe with a long needle to extract a blood sample from the neck of each of the subjects. Returning to his laboratory he begins to process and examine the specimens . . . Eureka! . . . The microbe is identified. The *love microbe* is displayed on the movie screen as seen supposedly by the professor through his microscope (perhaps the first time miscroscopic life was shown on film). The professor then seeks to test his microbe on a variety of subjects. In each of the tests the bacteria turns the individual into a tranquil, loving human being. Returning home after a satisfying day of inoculating people, the professor injects a large quantity of the microbe into a kettle of beer which is being carried home by a young lad. Meanwhile, at the boy's house a fierce argument has commenced between his mother and father. The fight reaches a peak when the woman pushes a blackberry pie into her husband's face and he retaliates by throwing dishes, pots, tables, and other objects. She flees for her life just as her son comes home carrying the *doctored* beer. The father halts his hurling of objects long enough to sip the brew, immediately becomes tranquil, and begs his wife's forgiveness. She suspects a trick and, approaching her husband, strikes him with a rolling-pin. While he is out cold, she and the boy sip the beer, and thus peace reigns over the entire household.

FORM NO. 1277 BULLETIN No. 110, October 19, 1907

LOVE MICROBE

The Tender Passion Microscopically Treated in a Biograph Comedy

LENGTH, 670 FEET. PRICE, 12 CENTS PER FOOT.

In *The Love Microbe* (1907), the professor creates a dangerous potion.

Back at his office, the professor decides to inject himself with the microbe and becomes imbued with an all-consuming passion. His passion causes him to make advances toward a young lady, who resists and escapes his grasp. She returns shortly with her angry husband who is carrying a gun, intent on ending the professor's career. One of the professor's earlier subjects, however, his housekeeper, sneaks up on the armed gentleman and jabs him with a syringe filled with solution. The lady and her husband depart, completely peaceful with the world, leaving the professor and the housekeeper in a tight embrace as the movie ends.

THE MECHANICAL STATUE AND THE INGENIOUS SERVANT

Release: 1907, Vitagraph Company of America
Description: Silent, 450 feet
Classification: SF-C
References: No. 50, p. 296; LC, H89462; MPW, Vol. 1, p. 62

Credits

Producer .... John Stuart Blackton
Director .... John Stuart Blackton

An old inventor finally perfects an automatic servant, but the device malfunctions, causing some humorous moments for the audience. This feature is the first American made SF film to contain robots and, while weak, it was popular during this era.

NATURE FAKIRS

Release: 1907, Kalem Company
Description: Silent, 490 feet
Classification: SF-C
References: No. 50, p. 329; MPW, Vol. 1, p. 472-73, 475

The film *Nature Fakirs* (an archaic spelling for the word *fakers*) features the discovery of an unusual set of animals and is set in a semi-cartoon format. The film introduces two real nature fakers, Dr. Short and Jack England. The pair are being considered for membership into the prestigious Ananias Club (a type of explorer's club), but they must prove their worthiness by participating in an expedition into the wilderness. The president of the club awards Dr. Short a camera to record his findings. Professor Short and Jack then embark on the trip into the countryside, examining the flora and fauna along the way. They have proceeded a great distance when they come to an old barn with strange vegetation growing about its exterior. They are in the process of examining the growth more closely when an enormous chicken-like creature leaps around the far corner of the barn. Cautiously the professor and Jack observe the creature's strange behavior while it performs some sort of rhythmic dance. The professor soon names the bird a *Dingbat* and instructs Jack to take a photograph, but the Dingbat attacks the pair. They beg for mercy and the Dingbat withdraws to the barn. The would-be explorers continue on their way, encountering a human-like bear, two Dandy Lions, and an Elkorina. Convinced that they have uncovered a group of unidentified animals, they hasten back to Lobster Bay where they find the president of the Ananias Club working in the hay field. They relate their strange tale of adventure to him but he angrily declares that he has never seen such *nature faking* in his entire life, and proceeds to chase the pair from his property with a pitch fork.

The use of special photographic effects to produce the Dingbat heralded a trend which would be the hallmark of future science fiction films. This movie also included a bit of a social satirical element in its depiction of the president of the Ananias Club—he seems to very closely resemble then President Teddy Roosevelt.

WORK MADE EASY

Release: 1907, Vitagraph Company of America
Description: Silent, 650 feet
Classification: SF-C
References: No. 23, p. 74; No. 50, p. 550; LC, H10315

Credits

Producer .... John Stuart Blackton
Director .... John Stuart Blackton

An attempt by Vitagraph to improve on a production released earlier in 1907, *Work Made Easy* depicts an inventor who develops a robot which can be used for performing extremely hazardous and difficult tasks. The robot performs these using its enormous strength, but somehow the communication between the inventor and the machine begins to deteriorate. The events which transpire during the remainder of the film provide many humorous moments.

This feature is much improved over the version released earlier in the year.

1908

THE AIRSHIP

Release: 1908, Vitagraph Company of America
Description: Silent, 450 feet
Classification: SF
References: No. 20, p. 25; No. 50, p. 6; LC, H1081061; No. 52, Vol. 2, p. 374, 377

The Airship (alternate title, *One Hundred Years Hence*) attempts to be prognostic about air travel during the 21st century. The airplane was a new and fascinating subject for writers and film makers during the early 1900's, and this venture explores the probable causal use of aircraft one hundred years in the future.

The film displays three types of aircraft: a lighter-than-air vehicle, a small winged craft suitable for one person, and a set of wings that attach to human arms to produce flight. A young man and woman are seen flying in the lighter-than-air craft above a large metropolitan area when she decides to hurl some fruit and vegetables on the populous below. Her main target appears to be a rabbi. He is pelted with various large fruits and vegetables. A policeman also becomes a victim of this *salad barrage*. An air-cycle patrolman is summoned to apprehend the culprits. Meanwhile, the rabbi has secured his own set of wings and joins in the chase of the air duo, but the air patrolman attempts to arrest the rabbi who he has mistakenly taken for the guilty party. The rabbi manages to escape by clubbing the pursuing policeman. Somehow during the struggle the rabbi lands on the moon (the viewer is never shown how—or why) and then falls back to earth, landing in the Atlantic Ocean where he is promptly swallowed by a whale. The whale is subsequently caught by a passing ship, cut open, and out pops—you guessed it—the rabbi.

This film is the first American-made science fiction movie to picture an advanced design aircraft, and while their prognostic eyesight was slightly myopic, the film did produce good entertainment for the movie viewers of the era.

Only a year later, Charles Urkan, a British film maker, produced a SF air epic that went unrivaled for years. The film, entitled *The Airship Destroyer*, had surprisingly realistic effects, depicting the bombing of London as well as an incredible radio controlled aerial torpedo. The success of both films paved the way for improvements on SF Concepts.

AN ANIMATED DOLL

Release: 1908, Essanay Film Manufacturing Co.
Description: Silent, 750 feet
Classification: SF-C
References: No. 50, p. 14; MPW, Vol. 2, p. 463

This film is the story of a young boy who wants to buy a present for his sister. He has five dollars to spend (a lot of money for 1908), and he knows an inventor who has a perfect present—an adult-sized automatic doll. He offers the inventor his five dollars for the doll, explaining his desire to surprise his sister. The inventor, however, rejects the offer. Frustrated, the lad conceals himself in the laboratory and awaits the inventor's departure. The boy then takes the doll, leaving his money as payment. The boy returns home and proceeds to his sister with the wonderful present. The doll is unwrapped and the crank turned until the doll begins to execute some beautiful ballet dances. The inventor soon appears on the scene demanding the return of his property. He participates in several dances with the doll and then picks up his creation and leaves the house. The film ends with the little girl crying inconsolably.

This is the third SF film to present a view of a robot-type device. However, this particular effort is not as effective as its predecessors, *The Mechanical Statue and the Ingenious Servant* (1907) and *Work Made Easy* (1907). Nevertheless, the dance scenes are very graphic in depicting the movements of a mechanical doll.

THE DOCTOR'S EXPERIMENT

Release: 1908, Gaumont Company
Description: Silent
Classification: SF-C
References: No. 6, p. 153; No. 50, p. 108

The Doctor's Experiment is a satire aimed at Darwin's theory of evolution. A scientist has perfected a chemical which will reverse the evolutionary process, turning men back into apes, but apes with human-like characteristics. This film could have been the forerunner of *Planet of the Apes*, but the extremely weak SF qualities, together with its humor, only result in an average film for its era.

DR. JEKYLL AND MR. HYDE

Release: 1908, Selig Polyscope Co.
Description: Silent, 1035 feet
Classification: SF
References: No. 50, p. 106; No. 52, Vol. 2, p. 194

Credits

Producer .... William N. Selig

The film *Dr. Jekyll and Mr. Hyde* attempts to follow the original book, *The Strange Case of Dr. Jekyll and Mr. Hyde*, written by Robert Louis Stevenson. This is the first American SF film to use a science fiction literary work as its basis. The film divided into four acts, represents a theatrical performance. In Act I the viewer sees a stage with the curtain rising on a garden scene behind a small church. Alice (Dr. Jekyll's fiancee) is waiting her lover's arrival. Just as Dr. Jekyll nears the garden area, however, a terrible transformation takes place and he turns into the ferocious monster Mr. Hyde. As Mr. Hyde attacks the unsuspecting defenseless Alice, her father, the vicar of the church, endeavors to beat off the man, but he is killed in the process of defending his daughter. Jekyll, as Mr. Hyde, then vanishes, leaving the grief stricken Alice in a state of shock. He soon appears as himself to comfort her, unaware that he is responsible for her despair.

Acts II and III continue to depict the struggle between Dr. Jekyll and Mr. Hyde and the intensity of the action builds causing the audience's emotions to peak by the end of Act III. The production, luckily, interjects just enough comedy to abate some of the realism of the scenes. But in Act IV the drama climaxes with Mr. Hyde consuming too large a dose of the terrible drug, thus destroying both Jekyll and Hyde.

This is a very fine production for the period, and one of the most lengthy (1035 feet) undertakings of this ten year span.

"The successful reproduction of this well-known drama has surpassed our expectations . . ."
The Moving Picture World, Vol. 2, p. 194

THE ELECTRIC HOTEL

Release: 1908, Vitagraph Company of America
Description: Silent, 495 feet
Classification: SF-C
References: No. 5, p. 16; No. 50, p. 120; BIO 11-6-08, p. 14, 23

Credits

Producer .... J. Stuart Blackton
Director .... J. Stuart Blackton

A young inventor creates a hotel of the future where every device is operated by electricity. Every item is as near as your fingertip and your slightest command is obeyed instantly. It is the system's aim to carry out every command to the letter—which sets the stage for the humor in the picture: the characters don't say what they mean and, naturally, the hotel's system doesn't know the difference.

This was an interesting film for 1908 especially considering the novelty of electricity hadn't worn off. Blackton seems to produce a number of films during this time using electricity as the focus.

ENERGIZER

Release: 1908, American Mutoscope & Biograph Co.
Description: Silent, 789 feet
Classification: SF-C
References: No. 16, p. 329, 431; No. 50, p. 123; MPW, Vol. 2, p. 44; BGB, No. 119, 1-11-08

Credits

Camera .... F. A. Dobson

A satire on the breakfast cereal food fad of 1908, the film centers on the production of a cold cereal that is guaranteed to turn the eater into a champion. With that theme set, the movie focuses on a young woman who is dismayed by her husband's lack of energy. She decides to supplement his breakfast with the new preparation called *Energizer.* he soon becomes a veritable storm of energy, performing all sorts of tasks, including the maid's household chores. Naturally, his wife is amazed, and the maid is ecstatic. The plot thickens when the maid, realizing the advantage of her employer's boundless energy, offers a hobo a generous portion of the palatable pabulum. The man soon becomes a giant of strength and performs feats that would have caught even Hercule's attention.

The science fiction theme of chemicals producing great strength is one that continued to be an important screenwriter's tool for many years.

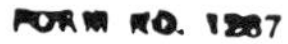

FORM NO. 1287 — BULLETIN No. 119, January 11, 1908

"ENERGIZER"

A Cereal Serial Satire on the Breakfast Food Fad

LENGTH, 789 FEET. — PRICE, 12 CENTS PER FOOT.

Wow, what a cereal! *Energizer* (1908).

GALVANIC FLUID

Release: 1908, Vitagraph Company of America
Description: Silent, 500 feet
Classification: SF-C
References: No. 14, p. 177; No. 50, p. 155; LC, H105646

Credits

Producer .... John Stuart Blackton
Director .... John Stuart Blackton

The alternate title for this film, *More Fun With Liquid Electricity*, indicates the film's forerunner, *Liquid Electricity* (1907). The opening scene is an exterior of the laboratory of Professor Watt, the inventor of *liquid electricity*. It seems the professor has uncovered an unusual property of this strange chemical—when applied to any object (or human being) it is able to fly for a short time. Professor Watt decides to experiment with this fluid as he goes for his morning walk in the park. He sprays a nursemaid who is wheeling a baby carriage and they immediately begin to fly about the flowers in the park. He then proceeds with his morning walk, indiscriminately spraying each and every individual he encounters. But when the professor sprays a trolley car and the car commences to fly, several policemen are attracted to the scene. They attempt to secure the professor but are all sprayed and sent flying off. However, they soon return with sufficient reinforcements and the inventor is forced to spray himself, thus avoiding capture. His speedy airborne journey takes him to his front doorstep with his pursuers running below and not far behind. Soon a large angry crowd begins to gather outside. The professor waits until they are near the door, then he quickly opens it and sprays the entire group causing them to disappear overhead. In doing so, he accidentally drops the syringe; a terrific explosion results, and when the smoke clears the professor and his house are nowhere to be found.

HEATING POWER

Release: 1908, Lubin
Description: Silent, 410 feet
Classification: SF-C
References: No. 14, p. 215; No. 50, p. 188; LC, H115285

Credits

Producer .... Sigmund Lubin

A famous chemist discovers a new compound that can transmit energy from the atmosphere to any object with which it comes in contact. To test it, the new powder is placed on a table in the laboratory and sets it ablaze. The chemist, now very excited over his discovery, carries a sample to his colleague. During the examination of the new substance, the chemist accidently spills a few grains of the powder on his friend's clothing. At this point in the movie the audience is treated to some excellent slapstick comedy.

THE INVISIBLE FLUID

Release: 1908, American Mutoscope & Biograph Co.
Description: Silent, 662 feet
Classification: SF
References: No. 2, p. 53; No. 16, p. 359, 437; No. 50, p. 221; MPW, Vol. 2, p. 531; BGB, No. 144, 6-16-08; LC, H11674

Credits

Camera .... G. W. Bitzer

An adaptation of the SF theme presented in H. G. Wells' novel *The Invisible Man* (1897), *The Invisible Fluid* has an erudite scientist discovering a mysterious fluid that contains properties which render objects, as well as people, invisible. When anything (or anyone) is sprayed with this liquid, it (or they) vanishes for about ten minutes. Realizing the impact of his discovery, but uncertain how to market it, the scientist pours his invention into an atomizer and proceeds to write a letter to his brother asking him to explore the market for such a product. He then dispatches the atomizer and letter by special messenger to his brother. His brother, however, after reading the letter, regards it as a joke and sprays himself with the fluid. To the messenger boy's amazement the man soon disappears. Not sure what had just happened, the boy reads the letter and, realizing what fun he can achieve using such a device, absconds with the atomizer.

FORM NO. 1318 BULLETIN No. 144. RELEASED June 16, 1908

THE INVISIBLE FLUID

Demonstration of the Powers of the Most Egregious Commodity of the Age

LENGTH, 662 FEET. PRICE, 14 CENTS PER FOOT.

***The Invisible Fluid* (1908) was the first film attempt to adapt H.G. Wells' novel, *The Invisible Man*.**

The lad immediately encounters a young girl walking her dog, and sprays the animal with the atomizer: the girl is left holding an empty chain. Next he sprays a fruitstand and its proprietor, resulting in the disappearance of both fruit and man. The boy merrily continues his escapade until he stops for a bite to eat. As he gets ready to pay his check, he decides it would be more fun to spray the cashier and steal the cash register. Having done so, he scurries from the restaurant hotly pursued by a mob of his previous victims. They embark on a lengthy chase, but the boy tires and confronts his pursuers, spraying each as they come near him. Now extremely confident of his ability to foil anyone, he fails to notice a stealthy-footed policeman creeping upon him from behind. He is captured and carted off to jail, and appears before a judge who is baffled by the tale of the defendant's misdeeds. He inquires of the boy how the strange *invisible fluid* works and the boy eagerly offers his assistance in demonstrating the invention—of course he does so by cunningly spraying himself, thus disappearing. The judge and police officer are left dumbfounded.

This film is an amazing piece of photographic achievement, and the combination of excellent special effects and good storyline make this a hallmark of science fiction films for the future.

LOVE GERMS

Release: 1908, Lubin
Description: Silent, 460 feet
Classification: SF-C
References: No. 50, p. 269; LC, H118065; VFI, Vol. 5, p. 7-8

Credits

Producer .... Sigmund Lubin

The content of this film is very similar to an earlier work entitled *The Love Microbe* (1907). The former work, however, was a higher quality production. The basic difference between this film and its predecessor is that aerobic germs are captured in a sample of air rather than the blood of the victim. The premise of *Love Germs* remains the same—locate and control the organism which causes love.

OH, WHAT AN APPETITE

Release: 1908, Essanay Film Manufacturing Co.
Description: Silent, 600 feet
Classification: SF-C
References: No. 50, p. 345; MPW, Vol. 2, p. 186

A young chemist develops a new compound which can add weight to cattle, but while he is out telling another chemist about his discovery, the cleaning man takes a bite of what he believes to be cake. It is not, but rather the new compound which was designed to increase the appetite of farm animals. The janitor nearly eats himself to death before the chemist perfects an antidote. This is a weak SF film, but a humorous one for the audience.

THE PROFESSOR'S ANTI-GRAVITATION FLUID

Release: 1908, Hepworth
Description: Silent, 380 feet
Classification: SF-C
References: BIO, 11-13-08, p. 14

An old scientist accidently discovers a remarkable new powder which seems to defy the laws of gravity. He gets great delight in sprinkling his powder on various unsuspecting people and enthusiastically watching as they sail about in the air. It seems that after a few moments, the effect of the powder wears off, returning all the people to earth and normal gravity. The victims soon unite to seek revenge and pursue the professor as he dashes for his laboratory. Reaching there only moments before the angry mob, he bolts the door behind him. The mob, however, manages to break into the laboratory and destroys all the scientific apparatus. Moreover, they make the professor vow never to conduct experiments again on human subjects.

This is a weak SF film, but an excellent example of good healthy fun and abundant humor.

1909

BRAIN-SERUM

Release: 1909, Lubin
Description: Silent, 305 feet
Classification: SF-C
References: No. 14, p. 389; No. 50, p. 8; BIO, 8-5-09, p. 28; LC, H127184

Professor Weise discovers a new brain serum which will increase intelligence. After several successful experiments with various subjects, the professor decides to try the drug on himself. The film ends, leaving the audience with the inference that the professor has made a great leap in mental ability. But the movie is too short to do justice to the plot.

This film had the alternate title of *Professor Weise's Brain Serum Injection*. This theme occurred again in several films from 1910 to 1915.

THE DIAMOND MAKER

Release: 1909, Vitagraph Company of America
Description: Silent, 490 feet
Classification: SF
References: No. 5, p. 10; No. 50, p. 101; LC, H128245; VFI, Vol. 25, p. 9

Credits

Producer .... John Stuart Blackton
Director .... John Stuart Blackton

This film had two alternate titles, *Fortune and Misfortune*, and *The Maker of Diamonds*. It centers on the process of making artificial diamonds through a mechanical condensation process. This process, however, is never fully explained to the viewer, resulting in a weak science fiction production.

THE EARTHQUAKE ALARM

Release: 1909, Schultze
Description: Silent, 300 feet
Classification: SF-C
References: No. 50, p. 118; BIO, 10-31-09, p. 43

A marvelous automatic invention which can detect earthquakes five minutes before they strike provides the impetus for this film's action. A young man purchases one of these new devices and becomes increasingly more nervous as he misinterprets some sounds to be signals from the earthquake alarm. His constant false alarms of the danger of what he believes to be impending earthquakes causes the neighbors to ignore a real warning when the alarm does detect a dangerous earthquake. The movie ends with the walls of the apartment crumbling and the young man hiding under his bed.

THE HAIR RESTORER

Release: 1909, Pathe
Description: Silent, 478 feet
Classification: SF-C
References: No. 50, p. 179; BIO, 2-10-10, p. 55

A remake of an earlier film entitled *Hair Restorer* (1907), the former is the superior production. The film's action is focused on a young man who is bald and in love with a girl who is not willing to marry him because of his bald appearance. He discovers a source of wonderful hair restorer, and the effect is amazing as an immediate thick crop of hair starts to develop on his head. He wins the affection of his beloved, but the woman and her mother are very curious about the fantastic transformation. They examine the bottle of hair restorer, during which a minute amount of the liquid spills on their handkerchiefs. Later when they wipe their faces with the infected hankies, thick facial hair results. The young man is horrified and employs the use of a hair remover antidote. The results, however, prove disastrous--the two women become completely bald.

INVENTIONS OF AN IDIOT

Release: 1909, Lubin
Description: Silent, 295 feet
Classification: SF-C
References: No. 50, p. 220; MPW, Vol. 2, p. 564; LC, H124443

A young inventor displays a potpourri of his inventions to a friend, the first of which is a new type of baby incubator which totally controls the environment. His friend obviously is impressed and asks to see more. The inventor invites his friend to step into a tonsorial cabinet, but he soon emerges angry at having lost his beard and hair in the process. The inventor shoves him back into the chamber and adjusts several dials and his friend emerges the second time with a luxurious growth of hair and beard. Next, the man and his friend board a *flymobile* and depart for a short aerial journey over the city. Soon the craft reaches a speed of 200 miles per hour, whereupon it explodes and the aircraft with its passengers inside are hurled to the ground. Disheveled, but unhurt (somehow) the friend begs the inventor not to show him any more of his creations. He gets his wish when the inventor pushes an ejection button which sends him abruptly tumbling out the door of the flymobile.

This film could have been a very good SF entry had it not been handicapped by its shortness (295 feet). Nevertheless, the devices exhibited during the film make it a worthwhile effort.

MEASURE FOR MEASURE

Release: 1909, Lubin
Description: Silent, 900 feet
Classification: SF-A
References: No. 50, p. 295; BIO, 10-7-09, p. 95; LC, H127187

Jules, a young inventor, has just perfected his latest device--a highly destructive submarine mine. Jules and his lab assistant, Dick, celebrate his new invention. Their work is lauded by the superintendent of armaments as a major weapon against naval attacks and Jules decides to give the plans for the weapon's development to the government. Dick, however, has different ideas. He drugs Jules and attempts to force him to reveal the weapon's secret. But Jules' resistance to the drug is successful and he vows never to divulge the secret. When a foreign power offers fifty thousand dollars for the plans, Dick is spurred on to try more drastic methods. He attempts to discredit Jules and steal the plans from the superintendent's vault. Meanwhile, Jules makes an escape by using his submarine mine. His captors are killed and Jules is badly injured. He is taken to a hospital where he relates his ordeal to the authorities. Dick is soon apprehended before he can deliver the stolen plans to the enemy.

This film contains lots of action and suspense to keep the viewer entertained. Additionally, a device such as the *submarine mine* has interesting science fiction qualities, made even more interesting by the fact that this SF invention has become a reality of our modern warfare.

THE PROFESSOR'S LOVE TONIC

Release: 1909, Essanay Film Manufacturing Co.
Description: Silent, 386 feet
Classification: SF-C
References: No. 50, p. 383; BIO, 4-13-11, p. xvii

A chemistry professor seeking to develop an elixir that will provide perpetual life develops instead a tonic that transforms the meanest of individuals into amorous Romeos. Not reaching his original experimental goal is a disappointment, but the professor plans to have some fun with the *love tonic*. After injecting several of his friends with the fluid, and relishing the observance of their amorous behavior, the professor rests in a nearby park. While asleep his friends turn the tables on him by injecting him with his own love tonic. They leave and he awakens and sees a jackass nearby. Hidden in the surrounding foliage, his comrades enjoy the hilarity of the amorous events.

THE RUBBER MAN

Release: 1909, Lubin
Description: Silent, 270 feet
Classification: SF
References: No. 50, 409; BIO, 12-30-09, p. 45; MPW, Vol. 5, p. 771, 799; VFI, Vol. 48, p. 12

A creative inventor has assembled a robot with a mechanical interior and rubber exterior. During an experiment the robot develops a short circuit and the *rubber man* goes on a devastating rampage, attacking his creator and his family, tossing them from their home. The police are summoned, but three policemen prove no match for the powerful robot. He escapes into the streets of the city, wreaking havoc wherever he goes. Eventually the robot is chased from the city but he doubles back and brings more destruction to the town. In the process of this wanton destruction, he stumbles into a horse trough, the water causes a complete breakdown of the robot's internal system, and he is left powerless—and harmless.

A TALKATIVE LADY

Release: 1909, Gaumont Co.
Description: Silent, 353 feet
Classification: SF-C
References: No. 50, p. 474; BIO, 12-30-09, p. 37

A man seeking a cure for his mute wife takes her to a doctor who has the mysterious ability to cure mutes. After the cure has been affected the wife begins to drive the husband mad with her incessant chatter. Enduring as much as he can, the man returns his wife to the doctor hoping to have the cure reversed. When the doctor demands a greater quantity of money to reverse the process, the husband does not understand. In desperation, the doctor begins to count money into the man's hand, which the husband quickly pockets as he exits with his wife.

This film is probably the weakest SF film of the period. The doctor's process is intended to be scientific, but the plot leaves the viewer very uncertain that anything *scientific* has taken place.

THE WONDERFUL ELECTRO-MAGNET

Release: 1909, Edison Film Company
Description: Silent, 400 feet
Classification: SF-C
References: No. 50, p. 548; EDK, Vol. 1, No. 8, p. 10-11; LC, J135663-66; MPW, Vol. 5, p. 807, 820, 841

A young inventor genius develops an electro-magnet which is capable of attracting people instead of magnetic metals. He demonstrates his marvelous new device to a motion picture theater owner who envisions vast financial gains by employing this device in his theater. The inventor agrees to sell the electro-magnet to the theater owner and immediately the theater's business takes a turn for the better. Inadvertedly the owner attracts a young minister to the day's film showing. Realizing his mistake the owner apologizes and offers an explanation. The minister accepts his apology and explains that his bishop is very unhappy with him because of his small congregation. Suddenly, the owner has a brilliant idea: he will take his electro-magnet to the minister's church and help him increase his congregation. The film ends with the bishop amazed by the sudden unexplained popularity of his young minister.

> "It is one of those trick films which seem satisfactory and which develop funny situations regardless of the environment or the uncertain element which sometimes controls people's actions."
>
> *The Moving Picture World*, Vol. 5, p. 841

CLASSIFICATION OF SCIENCE FICTION FILMS FROM 1897 TO 1909

Science Fiction

Airship, The 1908
Dr. Jekyll and Mr. Hyde 1908
Galvanic Fluid 1908
Invisible Fluid, The 1908
Brain-Serum 1909
Diamond Maker, The 1909
Rubber Man, The 1909

Science Fiction - Comedy

Sausage Machine, The 1897
Fun in the Butcher Shop 1901
Dog Factory 1904
Dr. Skinum 1907
Hair Restorer 1907
Liquid Electricity 1907
Love Microbe, The 1907
Mechanical Statue and the Ingenious Servant, The 1907
Nature Fakirs 1907
Work Made Easy 1907
An Animated Doll 1908
Doctor's Experiment, The 1908
Electric Hotel, The 1908
Energizer 1908
Heating Power 1908
Love Germs 1908
Oh What an Appetite 1908
Professors Anti-Gravitation Fluid, The 1908
Earthquake Alarm, The 1909
Hair Restorer, The 1909
Inventions of an Idiot 1909
Professor's Love Tonic, The 1909
Talkative Lady 1909
Wonderful Electro-Magnet, The 1909

Science Fiction - Adventure

Measure for Measure 1909

COMPANIES RELEASING FILMS FROM 1897 TO 1909

American Mutoscope & Biograph Co.

Sausage Machine, The 1897
Dr. Skinum 1907
Love Microbe, The 1907
Energizer 1908
Invisible Fluid, The 1908

Edison Film Company

Fun in the Butcher Shop 1901
Dog Factory 1904
Wonderful Electro-Magnet, The 1909

Essanay Film Manufacturing Co.

An Animated Doll 1908
Oh, What an Appetite 1908
Professor's Love Tonic, The 1909

Gaumont Company

Doctor's Experiment, The 1908
Talkative Lady 1909

Hepworth

Professor's Anti-Gravity Fluid, The 1908

Kalem Company

Nature Fakirs 1907

Lubin

Heating Power 1908
Love Germs 1908
Brain-Serum 1908
Inventions of an Idiot 1909
Measure for Measure 1909
Rubber Man, The 1909

Pathe

Hair Restorer, The 1909

Selig Polyscope Co.

Dr. Jekyll and Mr. Hyde 1908

Shultze

Earthquake Alarm, The 1909

Vitagraph Company of America

Liquid Electricity 1907
Mechanical Statue and the Ingenious Servant, The 1907
Work Made Easy 1907
Airship, The 1908
Electric Hotel, The 1908
Galvanic Fluid 1908
Diamond Maker, The 1909

Williams, Brown & Earle

Hair Restorer 1907

1910 – 1919

AN OVERVIEW OF 1910-1919

By 1910 the Motion Pictures Patent Company, made up of outstanding film producers like Thomas Edison, Biograph, Kalem, Lubin, Selig, Essanay, Pathe, and Gaumont, were easily turning out more films than all the independent studios combined. Their solid efforts to resist the independent movement had forced these outside companies into a lengthy legal battle, one which continued for some years. Nevertheless, the motion picture industry as a whole was beginning a new dawn. The productions increased and films improved continually in quality of acting and technique over the next decade.

Science fiction feature films began the metamorphosis toward a new film genre. A variety of variables influenced this change such as length of film, camera quality, film quality, and experienced players. As the film producers become more concerned about these variables, the quality of their productions vastly improved. During the first four years of the decade (1910-1919) probably one of the most noticeable changes was the length of movies as they became "2 reelers" (approximately 2000 feet).

In addition, we began to see actors that we had seen in other productions. Their experience in film making and in appearing before the cameras became assets, valued for their transference into audience revenues. Legitimate theatrical players who had first scoffed at the film industry as a passing fancy, were now beginning to take it seriously. Many of them were even clamoring to appear on the silver screen so that their images could be engraved in celluloid for posterity.

There are some factors that seemed to uniquely affect science fiction films: (1) the science of the era provided a rich reservoir of technological devices for the creative story writer; (2) the legacy of literature from such authors as H. G. Wells, Mary Wollstonecraft Shelley, Robert Louis Stevenson, Jules Verne, Arthur Conan Doyle, and Edgar Rice Burroughs; (3) and the general audience appeal for adventure, excitement and romance, coupled with a variety of science fiction paraphernalia.

The plausibility of air travel led to visions of spaceships and planetary exploration, and the first film in this section, *A Trip to Mars*, produced by Thomas Edison, was such a film. Even though it employs a great deal of fantasy, the feature does talk for the first time about a trip to the planet Mars.

Additionally, Edison's venture into electricity and the excitement of the general public for this new found energy source can be reflected in some of the earlier films of this period: *The Wonderful Electro-Magnet*, *Betty's Electric Battery*, *Electric Insoles*, and *The Electrified Pig*. Electricity held a great mystery and fascination for the audience, and this scientific advancement would remain a tool for science fiction films for some time.

This period also saw the producers becoming more aware of the plethora of SF literature which could be adapted successfully to screenplays. This trend is evidenced by such films as *Frankenstein* (1910, Edison Film Company), as well as the many remakes of *Dr. Jekyll and Mr. Hyde* (1912, 1913, and 1914).

In 1912 a truly unusual and prophetic event occurred. Thomas Edison's company produced a serial feature—a first in the industry—starring Mary Fuller and entitled *What Happened to Mary*? After seeing the excitement created by this new presentation, it didn't take the other producers long to climb aboard the band wagon; the serial era had begun. It was two years, however, before the first science fiction serial was made, and it began a trend in SF productions that occupied much film footage during this time.

The Exploits of Elaine (1914, Pathe), based on the Craig Kennedy mysteries created by Arthur B. Reeve, starred Pearl White in its 14 episodes. Kennedy, being a scientific detective, found himself in unbelievable spots only to produce a new scientific apparatus which allowed his escape and the rescue of Elaine, who was naturally in constant peril. *Exploits of Elaine* only cost $175,000 to produce, but the return to the investors was nearly ten times that amount. Certainly this was an economic indicator that pointed the way for future serials. It certainly did for Pathe, which followed *Exploits of Elaine* with two sequels: *The New Exploits of Elaine* (1915) and *The Romance of Elaine* (1915). These added 20 more episodes to the original 14 chapter serial.

From 1914 to 1919 theaters across the country became inundated with serials, each having a multitude of scientific gadgetry and diabolically sinister geniuses, each foiled in the end by the brilliant all-American hero. These produced exciting weekly adventures and audiences repeatedly returned to see their stars placed in jeopardy only to be freed or escape the following week in the next chapter.

One of the things that probably made these serials so fascinating to the public was the collaboration with the Hearst newspapers by the studios. The paper carried the weekly episodes in its several hundred affiliates across the nation. These synopses and the weekly theatrical presentations virtually assured the public's fascination and produced a voracious appetite for the next thrilling installment.

Creating sequels to serials became the vogue of the day. *The Million Dollar Mystery* (1914 serial, Thanhouser) was an example of this. It was said to have cost $125,000 to produce and returned over 1.5 million dollars to its producers. It was so successful that the studio advertised a contest in which the Chicago *Tribune* offered a $10,000 prize to anyone who created the best sequel. The winner was Roy L. McCardell for his entry entitled *The Diamond Sky* (1915).

In addition to the actors and actresses gaining more experience, the cameramen and their techniques had become equally experienced. The first underwater film, *20,000 Leagues Under the Sea* (1916), began a new dimension in cinematography and resulted in the first underwater filming studio. It was located in the Bahamas and cost nearly $500,000. The techniques employed became instrumental in film making over the next twenty-five years.

Two films of 1917 that almost went unnoticed were animated shorts, *The Dinosaur and the Missing Link* and *10,000 B.C.* Both of these were produced by Willis O'Brien, a man who became famous in SF special effects. O'Brien's expertise in animated special effects was one of the key assets that evolved from films of this decade. In fact, special effects became an accepted hallmark of good science fiction film making.

By the close of the period, screenplays became more elaborate. The quality of writing had improved and the actors had developed into respected artists. Many film companies had moved to the California sunshine where they could film year round, and by 1917 the Film Patents Company had been dissolved, and the war between the independents and the conglomerate had been waged and resolved. This resulted in many new companies springing up virtually overnight.

The size of the industry had grown to proportions that even the studios themselves found difficult to assess. At the annual board meeting of the Kodak Film company in May, 1920 the Kodak president reported a 17 year profit on film sales of $179,512,613.00—an unbelievable sum for an industry that only a few years before had sprung out of the dreams of a few creative men.

The previous "decade" (1897-1909) had spawned only 33 science fiction films from among the thousands produced. This decade (1910-1919), however, gave birth to 114 SF features, many involving serials of 10 or more episodes. In the earlier period 76 percent of these films were classified as science fiction-comedy (SF-C), while from 1910-1919 the classifications were almost equal; 37 science fiction (SF); 36 science fiction-comedy (SF-C); and 37 science fiction-adventure (SF-A). Moreover, the earlier films seemed to be produced by a small number of film companies which was not the trend during the 1910-1919 period.

In less than three decades, the film industry had created such momentum that America's fascination with the world of films promised an exciting future for science fiction features.

The prehistoric animals of our past and evolution; two themes which became popular with early science fiction film procedures.

1910

A TRIP TO MARS

Release: 1910, Edison Film Company
Description: Silent, 265 feet
Classification: SF-C
References: No. 50, p. 503; EDK, Vol. 2, No. 1, p. 5-6; LC, J138566-68; MPW, Vol. 6 p. 203, 267, 338

A famous professor of chemistry discovers two fascinating powders which, when combined, react to form a new compound that possesses antigravity characteristics. The professor places the mysterious substance on several objects, all of which begin to float about the room. Excited over this amazing discovery he darts from the room, waving the envelopes containing the two inert powders above his head. Accidentally, some of the powders spill on him and begin to react. Before he can grasp what is happening he is hurled out a window, through the clouds, and into space on his way to the planet Mars.

Tumbling onto the surface of Mars, the professor finds himself surrounded by a dense forest with trees of enormous height. The upper halves of the giant trees, however, appear to be semi-human monsters which reach out with a multitude of long arms trying to grasp the professor as he attempts to scurry from the woods. Escaping their clutches, he next scales an embankment and leaps onto the rocky terrain below. The surface begins to quake, it appears that just beneath the rocky terrain a huge half-human Martian was sleeping and the professor has landed on his lip! The Martian monster opens his eyes and issues a cloud of steam from his mouth that propels the professor high into the Martian atmosphere. During the professor's descent, the Martian reaches out and catches him in his enormous hand. Gaining his composure, the professor rests on his knees and finds himself staring into the gargantuan face of his captor. The Martian blows on the professor and the air surrounding him begins to chill, resulting in his body being encased in a snowball-like structure. The Martian holds the snowball over an open flame; suddenly it begins to increase in volume until it explodes. The concussion forces the professor into space and toward earth.

Reaching earth, the weary professor falls headlong into his laboratory. After a quick recovery, he decides he wants no part of his new antigravity compound. In his rage he hurls the two envelopes containing the substances to the opposite side of the room, which, naturally, causes them to combine and produce the dreaded antigravity compound—immediately one side of the room begins to rise. The final scene of the film shows the room spinning like a top with the professor sitting bewildered at the base of it.

The special effects of the movie are clever and unique for the period in which it was made. The story and setting show an originality not displayed in previous SF films.

"It [the film] is all amusing and is managed with consummate skill."

The Moving Picture World, Vol. 6, p. 338

BETTY'S ELECTRIC BATTERY

Release: 1910, Pathe
Description: Silent, 396 feet
Classification: SF-C
References: No. 14, p. 44; No. 50, p. 32; BIO, 9-15-10, p. 29, 40

Mischevious Betty possesses a unique electric battery which seems to be able to pass electric charges to people. Individuals receiving Betty's incredible electric shock appear to be possessed with boundless energy, resulting in their performing strange and unusual acts. The first of a long line of Betty's victims are a pair of elderly ladies who are given an electrical shock. They begin to spin faster and faster until they slump over, totally exhausted. Betty scurries through the city shocking people and sending each into a state of frenzied activity. Finally, she is apprehended and taken to police headquarters. Somehow she regains control of her electric battery and begins charging the policemen, who run frantically outside to escape. Observing their strange behavior from a nearby window, Betty's final prank is to pour water over her victims, causing them to short circuit: the end!

A very weak SF entry, Pathe did a much better job on earlier films. This work, however, does express the fear the general public had toward electricity at the beginning of the twentieth century.

THE COMET

Release: 1910, Kalem Company
Description: Silent
Classification: SF
References: No. 5, p. 149; No. 14, p. 90; No. 50, p. p-12

The passage of Halley's Comet in 1910 (The comet reached perihelion on April 20, 1910.) was the impetus for this film production. Many believed that we were in real danger of a collision with the comet and the earth's destruction was imminent. Prognosticators foretold of the earth being engulfed by a great ball of fire and the film translated those warnings into celluloid. The picture gives glimpses of the approaching orb and the catastrophic devastation being wreaked upon the earth: automobiles explode, houses are set on fire,and a miner watches his gold begin to melt. The population is terrified and seeks a refuge underground, safe from the comet's fury.

This is a well made film for the period, and uses a SF theme that has remained popular for many years (the film, *Meteor*, for example, made in 1979). This, coupled with the presence of the real comet, must have had an unique effect on the audience.

THE ELECTRIC INSOLES

Release: 1910, Essanay Film Manufacturing Co.
Description: Silent, 502 feet
Classification: SF-C
References: No. 14, p. 145; No. 50, p. 120; BIO, 4-14-10, p. 31; MPW, Vol. 6, p. 93

Poor Bill Smith is plagued with aching feet. His friend, Jim Brown, suggests that he visit the famous Dr. Wright, who has invented a new device. His *electric insoles* are guaranteed to relieve the discomfort of foot ailments. Bill, willing to grasp at anything which will ease his pain, purchases a pair of the insoles. He carefully fits the devices into his shoes, puts his shoes on his feet, and stands up—and his troubles really begin. It seems the electric insoles have mistakenly been given too great of an electrical charge. Bill's feet become uncontrollable, and he starts to run at incredible speeds, unable to slow himself or control his direction. He collides with two policemen and leaves them sprawled on the ground as he continues his unaltered, uncontrollable journey. Bill's escapades lead to many humorous encounters until his electrified feet are attracted by a manhole cover. Unfortunately, Bill's pursuers catch up to him and give him the beating of his life, during which (much to Bill's relief) his shoes are jarred off. Bruised and exhausted, he is left sitting on the sidewalk curb as the picture fades.

FRANKENSTEIN

Release: 1910, Edison Film Company
Description: Silent, 975 feet
Classification: SF
References: No. 6, p. 8-11; No. 14, p. 171; No. 46, p. 204; No. 47, p. 40; No. 50, p. 148; BIO, 5-5-10, p. 126; COF, Vol. 2, p. 20; COF, Vol. 3, p. 6; EDK, 3-15-10; FAM, Vol. 23, p. 45, Vol. 26, p. 57; LC, J139349-52

Credits

Producer .... Thomas Edison
Director .... J. Searle Dawley
Screenplay .... J. Searle Dawley

Cast

Monster .... Charles Stanton Ogle
Dr. Frankenstein .... Augustus Phillips
Sweetheart .... Mary Fuller

Charles Ogle used grease paint and hair to create Edison's *Frankenstein* (1910).

The monster (Charles Ogle) scares himself by gazing at his image in the mirror.

The EDISON
KINETOGRAM

VOL. 2 MARCH 15, 1910 No. 4

SCENE FROM

FRANKENSTEIN

FILM No. 6604

EDISON FILMS RELEASED FROM
MARCH 16 TO 31 INCLUSIVE

A copy of the advertisement which appeared in the Edison Kinetogram for Edison's feature *Frankenstein* (1910).

The monster was not that scary, but the overall effect of the feature gave the audience sufficient excitement. (*Frankenstein*, **1910**)

This film was the first American screen version of Mary Wollstonecraft Shelley's (1797-1851) famous literary classic. Unfortunately, the screen adaptation was a very liberal interpretation of the novel. Nevertheless, it presented an interesting and haunting story for the audience.

As the movie opens, young Frankenstein has left for college to study medicine. Both his father and his sweetheart are very distraught about his departure. At college Frankenstein excels and within two years has an experimental laboratory of his own. Believing he can create life without evil, Frankenstein begins his experiments toward achieving this goal.

The creation is brought about through a series of volatile chemical reactions. The young Dr. Frankenstein writes to his sweetheart, "Tonight my ambition will be accomplished. I have discovered the secret of life and death, and in a few hours I shall create into life the most perfect human being that the world has yet known. When this marvelous work is accomplished I shall return to claim you for my bride."

Frankenstein then begins the crucial experiment which he is convinced will make his name immortal in the annals of science and medicine. First, he ignites the fire that will heat the cauldron and send the chemicals flowing into the iron chamber in which the *being* will be formed. As Frankenstein observes the process through a portal in the chamber, his emotions move from excitement and joy to horror and disgust—he has not created the perfect being he sought, but a monstor, a hunchbacked, hairy creature with hideous facial features. As he stares in utter disbelief, the doors of the chamber are ripped open and the monster stands before its creator. The creature turns and bolts through an open doorway, escaping the confinement of the laboratory.

Dr. Frankenstein, sick with the realization of the terrible evil he has created, is nursed back to health by his sweetheart and his father. Regaining his strength, a marriage date is set. But Frankensteins still has no idea of the monster's fate. Soon, however, the being visits Dr. Frankenstein in an attempt to prevent the forthcoming marriage. The creature and its creator engage in a struggle, but the doctor is no match for the monster and is soon overpowered. As the being is about to leave the room, it sees its reflection in the mirror and is horrified by the sight. Somehow he realizes the concern his creator has for him and the love Dr. Frankenstein feels for the woman. As the creature gazes into the mirror, the intensity of these emotions cause him to fade into oblivion. The film ends with this concluding caption:

"The creature of an evil mind is overcome by love and disappears."

Although the film's story did not follow the novel as many would have preferred, it was an excellent film production. Unfortunately, few people have ever viewed the feature, as the movie became a victim of its decaying nitrate base film before it could be converted to the safer acetate base film and preserved by some archive. Nevertheless, there appear to be three copies in existence (held by private collectors located in France, England and U.S.A.) but, as of this date none of the collectors have offered this film to any major archive.

The characterization of the monster by Charles Ogle was described by viewers at the time to be extraordinary and superb. Ogle was already a seasoned actor prior to this role, and went on to act in more than 300 silent films.

The director and screenwriter, J. Searle Dawley created and directed more than 350 films in his career. His years with the Edison Manufacturing Company produced films of even higher quality.

This entry into the SF film collection provided two themes of interest: "Does man have the right to tamper with natural events," and, "What creations has science brought upon us?" These themes would form the basis for many science fiction endeavors in the future.

THE INVENTOR

Release: 1910, Pathe
Description: Silent, 900 feet
Classification: SF
References: No. 14, p. 249; No. 50, p. 221; BIO, 9-29-10, p. 27

An inventor, Lardier, attempts to construct a material which will make automobile tires puncture-proof. After investing his life savings and many countless hours of toil, Lardier develops a compound which resists all efforts to pierce it. Lardier, being a poor businessman, is convinced that his invention is useless by another manufacturer. The man, Chavard Bourron, agrees to purchase his worthless invention for a small sum of money. Discouraged, Lardier agrees to the purchase.

A few months later Chavard is given an award for his new non-puncturable tire and Lardier realizes he has been robbed. He attempts to kill Chavard, but his efforts are foiled and he is jailed. The manufacturer's daughter, however, comes to Lardier's aid when she reveals the true story. Lardier is then freed and given a large portion of the manufacturer's fortune.

LOOKING FORWARD

Release: 1910, Thanhouser
Description: Silent, 1000 feet
Classification: SF-C
References: No. 50, p. 264; MPW, Vol. 7, p. 1490, 1539, 1554

Jack Goodwin is a young chemistry student who seems to have mastered the area of physical sciences far more quickly than his peers. One of Jack's experiments has resulted in the creation of a powder that, when consumed, creates a state of suspended animation.

Jack, however, violates one of the cardinal rules of science when he tests a small quantity of the compound on himself. He is astounded when he awakens and finds it is a week later. Fascinated and thrilled by his discovery, Jack decides to consume a greater quantity of the powder. First, he acquires a large safety deposit box in a nearby bank and leaves instructions that it is not to be opened until 100 years have passed.

In 2010 the box is broken into and everyone is shocked: Jack is in the vault—he had slept for 100 years. He is surprised by the many new sights and changes in society. There is rapid transportation and there has even been a new kind of revolution: women's rights. He is soon befriended by the mayor—a woman—who attempts to aid him in his adjustment to their environment. The film ends with the mayor stating that "*there is no way back*," and we must keep "*looking forward*."

THE MECHANICAL HUSBAND

Release: 1910, LCC
Description: Silent
Classification: SF-C
References: No. 5, p. 53; No. 14, p. 314; No. 50, p. 295

A young girl falls in love with a very personable robot and, after much persuasion, the justice of the peace agrees to perform their marriage ceremony.

Very little information was available on this film, or its producer. Unfortunately, it appears to have been destroyed before the film restoration project of the Library of Congress was in effect.

1911

DR. GROWENQUICK'S FEEDING POWER

Release: 1911, Walterdaw
Description: Silent, 600 feet
Classification: SF
References: No. 14, p. 131; No. 50, p. p-17

Dr. Growenquick invents a special powder that is capable of causing infants to become adults within a matter of minutes. The good doctor administers some of this marvelous potion to a young baby boy. After one spoonful, the infant grows to a young boy. Even the doctor is surprised at the success of his new creation. After the next spoonful, the young boy becomes a young man. One minor defect in the growth formula is discovered, however, the young man still acts like an infant.

THE ELECTRIFIED PIG

Release: 1911, Cosmopolitan
Description: Silent, 395 feet
Classification: SF-C
References: No. 14, p. 145; No. 50, p. 120; BIO, 4-20-11, p. xiii

A butcher purchases a large pig at a local market and begins the journey home, but while aboard a cable car the pig is struck by a loose power line. The accident leaves the pig electrically charged and unable to be held by the butcher. The pig, having escaped the butcher's grasp, leaps from the cable car and is pursued by the bewildered man. The chase causes a great deal of turmoil within the community as the pig scurries about shocking all it touches. Finally the butcher acquires a pair of rubber gloves which enable him to capture the pig.

The pig is slaughtered and converted into sausages, which also are electrically charged. The butcher sells the sausages to many different customers, but when each of them attempts to cook them they leap from the pan and return to the butcher shop, where they all are attracted together, thus recreating the very much alive and electrified whole pig.

THE HOUSE OF MYSTERY

Release: 1911, Pathe
Description: Silent, 460 feet
Classification: SF-C
References: No. 14, p. 230; No. 50, p. 204; BIO, 1-4-12, p. viii; MPN, Vol. 13, p. 243

The House of Mystery depicts a newly designed house with an unusual ultramodern burglar alarm system. It is not long after the house is constructed that a burglar gains entry. He is suddenly bombarded with an avalanche of weights, and, while still stunned by this attack, he is next seized by several small robots, all of whom begin to strike him with their metal arms. In an effort to free himself, the intruder runs into the adjoining living room. Without warning the normally immobile furniture begins to move and pursue the burglar. The tired, confused man takes refuge in a large wicker basket and the lid slams down on his head, thus preventing his escape. The basket begins to move and within a few moments is shot down a chute leading to a neighboring police station. Here a large mechanical policeman takes charge of the criminal and thrusts him into a cell. The scene ends with the captured man looking almost relieved at being in a safe jail.

THE INVENTOR'S SECRET

Release: 1911, Biograph Company
Description: Silent, 468 feet
Classification: SF-C
References: No. 14, p. 250; No. 50, p. 221; BIO, 11-30-11; BIO, 1-29-14; LC, J167112; MPW, Vol. 10, p. 226

Credits

Producer .... D. W. Griffith

A similar story portrayed in an earlier science fiction film, *An Animated Doll* (1908), seems to be a much more complete production than this later effort. In the film a toymaker invents an automatic doll and attempts to secure a patent. Meanwhile, a young girl is lost and, naturally, resembles the automatic doll. Accusations are aimed at the inventor in regards to the missing girl. Finally, the issue is resolved when the young girl appears, and the movie ends with everyone apologizing profusely to the old toymaker.

1912

THE CAVEMAN

Release: 1912, Vitagraph Company of America
Description: Silent, 1000 feet
Classification: SF-A
References: No. 14, p. 79; No. 50, p. 60; BIO, 7-4-12; MPW, Vol. 12, p. 425

Credits

Director .... Ralph Waldo Ince

Cast

First Cavewoman .... Edith Story
Second Cavewoman .... Rose Tapley
Caveman Chief .... Teft Johnson
First Caveman .... Harry Northrup

This film takes the viewer back in time to the dawn of mankind, where a cave population is busy attempting to survive in a hostile world. With crude weapons they stalk and kill the denizens of the jungle. Their society is simple: the caveman chief is the ultimate authority; women perform the necessary chores to free the men to hunt for food and provide the necesssary protection for the community.

> "The camera work is perfect, and the backgrounds were so well chosen that they seem to breathe with the story."
>
> *Motion Picture World*, Vol. 12, p. 425

The Caveman was another attempt to display Darwin's controversial theory of evolution which, during this era, was considered by most to be more science fiction than science fact.

DR. BROMPTON-WATT'S AGE ADJUSTER

Release: 1912, Edison Film Company
Description: Silent, 325 feet
Classification: SF-C
References: No. 14, p. 130; No. 50, p. 104; BIO, 6-20-12, p. vi; LC, LP161020-23 EDK, Vol. 6, No. 5

Cast

Dr. Brompton-Watts .... John Sturgeon
Experimental Subject .... Edward Boulden
Experimental Subject .... Mrs. Wallace Erskine

Dr. Brompton-Watts has produced a new chemical that restores one's youth. An elderly couple

A couple attempts to regain their youth in Dr. Brompton-Watt's Age Adjuster (1912)

enters his sanatorium for this miracle age restoration treatment. The elderly man is, however, so excited about regaining his lost youth that he takes an overdose of the powerful elixir. The great amount results in 60 years being removed from his age, sending him back to the infant stage. He drinks more of the liquid and this time his infant age is sent even further back in time, to when man's ancient ancestor lived—Neanderthal Man. Dr. Brompton-Watts is able to correct his mistake by reversing the process, and returns the man to an age of 21 years.

Meanwhile, the wife decides that she is satisfied with her present age and declines any treatment. Her husband, not wishing to be young while his wife remained her true age, asks the doctor to restore him to his original elderly status.

A well executed SF-C film, revealing that Edison's endeavors in the film world had made significant technical strides in the past few years. The acting appeared to be more deliberate than many of its contemporaries of 1912.

DR. JEKYLL AND MR. HYDE

Release: 1912, Thanhouser
Description: Silent
Classification: SF
References: No. 14, p. 132; No. 50, p. 106; MPN, Vol. 5, p. 22; MPW, Vol. 11, p. 86, 128, 152, 305, Vol. 12, p. 87, 152

Credits

Producer .... Thanhouser
Director .... Lucius Henderson

Cast

Dr. Jekyll and Mr. Hyde .... James Cruze
Muriel Carew .... Marguerite Snow
Dr. Lanyan .... Harry Benham

This film's enactment of the Robert Louis Stevenson novel, *The Strange Case of Dr. Jekyll and Mr. Hyde*, is a worthy representation of the original work.

In this picture, Dr. Jekyll is portrayed as a young physician possessed with the idea that medicine can aid the soul, or human spirit, as well as the body. His constant and persistent experiments to achieve this goal must be conducted in secret as many of his colleagues lack understanding of his efforts.

Soon he discovers a strange chemical mixture which can divide a person's *evil* side from their *good* side. He believes he can eventually remove the evil completely from each individual. As he begins to experiment, using his own body as the subject, he devises an antidote which will reverse the process and restore the subject to his former self.

The experiment begins as Dr. Jekyll swallows the first dosage of the chemical. His body contorts and the gruesome figure of Mr. Hyde appears. At first, Dr. Jekyll is horrified by the creature he has unleashed. But at the same time he is comforted by the ability of the antidote to subdue this evil side. As time passes, the process requires larger and larger doses of the antidote to restore his *normal* self. Moreover, the emergence of Mr. Hyde becomes more frequent and his visits more lengthy. When Mr. Hyde brutely murders Dr. Jekyll's financee's father, the guilt of this action is too overwhelming for Jekyll. He vows to extinguish Hyde forever. Locking himself in the laboratory, he attempts to mix the final portion of the antidote, but accidently spills the chemicals. Suddenly, Hyde begins to take form again. This results in Jekyll's *conscience* being encased in Hyde's miserable form. From behind the

In this scene from *Dr. Jekyll and Mr. Hyde* (1912), a dying Mr. Hyde, who has transformed into Dr. Jekyll (James Cruze), is being embraced by his sweetheart, Muriel Carew (Marguerite Snow).

laboratory door, he pleads with an assistant to bring him the necessary chemicals to remake the antidote. The assistant, however, recognizes the voice of Hyde. He suspects that some disaster has befallen Dr. Jekyll and instead summons the police. As they arrive and attempt to gain entry to the laboratory, Mr. Hyde swallows a large dose of poison—thus ending the terrible dual existence.

> "We have long known that Thanhouser had designs on Robert Louis Stevenson's *The Strange Case of Dr. Jekyll and Mr. Hyde*, and therefore was not surprised to learn of its scheduling on that producer's list of *Greatest January* releases."
>
> *Moving Picture News*, Vol. 5, No. 1, p. 22

This film is extremely well done and vastly superior to an earlier version by Selig (1908). The acting, sets, and action sequences provide a sense of realism that was convincing to the 1912 audience.

THE HYPNOTIC CHAIR

Release: 1912, Majestic
Description: Silent
Classification: SF-C
References: No. 14, p. 237; No. 46, p. 290; No. 50, p. 209; MPW, Vol.12, p. 660, 832; MPW, Vol. 14, p. 1082

The Hypnotic Chair is a film in which a specially constructed chair has the capability of inducing an electrical charge to the person occupying it which has a hypnotic effect on all the chair's victims. A man uses the chair to control his rebellious wife, but has some misgivings about the results.

The movie is a good idea, but fails to develop either strong acting or a sufficient plot. Definitely a weak SF effort for the period.

IN THE YEAR 2000

Release: 1912, Solax
Description: Silent
Classification: SF-C
References: No. 14, p. 243; No. 46, p. 309; No. 50, p. 216

Credits

Producer .... Solax
Director .... Alice Guy

The film *In the Year 2000* attempts to prognosticate the future revealing that by the year 2000 women will be the dominant political and social force throughout the world. The film depicts women in every role previously held by man—even all the housework is done by men (reluctantly, of course).

The viewer of this work is never sure how the film maker is able to predict the future (i.e. what device is used), but the film provides several light and humorous moments for the 1912 viewer.

KISSING PILLS

Release: 1912, Lubin
Description: Silent, 1020 feet
Classification: SF-C
References: No. 14, p. 272; No. 46, p. 330; No. 50, p. 245; LC, H101443; MPW, Vol. 2, p. 144; BIO, 2-22-12, p. xxix

Credits

Producer .... Sigmund Lubin

A chemistry professor of great repute lives in Green-Top, a beautiful mountain community. The professor has noted for some time that husbands reduce their kissing frequency soon after the honeymoon. On the other hand, the wives continue their longings for affection far beyond the honeymoon. The women begin to expect a kiss only on New Year's Eve and on their birthdays. Their discontent is loudly echoed throughout the small town of Green-Top. In fact, their outcry becomes so vociferous that Professor Newton vows to end their plight of agony.

After much experimentation, the professor develops a *kissing pill* designed to make even the most reluctant suitor *pucker-up*. He begins to distribute free samples of this marvelous kissing drug. The results are, however, a mass kissing frenzy that would shame even the most ardent of lovers.

The film, having brought the audience to a state of complete *pucker-madness*, abruptly ends.

MAN'S GENESIS

Release: 1912, Biograph Company
Description: Silent, 1035 feet
Classification: SF
References: No. 1, p. 523; No. 2, p. 202; No. 3, p. 73; No. 23, p. 113, 114; No. 47, p. 32; No. 50, p. 289; LC, J171534; MPW, Vol. 13, p. 72, 343

Credits

Producer .... Biograph Company
Director .... D. W. Griffith
Screenplay .... D. W. Griffith and Frank Woods
Camera .... Billy Bitzer

Cast

Weakhands .... Robert Harron
Lily White .... Mae Marsh
Brute Force .... Wilfred Lucas
Old Man .... William Chrystie Miller
Boy .... Charles Mailes
Girl .... W. C. Robinson

The film opens with an old man telling a young boy and girl about the dawn of mankind. The scene fades to a quiet, fertile valley; the sun begins to rise over the nearby hills as Weakhands emerges from

Weakhands captures Lily White in the film *Man's Genesis* (1912).

his cold damp cave overlooking the valley far, far below his rocky ledge. He can barely distinguish Brute Force coming out of his thatch hut. His intense dislike for Brute Force is quite apparent. Brute Force has successfully driven Weakhands away each time he has entered the valley seeking a mate. As the names imply, Brute Force is the antithesis of Weakhands with his frail, anemic body, and thus the reason he has been unable to overpower Brute Force.

Lily White is forced out of her cave after the death of her mother and while gliding across the parapits high above the valley encounters Weakhands. They immediately have a physical attraction toward each other and begin to make a home in a nearby cave. Lily White goes to the mouth of the cave to gather small bits of wood for a fire when Brute Force suddenly springs from behind a large rock and attempts to carry her away. Weakhands makes futile efforts to overcome Brute Force, but ends up rolling down the rocky terrain. Badly bruised and cut, he crawls back to the cave to save Lily White. As he nears the entrance, he grasps a large stick to use as a weapon. Lily White remains silent as she sees Weakhands' approach. As he climbs atop a level rock ledge, Brute Force turns and attacks. Swiftly, Weakhands strikes him with his new weapon, each blow finding its way to a vital area. Soon Brute Force is seen sprawled upon the rocks below. Weakhands and Lily White enter their cave dwelling, thus ending the old man's tale and the film.

This movie is by far the best SF production of those listed thus far, and is a classic SF endeavor. In fact, it became the necessary evidence to convince the public and the film industry of D.W. Griffith's genius. Vachel Lindsay in his book, *The Art of the Moving Picture*, lauded *Man's Genesis*, exclaiming the film to be, "A Griffith masterpiece, and every actor does sound work. The audience, mechanical Americans, fond of crawling on their stomachs to tinker with their automobiles, are eager over the evolution of the first weapon from a stick to a hammer. They are full of curiosity as they could well be over the history of Langley or the Wright Brothers."

This is the first SF film to have an experienced director and cast. Robert Harron (Weakhands) played in an earlier SF film, *Dr. Skinum* (1907), as well as being a veteran of over 20 other films prior to this role. He went on to act in more than 120 films in his career. Wilfred Lucas had starred or acted in more than 50 films before his role in *Man's Genesis*, and eventually appeared in nearly 300 films. For Mae Marsh, this was her screen debut, but her talent was obvious even in this, her first film. She later became known as Samuel Goldwyn's original *Goldwyn Girl*, and was named one of the five leading actresses of the silent era. (She received the George Eastman Award in 1957).

This film was such a huge financial success for the Biograph Film Company that they took the movie and shot another 1000 or so feet of film, and released it the following year under the title *The Primitive Man*.

NAVIGATION BY WIRELESS

Release: 1912, Danube
Description: Silent, 360 feet
Classifictation: SF
References: No. 1, p. 349; No. 50, p. 329; BIO, 2-1-12, p. xxiii

A brilliant inventor, Professor Wirth, succeeds in devising an instrument which can control the path of cars, ships, and trains without a human present. The film presents a future glimpse of the potential of wireless current.

THE SERPENTS

Release: 1912, Vitagraph Company of America
Description: Silent, 1000 feet
Classification: SF
References: No. 14, p. 423; No. 50, p. 427

Credits

Producer .... Vitagraph Company
Director .... Ralph Ince

Cast

Eric .... Ralph Ince
Chloe .... Edith Storey
Haakon .... Taft Johnson
Linda .... Helen Gardner
Idiot .... William V. Raynous

The film takes the viewer back into the primitive beginnings of mankind. It tells us that from the crude times right down through the ages man has battled the forces of good and evil. In the movie this struggle between good and evil comes into sharp focus as each of the players act their parts.

Eric and Chloe, who live in a secure cave high above the lush primeval valley, are herding sheep along a narrow ledge toward their dwelling. They encounter a friend, Haakon, along the path. After greetings are exchanged, Haakon accompanies the pair to their cave and stays the night. It becomes apparent that Haakon covets Chloe and begins to tempt her with various gifts. But Chloe will not be blinded by the gifts offered—her love for Eric is too great.

In a nearby cave dwells a pagan priest whose powers are as awesome as they are mysterious. This sorcerer and his idiot apprentice are responsible for the nefarious traffic of poisons, responsible for many deaths within the primitive society. The mysterious power of the priest is summoned by Haakon (for a handsome price) to aid in his quest for Chloe.

Soon Linda, Chloe's sister, arrives for a short visit and the evil plan is set in motion. Mysteriously, Linda begins to have strong desires for Eric. When Chloe finds them in each other's arms, she becomes bitter, but believes that Eric is not to blame. Haakon must resort to more drastic means. He administers a special potion to Eric that will induce the *sleep of death*. Meanwhile, Linda has sought a similar drug to give to Chloe, but finds she has no means of paying the priest. The priest offers a suggestion for a form of payment—and leads Linda to the rear of his cave. At this, the idiot becomes inflamed with jealousy and dislodges a large stone which falls and crushes the evil priest. The idiot then poisons Haakon and carries Linda back to his cave—his prize for having rid the society of the evil priest. Soon Eric awakens and the cave community becomes a tranquil environment once again.

This is a weak SF film, but is significant in that Darwin's theory of evolution was a highly controversial subject during the early 1900's. The following excerpt depicts the climate into which this film was introduced:

> "For audacity this picture has not been approached for sometime. It remains to be seen how well it will take with the public."
>
> *The Moving Picture World*, Vol. 12, p. 316

This film contained two sections of an earlier Vitagraph film, *The Caveman* (1912), and even used much of the same cast.

THE THEFT OF THE SECRET CODE

Release: 1912, Vitascope Company
Description: Silent
Classification: SF-A
References: No. 50, p. 485; LC, LU183; MPW, Vol. 15, p. 703

This film provides a great deal of adventure for the viewer. A race between a high speed automobile and a military airplane provides the action. The plot centers around an international adventuress who steals a secret code from a famous statesman. The spies employ a new living x-ray machine which can detect objects under a person's clothing. The film becomes daring for the 1912 era when the American agents search the female adventuress using the *living* x-ray machine.

1913

A BOLT FROM THE SKY

Release: 1913, Kalem Company
Description: Silent, 1 reel (less than 1000 feet)
Classification: SF
References: No. 3, p. 17; No. 14, p. 62; No. 46, p. 59; No. 50, p. 43; BIO, 9-11-13; MPW, Vol. 17, p. 537

Cast

Young Girl .... Alice Joyce
Young Man .... Tom Moore

A belligerent old astronomer refuses to allow his daughter to wed a handsome young man from a nearby town. The young man and the astronomer have quite an argument, but the result is unchanged—no marriage to his daughter. The astronomer returns to his laboratory and continues to observe an object of considrable size approaching the earth. As his observations continue, he identifies the object as a large meteor, and becomes ecstatic about the possibility of the meteor landing near his laboratory. It does, indeed, land nearby—in fact, on top of the laboratory, crushing it and killing the crotchety old astronomer.

After a few minutes of remorse, the daughter realizes that she is now free to marry the man she loves. As the film ends the young couple are found in each other's arms gazing toward the heavens in thankful response.

This film is one of the few SF films in which the scientist gets what he deserves, and gives the audience a happy ending. Nevertheless, it is a weak science fiction effort for 1913, especially when so many films preceding it were vastly superior.

BUMBLE'S DIMINISHER

Release: 1913, Universal Film Manufacturing Co.
Description: Silent, 360 feet
Classification: SF-C
References: No. 14, p. 69; No. 50, p. 50; BIO, 9-11-13

An awkward young lad (Bumble) accidentally discovers a powder that has the ability to reduce the size of any object. His use of this powder causes him a great deal of difficulty, but provides many a humorous moment for the audience.

A weak SF entry, this film is far too short to adequately develop a decent plot. This was Universal's first SF production and was at a time when all their film efforts took place on the East Coast.

BUMKE DISCOVERS THE TURNING MICROBE

Release: 1913, Elite Film Company
Description: Silent, 600 feet
Classification: SF-C
References: No. 14, p. 69; No. 50, p. 50; BIO, 6-12-13, p. xv

Bumke's uncle gives him a microscope for his birthday, and this little genius sets to work making scientific investigations. Not long afterward, Bumke makes a startling discovery: an unusual microbe which has the power to make objects rotate. Bumke, with all his genius, has not learned proper and safe laboratory procedures, and accidently infects himself with this unique microbe.

Soon he gains the power to rotate objects. At first this appears to be quite a lark, but as the microbe further invades his body, the power becomes too great for him to control. The film ends with Bumke being led away by policemen with certain incarceration as his fate.

The film clearly points out the dangers of an uncontrolled experiment and firmly establishes an experimenter's motto: never use thyself.

THE CAVEMAN'S WAR

Release: 1913, Kalem Company
Description: Silent, 2000 feet
Classification: SF
References: No. 14, p. 79; No. 46, p. 92; No. 50, p. 60; BIO, 2-15-14; MPW, Vol. 18, p. 973, 1036, 1412

This film contains similar scenes and dialogue as seen in the earlier primitive man epics. The only unique facet of this film is the invention of a new weapon—the bow and arrow. The sequences of events which pictorially describe this devastating new weapon makes the movie a worthwhile SF entry.

The prehistoric drama begins with Red Axe being ostracized from the Cave Dwellers society for lusting and attempting to steal another's mate. Removal from the society was obviously a serious action as all the male members of the community hurl stones, clubs, and sharp spears at Red Axe as he makes his hasty departure. Unfortunately, he was not as fast on foot as he should have been—one of the spears tears a deep gash in his side. Somehow he continues to move away from the village and out of range of the spear-throwers. The loss of blood makes him weak and he staggers forward, tumbling down a shallow slope, and coming to rest in a narrow gully.

After a short time, he is discovered by Strong Arm and a small hunting party of Shell People. Strong Arm, being of a generous mood (he had just taken Light foot, daughter of Scarface, as his mate), instructs his men to take the wounded man to the village. Immediately Strong Arm and Lightfoot begin to care for the injured stranger. Soon he regains his strength, and--very ungraciously--attempts to steal Lightfoot from Strong Arm. Again, his lustful, evil ways are foiled. This time, however, he escapes the Shell People's wrath and returns to the village of the Cave Dwellers.

Once home, he organizes the Cave Dwellers in an attack against the Shell People in hopes of gaining Lightfoot during the ensuing battle. As he suspected, the Shell People are no match for the Cave Dwellers, whose strength and size give them a decided advantage. Strong Arm, fighting with blind fury, begins to tire. But seeing Red Axe grab Lightfoot and carry her away gives him new strength. Almost without thinking he picks up a long stick with a taut vine attached and uses it to propel a second stick in the direction of Red Axe. He is surprised at the distance the stick travels, but not half as surprised as Red Axe when the sharp stick strikes him in the chest. This time Red Axe's wound is fatal. The other Cave Dwellers are struck with terror at the sight of this new device and flee. Meanwhile, Lightfoot has escaped and returns to Strong Arm's side. The Shell People rejoice over their victory.

The final scene displays the concerned face of Strong Arm wondering where this new weapon technology will lead his people.

CURSED BE WAR

Release: 1913
Description: Silent
Classification: SF
References: No. 13, p. 38; No. 50, p. 84

Credits

Director .... Alfred Machin

This film anticipates the horrors of a global conflict involving massive ground forces, fast moving aircraft, and diabolical men driving their armies to destruction. The techniques of this production makes it a truly unique SF entry. Unfortunately, the film was lost before the restoration projects began.

DANCES OF THE AGES

Release: 1913, Edison Film
Description: Silent, 1000 feet
Classification: SF-F
References: No. 14, p. 106; No. 46, p. 129; No. 50, p. 86; BIO, 7-31-13, p. xv; EDK, 5-15-13; LC, LP723

Cast

Dancing Master .... Duane Wagar

A weak SF entry, but worthy of mention because of its special effects, the film involves dream sequences of an old dancing master as he visits a wonderful world of miniature dancers. Suddenly the dancing master and his company of miniatures are hurled back into the annals of mankind where they perform syncopated movements, primitive style, to the accompaniment of a distant undulating drum. As they continue, their tempo increases as time advances. The viewer is taken forward in time by means of period dances—the Dance of the Priest of Ra (1200 B.C.), dances from the oriental past (200 B.C.), the minuet (1760), and many more—as they progress toward the (then) modern Rag. Finally, the dance master and the miniatures return to the present where the tired old man awakens. He is stunned by the dream he has just experienced ("It was a dream, wasn't it?" he wonders).

> "The picture is a decided novelty, and one that is bound to attract a great deal of attention."
>
> *Bioscope*, 7-31-13, p. xv

DEMONYTE

Release: 1913, Film Releases of America
Description: Silent, 2000 feet
Classification: SF
References: No. 14, p. 118-19; No. 46, p. 138; No. 50, p. 94; BIO, 11-13-13, p. iii; MPW, Vol. 13, p. 1338

Lincoln Whatley, a noted professor of chemistry, after many hours of labor has developed a new explosive. Naturally this new device has great value as a new weapon—heads of nations begin to bid for its exclusive ownership.

Meanwhile, a group of anarchists plot to acquire the new explosive. This sinister league is led by the infamous Lydia, Countess of Orloff. Lydia manages to become employed as companion to Professor Whatley's daughter. Not long after her employment she uncovers a box of demonyte caps which were hidden in the Professor's secret laboratory. Quickly she steals one of the caps; she has been observed, however, by Lieutenant Turner, Mary Whatley's fiance, and he and Professor Whatley capture her. They imprision Lydia in the x-ray cabinet. He turns the powerful x-ray machine on which reveals the location of the demonyte cap in Lydia's mouth. But in their haste to recover the cap, the two allow Lydia to escape.

The Lieutenant decides to return to Washington, D.C. with the secret formula and the box of demonyte caps. While aboard the train to Washington he is again confronted by Lydia, this time with her cohorts. Fleeing for his life, the Lieutenant seeks safety on the roof of the train but his pursuers are relentless. As the anarchists are about to grab the brave man, a train appears going in the opposite direction. In a futile attempt to escape, the Lieutenant leaps for the passing train, but falls short of his mark which causes an explosion that destroys him, his pursuers, and the trains.

The professor, upon learning of the Lieutenant's fate, decides to destroy the demonyte and his secret laboratory.

This film may remind many SF fans of another plot, as well it should: Jules Verne's *A Trip from the Earth to the Moon* (1865) had already established the plot upon which this film is based. Unfortunately, the movie does not go far enough with the story to do justice to the Jules Verne book.

THE DIAMOND MAKERS

Release: 1913, Rex Motion Picture Company
Description: Silent, 2000 feet
Classification: SF
References: No. 1, p. 394; No. 14; P. 126-27; No. 46, p. 142; No. 50, p. 101; MPW, Vol. 17, p. 726, 1100, 1178

Credits

Producer .... Edwin S. Porter

Cast

High Priestess .... Margarita Fischer
Felix Westerly .... Robert Leonard

The story begins with an old *Hindoo* alchemist's discovery of the delicate technique for creating perfect diamonds. His process, furnace, and laboratory are kept with utmost secrecy by his fellow Buddhists. Finally, the alchemist convinces the high priest that his diamonds should be sold in America and the money used to rehabilitate the Buddhist religion. Reluctantly, the high priest agrees, and decides to send the high priestess and two native attendants to sell the precious stones. There appears to be speculation among the other American diamond dealers that the stones may be fake and they engage the great detective, Felix Westerly. With impeccable sleuthing, the famous private eye tracks down the diamond sellers, but the priestess is very sly and provides a good match of wits for Mr. Westerly, which in turn provides a good deal of excitement for the audience.

> "The picture is full of quick detective stuff and clever getaways. It is highly exciting. One poor fellow gets burned to death on a live wire. The old Alchemist blows up his furnace and takes his life rather than reveal his secret. Escapes are made by means of roofs, panel doors, automobiles, yachts, and other things.Margarita Fischer as the oriental woman is superb. Bob Leonard makes a very convincing detective and is highly acceptable in the part. He bagged the whole gang and then fell in love with the priestess, but a Joe Brandt or Rudyard Kipling might say, 'that's another scenario.' "
>
> *The Moving Picture World*, Vol. 17, p. 726

As an added note, both Margarita Fischer and Robert Leonard were veteran performers and appeared in many more silent films. Margarita never made a sound picture and Robert made only one in 1945. Robert Leonard was more renown for his directorial skills than his acting accomplishments.

DR. JEKYLL AND MR. HYDE

Release: 1913, Independent Moving Picture Co.
Description: Silent, 2000 feet
Classification: SF
References: No. 14, p. 132; No. 46, p. 147; No. 47, p. 41, No. 50, p. 106; BIO, 6-15-13, p. 909; 7-17-14, p. 156; 8-14-13, p. 479; 5-28-14, p. 992; FAM, Vol. 11, p. 39; MPW, Vol. 15, p. 899, 997, 1105, Vol. 25, p. 1727

Credits

Producer .... Carl Laemmle
Director .... Herbert Brenon
Screenplay .... Herbert Brenon

Cast

Dr. Jekyll & Mr. Hyde .... King Baggot
Alice .... Jane Gail
Alice's Father .... Matt Snyder
Dr. Lanyon .... Howard Crampton
Lawyer Utterson .... William Sorelle

This film version continues many of the departures from the original work by Robert Louis Stevenson that began with the 1912 film rendition by Thanhouser. Dr. Jekyll is a young practicing physician in the metropolitan area of London, who devotes some of his valuable time to work in the slum charity wards. Dr. Jekyll openly conducts drug experiments on many of these charity patients, and his two friends, Dr. Lanyon and his Lawyer Utterson, openly joke about this experimentation. Unbeknownst to his friends or colleagues, Dr. Jekyll believes that he has found a new drug which can rid these wretched people of their evil ways. For some reason the good doctor finds himself unable to inject this strange serum into anyone else's body, and so uses his own. Immediately a hideous transformation takes place: the once kind and handsome doctor is now the hideous, deformed Mr. Hyde. But, Dr. Jekyll's mind continues to function as his own even while he is Mr. Hyde, and he creates a note that reads, "To my household servants: the bearer of this message, Mr. Hyde, is my best friend; treat him as you would me."

As time passes, the transformations from Dr. Jekyll to Mr. Hyde become more frequent resulting in Mr. Hyde becoming the dominate personality. The antidote dosage must be greatly increased to restore Dr. Jekyll. When Mr. Hyde takes form, he becomes increasingly more violent—a violence which results in the death of Alice's father (Jekyll's future father-in-law). Hyde returns to the laboratory, hoping to transform into Dr. Jekyll before his evil can be detected. Accidentally, the valuable antidote is spilled, making the transformation impossible. Hyde, in a raving, fiendish fury, attempts to destroy the laboratory. The physical and mental strain, however, have been too great, and he drops dead.

Dr. Lanyon and the police finally break open the door of the laboratory and find it in shambles with Hyde's corpse lying across an overturned workbench. The grotesque, twisted Hyde is a gruesome sight and Dr. Lanyon carefully covers it with his cloak. Moments pass in silence and disbelief until Alice appears in the doorway. Calm, she glides across the room to the covered body and carefully lifts the edge of the cloak to get a glimpse of the monster that killed her father. But it is not the body of the hideous Hyde she sees, but that of her fiance, Dr. Jekyll. Her grief is now magnified by the sudden loss of two loved ones and the realization that Jekyll was the monster Hyde. Dr. Lanyon attempts to console her by proclaiming that Dr. Jekyll was a noble martyr in the medical sciences.

> "There are many thrilling moments in this picture—moments that serve to make more complete the illusion. The refinements of Kimematography lend material aid in the creation of this illusion. It is through the means of the dissolving process that the transformation is made peculiarly effective. You see the change from the man of good to the man of evil right before your eyes.
>
> "The story is coherently and lucidly told."
>
> *The Moving Picture World*, Vol. 15, p. 899

This film version of *Dr. Jekyll and Mr. Hyde* was only slightly better than its predecessor, and this may be credited to the photographic special effects and the strong performance by King Baggot. Nevertheless, this is the third version of the same story within a five year period. I guess the old saying is true, "Keep trying until you get it right," and Hollywood was no quitter.

DR. MAXWELL'S EXPERIMENT

Release: 1913, Lubin
Description: Silent, 1053 feet
Classification: SF
References: No. 14, p. 33; No. 46, p. 147; No. 50, p. 106; BIO, 4-10-13, p. xxiii; MPW, Vol. 15, p. 804

Credits

Producer .... Sigmund Lubin
Director .... Arthur Johnson

Cast

Dr. John Maxwell .... Arthur Johnson
Alice Maxwell .... Lottie Briscoe
Bill Dawson .... Charles Brandt

Dr. John Maxwell, a brilliant surgeon, returns home after a fatiguing day of operations and finds his daughter asleep on the couch. He sends her off to bed and settles down to puruse the latest medical journals. In one of the journals an article about a new brain alteration technique captures his attention. The new information will aid him in completing a new surgical procedure which may alter an individual's personality. As he is about to retire for the evening a noise from the rear of the house causes him to become alarmed. When he investigates he captures a would-be burglar, Bill Dawson. After the apprehension of the intruder, a lengthy conversation takes place during which Dr. Maxwell offers Bill a choice between his operating table or jail. Reluctantly, Bill selects the operation which will hopefully change his personality and remove his tendencies to steal.

The operation is a success. After a sufficient recovery period, Bill moves to a nearby city to begin a new life. During the next two years, Dawson becomes a very successful businessman but Dr. Maxwell's fortunes take a serious turn for the worse.

Alice is now working as a stenographer and one day she meets Bill by accident. Naturally, he quickly offers to help in anyway he can—after all he owes a great debt to Dr. Maxwell. But Alice has not seen her father for some time, his most recent letter is several months old and quite worn from her constant reading. She offers Bill the tear-soaked letter: "Dear Alice," it reads, "Speculation and morphine have ruined me. Save what you can of the house, I cannot face you; am going...God knows where. Your Father." Bill offers Alice a job at his office and within a year they are married.

Some time later, late at night in their new home, Bill hears a strange sound coming from their dining area. He quietly investigates and captures a burglar attempting to steal the silver. When he turns on the light, he and the burglar are both shocked: Dr. Maxwell is the thief! After much discussion, Bill decides to take care of the old doctor, and all three of them live happily together.

This film offered the interesting SF twist of corrective physiosurgery, which would appear many times over the next 60 years of film making.

Each of the players were veteran actors: Arthur Johnson had appeared in many films; Lottie Briscoe and Charles Brandt were equally experienced. This trio appeared in several more pictures together, but all died before the end of the silent era.

THE INDESTRUCTIBLE MR. JENKS

Release: 1913, Kalem Company
Description: Silent, 370 feet
Classification: SF-C
References: No. 14, p. 245; No. 46, p. 295; No. 50, p. 217; BIO, 6-29-13, p. vii; MPW, Vol. 16, p. 82, 380

Credits

Producer .... Sigmund Lubin

Cast

Mr. Jenks .... John E. Brennan
Mrs. Jenks .... Ruth Roland

Mr. Jenks, an amateur inventor, after many unsuccessful experiments to render himself indestructible, accidentally spills some chemicals on the kitchen stove. Unexpectedly, there is a terrific explosion and the kitchen is nearly destroyed. Mrs. Jenks, though horrified by the disaster, is thankful that her husband is safe.

After cleaning up a bit, Mr. Jenks goes to get the evening paper. On the way there a thug attacks him and attempts to bludgeon him. When the violent attack has no effect on his victim, the burglar runs down a nearby alley. This event causes Mr. Jenks to wonder if he has discovered the secret of indestructibility. Still in a perplexed mood, he inadvertedly steps in front of a steam roller—but he is unharmed. Excited by the turn of events, he hurries home to inform his wife of his success. Poor Mr. Jenks! As he is walking up the sidewalk to his home, his wife throws a pan of burned biscuits out the window. One of them strikes Mr. Jenks on the head and kills him. (Now that's a *h-a-r-d* biscuit!)

This is a weak SF entry for 1913. John Brennan appeared in very few films after this production, but Ruth Roland went on to become a queen of silent serials.

THE PRIMITIVE MAN

Release: 1913, Biograph Company
Description: Silent, 2000 feet
Classification: SF
References: No. 3, p. 73; No. 14, p. 67; No. 46, p. 74; No. 50, p. 49; LC, LU1651, LP1806

Credits

Producer .... Biograph Film Co.
Director .... D. W. Griffith
Screenplay .... D. W. Griffith
Special Effects .... Howard Gaye
Camera .... Billy Bitzer

Cast

Weakhands .... Robert Harron
Lily White .... Mae Marsh
Brute Force .... Wilfred Lucas
Caveman .... Charles Hill Mailes
Caveman .... Alfred Paget
Caveman .... Edwin Curglot
Caveman .... William J. Butler
Cavewoman .... Jenny Lee

The film *The Primitive Man* was also released under two alternate titles: *Brute Force* and *Wars of Primal Tribes*. The first 1000 feet of the film are from an earlier Griffith epic, *Man's Genesis*, with the remainder of the footage devoted to the struggle of primitive man to survive.

For the details of the initial events of the story, refer to *Man's Genesis* (1912). It will suffice to say that there was a struggle between Weakhands and Brute Force over Lily White, and Weakhands won the battle and Lily White's companionship.

Because of the skins they wear, the weapons and tools they use, the society depicted would be a Cro-magnon society existing some 35,000 years ago. Their society was very structured, with the men doing the hunting, the women cooking and bearing the children. The days and years flow steadily onward in this pattern.

Suddenly, this tranquil valley and its inhabitants are threatened by a neighboring tribe of Neanderthalers (a type of man looking more ape-like than Cro-magnon), and the men of the society gather together to protect their community. After a fierce battle the Cro-magnons pursue the Neanderthalers outside the safe boundaries of the valley where they encounter several enormous denizens of the jungle—which, based on current data, should not have been present during this part of earth's evolution. Nevertheless, the men battle several large beasts, including a reptilian-like creature that appears to be a cross between an alligator and a Tyrannosaurus Rex.

This film was as successful as its predecessor and offered Griffith the opportunity to explore some unusual special effects and camera techniques. The success of *The Primitive Man* and *Man's Genesis* set the stage for one of his most famous epics, *The Birth of a Nation*. Many of the actors and actresses in these films appeared again in *The Birth of a Nation*.

The film *The Primitive Man* is of SF interest as it carefully explores the possible foundation for Darwin's theory of evolution which was still skeptically held by many within the scientific community and most distastefully by the general public. In addition, this film marked a change for SF films as it was the first two-reel SF film and coined a new word: intermission.

THE WHIRL OF DESTINY

Release: 1913, Mundstuk Features
Description: Silent, 1000 feet
Classification: SF
References: No. 50, p. 537; MPW, Vol. 19, p. 472

This film is an unusual SF entry. It is the first science fiction semiwestern. A truly unique film is the result. Unfortunately, it was destroyed before it could be converted to acetate base film.

The picture begins with Louise marrying Dr. Hortz, a noted chemist. Louise is getting married against her will. Her father insists that she marry Dr. Hortz and not her lover, Richard Marx. She reluctantly complies with his wishes though obviously disturbed by it.

After several years have passed, Dr. Hortz devotes himself exclusively to his experiments to convert organic matter into cellulose. During this time he has virtually ignored Louise except for the time required to father a son. Finally, his experimenting is rewarded when the transformation of any organic matter into cellulose becomes a reality.

Circumstances and finances prevent Dr. Hortz from manufacturing the chemical for distribution, but as fate so often does (at least in the movies), Richard Marx returns a wealthy man and agrees to support the project. Sometime later a fire breaks out in the manufacturing plant and Dr. Hortz in an attempt to save his and Richard's notes uncovers love letters written to Richard by his wife prior to their marriage. Realizing that his wife was forced into their marriage, he decides to go West so she can finally be happy.

Unfortunately, everyone believes Dr. Hortz was killed by the fire. Louise and their son, Frank, are stricken with grief. Louise has come to love her husband very deeply over the years, and no longer desires Richard.

Frank is so upset he decides to go West to seek his fortune. However, misfortune instead follows when he becomes involved in a saloon card game during which a famous cowboy is killed. Naturally, Frank, as the stranger in town, is blamed. An angry mob is about to lynch him when the sheriff realizes that the man is his son. (It seems Dr. Hortz had become the county sheriff.) He quickly disarms the mob and frees his son. The pair quickly departs for home. Louise, alas, is so overcome by the sight of her husband alive, that she dies in his arms.

1914

A SURE CURE

Release: 1914, Crystal
Description: Silent
Classification: SF-C
References: No. 14, p. 464; No. 46, p. 587; No. 50, p. 470; LC, LP1703; MPW, Vol. 19, p. 718

Mrs. Stout is constantly yelling at her fat husband and servant Lizzie for their laziness. When all her efforts to encourage them to get to work fail, Mrs. Stout procures a bottle of special medicine called *Vitalo*. She carefully slips a drop of this strange substance into Lizzie's milk as she talks to her boyfriend, the neighborhood policeman. They both drink from the glass of doctored milk and immediately become imbued with boundless energy.

Mrs. Stout is now convinced she must administer this drug to her husband. She puts several drops into a cup of his coffee and the man immediately energetically performs many of the household chores he has neglected for years. Afterwards he invites his wife for a drive into the country. On the way back the car runs out of gas, so Mr. Stout gets out and pulls the car home! Upon arriving home, Mr. Stout and Lizzie use their excess energies to rearrange the house, but they make such a mess of it that Mrs. Stout vows never to use the *Vitalo* again.

AN ABSENT-MINDED MOTHER

Release: 1914, Edison Film Company
Description: Silent, 500 feet
Classification: SF-C
References: No. 46, p. 2; No. 50, p. 2; BIO, 5-14-14, p. v; LC, LP2163

Credits

Producer .... Thomas Edison
Director .... Charles H. France

Cast

Father .... John Daly Murphy

A very weak SF work in which a mother loses her infant and, in the process of searching for the tot, discovers an astounding hair restorer chemical. The film is less impressive than earlier productions using the *hair restoring* theme.

THE BIRTH OF EMOTION

Release: 1914, Alhambra: Krilerion
Description: Silent, 2000 feet
Classification: SF
References: No. 14, p. 48; No. 46, p. 51; No. 50, p. 36; LC, LU4478; MPN, Vol. 11, p. 45

Credits

Producer .... Alhambra
Director .... Henry Otto
Screenplay .... Marty Martin

This film uses an invention to go back in time in an effort to uncover the origin of psychological makeup. The production includes only three players, two men and a woman. Through these characters we see the initial emergence of human emotions as displayed by the actors: vanity, lust, passion, love, jealousy, revenge, and grief.

As you may have guessed, the plot calls for one of the men to fall in love with the only woman; the second man then becomes jealous and kills the other man. But the woman becomes so filled with grief she kills herself. The surviving man sits upon a rock and dwells on the misdeeds he has been a part of, thus providing us with the last emotion displayed: a guilty conscious.

> "The three members of the cast are fully expressive of the varying emotions that possess them. Not much chance is given them to exercise any dramatic ability."
>
> *Motion Picture News*, 1-16-15, p. 45

BLOWN UPON

Release: 1914, Kriterion
Description: Silent, 1 reel
Classification: SF-C
References: No. 14, p. 60; No. 46; p. 56; No. 50, p. p-7; LC, LU4091, MPW, 1-30-15

Credits

Director .... Alexander Frank

Cast

Doctor .... William Rising
Male Patient .... Robert Roberts

An extremely weak SF movie, *Blown Upon* depicts a chemist who develops an amazing liquid that can cause instant freezing. It seems that when this liquid is drunk it converts the person's breath into a freezing gas. This action becomes the basis for the comedic performance.

THE BOMB

Release: 1914, Lubin
Description: Silent, 2000 feet
Classification: SF
References: No. 14, p. 62; No. 46, p. 59; No. 50, p. 43; LC, LP3923; PHO, Jan. 1915, p. 63

Credits

Producer .... Sigmund Lubin
Director .... Joseph Smiley

Cast

Scientist .... Harry Chandler

A clever chemist invents a new explosive which is many times more powerful than dynamite. The liquid chemical can destroy an entire mountain or a small town using only five drops. The chemist attempts to force the various countries of the world into peaceful coexistence using his explosive as the threat.

The plot of this SF film is a combination of three of Jules Verne's classic tales, *A Trip to the Moon, Master of the World,* and *Robur, the Conqueror*. Unfortunately for the viewer the production effort was poor and, according to the critic's reviews of the time, the acting was extremely weak.

THE BULLY'S DOOM

Release: 1914, Lubin
Description: Silent, 353 feet
Classification: SF
References: No. 46, p. 75; No. 50, p. 49; BIO, 6-18-14, p. vii

Credits

Producer .... Sigmund Lubin
Director .... Arthur Hotaling
Screenplay .... Frank E. Griffin

Cast

Mugsy .... Frank E. Griffin
Pug .... Frances NeMoyer
Gang Member .... Jerald Hevener

This is probably the weakest SF entry of this period. Mugsy purchases some *electric snuff* which gives increased speed and agility to the user. He thereby overpowers the *bully* and becomes the ruler of the block and especially the keeper of the favorite alley territory. This production was Lubin's worst effort.

BY RADIUM RAYS

Release: 1914, Gold Seal
Description: Silent, 1959 feet
Classification: SF
References: No. 14, p. 70; No. 46, p. 80; No. 50, p. 51; BIO, 6-18-14, p. xiv; MPW, Vol. 19, p. 1090, 1107, 1158

The story centers around twin brothers, Jim and Tom, who are identical in appearance but completely opposite in personality. Both are madly in love with Sarah, the old miner's daughter. Sarah falls in love with Tom, the brother with the evil personality and Jim decides to give his part of the mine to them as a wedding gift. Naturally, as soon as they are married, Sarah realizes the mistake she has made. Things go from bad to worse when Tom steals a United States mint gold shipment. He is

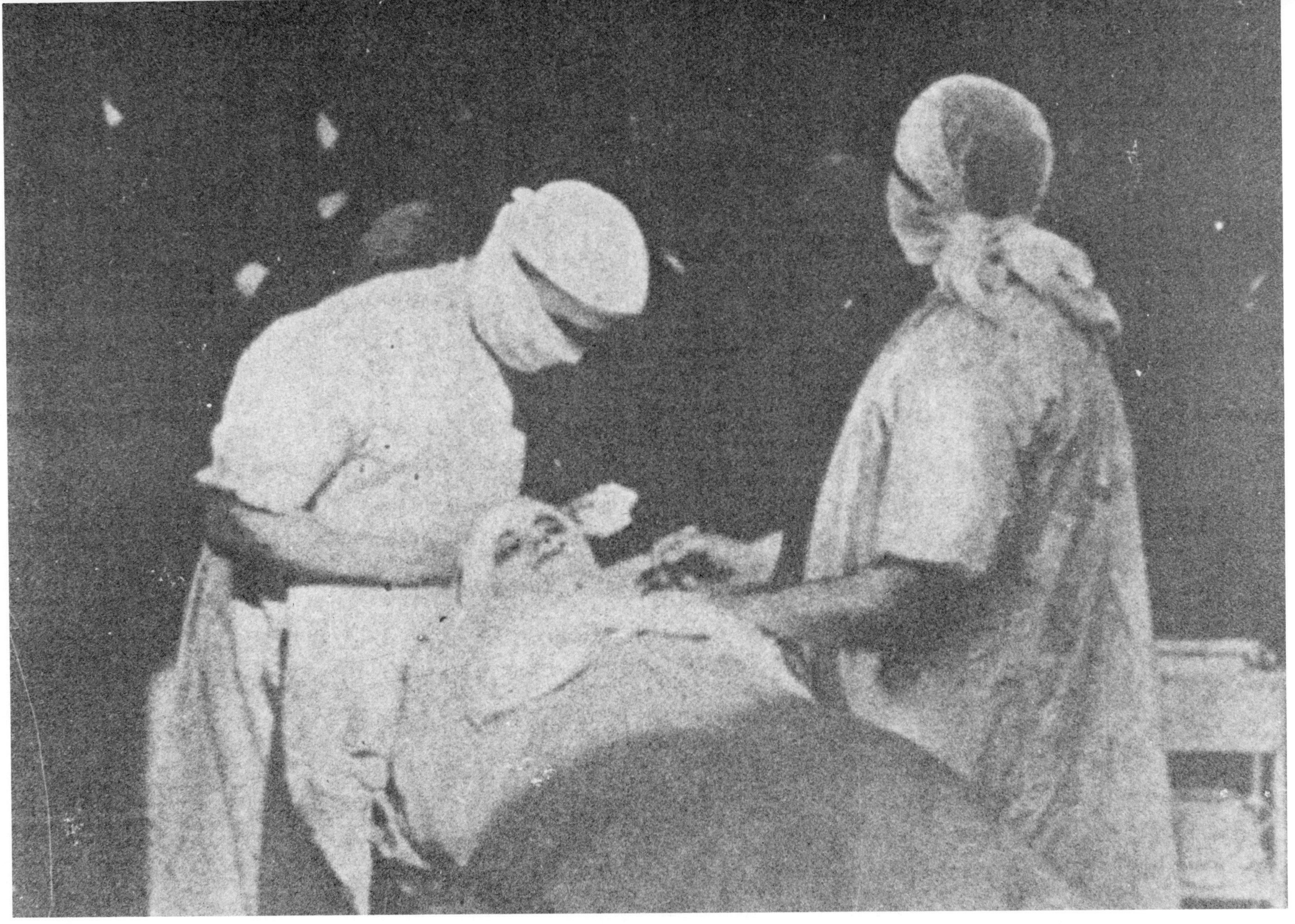

In an attempt to cure the insane, the physician uses Sarah as his demonstration case. *By Radium Rays*, 1914.

caught and sentenced to fifteen years in the state penitentiary, but he refuses to reveal the gold's hiding place. Meanwhile Sarah's baby dies of some childhood disease. This is apparently the final straw for Sarah: she loses all sense of reason and is declared insane; the local authorities have her removed to the nearby insane asylum. Fortunately for Sarah a young physician is performing some new experiments using radium rays, and offers new hope to her through this new method.

With the slim promise of a cure, Jim and Sarah's father visit the asylum. During their visit they show her some new ore they have recently mined which contains a significant gold content. She asks to keep the shining rock and they leave it with her.

The doctor then explains the radium process to the men, quickly adding that the treatment is extremely expensive. Both men dispel the doctor's worry about payment and give him their permission to proceed. Jim now decides he must visit Tom and attempt to secure a portion of the stolen money for Sarah's treatment. Tom, however, has other plans and refuses to tell his twin brother the gold's whereabouts. Finally they agree to switch places so Tom can get the necessary funds for the doctor's cure.

Meanwhile, the good doctor has used Sarah as his demonstration case and her cure is almost immediate. In addition, the doctor discovers the rock left with Sarah is rich in radium, and he and Sarah proceed to the mine to inform her father. He is ecstatic over Sarah's cure and overwhelmed by the doctor's detection of the radium ore. The old miner decides to blast out an area in order to determine how much of this strange and valuable ore his mine contains. After he detonates the charge he hears a voice from within the mine yelling for help. Much to his surprise, he finds Tom, who was near the rear of the mine searching for the stolen gold when the explosion occurred. He has been gravely wounded by the explosion and the doctor reluctantly tells them there is no hope for his survival. Hearing this, Tom tells Sarah and the others that Him has traded places with him and is still in prison. As he dies, the group hurries to the state prison to secure Jim's freedom.

> "The scenes in the first reel are very disconnected and obscure in meaning and throughout the picture the photography is at fault. In spite of these defects some of the scenes are interesting, but as a whole the production is not strong."
>
> *The Moving Picture World*, Vol. 19, p. 1090

The above says it best: a definitely weak SF entry, but an interesting use of radium at a time when the public's interest, as well as the scientific community's, was very intense. The film attempted to capitalize on that interest.

THE DIAMOND-MAKER

Release: 1914, Eclair
Description: Silent, 2989 feet
Classification: SF-A
References: No. 14, p. 126; No. 46, p. 142; No. 50, p. 101; LC, LU2124; MPW, Vol. 19, p. 1158

This film is very similar to *The Diamond Maker* of 1909 and *The Diamond Makers* (1913), but the 1914 effort involves a good deal more action and suspense. In addition, this is the longest SF production yet referenced. Too little time, however, seems to have been spent on the scientific aspects of the artificial diamond.

As this film begins we are introduced to Thomas Kellner, an eccentric chemist who has spent a number of years researching the process by which diamonds could be made artificially. Finally, Dr. Kellner, with the aid of his son Jack, has succeeded in replicating nature's handiwork: he has manufactured an imitation diamond. The material is of such fine quality that even the leading experts are unable to detect any difference. Jack becomes so excited that he suffers a heart attack and dies, taking with him most of his secret process for the diamond's creation. Dr. Kellner is distraught over his son's death and vows never to return to the laboratory.

Fifteen years later Jack's daughter, Doris, has grown to womanhood and is engaged to Wynne Browning. During the past years Doris has hoped for revenge on the diamond community for her father's death. She tells her plan to Wynne and he agrees to aid her in any way possible. They then tell Tiffany & Co. that unless they deposit ten million dollars in Doris' foreign bank account, she will mass produce the imitation diamonds using her father's process. During the next two-thirds of the movie the action centers around Doris and Wynne as they are pursued by a famous detective. In the final moments of the film the diamond barons agree to pay Doris' price. She and Wynne are married and vow never to reveal the manufacturing secret.

DR. JEKYLL AND MR. HYDE

Release: 1914, Starlight
Description: Silent
Classification: SF-C
References: No. 14, p. 132; No. 46, p. 147; No. 50, p. 106; MPN, 11-28-14, p. 50

This film was an attempt to make *Dr. Jekyll and Mr. Hyde* into a comedy. It failed miserably. The evidence indicates that it was only shown in a few theaters because it did so poorly. It was discarded when all the critics had nothing favorable to say about the production.

THE EXPLOITS OF ELAINE

Release: 1914, Pathe
Description: Silent, 14 episode serial, each episode approx. 2000 feet
Classification: SF-A
References: No. 8, p. 27, 28; No. 14, p. 150; No. 31, p. 6-8; No. 32, p. 15-18, 39, 54, 496; No. 46, p. 155; No. 50, p. 127; MPW, Vol. 23, p. 1297, 1529, 1642, 1789, 1790, 1791; Vol. 24, p. 8, 9, 179, 628, 717, 934, 935

Credits

Producer .... Theodore W. and Leopold V. Wharton
Director .... Louis Gasnier and George B. Seitz
Screenplay .... Arthur B. Reeve and Charles L. Goddard

Cast

Elaine Dodge .... Pearl White
Jameson .... Creighton Hale
Craig Kennedy .... Arnold Daly
Clutching Hand .... Sheldon Lewis
Michael .... Floyd Buckley
President Taylor Dodge .... William Riley Hatch
Perry Bennett .... Raymond Owens
Limpy Red .... Robin Towney
Wu Fang .... Edwin Arden
Wong Long Sin .... M. W. Rale

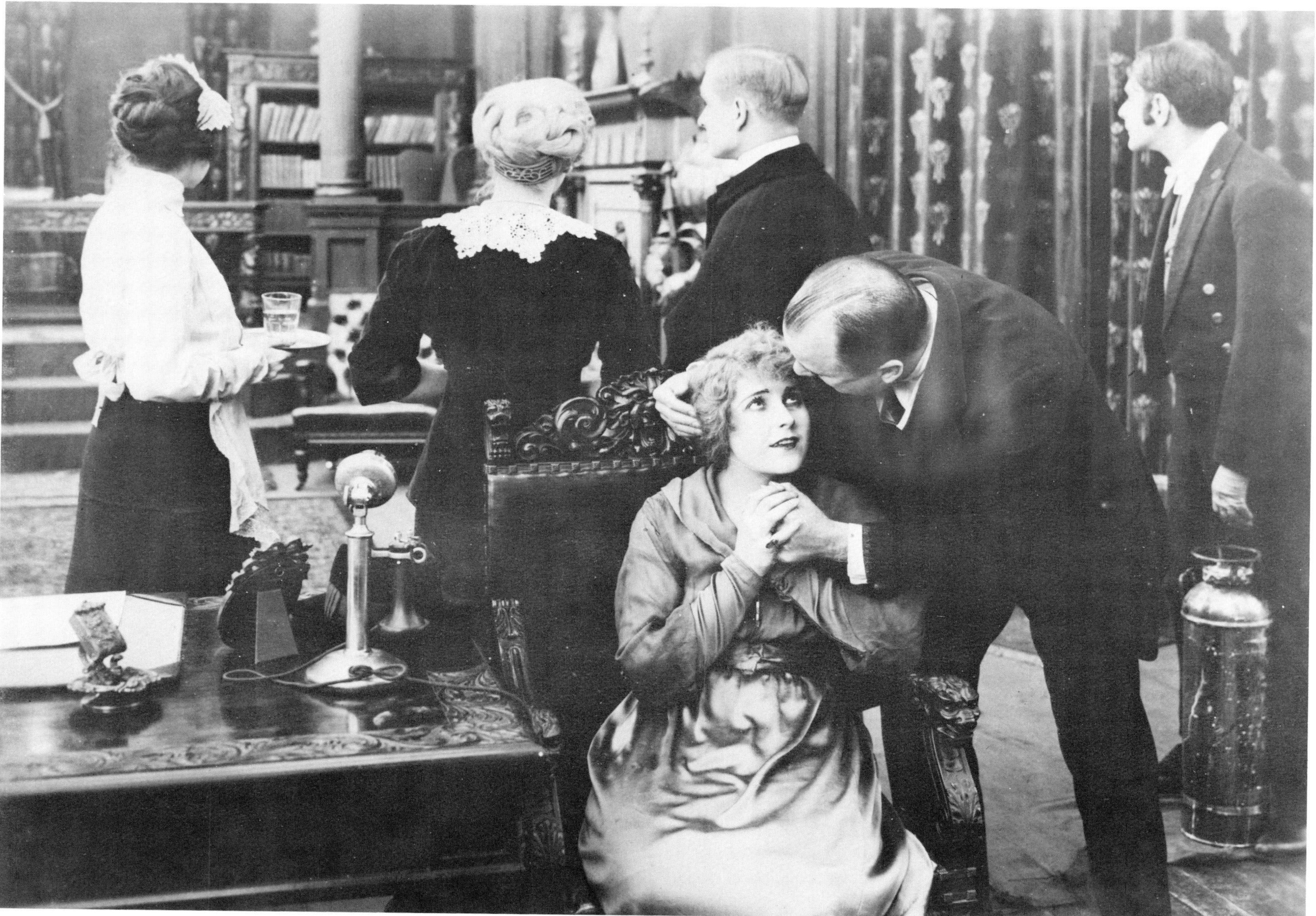

Elaine Dodge and her father are distraught over the robberies which have plagued the Dodge mansion in *Exploits of Elaine* (1914).

Chapters 1-14 of *The Exploits of Elaine*

Chapter 1: The Clutching Hand
References: LC, LU4257; MPW, Vol. 23, p. 80, 276, 278
Chapter 2: The Twilight Sleep
References: LC, LU4258; MPW, Vol. 23, p. 278
Chapter 3: The Vanishing Jewels
References: LC, LU4344; MPW, Vol. 23, p. 498, 575
Chapter 4: The Frozen Safe
References: LC, LU4345; MPW, Vol. 23, p. 575, 584, 829
Chapter 5: The Poisoned Room
References: LC, LU4522; MPW, Vol. 23, p. 740, 842
Chapter 6: The Vampire
References: LC, LU4523; MPW, Vol. 23, p. 740
Chapter 7: The Double Trap
References: LC, LU4799; MPW, Vol. 23, p. 900, 1148
Chapter 8: The Hidden Voice
References: LC, LU4800; MPW, Vol. 23, p. 900, 1449
Chapter 9: The Death Ray
References: MPW, Vol. 23, p. 1052, 1460
Chapter 10: The Life Current
References: LC, LU4829; MPW, Vol. 23, p. 1200
Chapter 11: The Hour of Three
References: LC, LU4830; MPW, Vol. 23, 1198, 1774
Chapter 12: The Blood Crystals
References: LC, LU4831; MPW, Vol. 23, p. 1682, 1774
Chapter 13: The Devil Worshippers
References: LC, LU6621; MPW, Vol. 23, p. 1846; Vol. 24, p. 237
Chapter 14: The Reckoning
References: LC, LU6622; MPW, Vol. 23, p. 2002; Vol. 24, p. 246

By the end of 1914 (this film was released on December 28, 1914) the success of serials had motivated each of the major producers to film an epic. The unbelievable success Miss Pearl White enjoyed from the Pathe serial, *The Perils of Pauline*, prompted the studio to build another serial around her tremendous drawing power. *The Exploits of Elaine* was more carefully written and filmed than any of its serial predecessors, and the cast contained many experienced actors and actresses. To secure the proper public attention Pathe desired for this production, they joined with Hearst Publications to publish each episode of *The Exploits of Elaine* in more than 400 newspapers across the country.

The fourteen chapters of the serial focus on Elaine Dodge's search for her father's murderer, a mysterious villain known only as the *Clutching Hand*. In her quest for justice, Elaine is aided by the extraordinary *scientific* detective, Craig Kennedy, whose constant bandishment of scientific paraphernalia never ceased to amaze the audience.

The first episode of the serial, *The Clutching Hand*, begins with Taylor Dodge, president of the Consolidated Insurance Company, expressing deep concern over the financial losses suffered by the company during several recent and mysterious robberies. The clues, though vague, lead them to

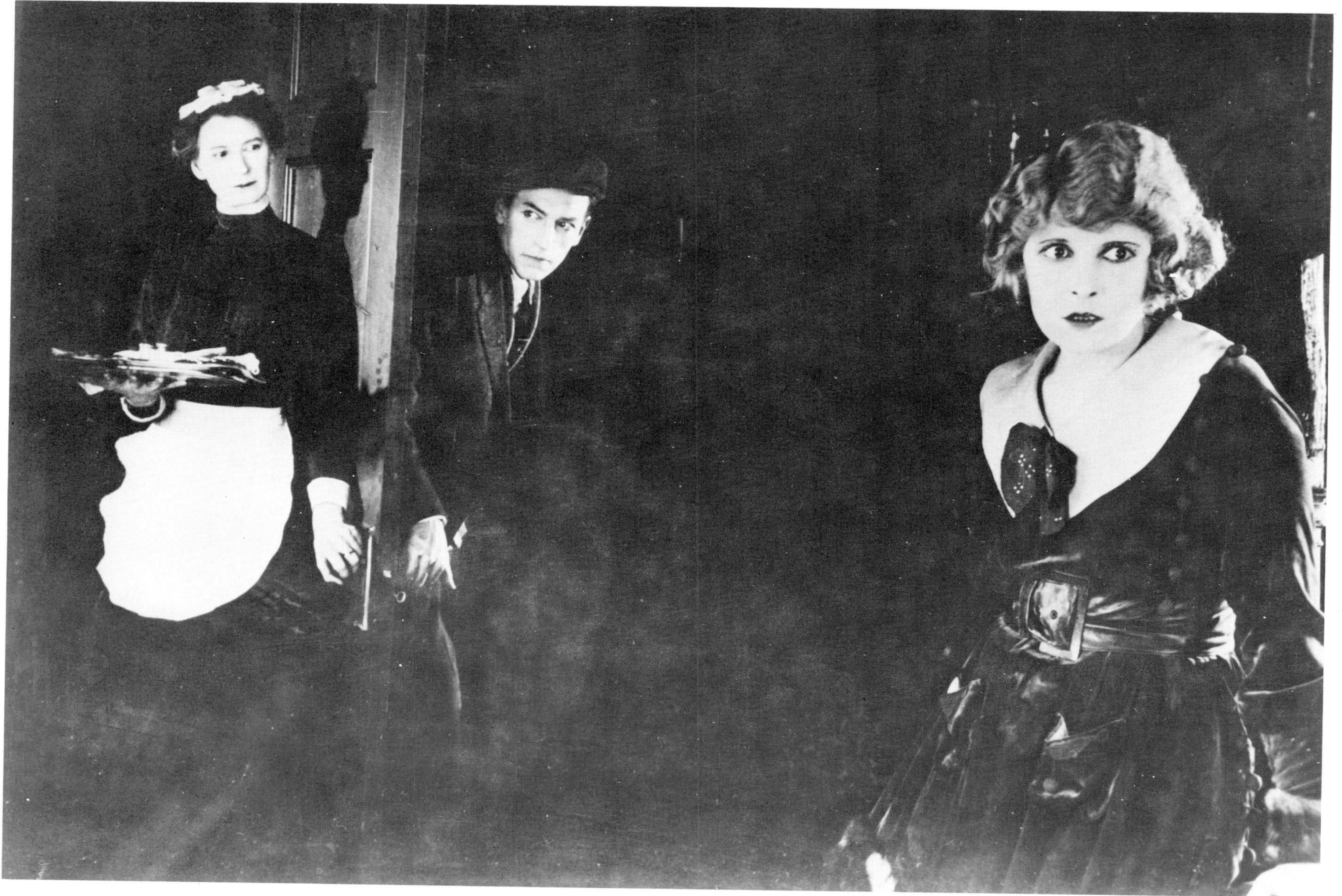

Elaine (Pearl White) fears for her life as the "Clutching Hand" delivers an ultimatum. But Craig Kennedy's (Arnold Daly) presence helps provide a sense of security.

believe that this is the work of the master criminal known as the *Clutching Hand*; the anonymous notes warning Dodge to cease his pursuit seem to confirm his suspicions.

Perry Bennett, a lawyer and special assistant to president Dodge, is also attempting to uncover the identity of this dastardly villain. Suddenly, he and Dodge are visited by a small time crook known as Lumpy Red. It seems he was wronged by the *Clutching Hand* and seeks revenge. Red gives them the directions which will lead them to the source of their robberies. Dodge carefully records the directions and places them in an envelope. He and Bennett then leave the office for the evening, vowing to track down the culprit first thing in the morning.

When Dodge arrives at his home he is greeted by his daughter, Elaine, and Jameson, a newspaper reporter. After a quiet dinner, Dodge relates the events of the day. The mystery excites Jameson; upon leaving the Dodge mansion, he can't wait to tell his friend Craig Kennedy (a famous detective) the news that Dodge has discovered the *Clutching Hand's* hideout.

Meanwhile, before retiring, Dodge hides the directions in a recess in the library wall, and places the now empty envelope in the safe. No sooner is the safe closed than the telephone rings. Turning to answer it he steps on the iron floor register; as he picks up the receiver, a powerful blinding electrical flash occurs and he slumps lifelessly to the floor. Soon after, a mysterious masked man enters the library and blows open the safe. He removes the contents and quietly disappears. Elaine discovers her father and summons the police and her friend Jameson. Jameson, in turn, immediately notifies Craig Kennedy and the pair meet at the Dodge mansion, where the group is joined by Perry Bennett, as each attempts to comfort the grieving Elaine. Meanwhile, Kennedy begins his investigation of the library. He is mystified when he discovers his own fingerprints are on the safe and several objects within the room. Now he begins to realize the cunning of the villain with whom he must cope. The first chapter ends with each member of the household vowing to devote their entire efforts to bringing the *Clutching Hand* to justice.

In chapters two through four Elaine and Craig Kennedy draw closer to the identity, but each clue unveiled represents an increased danger to their safety. In episode two, Elaine is injected with a drug known as *scapolarium*, developed by a German scientist working for the *Clutching Hand*. She enters a *twilight sleep* during which she obeys any external suggestion. Luckily, Craig arrives just in time to prevent her from causing any harm.

In episode three Elaine and Craig attempt to foil a large jewel robbery planned by their arch rival, the *Clutching Hand*, but the cunning crook manages to divert their attention while absconding with the precious gems. Nevertheless, Craig and Elaine manage a glimpse of the crook as he flees and they give chase. Craig, however, is struck from behind and Elaine is bound and gagged. She is sealed in an old boiler which sits by the water's edge; as the tide begins to rise, so does the water in the boiler... will this be the end of Elaine?

Meanwhile, Craig has been helped back to consciousness by Jameson. The pair attempt to follow the gang's trail, hoping to free Elaine from her captors. They discover her trapped in the boiler and quickly grasp the seriousness of her plight. Craig employes the use of one of his new scientific inventions, a miniature oxyacetylene welder, to cut a hole in the boiler and free Elaine.

In chapter four Craig attempts to bait the *Clutching Hand* by claiming to have invented a fool-proof safe. Near the safe he installs another new device, the *kinograph*, which reacts to pressure of a person's feet and records their picture. The fiendish thief, however, carefully avoids Craig's snare while placing a few fatal booby traps of his own, one which nearly kills Craig.

The *Clutching Hand*, disguised as a telephone inspector, gains entry to the Dodge mansion and sprays Elaine's bedroom with an invisible powder which will produce a fatal illness. Michael sees the telephone man spraying the strange substance throughout the room, but the man threatens to perform vile acts on Michael if he reveals the secret. That night Elaine and her dog become very sick and the doctor is unable to diagnose the strange ailment. Kennedy, seeing the dog's condition, takes him to his own laboratory for more extensive examination. He discovers arsenic in the animal's blood and, thus, can now save Elaine. Meanwhile, Michael has contacted Craig, but before they can meet he is killed by a poisoned blow-gun dart.

The "Clutching Hand" appears to be just another costumed guest to Craig Kennedy and Elaine in *The Exploits of Elaine* (1914).

Messages from the *Clutching Hand* continue to plague Elaine and Craig. The threats become more sinister and vile in chapter six. Finally, in chapter seven, a furious battle ensues which leaves both Elaine and Craig wounded, but for the first time they openly express their love for each other.

In chapter eight, Craig unveils his newest invention, the ultra-modern *vocaphone*. This device allows two-way communication between any room in the mansion. The vocaphone saves Elaine from certain death at the hands of the *Clutching Hand's* henchmen as Craig overhears their evil plan and foils their bold attempt to kill Elaine.

Each week the great detective demonstrates his remarkable resourcefulness and scientific genius in the continuous conflict with the *Clutching Hand* who makes an all-out effort to hide himself from Craig and Elaine. In chapter nine the culprit utilizes an infra-red ray which claims several victims before being directed at Craig and Jameson. Kennedy shields their bodies with a newly designed diverting shield, causing the flow of energy to ignite the infra-red device. In chapter ten Elaine is imprisioned in a sewer and becomes asphyxiated by the vile gases. She is pronouced dead by the attending physician, but Craig's superior knowledge of ultra modern medical science enables him to apply the famous Professor Leduc's method of electrical resuscitation and Elaine is again pulled from the jaws of death. In chapters eleven through thirteen, the *Clutching Hand* senses the end is near as he prepares for a hasty retreat from the relentless pursuit of Craig and Elaine. During these three chapters, he forms an affiliation with a corrupt chinese element led by Wu Fang. (Wu Fang will appear again as the villain in the 1915 Pathe serial epic, *The New Exploits of Elaine*.)

One of Wu Fang's lieutenants, Wong Long Sin, was saved from certain death by Craig Kennedy in chapter thirteen and has now become a trusted ally of the ingenious detective. A bomb which is intended for Wong Long Sin gives the ultimate clue which will lead to the *Clutching Hand's* identity. Kennedy calls the entire group together at the Dodge mansion: Perry Bennett, Jameson, Elaine Dodge, Wong Long Sin, and other relatives. Using a specially designed x-ray device, he discovers metal fragments similar to those of the bomb on Perry Bennett's clothing—he is the *Clutching Hand*! Alas, Bennett quickly drinks a fast-acting poison and thus dies before the secret of the *Clutching Hand's* hidden treasure can be discovered.

> "One of the most noticeable points about *The Exploits of Elaine* is the manner in which it is being directed and put together. Too much praise cannot be given to the clean-cut methods employed, and the smoothness and consistency of action."
>
> *Moving Picture World*, Vol. 23, p. 498

Pearl White's stardom was guaranteed after this serial. Her silent screen performances led her to become the *queen* of the silent serials. *The Exploits of Elaine* netted Pathe in excess of one million dollars during the year it was released. This venture proved to be only the first installment on a series which was one of the most popular epics ever.

Creighton Hale's film career began with this serial and continued into the talkies. His last film was made in 1949. Few of the other main characters of the series appeared in additional films and none in any talkies.

This serial helped introduce audiences to the Craig Kennedy mysteries. These stories fascinated the movie-makers of the day that more than 246,000 feet of film was used from 1914 to 1921 to display them to the public. This is more film footage than any other science fiction topic from 1887 to 1979 . . . truly a unique accomplishment.

HIS PREHISTORIC PAST

Release: 1914, Keystone
Description: Silent, 1157 feet
Classification: SF-C
References: No. 14, p. 222; No. 46, p. 273; No. 50, p. 195; LC, LP3900; NYT, 3-31-19

Charles Chaplin portrays a harmless, sex starved caveman in a humerous satire of Darwin's theory of evolution in *His Prehistoric Past* (1914).

Credits

Producer .... Keystone
Director .... Charles Chaplin
Screenplay .... Charles Chaplin

Cast

Caveman .... Charles Chaplin
Caveman .... Mack Swain
Caveman .... Gene Marsh
Caveman .... Fritz Schade
Caveman .... Al St. John
Caveman .... Frank D. Williams
Caveman .... Cecile Arnold
Caveman .... Hank Mann
Cavewoman .... Alice Howell

In this film a young man is taken back in time to the caveman era where he attempts to use modern methods and techniques in this prehistoric world. The events which take place during the last part of the Cretaceous epoch produce extremely humorous moments for the audience. The result is a classic Chaplin film, deserving of the viewer's full attention. Nevertheless, the production remains a weak science fiction effort.

THE MISER'S REVERSION

Release: 1914, Thanhouser
Description: Silent, 3023 feet
Classification: SF-C
References: No. 6, p. 153; No. 14, p. 321; No. 50, p. 305; BIO, 6-25-14, p. xiv

An old taxidermist is about to pledge his daughter in marriage to a disgraceful man, but the act will bring extreme wealth into their family. As the old man sits in his easy chair thinking about the coming events he dozes off and is soon dreaming of his ancestors from his prehistoric past. He sees himself as an ape-like creature moving about a small group of thatched huts. The events which follow are indeed humorous and relate to the old miser the true meaning of life and family. Upon awakening, he rushes to stop the planned wedding and then encourages his daughter to elope with the man she truly loves.

This film is a weak science fiction work. The prehistoric scenes are not as well done as previous ones, such as *Man's Genesis* (1912) or *The Primitive Man* (1913).

NAIDRA, THE DREAM WOMAN

Release: 1914, Thanhouser
Description: Silent
Classification: SF
References: No. 14, p. 347; No. 46, p. 425; No. 50, p. 327; MPN, 12-19-14, p. 85; MPW, Vol. 22, p. 1524, 1586

Credits

Producer .... George Kleine

Cast

Naidra .... Mignon Anderson
Scientist .... Riley Chamberlain
Organist .... Morris Foster
Father .... Carey L. Hastings

An old scientist has labored for many years to discover the secrets for chemically producing human life. Quite by accident, he comes by an ancient alchemist's notebook, the contents of which contain several unusual formulas. One of these is very nearly the same as the one the old man had been working on all these years. This slight difference between his formula and the ancient one gives him the clue to an error he thinks he has been making. The scientist hurries back to his laboratory to test his new hypothesis. Much to his amazement, the formula works and before his very eyes a body of a beautiful woman begins to take form. He soon discovers that this woman, despite all her beauty, is incapable of love.

He begins a new set of experiments designed to show his creation the meaning of love. All his efforts, however, seem to fail and he experiences a deep despair.

A young organist visits the man, and Naidra and the visitor seem to be attracted to each other. Soon the two are madly in love, but the scientist suddenly realizes that he is in love with her, too! He reaches out to take Naidra from the organist—but there is no Naidra. It was all a dream: the ancient formula had the power to induce very real dreams and not real human beings.

> "The acting is good and it has many poetical and very pleasing pictures. It may be called an artistic offering."
>
> *The Moving Picture World*, Vol. 24, p. 1524

PROFESSOR OLDBOY'S REJUVENATOR

Release: 1914, Kalem Company
Description: Silent, 613 feet
Classification: SF-C
References: No. 14, p. 389; No. 46, p. 490; No. 50, p. 383; BIO, 5-28-14, p. xi; MPW, Vol. 20, p. 366

Credits

Producer .... George Kleine

An eccentric, but brilliant, professor has succeeded in devising a chamber which has the power to restore youth. After several successful experiments on animals, the professor is tempted to try it on himself. He instructs his daughter on the delicate operation of the machine's controls, admonishing her to pay close attention to the time setting. After all, he only wants to be a few years younger. Cautiously, he enters the chamber and closes the door tightly behind him. His daughter carefully sets the control knobs. Slowly the machine's process begins to turn back the years and the professor appears more youthful each passing moment. Suddenly, the door bell rings and the young girl goes to answer it. She is gone an unreasonably long time. When she finally remembers her poor father, she scurries back to the laboratory and turns off the rejuvenator. But, she is too late—for inside the chamber is not her father but an infant boy!

THE READER OF MINDS

Release: 1914, Thanhouser
Description: Silent, 2000 feet
Classification: SF-A
References: No. 50, p. 394; MPW, Vol. 22, p. 1434

Credits

Producer .... Edwin Thanhouser
Director .... Lester Lonergan
Screenplay .... Philip Lonergan

Cast

Lieutenant Esmond .... Philip Longergan
Heinrick Hoevler .... Lester Lonergan

A young American army officer, Lieutenant Esmond, invents a wireless device that seems to be able to seek out naval vessels and destroy them. He successfully demonstrates his machine as a weapon for destroying enemy warships. It is not long before secret agents are pursuing him in an effort to steal the secret of this new device. The foreign agents call on Heinrick Hoevler, an old German inventor who has recently perfected an instrument capable of reading a person's mind from a reasonable distance. The foreign agents and Dr. Hoevler attempt to use his instrument on the unsuspecting Lieutenant. Esmond foolishly accepts an invitation to a dinner party being given by the foreign agents. It seems Esmond believes he has thwarted their pursuit and his secret invention is secure. What the Lieutenant does not know is that the professor has his ingenious device in the next room recording all of Esmond's thoughts. The smug Lieutenant departs the party confident he has foiled the foreign agents.

The next day, he is astonished to learn the enemy has gained the secret of the wireless device. Army officials believe that the Lieutenant has sold his weapon to the enemy and he is arrested, followed by a dishonorable discharge from the military service.

Thereafter, the shamed man and his sweetheart, who believes he is innocent, begin their quest to uncover the enemy agents. Esmond's girlfriend works as a telephone operator for a large metropolitan hotel. One evening she overhears a conversation which may prove her lover's innocence. The pair investigate and uncover Professor Hoevler and his mind reading machine. They turn the professor and his machine into the authorities, and the Lieutenant is reinstated. As the movie ends, the Lieutenant and the army are using the mind reading device to defeat the foreign power.

This is a well done SF film for the year 1914. The foreign government, as you might have inferred, is Germany. No direct reference was made in the film to this, but none was needed for the 1914 audience.

THE SILENT PERIL

Release: 1914, Bison
Description: Silent, 2000 feet
Classification: SF-A
References: No. 14, p. 434; No. 46, p. 538; No. 50, p. 439; MPN, Vol. 10, p. 51; MPW, Vol. 22, p. 828, 1077

Credits

Producer .... Adam Kessel, Jr.
Director .... Charles O. Bauman

Cast

Marie Von Glahn .... Marie Walcamp
Jack Parsons .... William Clifford
Professor Von Glahn .... Sherman Bainbridge

Jack Parsons, an undercover agent for the secret service, is also an expert on wireless devices. He appears to all who know him as a playboy and *man about town*. But Jack has been secretly working on a new powerful wireless invention which can send out an electrical wave that destroys any object upon which it focuses. He believes that the device has been perfected but has been unable to test it.

During the next few days, the newspaper begins to publish reports about a *powerless boat* developed by a foreign government. A fleet of these boats, controlled by a remote wireless device, could destroy a nation's navy. The United States Secretary of State receives a coded message from one of our European agents which confirms that the wireless boat is operational, and in a test run has indeed destroyed two naval vessels with apparent ease. The Secretary contacts Jack Parsons who has been away on special assignment. Unfortunately, an enemy agent intercepts his transmissions and learns of Jack's true identity. The Secretary orders Jack to interrupt his work and somehow destroy the wireless vessel.

As the plot, shall we say, "thickens," the enemy agent sells Jack's secret identity to the infamous Baroness Alda, who, with another fellow enemy agent, seeks to stop Jack from reaching his destination. They board the ship Jack is taking to Europe. The journey soon reveals many perils for Jack, but he manages to survive all attempts to foil his mission as they cross the Atlantic.

During the voyage he meets Marie Von Glahn, with whom he falls in love. Always the professional, Jack cannot think of personal affairs until his job is done . . . As the ship nears the port, he slips into the Baroness' stateroom and sprays the entire area with *Kelene*, a powerful anesthetic. The agents are overcome by the Kelene which prevents them from following the pair as they leave the ship.

Jack and Marie disembark and are met by Marie's father, Professor Von Glahn. The Professor is the inventor of the boat Jack has been ordered to destroy! Allowed to move freely and unsuspected about the Von Glahn estate, he soon discovers the boat's location. He places his own device *the interrupter* under the canvas in the bow of the vessel, and returns to the house. After dinner Jack sees the boat on the lake for a test run; quickly he goes to his room, and switches on his transformer. Immediately the boat explodes; his mission is a success. Alas, Jack soon learns that the Professor was aboard the boat—he has killed his new love's father.

This is a good SF adventure film. During this time the movie industry seemed to be greatly influenced by the German efforts in Europe. William Clifford (Jack Parsons in this film) went on to star in a number of silent adventure films but never appeared in any *talkies*.

THE SURGEON'S EXPERIMENT

Release: 1914, Majestic
Description: Silent, 2000 feet
Classification: SF
References: No. 14, p. 464; No. 46, p. 588; No. 50, p. 470; MPW, Vol. 20, p. 58, 116

Credits

Producer .... Harry Aitken

Cast

Dick Clayton .... Paul Scardon

The famous surgeon, Dr. Gale, theorizes that criminal tendencies are the result of insufficient cranial capacity. Dr. Gale explains to Senator Brady that a protuberance at the base of the skull prevents proper brain expansion. The doctor pleads with the Senator to introduce a bill which will allow surgeons to operate on criminals. The Senator, however, reminds the doctor that this is only his theory and that if he can produce one criminal who has been reformed through this process, he will take him more seriously.

That night, the doctor is a victim of the notorious burglar *Red Dick*, alias, Dick Clayton. Somehow Dr. Gale overpowers Clayton and succeeds in anesthetizing him. He immediately removes his prey to his private operating room and begins the delicate surgery that will free this wretched soul from a life of crime. After explaining the nature of the completed operation to the now awake Clayton, and allowing sufficient time for a complete recovery, Dr. Gale persuades the Senator to give the reformed Dick Clayton a job.

The Senator proceeds to test the doctor's claims by giving Clayton some very expensive bonds to deliver to a bank across town. When Clayton fails to make the expected delivery, the doctor is shocked and discouraged. But Clayton shows up the next morning with the bonds explaining that he had undergone a strange attack of vertigo. Relieved, the surgeon explains that this must be an unexpected side effect of the operation. He urges the Senator to proceed with the bill that will allow many more of these operations to take place.

The movie seems to be based on a plot which was used in an earlier film. *Doctor Maxwell's Experiment* (1913). Even though the two films deal with the burglars in slightly different ways, there are many similarities between them.

Paul Scardon, the actor who portrayed Dick Clayton, had an unusual film career: He appeared in one more film after this production but did not act on the silver screen again until 1941. From 1941 to 1947 he appeared in 12 films, the exact same number in which he played from 1911 to 1915.

WON IN THE CLOUDS

Release: 1914, Universal Film Manufacturing Co.
Description: Silent, 2980 feet
Classification: SF-A
References: No. 46, p. 697; No. 50, p. 548; MPW, Vol. 20, p. 214, 274

Credits

Producer .... Universal
Director .... Otis Turner
Screenplay .... Otis Turner

Cast

Cecil James .... Herbert Rawlinson
Grace James .... Marie Walcamp
Portugese Jack .... Rex De Rosselli
Mary Bjornsen .... Essie Fay
Roy Knabenshue .... Frank Lloyd

This SF adventure epic involves a dirigible capable of flying around the world. It seems to have much greater speed than any dirigible of the era.

As the story begins, Cecil James, an English nobleman, is accompanied by his daughter Grace on a safari. A young native bearer, Bangula, steals a rifle from the encampment. After he has been apprehended, and is about to be executed by the head guide, James intercedes to save the young lad's life. Out of gratitude for stopping the execution, Bangula offers to lead James and his daughter to the secret diamond mine of the Kabangan tribe.

Meanwhile, in the nearby city of Bloernfontein, Roy Knabenshue, a world famous American aeronaut, arrives in his new shining, sleek dirigible. Roy's passengers, Mr. Bjornsen and his daughter, Mary, have traveled a great distance to perform the annual audit on one of his branch banks. He is also the banker for the large diamond syndicate in this part of Africa. After a brief examination of the books, Bjornsen discovers the bank is in serious financial trouble. Within days, the bank fails and Bjornsen and his daughter are left penniless.

Knabenshue must find another mission for his dirigible and make his way back to America. It is on his way from Bloernfontein that he encounters Cecil James and his daughter, Grace. James has by this time found the diamond mine, but was unable to secure any diamonds because of the native guards. After a lengthy discussion, James persuades Roy to help them steal the diamonds by promising that they will all be wealthy within a week. After Roy enlists the services of a renegade named Portugese Jack to help handle the airship, the group disembarks. They approach the Kaffer village slowly and quietly. Roy lets James, Grace, and the renegade off near the feast house where the loot is stored. They proceed to fill the canvas sacks with diamonds. Meanwhile, Roy turns the airship around and makes another pass to pick up his comrades. The renegade, however, doublecrosses them and warns the natives who begin to attack James and his daughter. But they see the flying ship and are struck with awe and fear. Quickly James and Grace board the ship with their sacks of diamonds. The renegade finally convinces the natives that the airship can be killed by their spears, but by the time the natives are within spear-range, the dirigible has made its escape by dropping lyddite bombs upon the unsuspecting natives. Roy Knabenshue makes good their escape from the fearsome Kaffer tribe. As the film ends, Roy returns to Bloernfontein and with his wealth, re-establishes Bjornsen's bank and weds his daughter Mary.

> "It is an adventure story, clean-cut and full of atmosphere. It runs like one of the romances of H. Rider Haggard combined with a Jules Verne novel . . . all well pictured and convincing."
>
> *Motion Picture News*, Vol. 20, p. 214

Frank Lloyd acted in very few films from 1910 to 1916, but became an outstanding director, winning two Academy Awards for best director--one in 1928-29 for *The Divine Lady,* and the other in 1932-33 for *Cavalcade.*

Herbert Rawlinson who played the lead in this film acted in more than 400 films from 1910 to 1951.

1915

THE AUTOMATIC HOUSE

Release: 1915, Empress Film Company
Description: Silent, 960 feet
Classification: SF-C
References: No. 46, p. 28; No. 50, p. 21; LC, LP4260; MPW, Vol. 24, p. 466

This film was made by Gaumont Film Company, but in 1915 the company changed its name to Empress Film Company. Additionally, the film was distributed through United Film Service, which was the trade name for Warner Brothers. This leading paragraph is not intended to confuse, but to provide adequate details for those who might attempt to research *The Automatic House*.

The movie is about a Mr. Brown who designs a totally electric house with many labor saving devices—a true house of the future. Nearly every device within the house is operated by a push button. It even comes with an electronic robot *maid* who can perform a variety of household duties. Mr. Brown's mother-in-law pays them a visit but her stay is cut short when she accidently engages the automatic fire sprinkling device. The sequences involving the mother-in-law's interaction with the automatic house provide the most amusing moments of the production.

BENEATH THE SEA

Release: 1915, Lubin
Description: Silent, 2000 feet
Classification: SF-A
References: No. 14, p. 44, p. 44; No. 46, p. 43; No. 50, p. 31; LC, LP4461; MPN, Vol. 11, p. 54

Credits

Producer .... Sigmund Lubin
Screenplay .... Wilbert Melville and S. Rowland White, Jr.

Cast

The Inventor .... Charles Fowler
President .... Melvin Mayo
Young Girl .... Velma Whitman
Crewman .... W. E. Parsons
Mechanic .... George Routh

A young ingenious inventor designs a new high speed submarine, and he and his construction drawings are rushed to Washington. The President and the Secretary of the Navy are impressed with the young inventor's talent and urge him to begin construction work at the naval yard immediately. During the submarine's construction the inventor meets the President's daughter and quickly falls in love with her. They plan to marry when the submarine has completed its trial run. But another man loves the young girl, also, and he vows to destroy the submarine and its inventor. He hires a crooked mechanic to sabotage the new submarine. During its trial cruise the boat nearly sinks and the young inventor narrowly escapes death. Somehow he manages to get the ship back to shore, where the authorities are in the process of arresting the saboteur. As the film ends, the young inventor and the President's daughter are getting married.

THE BLACK BOX

Release: 1915, Universal Film Manufacturing Co.
Description: Silent, 15 episode serial, each episode approx. 2000 feet
Classification: SF-A
References: No. 8, p. 30, 31, 160, 161; No. 14, p. 49; No. 46, p. 52; No. 50, p. 36

Credits

Producer .... Otis Turner
Director .... Otis Turner
Screenplay .... Otis Turner

Cast

Sanford Quest .... Herbert Rawlinson
Lenora MacDougal .... Anna Little
Prof. Ashleigh .... William Worthington
Lord Ashleigh .... William Worthington
Police Officer .... Mark Fenton
Laura .... Laura Oakley
Craig .... Frank MacQuarrie
Ian MacDougal .... Frank Lloyd
Mrs. Reinholdt .... Helen Wright
Ashleigh's Daughter .... Beatrice Van

Chapters 1-15 of *The Black Box*

Chapter 1: An Apartment House Case
References: LC, LP4538; MPN, 3-13-15, p. 53
Chapter 2: The Hidden Hands
References: LC, LP4602; MPN, 3-20-15, p. 59
Chapter 3: The Pocket Wireless
References: LC, LP4735; MPN, 3-27-15, p. 54
Chapter 4: An Old Grudge
References: LC, LP4762; MPN, 4-3-15, p. 59
Chapter 5: On the Rack
References: LC, LP4866; MPN, 4-10-15, p. 58, 59
Chapter 6: The Unseen Terror
References: LC, LP4934; MPN, 4-17-15, p. 73
Chapter 7: The House of Mystery
References: LC, LP5001; MPN, 4-24-15, p. 69
Chapter 8: The Inherited Sin
References: LC, LP5078; MPN, 5-1-15, p. 66
Chapter 9: Lost in London
References: LC, LP5122; MPN, 5-8-15, p. 74
Chapter 10: The Ship of Horror
References: LC, LP5161; MPN,5-15-15, p. 68
Chapter 11: A Desert Vengence
References: LC, LP5257; MPN, 5-22-15, p. 74
Chapter 12: Neath Iron Wheels
References: LC, LP5327; MPN, 5-29-15, p. 72
Chapter 13: Tongues of Flame
References: LC, LP5372; MPN, 6-5-15, p. 71

Chapter 14: A Bolt from the Blue
References: LC, LP5452; MPN, 6-12-15, p. 75
Chapter 15: The Black Box
References: LC, LP5993; MPN, 6-26-15, p. 79

This serial is based on the novel *The Black Box* by E. Phillips Oppenheim. Each of the fifteen installments (one each week) was accompanied by a short version of the story which appeared in many of the newspapers throughout the country.

The plot involves a *super science* detective, Sanford Quest, who has an impressive array of scientific devices at his command. The character and characterization have a strong resemblance to the much later James Bond (007) films.

> "In as much as *The Black Box* has developed into an exciting detective mystery it is just to give the producers great praise for turning out a picture of this nature, that instead of growing unfathomably complicated with each succeeding foot, it is pleasingly clear. But the mystery sticks to the story as well, it lends another touch of suspense to the picture which in other respects as well is most magnetic."
>
> *Motion Picture News*, 3-20-15, p. 59

As the first chapter opens, Sanford Quest is summoned to the Ashleigh household when Lord Ashleigh's daughter is found murdered in her bedroom. Quest subsequently discovers that a valuable diamond necklace is missing from the young daughter's jewel case. He employs the use of an electronic mind reading device which causes the girl's maid, Lenora, to reveal that her husband, Ian MacDougal, is the culprit.

The next four chapters involve MacDougal's escape from imprisonment and his plot to destroy Quest. A strange *Neanderthal* like creature begins to appear in chapter 2 and continues to plague Quest as he searchs for the villain. Additionally, clues begin to mysteriously appear in a small black box in the Ashleigh manor. Early in chapter 2 Lord Ashleigh's twin brother appears, having recently returned from Africa where he had been in pursuit of evidence to support the Darwinian theory.

Quest continually avoids being captured or killed by using various electronic gadgets and by enlisting the aid of his trusted assistant, Laura. As episode five unfolds, Quest has been framed for two murders and the theft of Mrs. Reinholdt's jewels. Only Laura's aid and Quest's own genius permit his escape from jail in an effort to prove his innocence. Throughout the first five episodes a mysterious pair of unseen hands keep stealing precious jewels or killing people. The viewer (and Quest) believe the ape-like creature, or Professor Ashleigh, or his servant, Craig, are the perpetrators of these hideous deeds. During each of the chapters Quest uses his wit and scientific devices to locate more clues surrounding the black box mystery.

In chapter 6, Quest clears himself of all charges, but nearly meets a fiery death in the servant's quarters as he searches for clues that will help him identify Craig as the prime suspect. During the next six episodes Quest continues to pursue Craig. He follows him to England and then to South Africa. While the trail is treacherous, it is not terribly difficult to discern as it seems to be littered with corpses. Even poor Lord Ashleigh meets an untimely end in episode 9 when he comes into contact with the mysterious reappearing hands. The amazing Sanford Quest continues to astonish the audience with his marvelous scientific devices and cunning skill for escaping sure death. By episode eleven the audience is convinced of Craig's evil treacherous character, but Professor Ashleigh still continues to appear involved somehow with the mystery of the black box.

In episodes twelve through fourteen, the chase returns to the Pacific Coast of the United States. Craig is captured by Quest, but continually pleads his innocence. During these three chapters, Craig becomes less of a villain and events which transpire make his story more believable. Quest begins to focus his attention on Professor Ashleigh as the force behind the mysterious hidden hands. Yet, he senses that Craig knows more than he is telling. Because of this, he attempts to force a confession out of Craig by using his electric-thought transference device, but during the process Craig dies.

In the final chapter of *The Black Box*, we learn Professor Ashleigh is the perpetrator of every crime which has transpired since chapter 1. Moreover, it was Craig who left the clue within the mysterious box. It seems while in darkest Africa, the professor was bitten by a wild savage ape. He contracted a disease similar to hydrophobia. This unique disease resulted in the professor's becoming sharp and cunning, but also very evil. Quest uncovers the mystery of the hidden hands when he discovers a special black costume which, when charged with an electrical current, causes the individual to become invisible except for the hands.

Sanford Quest's adventures stimulated the audience so greatly that Universal was convinced serials were vital to their future financial successes.

Two actors in this serial had appeared in previously referenced SF films: Herbert Rawlinson (*Won in the Clouds*), 1914) and Frank Lloyd (*Won in the Clouds*, 1914). Each went on to make outstanding achievements during their film careers, but this serial was the turning point for both.

THE DIAMOND FROM THE SKY

Release: 1915, North American Film Company
Description: Silent, 30 episode serial, each episode approx. 2000 feet
Classification: SF-A
References: No. 1, p. 510, 511; No. 8, p. 6, 31, 32, 161, 162; No. 14, p. 126; No. 46, p. 142; No. 50, p. 101; MPW, Vol. 25, p. 65; Vol. 26, p. 1436, 1501, 1910

Credits

Producer .... Samuel S. Hutchinson
Director .... William Desmond Taylor and Jacques Jaccard
Screenplay .... Roy L. McCardell
Camera .... George Hill

Cast

Esther Cummings .... Lottie Pickford
Blair Stanley .... William Russell
Arthur Stanley .... Irving Cummings
Vivian Marston .... Charlotte Burton
Luke Lovell .... George Periclat
Hagar .... Eugenie Ford
Dr. Lee .... Orral Humphrey
Chinaman .... W.J. Tedmarsh
Mother Stanley .... Lillian Buckingham
Marmaduke Smythe .... Charles Watt

Chapters 1-30 of *The Diamond from the Sky*

Chapter 1: The Heritage of Hate
References: LC, LU5360
Chapter 2: An Eye for an Eye
References: LC, LU5361
Chapter 3: The Silent Witness
References: LC, LU5362

Chapter 4: The Prodigal's Progress
References: LC, LU5598
Chapter 5: For the Sake of a False Friend
References: LC, LU5605
Chapter 6: Shadows at Sunrise
References: LC, LU5602
Chapter 7: The Fox and the Pig
References: LC, LU5600
Chapter 8: A Mind in the Past
References: LC, LU5604
Chapter 9: A Runaway Match
References: · LC, LU5597
Chapter 10: Old Foes with New Faces
References: LC, LU5955
Chapter 11: The Web of Destiny or Plaything of the Papoose
References: LC, LU5950
Chapter 12: To the Highest Bidder
References: LC, LU5949
Chapter 13: The Man in the Mask
References: LC, LU6226
Chapter 14 For Love and Money
References: LC, LU6227
Chapter 15: Desperate Chances
References: LC, LU6367
Chapter 16: The Path of Peril
References: LC, LU6363
Chapter 17: *King of Diamonds and Queen of Hearts
Chapter 18: Charm Against Harm
Chapter 19: Fire, Fury and Confusion
Chapter 20: The Soul Stranglers
Chapter 21: The Lion's Bride
Chapter 22: The Rose in the Dust
Chapter 23: The Double Cross
Chapter 24: The Mad Millionaire
Chapter 25: A House of Cards
Chapter 26: The Garden of the Gods
Chapter 27: Mine Own People
Chapter 28: The Falling Aeroplane
Chapter 29: A Deal with Destiny
Chapter 30: The American Earl
*These episodes were not submitted for copyright.

This serial is based on a meteorite striking earth sometime in the 1600's. Sir Arthur Stanley, while journeying through Virginia, is captured by Indians and is about to be burned at the stake. Suddenly, a meteoroid lights up the sky overhead and strikes the earth, sending smoke and dust in all directions. The Indians believe that this is a sign to free their prisoner. Sir Arthur stumbles upon a meteorite fragment after his release. The piece turns out to be a large diamond. He believes that this diamond is a *charm against harm* and decides it shall never leave his family.

Some 250 years later we encounter Colonel Stanley and Judge Lamar Stanley, brothers who have adjoining Virginia plantations. The colonel's wife is expecting a child, and if it is a boy, the Stanley property in England and the diamond will be passed to his son. However, should they have a girl, the inheritance will be passed on to Judge Stanley's son. The child born to the colonel's wife is indeed a girl. Outraged, the colonel exchanges the baby girl for a gypsy boy born at the same time as his real daughter. Naturally, the colonel gives the gypsies a large sum of gold to ensure their silence.

The adventure begins with the principal actors in episode two when Esther, the real daughter of the colonel, seeks to find her true identity. Arthur, the gypsy child, by now is heir to the Stanley fortune. Blair, his cousin, somehow learns of Esther's true identity but keeps silent. Soon, Arthur falls in love with Esther. The rest of the film involves their attempt to secure the diamond Blair has wagered away while gambling, and their ensuing struggle with Blair and interactions with the other characters to this end.

From the reviews this appears to have been a very successful serial, but it is still a very weak SF epic, and certainly is nowhere near the caliber of *The Black Box* (1915). This was probably the most expensive serial ($800,000) attempted thus far in the film industry. The producer tried, without success, to interest Mary Pickford in the female lead. Her other commitments, however, would not permit her to accept the role. Mary therefore suggested they give her sister a chance at the part. Reluctantly, North American agreed. Lottie Pickford (her real name was Lottie Smith) turned in an excellent performance in her role as Esther. In fact, this would be her finest performance of her career.

The film received rave reviews during the period in which it was released, and many fans followed the serial because of a promised contest at the conclusion of the last episode.

This advertisement appeared in the final chapter of *The Diamond from the Sky*:

"Who will make the suggestion for a sequel, the suggestion in 1000 words or less, that will gain the prize of $10,000."

Moving Picture World, Vol. 26, p. 1910

"The two thrillers given so much advance notice by the producers of this continued story fall in this chapter. They are so daringly sensational that they materially elevate this number from the two preceding ones in point of excitement. In fact, they are unusually breath-taking feats.

In both of these death-defying events Irving Cummings figures in glorious solitude. Loss of life must have threatened him in both instances. That fact is obvious and it is this pointed risk which Mr. Cummings ran while executing the thrillers that will be responsible for their unlimited power to excite and startle."

Motion Picture News, Vol. 11, No. 14, p. 69

THE ELECTRIC ALARM

Release: 1915, Majestic
Description: Silent
Classification: SF-A
References: No. 46, p. 161; No. 50, p. p-19; MPW, Vol. 11, p. 78; Vol. 24, p. 1432

Credits

Producer .... Harry Aitken

Cast

Engineer .... Charles Gorman
Sweetheart .... Lillian Webster

A young engineer invents an electrical fire alarm system, but before he has completed the installation disaster strikes. A railroad trestle is being consumed by fire only minutes before a train carrying the young engineer's sweetheart is due to arrive. The young man completes the electrical circuit using his body. The resultant charge passing through his body nearly kills him, but miraculously he survives the shock. Upon recovering, he is rewarded by the railroad. In addition, they agree to install his device throughout the railroad line.

THE FOSTER BROTHER

Release: 1915, Mica Film Corporation
Description: Silent
Classification: SF
References: No. 46, p. 203; No. 50, p. 146; BIO, 2-6-15; LC, LU4423

Credits

Producer .... All Comedy Films, Inc.
Screenplay .... Thomas M. Metcalf

Cast

Medical Researcher .... Justina Wayne
Surgeon .... Crawford Kent

A team discovers a cure for cancer, but the treatment has great risk. A surgeon's foster brother is diagnosed as having terminal cancer, and the patient agrees to the highly experimental technique. After what seems like a rather lengthy recovery, the patient and members of the research team rejoice: the cure for cancer has been perfected through their medical research.

The claim at the end of the film resulted in problems for the producers. Many viewers took the movie as a documentary, not a drama, and they immediately sought the new cancer cure. But, of course, none was to be found--except on celluloid.

The producer of this venture, All Comedy Films, Inc., used the code names *Punch* for his comedic productions, and *Trump* for the dramas.

HATTIE, THE HAIR HEIRESS

Release: 1915, Falstaff
Description: Silent
Classification: SF-C
References: No. 14, p. 208; No. 46, p. 241; No. 50, p. 185; MPN, 10-23-15, p. 101

Credits

Producer .... Falstaff Films

Cast

Hattie .... Frances Keyes
Hattie's Fiance .... Claude Cooper
Hattie's Father .... Arthur Cunningham

Hattie's father is a well known and wealthy hair tonic manufacturer. Suddenly, he passes away and she becomes the heiress to millions of dollars, plus the hair tonic factory. She is immediately beseiged by hordes of suitors, all displaying luxurious heads of hair, produced overnight, they claim, by her father's secret formula. But, Hattie rejects them all. Finally, she displays a photograph of her fiance. The crowd is astounded: the man is totally bald. Hattie announces that she will soon marry and devote her entire research efforts toward finding a solution to her husband's baldness.

THE INVENTOR'S PERIL

Release: 1915, Lubin
Description: Silent, 2000 feet
Classification: SF-A
References: No. 14, p. 249, 250; No. 46, p. 310; No. 50, p. 221; LC, LP5403; MGY, 6-5-15; MPN, 6-5-15, p. 77

Credits

Producer .... Sigmund Lubin
Director .... Joseph W. Smiley
Screenplay .... Adrian Gil-Spear

Cast

Marvelli .... Joseph W. Smiley
Lola .... Lulu Leslie
John Alden .... Jack Standing
Mrs. Baldwin .... Florence Williams
Michaels .... John Smiley

Michaels, a young inventor, believes that Marvelli, the great genius of the world, has stolen his latest wireless invention. Michaels vows to kill Marvelli and follows him to Mrs. Baldwin's dinner party. While at the party, Marvelli is introduced to another young inventor, John Alden. He seems impressed by John's intelligence and his new wireless research. The two arrange a series of meetings for the coming week. Mrs. Baldwin is especially interested in John as she hopes he and Lola, her daughter, will find each other attractive.

After the party, John returns to his laboratory to continue working on his wireless device. His enthusiasm is obviously a result of Marvelli's praise. Meanwhile, Marvelli continues his own research in a loft in the Baldwin mansion.

Michaels attempts to murder Marvelli, but is interrupted by Lola's untimely entrance. He makes several other attempts to end Marvelli's life. One of these nearly kills Lola, but she is saved and the murder foiled by John's sudden appearance.

John convinces Marvelli and Lola to come to his laboratory away from Michaels' manic-like behavior. The trio is no sooner at the lab than Michaels springs his trap, barricading them in John's laboratory. John and Marvelli work feverishly to complete John's wireless device believing it is their only apparent means of escape. Their efforts are rewarded; the device works perfectly, and they make their escape. Michaels is caught and taken to jail. Mrs. Baldwin is ecstatic as John and Lola announce their plans to wed.

"Joseph Smiley does some fine directing here, as well as capably acting Marvelli."
Motion Picture News, 6-5-15, p. 77

JACK SPRATT AND THE SCALES OF LOVE

Release: 1915, Essanay Film Manufacturing Co.
Description: Silent
Classification: SF-C
References: No. 14, p. 259; No. 46, p. 314; No. 50, p. 228; LC, LP7032; MPN, 12-4-15, p. 103

Cast

Mustang Pete .... Victor Potel
Sophie .... Margaret Joslin
Slippery Slim .... Harry Todd

This film is a weak SF production, but does deserve mention because of the creation of compounds which can increase or decrease an individual's weight almost overnight.

Sophie and Slippery Slim have just been married and each vows to change their appearance. Sophie agrees to shed some of the mountains of fat which make up her enormous stature, and Slim agrees to add some flesh to his emaciated frame. The pair seeks the aid of a nearby druggist who offers two experimental potions, *Fato* for thin people, and *Thino* for fat people. sometime during the evening, Mustang Pete, who takes pleasure in playing jokes on Slim, switches the labels on the druggist's bottles.

Within a few hours, Sophie tips the scales at 290 pounds, and Slim has dropped to a mere 85. Pete becomes concerned about Slim's health and confesses the prank. Meanwhile, Sophie has returned to the druggist to demand the return of her money and an explanation. The last few minutes of the film provide the audience with some very funny scenes.

THE JUNGLE LOVERS

Release: 1915, Selig Polyscope Company
Description: Silent, 2960 feet
Classification: SF-A
References: No. 14, p. 264; No. 46, p. 323; No. 50, p. 236; LC, LP6327; MPW, Vol. 25, p. 2059, 2062

Credits

Producer .... Selig
Director .... Lloyd E. Carleton
Screenplay .... James Oliver Curwood

Cast

Naida Rand .... Bessie Eyton
Van Cleeve .... Edward J. Peil
Starling .... Richard Morris
Jan Blaas .... Tom Bates
Herman Blaas .... Edwin Wallock
Peter Rand .... Cash Darrell

A brilliant, but eccentric chemist, Van Cleeve, seeks seclusion in a remote corner of the African jungle—a place to pursue his research on a new type of explosive—away from the pressures of foreign governments. Van Cleeve begins his experiments from this desolate place unaware that Peter Rand and his family are developing their small farm a few miles away.

After a short passage of time, Herman Blaas and his little son, Jan, visit the Rands. Naida Rand and Jan go into the nearby jungle to play. Within moments, the farm is attacked by savage Zulu warriors. All the adults are killed as Naida and Jan hide in the dense jungle foliage. The children, frightened, alone, and homeless, are found by Van Cleeve. He takes them home and cares for them as though they are his own.

Fifteen years pass, during which Naida has grown into a beautiful young woman, and Jan into a handsome young man. He and Naida fall in love and wish to be married soon. During this same time, Van Cleeve has come close to perfecting his explosive but it always seems to lack something.

Their encampment is visited by Starling, a gruesome ivory trader. He, of course, immediately desires Naida's hand in marriage, but Van Cleeve orders him from their settlement; Starling vows to return and take Naida by force.

Starling is a man who doesn't have many friends in the jungle. He has made countless slaves of the native population, and Wamba, a nearby native chief, summons his warriors when he learns of Starling's presence. Meanwhile, Van Cleeve has perfected his explosive and is testing it. Starling returns to the Van Cleeve camp and finds Naida alone. He attempts to abduct her, but Jan opportunely appears and averts his efforts. Naida escapes to a nearby cave, but Jan is made Starling's prisoner.

As fate would have it, Naida's hiding place is the very place Van Cleeve is testing his new explosive. A stray bullet from one of Starling's native's guns accidently sets off the explosive which renders Van Cleeve unconscious. Naida attempts to revive him, but the flames and smoke become too great. She goes to the mouth of the cave for fresh air as Wamba and his warriors arrive. They see Naida behind a background of smoke and flames and infer that she is a witch. She takes advantage of this deception and leads the warriors against Starling. He and his evil natives are killed and her beloved Jan is freed. They return to rescue Van Cleeve who then urges them to marry with the natives serving as witnesses.

Selig produced many jungle films after his 1912 acquisition of the Jungle Zoo in Los Angeles. This, however, was his best jungle production to date, though certainly not the best SF attempt.

THE KITE

Release: 1915, Kay-Bee
Description: Silent
Classification: SF-A
References: No. 14, p. 272; No. 46, p. 330; No. 50, p. 245; MPW, Vol. 24, p. 981

This SF film depicts an electric kite which can aid in the detection of approaching storms. However, murder and mystery surround this new invention.

As the plot begins, Benjamin Wheeler and his daughter, Marion, are entertaining David Watts, an eccentric capitalist. Since the evening is warm the group dines on the roof garden. Watts is interested in the electric kite developed by Wheeler and his laboratory assistant, Hammond. When dinner is finished, he seats himself in Professor Wheeler's favorite chair as the Professor and Marion prepare a musical interlude. Suddenly, Watts falls forward in the chair—very dead.

Because of serious indebtedness to Watts, Wheeler is immediately suspected of killing him, and is soon taken into custody. Marion, extremely upset by her father's arrest, enlists the aid of Norman Dunbar, a famous scientific detective. After a series of interesting revelations, Dunbar concludes that Hammond is the real murderer. He suspects that Hammond, who wishes to wed Marion and could not get her father's consent, intended to kill Wheeler when Watts mistakenly sat in his chair.

In the final scenes of the movie, Dunbar confronts Hammond with the hideous crime, and he breaks down and confesses. Thus, through Dunbar's brilliant detective work, Benjamin Wheeler is freed and can continue his research on the electric kite.

LADY BAFFLES AND DETECTIVE DUCK

Release: 1915, Universal Film Manufacturing Co.
Description: Silent, 11 episode serial, each episode 1 reel
Classification: SF-A
References: No. 4, p. 14

Credits

Producer .... Gale Henry
Director .... Allen Curtis
Screenplay .... Clarence C. Badger

Cast

Detective Duck .... Max Asher
Lady Baffles .... Lillian Peacock
All Other Characters .... Gale Henry
.... William Henry
.... Milburn Morante
.... William Franey

Chapters 1-11 of *Lady Baffles and Detective Duck*

Chapter 1: The Great Egg Robbery
References: LC, LP5349; MPW, Vol. 24, p. 1326
Chapter 2: The Sign of the Sacred Safety Pin
References: LC, LP5458; MPW, Vol. 24, p. 1674
Chapter 3: The 18 Carrot Mystery
References: LC, LP5572; MPW, Vol. 24, p. 2002
Chapter 4: Baffles Aids Cupid
References: LC, LP5721; MPW, Vol. 25, p. 130
Chapter 5: At the Sign of Three Socks
References: No. 14, p. 29; No. 50, p. 19; LC, LP5814; MPW, 7-17-15, p. 80; MPW, Vol. 25, p. 555, 558
Chapter 6: Saved by a Scent
References: No. 14, p. 414; No. 50, p. 419; LC, LP5935; MPN, 8-7-15, p. 83; MPW, Vol. 25, p. 862
Chapter 7: The Dread Society of the Sacred Sausage
References: LC, LP6082; MPW, Vol. 25, p. 1215
Chapter 8: The Ore Mystery
References: LC, LP6438; MPW, Vol. 26, p. 140

Chapter 9: When the Wets Went Dry
References: LC, LP6572; MPW, Vol. 26, p. 503
Chapter 10: The Lost Roll
References: LC, LP6724; MPW, Vol. 26, p. 848
Chapter 11: Kidnapping the King's Kids
References: LC, LP6980; MPW, Vol. 26, p. 1549

This is an interesting and entertaining serial with a weak SF emphasis. Detective Duck displays various scientific gadgets and inventions from Chapter 1 through the final installment, but their premises are never clearly explained. Lady Baffles is a *lovable* crook who takes great delight in providing perplexing situations for the famous Detective Duck. At the end of each episode one of the characters (either Lady Baffles or Detective Duck) leaves a charming message for the other. Detective Duck somehow always seems to foil Lady Baffles pranks. Always the scientific detective, Duck uses his inventions throughout the serial.

In Chapter 2 Duck foils Lady Baffles' attempt to steal the secret formula for a new noiseless explosive ingeniously labeled *noiselessite*. In each of the adventures these two protagonists become involved with each other and as the serial progresses, Duck always seems to know Lady Baffles' next move.

In Chapter 5, Duck reveals another device, the *rubberscope*, which allows him to spy on Lady Baffles completely undetected. The *rubberscope* resembles a modern closed circuit television system. In Chapter 6, Duck unveils his *smellograph*, a device designed to send fumes through the thickest of walls forcing crooks into the open. In Chapters 7 through 11, Duck continually outwits Lady Baffles, and just when you think Duck is stumped, he brandishes another marvelous scientific device.

LET THERE BE LIGHT

Release: 1915, American Film Manufacturing Co.
Description: Silent, 1920 feet
Classification: SF
References: No. 14, p. 272; No. 50, p. 256; MPN, 10-23-15, p. 87

Credits

Producer .... John R. Freuler
Director .... William Bertram

Cast

June Sterling .... Helen Rosson
Peter Sterns .... Charles Newton
Actor .... E. Forrest Taylor
The Maid .... Queenie Rosson
Mr. Sterling .... Perry Banks

Peter Sterns is an inventor who has devoted a large part of his life to electrical experiments. One of his fondest goals is to produce a brilliant electric ray for household illumination (fluorescent lighting had not yet been developed).

He soon hears of his close friend's death, and adopts his orphaned daughter, June Sterling. After considerable time had passed, the lonely bachelor realizes how much he cares for June and asks her to marry him. She consents. Peter's work, however, requires his full attention for lengthy periods of time, forcing June to rely on her own resources for companionship. She meets a famous actor and begins to spend a great deal of time with him. Soon she believes that she wants her freedom from Peter in order to be with the other man. Meanwhile, Peter has finally perfected his wonderous new light and tests it by shining it fully on the garden. What his new light shows, however, is June in the arms of the actor. Realizing how much he has neglected his wife, he offers to give her freedom so she may marry this man. But June suddenly realizes how much she truly cares for Peter and they resolve their differences, vowing "to keep each other before all else".

LIFE WITHOUT SOUL

Release: 1915, Ocean
Description: Silent, 4970 feet
Classification: SF-H
References: No. 14, p. 280; No. 41, p. 63-66; No. 46, p. 345; No. 50, p. 258; MPN, 12-11-15, p. 92; MPW, Vol. 26, p. 1422, 1423, 1846

Credits

Producer .... George DeCarlton
Director .... Joseph W. Smiley
Screenplay .... Jesse J. Goldburg

Cast

The Monster .... Percy Darrell Standing
Dr. Frankenstein .... William A. Cohill
Victor .... Jack Hopkins
Elizabeth .... Lucy Cotton
Dr. Frankenstein, Sr. .... George DeCarlton
Sister .... Pauline Curley
Servant .... David McCauley
Maid .... Violet DeBiccari

This is the second film adaptation of Mary W. Shelley's famous novel, *Frankenstein* (1818). In the first version (1910, Edison), Charles Ogle portrayed the monster, adorned with an array of grotesque trappings. While in this celluloid production the monster, as acted by Percy Darrell Standing, wears little or no makeup. Mr. Standing displays the anger and horror of the creature using his rather husky size and terrible brutish scowl as special effects.

This film also differs from the previous one in that the introduction of a prologue and epilogue lessen the gruesomeness of the monster's actions. The creature seems to kill more persons than in the 1910 version or in the original novel. The emphasis is focused on his deficiencies--extremely low intellect and lack of human *soul.* The torment of the young Dr. Frankenstein reaches a high point when the monster thoughtlessly murders the doctor's sister, his best friend, and, finally, his wife. These events shatter his sanity as he slumps to the floor with an upward glance, as if to plead for forgiveness. Exhausted, he fires a shot which kills his creation. The monster and its creator, Dr. Frankenstein, die together on the laboratory floor.

Immediately following this scene the audience sees the entire cast gathered around one member reading the story of the film from a large old book. The effect was meant to treat the story as a fairy tale in order to lessen the horrific impact on the audience. It was felt that the viewers could never accept Frankenstein as a real story; therefore, it must be presented in storybook fashion.

Victor (Jack Hopkins) wishes Dr. Frankenstein (William Cohill) and Elizabeth (Lucy Cotton) best wishes on their forthcoming marriage in *Life Without Soul* (1915).

Obviously, the audience favored this film presentation of Frankenstein as the reviews for the film were most favorable.

> "The picture easily fulfills its mission. Supplemented by the resources and excellent judgment of the director, Joseph W. Smiley, and the equally efficient acting of the cast, the author of *Life Without Soul* has wrought a photoplay of distinct merit. Great diversity of incidents and scenes, of views of deep chasms, wild glades, desert sands and the ocean's wide expanse, are intermingled with glimpses of the young scientist bending over his creation in his laboratory and then of tranquil home life."
>
> *Motion Picture World,* 12-4-15, p. 1846

The film's debut, November 21, 1915, 3:45 p.m., at the Candler Theatre in New York, was marred by some projectionist's errors:

> "Since the picture's special showing to the trade at the Candler Theatre, much has been done that contributes towards its improvement. Many more titles have been added which clears the action considerably. Moreover the Candler operator cut short each reel, depriving the picture of its even continuity.
>
> In its present state, *Life Without Soul* is a feature that bids fair to please because of its unconventionality. The scenario, though it is inclined to disregard distances and time slightly, is logical."
>
> *Motion Picture News,* December 11, 1915, p. 92

Even these errors could not detract from the film's photography, with scenes shot in Florida, Georgia, Arizona, New York, and aboard an ocean liner.

THE MECHANICAL MAN

Release: 1915, Universal Film Manufacturing Co.
Description: Silent
Classification: SF-C
References: No. 14, p. 314; No. 46, p. 391; No. 50, p. 296; LC, LP5624; MPW, Vol. 24, p. 2118, 2163; Vol. 25, p. 65

Credits

Producer .... Joker Films
Director .... Allen Curtis
Screenplay .... Clarence Badger

Cast

The Mechanical Man .... Phroso
Professor Shultz .... Max Asher

Professor Shultz invents an adult mechanical man which appears quite human, and will dance and sing if the correct button is engaged. A very wealthy man, Heinie Gotrocks, reads of the professor's marvelous new invention and decides it would be a perfect gift for his young daughter. Gotrocks offers the professor $20,000 for the mechanical man upon delivery to his home. Shultz agrees and begins to pack the mechanical man for the journey. He and his helper go into the adjacent room to get more packing material when a sudden terrible commotion from the area where the invention is stored causes them to hurry back. The professor cannot believe his eyes--his mechanical man lies shattered upon the floor. It seems the janitor inadvertedly knocked over the shipping container. Professor Schultz convinces his assistant to take the robot's place in the Gotrock's home until he can repair the damage to the real mechanical man.

During the remainder of the film, the episodes of the mechanical man (Phroso) in the Gotrocks household provide the audience with a good deal of entertainment. In the end the professor repairs his invention and makes the necessary substitution that frees his assistant.

Evidently, *Phroso* was a well-known impersonator of mechanical manikins as the reviewers lauded his performance saying, "Phroso was even better on the screen than in person."

Max Asher, a veteran actor, appeared in another science fiction production in 1915. He starred in the serial *Lady Baffles and Detective Duck*. In all, Asher performed in nearly 300 films during his career.

Joker Film Company was an independent motion picture producer who released exclusively through Universal and produced only one-reel comedies. While most of their work showed originality and creativity, the plot of this particular movie was very similar to the screenplay for *An Animated Doll* (1908).

MR. JARR'S MAGNETIC FRIEND

Release: 1915, Vitagraph Company of America
Description: Silent, 960 feet
Classification: SF-C
References: No. 14, p. 323; No. 46, p. 406; No. 50, p. 307; LC, LP4930; MPN, 4-17-15, p. 62; MPW, Vol. 24, p. 280, 902

Credits

Producer .... J. Stuart Blackton
Director .... Harry Davenport
Screenplay .... Roy L. McCardell

Cast

Mr. Jarr .... Harry Davenport
Mrs. Jarr .... Rose Tapley
Willie Jarr .... Paul Kelly
Emma Jarr .... Audrey Berry
Fritz .... Frank Bunny
Dinkston .... Charles Eldridge

This was a series of twelve films depicting the misadventures of Mr. Jarr. Each of the movies seems to have been very entertaining to their audiences, but only one of the twelve, *Mr. Jarr's Magnetic Friend,* can be classified as science fiction.

On a peaceful Sunday afternoon, Fritz calls on the Jarr family and tells Mr. Jarr that his sister, Fatima, has fallen in love with Dinkston, the poet. She is ready to end her life if Dinkston doesn't pay her some attention. After much encouragement from Mrs. Jarr, Mr. Jarr and Fritz go to Fatima's home to aid her in this time of great despair. After pleading with Fatima for some time, they are interrupted by Vera Grimm, the infamous lady reformer. After relating Fatima's sad tale to Vera, she decides to confront Dinkston with the problem. She finds him and forces him to return to Fritz's house with her. Upon their arrival, they see Jarr, Fritz, and Fatima struggling with an old folding bed. They all lend a hand and are soon joined by a police officer and Hogan (Dinkston's rival). The episode gets rather rough and disorderly with Dinkston slipping out of Vera's grasp and thus escaping. Realizing Dinkston has gotten away, everyone proceeds to chase after him. Dinkston seeks refuge in a local power station under a large dynamo. Hogan sees Dinkston hiding there and engages the switch which starts the dynamo. Enormous quantities of electrical current appear to pass through Dinkston's body, until finally a supervisor rushes to the switchboard and halts the dynamo. It is too late—poor Dinkston has been magnetized. Fatima arrives and throws herself into Dinkston's arms, immediately receiving the shock of her life. Dinkston, realizing that he will pass on electrical current to anyone who dares approach him, hurries out of the power station toward home.

Finally, the police capture Dinkston and discharge him, using copper wire. Dinkston and Fatima wander off, making plans for an early wedding. Meanwhile. Mr. Jarr returns home and blames his wife for getting him involved in the first place.

The excellent experience of the cast made this film, and the entire series, one of the most popular of 1915. Harry Davenport, the star of the series, acted in nearly 500 films from 1912 to 1950. Paul Kelly, who also appeared in all the installments, likewise appeared in 500 films from 1911 to 1957.

While this film was weak in SF content, it was rich in entertainment for its audiences.

THE MONOPOLIST

Release: 1915, Pathe
Description: Silent, 3000 feet
Classification: SF-A
References: No. 14, p. 327; No. 46, p. 413; No. 50, p. 312; MPN, 8-21-15, p. 87

A rather interesting, but weak, science fiction film which centers around a young man who develops a device which will double the speed of merchant vessels. A young assistant to a large ship owner (Hopkins) falls in love with his daughter. Hopkins, however, reacts by firing the young man. A few months later the young man has perfected his speed process and begins to reap the rewards of his new device. Before long he is a very wealthy man and has everything he wants--except his true love. Meanwhile, Hopkins has experienced serious financial problems. His former employee offers to aid him if he will command his daughter to marry him. Hopkins agrees and the two are wed, but his bride declares that she does not love him and never will.

The young inventor and his marvelous invention have nearly perfected a monopoly in the shipping industry and he is obviously resented by the other large shipping firms. His enemies try to capture him, but somehow he escapes. During this conflict, his wife seems to lose her antipathy toward him and the film ends with the two lovers sailing into the sunset on a belated honeymoon.

THE MYSTERIOUS CONTRAGRAV

Release: 1915, Universal Film Manufacturing Co.
Description: Silent, 2000 feet
Classification: SF
References: No. 14, p. 341; No. 46, p. 420; No. 50, p. 322; LC, LP4867; MPW, Vol. 24, p. 132-134

Credits

Producer .... Gold Seal Films
Director .... Henry McRae
Screenplay .... Henry McRae

Cast

Professor Coxheim .... Frank Stites

Dr. Coxheim, a famous professor of science and well-known inventor, has recently extended his research of negative electricity by developing an anti-gravity device. Dr. Coxheim, with the timeless efforts of his son, Willard, and daughter, Laline, has successfully applied this new scientific wonder to an airplane. The experimental data reveals that the airplane not only flies faster and is more maneuverable, but needs little or no fuel to stay aloft. Williard and Laline, both extremely adroit aviators, have arranged a special demonstration for government officials.

Dr. Coxheim is concerned about what he should name his new discovery. Laline suggests that they call it *contragrav* as it appears to be contrary to gravitation. Her father is delighted with her suggestion and announces the new name of this discovery to the government officials. Laloud, one of the government officials at the contragrav demonstration, takes copious notes on all the marvelous invention's attributes. Unknown to the others, he is an undercover agent for a foreign government, and he transmits the details of the demonstration to his home office. Realizing the military value of such an invention as contragrav, the foreign power begins a plan which will result in its possession of the invention. It summons one of its most notorious agents, Olga Belgram, to obtain the device.

Olga gains the attention of the Coxheims when she wrecks her car near their mountain retreat. Laline, believing that she is injured, cares for her until she has sufficiently recovered, and by that time Olga has gained the confidence of the entire family. She wastes little time in uncovering the secret of contragrav. In addition she learns the hiding place of the conveted invention. Olga leaves the Coxheim household thanking them for aiding her in her recovery. She immediately summons her fellow agents, who devise a plan to steal the invention that very night.

Using the information provided by Olga, the agents have little difficulty in getting the prized invention in their possession. They quickly return to their ornate suburban villa to more closely examine the device.

Upon discovering the theft, and not wishing to notify the authorities or the public to the invention's disappearance, Dr. Coxheim hires a group of excellent detectives. Within days, the group has determined that Olga was the principal agent behind the theft. Moreover, it has located her headquarters in a remote suburban villa.

Laline and Willard thank the detectives for their fine efforts, but quickly add that they will pursue the matter from this point on. They feel responsible for Olga's gaining the information which made the theft possible and wish to recover the invention themselves. Using Willard's airplane, the duo demonstrates why their father was so proud of their aeronautic skills by landing quietly and undetected beside Olga's villa. After a fierce battle, the pair quickly recovers the plans and the contragrav device and returns to their airplane to make their escape. They are no sooner airborne than they notice a plane in fast pursuit. One of Olga's agents has orders to kill them both and destroy their device. Willard, realizing the impending peril advises Laline to strap the contragrav to her body and jump as he flies close to the next mountain ridge. Laline does as her brother instructs and floats gently to the ground. Gazing skyward, she sees her brother's airplane burst into flames as it is struck by a bomb from the foreign agent's plane. Laline makes her way back to the Coxheim mountain retreat where she relates the sad events to her father. Dr. Coxheim summons the authorities, who destroy the enemy agents and their headquarters.

This was certainly a very entertaining SF film, and appeared to be well done. The stunts performed by Frank Stites resulted in his changing his profession from actor to stuntman.

THE NEW EXPLOITS OF ELAINE

Release: 1915, Pathe
Description: Silent, 10 episode serial, each episode approx. 2000 feet
Classification: SF-A
References: No. 8, p. 28, 164; No. 14, p. 351; No. 46, p. 430; No. 50, p. 331

Credits

Producer .... Theodore W. and Leopold V. Wharton
Director .... George B. Seitz
Screenplay .... Arthur B. Reeve and Charles L. Goddard

Cast

Elaine Dodge .... Pearl White
Jameson .... Creighton Hale
Craig Kennedy .... Arnold Daly
Wu Fang .... Edwin Arden
Wong Long Sin .... M. W. Rale

Chapters 1-10 of *The New Exploits of Elaine*

Chapter 1 (15): The Serpent Sign
References: LC, LU6660; MPW, Vol. 24, p. 401
Chapter 2 (16): The Cryptic Ring
References: LC, LU6661; MPW, Vol. 24, p. 569
Chapter 3 (17): The Watching Eye
References: LC, LU6659; MPW, Vol. 2, p. 642, 740
Chapter 4 (18): The Vengeance of Wu Fang
References: LC, LU6658; MPW, Vol 24, p. 808
Chapter 5 (19): The Saving Circles
References: LC, LU6662; MPW, Vol. 24, p. 986, 1094
Chapter 6 (20): The Spontaneous Combustion
References: LC, LU6663; MPW, Vol. 24, p. 1168
Chapter 7 (21): The Ear in the Wall
References: LC, LU6678; MPW, Vol. 24, p. 1340, 1442
Chapter 8 (22): The Opium Smugglers
References: LC, LU6679; MPN, 6-12-15, p. 72; MPW, Vol. 24, p. 1340
Chapter 9 (23): The Tell-Tale Heart
References: LC, LU6680; MPW, Vol. 24, p. 1690, 1941
Chapter 10 (24): Shadows of War
References: LC, LU6681; MPW, Vol. 24, p. 1856, 1948

Due to the extraordinary success of *The Exploits of Elaine* (1914), Pathe added ten more chapters and called the expanded serial *The New Exploits of Elaine.* All of the primary actors, save Raymond Owens who played the *clutching hand* in the original (his character died in the final chapter of *Elaine*), returned to appear in the continuation of the Craig Kennedy feature.

The master villain in the serial is the mysterious Wu Fang, who searches for the seven million dollar treasure of the *clutching hand.* At first Wu Fang's interest appears to be solely monetary, but as Craig Kennedy and Elaine Dodge foil his every attempt to acquire the hidden wealth, Wu Fang's focus is redirected toward the maniacal elimination of Craig and Elaine.

In the first three episodes Craig and Elaine, and Wu Fang and his band of ruthless killers, each are seeking the secret vault containing the *clutching hand* treasure. The first place each searches is the Perry Bennett estate. Craig and Elaine uncover a secret passage which leads to a large underground chamber. Within the chamber they discover a large chest, but it does not contain the treasure, only an oddly shaped ring. Returning to the main section of the house and daylight. Craig discovers that the ring contains some unidentified message—a *cryptic ring.*

In Chapter 2, Craig, Elaine, and Jameson attempt to decode the secret of the ring. Meanwhile, Wu Fang schemes to steal the ring and learn its secret, thereby revealing the unfound treasure's location.

Pearl White, the most famous of all serial heroines, in a 1918 portrait.

In one attempt to steal the ring, Wu Fang's gang captures Elaine and presents her to their chief. Craig and Jameson continue their quest for the secret of the ring during which Craig employs the use of a mathematical device which crudely resembles a computer.

In Chapter 3 Craig learns the ring's secret, thereby discovering the underground treasure vault. With the bounty secure, Craig and Jameson devote all their efforts to locating Elaine, who remains a captive of the sinister Wu Fang.

Wu Fang's anger is displayed in Chapter 4 as he seeks vengeance on Craig Kennedy. He attempts to use Elaine, who is still under his power through some sort of drug injection, as bait for the most fiendish plot ever perpetrated on Craig. Wu Fang tells Elaine that she will witness each of her friends' deaths and will be helpless to stop the vengeance of Wu Fang. Meanwhile, one of the agents, Weepy Mary, places a deadly African tick in Craig's telephone receiver. After several annoymous calls, Craig and Jameson become stricken with the malignant fever as the infection spreads throughout their entire system. A specialist is summoned who happens to recognize the strange symptoms of their ailment. But before the antidote can be administered, Weepy Mary, disguised as a nurse, arrives on the scene. She attempts to destroy the antidote, but is foiled by the unexpected appearance of Elaine who immediately denounces her as an agent of Wu Fang. Weepy Mary quickly makes her escape, and Craig and Jameson are given the antidote which enables them to recover completely from the dread disease, thanks to the timely arrival of Elaine.

In Chapters 5 through 10 Wu Fang's maniacal desire to rid the world of Craig and Elaine provides thrilling adventures and narrow escapes for the intrepid duo. The accelerated attacks begin in Chapter 5 when Wu Fang manages to steal a large quantity of the ultra-powerful Trodite, a secret government explosive being used to create a new bomb for use by airplanes. Wu Fang employs several expert aviators to seek out and destroy Craig and Elaine. The agents paint a large white ring on Kennedy's house so the aviators will be able to easily identify the target. Jameson discovers the circle on the roof and reports the incident to Craig. The two quickly rub out the circle and place a similar circle on the house containing Wu Fang's agents. Needless to say, the bombs destroy a large portion of Wu Fang's labor force, only adding to the deep hatred he holds for Craig Kennedy. In a spectacular air and ground battle, Craig and Jameson manage to effect a direct hit on each of the aircraft causing them to plunge to earth.

In Chapter 6, Elaine is saved from a fiery death by a clever new device invented by Craig. Meanwhile, Wu Fang has planted an agent in the Dodge household--the new maid. Within days after her arrival, a new chair is delivered and the maid has the chair taken to Elaine's bedroom. The chair is a special creation of Wu Fang and it will burst into spontaneous combustion the moment anyone sits in the seat. Only Craig's suspicious nature foils Wu Fang's attempt on Elaine's life.

In Chapters 7 through 9 Craig continues to foil each of Wu Fang's attempts on his and Elaine's lives. Finally, Craig employs the sphygmograph (a type of lie detector) on a captured agent of Wu Fang's. After careful questioning Craig learns the hideout of Wu Fang. At the same time, Wu Fang is attempting to steal a new model torpedo Craig just completed for the United States government. As Wu Fang returns to his waterfront hideout, having successfully stolen the new secret torpedo, he is greeted by Craig and Jameson who have been awaiting his arrival. A fierce battle ensues, sending Wu Fang scurrying across the docks hotly pursued by Craig. The forms of the two warriors are silhouetted against the moonlit sky but suddenly the pair plunge into the murky bay only a few tell-tale bubbles on the silent surface revealing any evidence of their demise. On the morning tide the half eaten body of Wu Fang washes ashore, the obvious victim of a vicious shark attack. But what has become of the dauntless scientific sleuth, Craig Kennedy? Poor Elaine--her only love lost when victory was within their grasp!

Forsake not, faithful serial lovers, perhaps the next series, The Romance of Elaine, will shed some light on the mysterious disappearance of Craig Kennedy!

> "Watching week after week the defteness with which each episode of the now famous Pathe-Hearst serial is being handled it is astounding to note the limitless manner in which thrills and innovations of all sorts make their appearance. In fact, we wonder how much longer the pace can be kept up; and we have not finished wondering before another remarkable episode follows in the trail of the last one."
>
> *Motion Picture World,* Vol. 24, p. 1094

John Temple first meets Florence at a party; too soon though their new found love is savagely tested as war breaks out in *Pawns of Mars* (1915).

PAWNS OF MARS

Release: 1915, Vitagraph Company of America
Description: Silent, 2980 feet
Classification: SF
References: No. 14, p. 373; No. 46, p. 468; No. 50, p. 360; LC, LP5045; MPW, Vol. 24, p. 438, 571, 572

Credits

Producer .... Broadway Star
Director .... Theodore Marston
Screenplay .... Donald I. Buchanan

Cast

Florence Lefone .... Dorothy Kelly
John Temple .... James Morrison
Dr. Lefone .... Charles Kent
Rizo Turbal .... George Cooper

Mars, the mythical Greek god of war, appears to spur men into global conflict when reason would serve them better. Such is the case with this film epic in which men are driven to produce new and more powerful weapons so they can more efficiently destroy each other.

The opening scene takes the viewer to the small European country of Cosmotania and into the laboratory of Dr. Lefone. Dr. Lefone is a celebrated chemist whose field of expertise is explosives. He has developed a new one which seems to dwarf its predecessors in power of destruction. Somehow, the formula's secret is stolen by the shrewd spy, Rizo Turbal, who, in turn, sells it to the bellicose foreign government of Mapadonia.

Dr. Lefone, upon discovering the theft, confides in John Temple, a young physicist working on a device which can project a high intensity electrical beam at any target. John and Dr. Lefone immediately report the theft to the Secretary of War, who requests a demonstration of the new invention. During this, Florence, the professor's daughter, accidently spills some of the chemicals in her father's laboratory, resulting in an explosion which leaves her badly injured and blinded. The professor becomes very despondent after this, but Florence and John manage to instill within him the desire to complete his work. Dr. Lefone succeeds in producing several bombs about the size of a pigeon's egg, each with enough explosive to destroy an entire building.

Rizo and an accomplice manage to steal several of these new bombs and deliver them to the emperor of Mapadonia who is continuously setting in motion war planes against Cosmotania. The Secretary of Cosmotania learns of the impending invasion and begins to marshal his forces. John is ordered to complete his electric ray device with the utmost dispatch.

A large scale air and ground battle begins near the western border of Cosmotania. Airplanes on both sides are using Professor Lefone's bombs quite successfully as they destroy numerous ground troops. As the battle progresses, the Mapadonia forces seem to have the superior air power and victory appears only moments away. But wait! John arrives (just in the *nick of time*, as the saying goes) on the battlefield with his electric raygun fully operational and ready for action. Within a flash. John has destroyed the enemy airplanes and changed the tide of battle. The Emperor of Mapadonia realizes there is certain defeat ahead for his forces and sues for peace. The war now ended, John returns to Florence and asks her to marry him. She naturally consents, but remarks, "We are but *Pawns of Mars.*"

> "The spectacular quality of many of the scenes and the interest aroused by a very well presented story should make *Pawns of Mars* a popular offering."
>
> *The Moving Picture World*, Vol. 24, p. 572

Pawns of Mars is one of the few SF films referenced thus far which provides all the necessary ingredients to make it an outstanding SF movie. The character action and the technological devices capture the audience's attention and provide an imaginative interplay between the SF inventions and the actors, resulting in one of the better SF features of the decade.

THE PLAGUE SPOT

Release: 1915, Vitagraph Company of America
Description: Silent, 900 feet
Classification: SF
References: No. 14, p. 383; No. 46, p. 477; No. 50, p. 372; LC, LP6309; MPW, Vol. 25, p. 2234

Credits

Producer .... Vitagraph Company of America
Director .... Theodore Marston
Screenplay .... R. Norman Grisewood

Cast

Dr. John Farley .... Donald Hall
Eben Greggs .... Harry Northrup
Crook .... Billy Billings
Policeman .... Richard Clarke
Daughter .... Mildred Platz

A wealthy, elderly gentleman, Eben Greggs, visits his old friend and physician, Dr. John Farley. He finds Dr. Farley in a state of euphoria. His tireless research efforts have been rewarded—he has perfected a cure for the deadly bubonic plague. Greggs participates in the celebration and wishes his friend a warm and sincere congratulations.

A few days later, Greggs' daughter (his only child) is kidnapped. The culprit demands a large ransom be paid immediately. As fate would have it, the good Dr. Farley is visiting Greggs' house when the old man learns of the kidnapping. Farley devises a plan which will guarantee the safety of the woman and will likewise not force Greggs to give in to the ransom demand.

He pretends to cooperate with the kidnapper by meeting him. Farley, who has accompanied him, carelessly drops his fountain pen onto the kidnapper's hand, causing the sharp tip to make a superficial wound. Dr. Farley examines the injury and announces that the crook has but a few hours to live. Puzzled by the events, the kidnapper questions the doctor as to the meaning of his statement. Dr. Farley replys that the tip of the pen had been previously dipped in a vial containing a culture of bubonic germs. Moreover, Farley admonishes the man that unless he receives an innoculation of his new vaccine, he will die before he can spend a single dollar of the ransom. A few moments pass during which the crook is reduced to a whimpering shell of a man, pleading for the doctor to save his life. Dr. Farley provides the necessary injection only after learning the whereabouts of Greggs' daughter.

The film ends with the kidnapper being carted off to jail, while Eben Greggs and his daughter express their gratitude to Dr. Farley.

This was an interesting, but weak film, and certainly not the standard Vitagraph SF feature for this period. Harry S. Northup appeared in an earlier SF effort, *The Cave Man* (1912), as well as others after *The Plague Spot*. The other players, however, appeared in few, if any, subsequent films.

THE RETURN OF MAURICE DONNELLY

Release: 1915, Vitagraph Company of America
Description: Silent, 3000 feet
Classification: SF
References: No. 14, p. 401; No. 46, p. 511; No. 50, p. 399; LC, LP4939; MPN, 4-17-15, p. 77

Credits

Producer .... Broadway Star
Director .... William Humphrey
Screenplay .... William Addison Lathrop

Cast

Young Man .... Leo Delaney
Wife .... Leah Baird
Physician .... Anders Randolph
Mother .... Mary Maurice

District Attorney .... Denton Vane
Warden .... Garry McGarry
Nurse .... Josephine Earle
Crook .... William Dunn
Crook .... Daniel Hages

This is the story of a young man framed and convicted of a murder he did not commit. The judge sentences him to die in the electric chair and the warden carries out the sentence, electrocuting the young man. His body is claimed by a physician wishing to test a new electrolysis device. The doctor succeeds in restoring life to the young man who now begins the quest for the real murderer in order to prove his own innocence. The criminals are so terrified by the sight of a man they believed to be dead, they make a complete confession to the authorities.

The young man returns to his wife and family; his name is cleared, and thanks to the physician's marvelous invention, he is alive and well.

The purpose for producing this feature was to expose the risks of capital punishment, and was shown by groups as an appeal for the abolishment of this type of sentence. The movie failed, however, to have significant impact on the audiences. It is also considered a definitely weak SF endeavor.

> "It is our opinion and that of several others who saw the picture that it would have been much stronger if the end had come with the execution of the man."
>
> *Motion Picture News*, 4-17-15, p. 77

THE ROMANCE OF ELAINE

Release: 1915, Pathe
Description: Silent, 12 episode serial, each episode approx. 2000 feet
Classification: SF-A
References: No. 8, p. 28, 165, 166; No. 14, p. 408; No. 46, p. 519; No. 50, p. 408

Credits

Producer .... Theodore W. and Leopold V. Wharton
Director .... George B. Seitz
Screenplay .... Bertram Millhauser, Charles W. Goddard & George B. Seitz
Camera .... Joseph Dubray

Cast

Elaine Dodge .... Pearl White
Jameson .... Creighton Hale
Craig Kennedy .... Arnold Daly
Marcus Del Mar/Mr. X .... Lionel Barrymore

Chapters 1-12 of *The Romance of Elaine*

Chapter 1: The Lost Torpedo
References: LC, LU6682; MPW, Vol. 24, p. 2109, 2178
Chapter 2: The Gray Friar
References: LC, LU6683; MPW, Vol. 25, p. 205, 321, 322
Chapter 3: The Vanishing Man
References: LC, LU6684; MPW, Vol. 25, p. 396

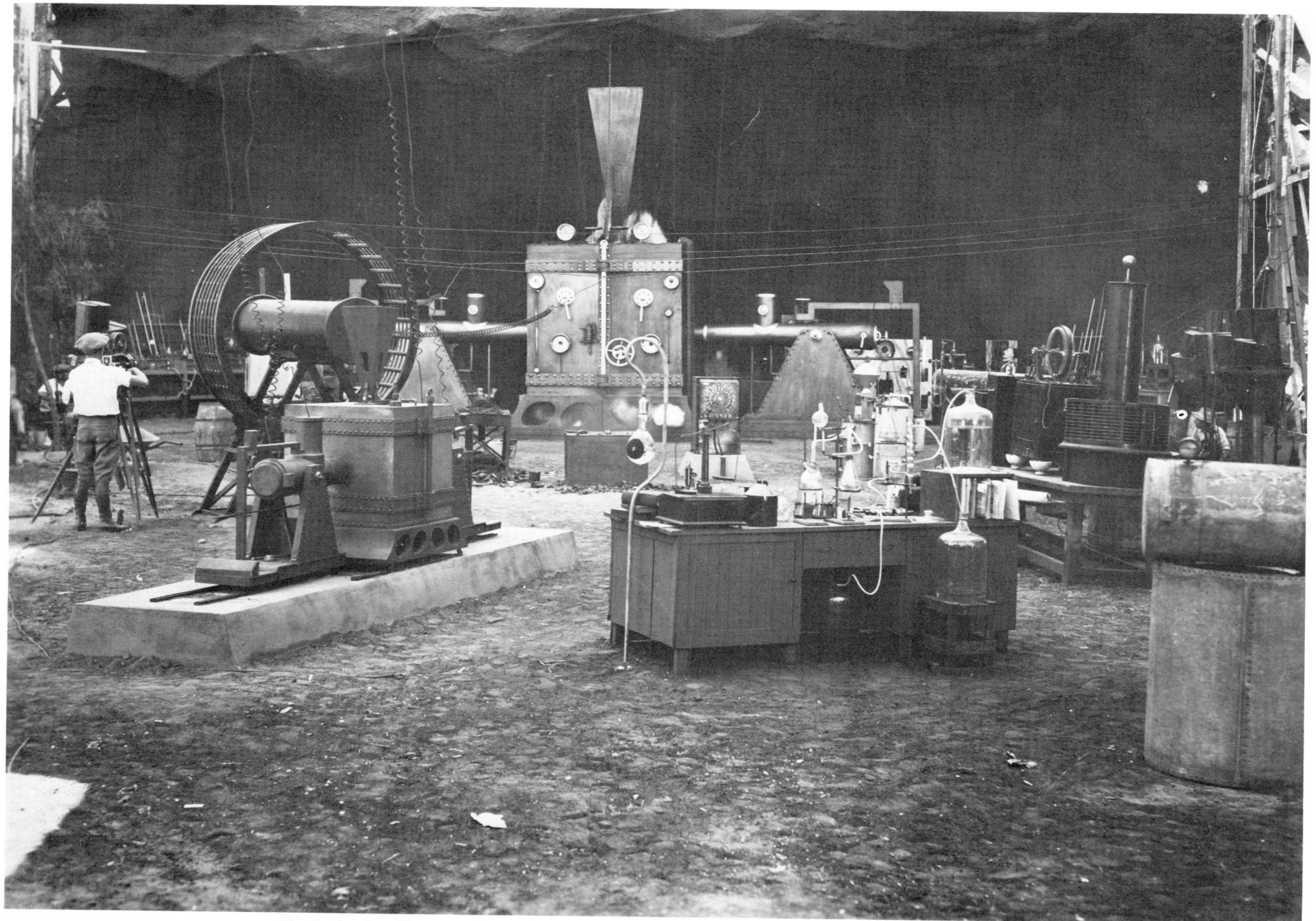

Typical scientific paraphernalia used in the film, *The Romance of Elaine* (1917).

Chapter 4: The Submarine Harbor
References: LC, LU6685; MPW, Vol. 25, p. 398, 509
Chapter 5: The Conspirators
References: LC, LU6686; MPW, Vol. 25, p. 566
Chapter 6: The Wireless Detective
References: LC, LU6687; MPW, Vol. 25, p. 904
Chapter 7: The Death Cloud
References: LC, LU6688; MPW, Vol. 25, p. 728
Chapter 8: The Searchlight Gun
References: LC, LU6689; MPW, Vol. 25, p. 987
Chapter 9: The Life Chain
References: LC, LU6690; MPW, Vol. 25, 1076
Chapter 10: The Flash
References: LC, LU6691; MPW, Vol. 25, p. 1231
Chapter 11: The Disappearing Helmets
References: LC, LU6692; MPW, Vol. 25, p. 1396
Chapter 12: The Triumph of Elaine
References: LC, LU6693; MPW, Vol. 25, p. 1396

The Craig Kennedy mysteries obviously captured the imagination and hearts of the public, and the movie makers of 1915 continued with *The Romance of Elaine,* which represented the final 12 chapters of the 36 chapter production. This serial had all the necessary ingredients for huge financial success: good acting, good scripts, and magnificent advertising through Hearst Publications. Not only were all 36 episodes published in their newspapers, but the trade journals, *The Moving Picture World* and *The Motion Picture News* contained more than 125 advertisements for the serial during 1915.

You might recall that in the final episode of *The New Exploits of Elaine*, Craig Kennedy, that marvelous scientific detective, had mysteriously disappeared while battling with Wu Fang. While Wu Fang's body was recovered with the morning tide waters, the audience and poor despondent Elaine were left perplexed by Kennedy's absence. In continuation of this epic SF adventure tale, chapter 1 of this series, *The Lost Torpedo*, offers a slim glimmer of hope that Craig may yet be alive and on the trail of one of the most sinister villains encountered thus far—the mysterious Mr. X.

The scene opens with a slim silhouette gliding across the moonless night, making only the slightest of ripples as it moves through the ocean's waters. The distinct shape of the periscope identifies the craft as it moves to an isolated dock along the deserted coast. Soon a man emerges from the submarine and moves along the dock toward the city as the vessel quietly submerges once again into the dark silent sea.

Later that evening, at a fashionable hotel in the New York area, a distinguished looking foreigner, resembling the shadow that departed from the submarine earlier, registers under the name Marcus Del Mar. The man has been unknowingly followed by a crusty old fisherman.

Del Mar wastes little time in seeking out Elaine and Jameson. He identifies himself as a secret service agent from Washington who is in search of Craig Kennedy's torpedo model and/or the plans for the model. Elaine and Jameson appear to offer little aid to Del Mar in his quest for the missing torpedo. Their concern is more directed toward locating Kennedy. Meanwhile, Elaine's dog uncovers the torpedo model in a large flower pot. He removes the model to the attic where he has stored other treasures. Del Mar discovers the miniature torpedo propeller near the flower pot and, therefore, believes Elaine has been lying. Within moments, the old fisherman enters Elaine's house and injects a paralyzing gas into the heating system, rendering Del Mar and Elaine unconscious. He then vanishes with the torpedo propeller.

In episodes 2 through 4 the inscrutable Mr. X (alias Marcus Del Mar) continues to try and uncover the model with little success. His plans seem to be foiled at every turn by some mysterious stranger or by Elaine's own investigation. The audience is treated to numerous fight scenes, all involving an array of elaborate weapons and gadgets. In episode four we learn the secret mission of Del Mar: to mine the harbors in the United States. It seems he and his crew had been successfully mining all the harbors on the East Coast. In this episode Elaine and Jameson accidently discover the harbor sabotaging efforts of Mr. X. They attempt to race back to the city with the vital information, but a heliograph signal is flashed to one of Mr. X's men to destroy the bridge their automobile is attempting to cross. Before this task can be completed, however, a mysterious stranger renders the man unconscious, thus allowing Elaine and Jameson safe passage to the city.

In episodes 5 through 11, Elaine gets help from Lieutenant Woodward (Commander at Fort Dale), Professor Arnold (Woodward's friend and chief science advisor to the United States aerial corps), Jameson, and the mysterious good samaritan. In these episodes Elaine displays a searchlight gun (which closely resembles a laser) to combat a horde of henchmen working for Mr. X. By chapters 10 and 11, Elaine's forces battle Mr. X and seem to be winning--they have discovered his secret base and destroy his mining operation of the harbors. But Mr. X, whom they have discovered is Del Mar, makes a spectacular underwater escape and joins his crew aboard their submarine. Del Mar prepares for a surface attack against all the ships in the harbor.

In chapter 12, *The Triumph of Elaine,* this bold attempt of Del Mar's to destroy all the defenseless ships in the harbor is foiled by an attack led by Professor Arnold who uses *hydroaeroplanes* mounted with wireless torpedos. The submarine proves an easy prey for this sophisticated weaponry as the first barrage sends the submarine crashing to the depths of the ocean floor, carrying with it the perfidious Del Mar. As the professor returns to the naval dock where Elaine is waiting, she learns, as does the audience, that Craig Kennedy has returned. The final scene shows Elaine and Craig tightly bound in tender embrace, confident that endless days of happiness await them.

The 36 episodes, which make up the three *Elaine* serials, had a significant impact on each of the actors' careers. Each became highly priced--and prized--professionals and they received an abundance of opportunities. The impact on Pathe Productions was unbelievable. They made millions off the three ventures and were able to produce even more films which affected the entire movie industry. Without question, this is one of the most outstanding SF endeavors of this entire period.

THE SECRET ROOM

Release: 1915, Lubin
Description: Silent, 2000 feet
Classification: SF
References: No. 14, p. 422; No. 46, p. 538; No. 50, p. 426; LC, LP6866; MPN, 2-27-15, p. 54: MPW, Vol. 23, p. 1146

Credits

Producer .... Sigmund Lubin
Director .... Tom Moore

Cast

Doctor .... Tom Moore
Daughter .... Marguerite Courtot
Boyfriend .... Robert Ellis
Mother .... Ethel Clifton
Idiot .... Paton Gibbs
Nurse .... Betty Peterson

This is a rather weak SF entry. The story centers around a physician's attempt to transplant a *soul* by employing a newly developed electrical device. The doctor captures his daughter's boyfriend and attempts to transplant his soul into the body of his imbecile son. Midway through the process, the system begins to fail resulting in the doctor's son's death. The young boyfriend is restored to good health and he and the daughter decide to run away to get married, leaving the doctor in despair after having killed his own son.

THE VENTURES OF MARGUERITE

Release: 1915, Kalem Company
Description: Silent, 16 episode serial, each episode approx. 2000 feet
Classification: SF-A
References: No. 8, p. 167; No. 14, p. 453, 512; No. 46, p. 571; No. 50, p. 459, 522

Credits

Producer .... Kalem Company
Director .... Hamilton Smith, John E. Mackin, and Robert Ellis

Cast

Marguerite .... Marguerite Courtot
Peter Enright .... Richard Pudon
Ferris .... E. F. Roseman
Fenton .... Phil Hardy
Bob Winters .... Bradley Parker
Kagler .... R. A. Bennett
Wharton .... Joseph Sullivan
Jones .... Harry Edwards
The Maid .... Paula Sherman
Helen .... Helen Lindroth
Leo .... Frank Holland
Crook .... Robert Vaughn
Crook .... Harry Edwards
Hal Worth .... F. B. Venocy
Dunbar .... Walter McErven
Martha .... Anna Reader
Carlow .... Otto Neimeyer
Manforth .... Freeman Barnes
Rudolph .... William Sherwood
Carrie .... Julia Hurley
Bolton .... H. E. Barrows
Irene .... Stella Jenno
Gungha .... A. Lever
Alota .... Eleanor Lewis
Bertha .... Losis Howell

Chapters 1-16 of *The Ventures of Marguerite*

Chapter 1: When Appearances Deceive
References: MPW, Vol. 25, p. 986
Chapter 2: The Rogue Syndicate
References: MPW, Vol. 25, p. 1016
Chapter 3: The Kidnapped Heiress
References: MPW, Vol. 25, p. 1189, 1190
Chapter 4: The Veiled Priestess
References: MPW, Vol. 25, p. 1189, 1190
Chapter 5: A Society Schemer
References: MPW, Vol. 25, p. 1363
Chapter 6: The Key to a Fortune
References: MPW, Vol. 25, p. 1715
Chapter 7: The Ancient Coin
References: MPW, Vol. 25, p. 1716
Chapter 8: The Secret Message
References: MPW, Vol. 25, p. 1889
Chapter 9: The Oriental's Plot
References: MPW, Vol. 25, p. 2063
Chapter 10: The Spy's Ruse
References: MPN, 1-1-16, p. 93; MPW, Vol. 25, p. 2239
Chapter 11: The Crossed Clues
References: MPW, Vol. 25, p. 2425
Chapter 12: The Tricksters
References: MPW, Vol. 26, p. 242
Chapter 13: The Sealskin Coat
References: MPW, Vol. 26, p. 381
Chapter 14: The Lurking Peril
References: MPW, Vol. 26, p. 381
Chapter 15: The Fate of America
References: MPW, Vol. 26, p. 522
Chapter 16: The Trail's End
References: MPW, Vol. 26, p. 614

This is the weakest SF serial of 1915. The film's producers obviously attempted to pattern *Marguerite* after *Elaine*, the character portrayed by Pearl White in *The Exploits of Elaine* (1914), *The New Adventures of Elaine* (1915), and *The Romance of Elaine* (1915), but their efforts fell miserably short. The serial lacks the mystery and the villainous characters of its predecessors. Moreover, there appears to be a lack of continuity from one episode to the next. Each seems to represent a single film rather than sixteen chapters, linked together by a common thread.

In chapters 1 through 4, Marguerite becomes involved with some very shady characters, but her naivite keeps her from falling into serious trouble. In these episodes, few scientific or technological devices are displayed, except for an unusual gun Marguerite uses to free herself when captured and locked in a steel room. The gun contains shells which explode with the force of a light explosive.

In chapter 10, *The Spy's Ruse*, Bob Winters invents an electric torpedo deflector which the Navy begins to test. Wharton and Jones are hired by a foreign power to steal the new weapon. They almost succeed, but are finally caught by Marguerite and Peter during a fierce gun battle. (A similar device was invented by Craig Kennedy in *The New Exploits of Elaine* [1915].)

In the remaining six episodes of the serial, Marguerite uncovers some exotic chemicals which have enormous explosive power and one which appears to be a form of nerve gas. Unlike earlier, or even its contemporary serials, the scientific devices discovered do not seem to relate well to the action of the characters, or the plot of the overall serial. The various scientific apparati appear to be added to the serial as *dressing* only. The characters rarely use the devices for any useful or logical purpose.

THE WAR O'DREAMS

Release: 1915, Selig Polyscope Company
Description: Silent, 2900 feet
Classification: SF
References: No. 14, p. 517; No. 46, p. 658; No. 50, p. 530; LC, LP56631; MPN, 7-3-15, p. 73; MPW, Vol. 25, p. 125

Credits

Producer .... Selig
Director .... E. A. Martin
Screenplay .... W. E. Wing

Cast

Prof. Arthur Ensign .... Edwin N. Wallock
Mrs. Ensign .... Lillian Hayward
Bessie Ensign .... Bessie Eyton

Arthur Ensign, a famous but impoverished chemist, has labored for a decade or more to perfect a new explosive material. He and his wife have made great sacrifices so that their daughter, Bessie, might have a better education. Bessie has just informed her parents that following her forthcoming graduation from college she and Lieutenant Leighton will marry. Her parents are delighted with her announcement, but their financial condition continues to deteriorate and they are forced to sell their kitchen stove. Professor Ensign uses part of the funds from the sale of the stove to purchase some badly needed chemicals.

That evening, quite by accident, Arthur discovers the correct combinations of chemicals to produce his long awaited discovery *trixite*. Trixite proves to be even more powerful than the professor had calculated. Moreover, the professor can detonate trixite at any desired location using an ether wave medium. The professor presents his discovery to the United States War Department. The Secretary of War is ecstatic and offers the professor a large sum of money for his formula. Ensign, his financial troubles at an end, rests peacefully with Mrs. Ensign that evening. But, during the night he has a nightmare in which he envisions his daughter and future son-in-law, along with tens of thousands of others, killed by trixite explosives. Ensign awakens from the horrifying nightmare and destroys the trixite formula, vowing to live in poverty rather than live in wealth that is stained with the blood of others.

An interesting feature, but this SF film plot was already old by 1915. It failed to capture the enthusiasm of the audiences.

WHEN THE MIND SLEEPS

Release: 1915, Kalem Company
Description: Silent, 2950 feet
Classification: SF-A
References: No. 14, p. 524; No. 50, p. 536; MPW, Vol. 24, p. 1786, 1826

Cast

Bess .... Myrtle Tannehill

A middle-aged gentleman, Roberts, inherits a fine estate but a condition is attached to it: he must care for Bess, an 18 year old child who is severely retarded. Roberts agrees to the conditions and after a few weeks attempts to make love to Bess. She does not understand and becomes terrified. Rejected and feeling guilty about his advances toward Bess, Roberts plans to get rid of her. Tom, a young violinist, is attracted to her, and she returns his affections. Roberts encourages Bess to go with Tom.

Sometime later, after Bess and Tom have been together for a while, Tom tells a friend, Dr. Carlson, about Bess' condition. He is the head of a large sanitarium and believes a new process called *cretinism* may restore Bess' mind to some semblance of normalcy. Bess and Tom agree to the operation. Afterward, Bess appears to have a normal mind, but only so long as she receives the proper dosage of a secret stimulant. The secret formula for this stimulant is known only by Dr. Carlson who personally administers it to all his patients. Bess has experienced a loss of memory, a side effect of the medication. She does not remember Tom or any of her past. Meanwhile, Dr. Burke, an assistant to Dr. Carlson, falls in love with Bess. Poor Bess—she becomes the pawn in a vicious love triangle between Dr. Burke, Tom, and Dr. Carlson. Dr. Carlson refuses to give Bess additional medication unless she returns his affections. Burke, Carlson, and Tom become involved in a vicious fight where Burke and Tom slay Carlson. Burke manages to seize the bottle containing Bess' needed medication, but sustains a mortal wound in the process.

Bess, seeing the terrible consequences of being normal, slams the vial to the floor, destroying its precious contents. She decides that she was far happier when ignorant of the *real* world. She and Tom then move toward Tom's cabin as Bess' mind slowly reverts to the mind of a child.

1916

THE BEGGAR KING

Release: 1916, Lubin
Description: Silent, 1500 feet
Classification: SF-A
References: No. 14, p. 42, 43; No. 50, p. 29; LC, LP8248; MPN, Vol. 13, p. 3271

Credits

Producer .... Lubin
Director .... Wilbert Melville
Screenplay .... Wilbert Melville

Cast

Reporter .... Robert Gray
Father .... Jay Morely
Beggar .... Louis Fitz Roy
Beggar .... M. De la Pacelle
Young Girl .... Eleanor Blevins

The film depicts the usage of automatic typewriters to transmit newspaper stories from one city to the next (prognosticator of the modern day teletype).

A reporter falls in love with a young girl whose prominent father turns out to be the head of a large group of professional beggars. Rather than write the story, the reporter resigns. But a bullet, meant for the reporter, misses and strikes the *beggar king* killing him instantly, and he vows to keep the old man's secret from the world.

Definitely a weak science fiction film, but the automatic typewriter makes it worthwhile.

THE COMET'S COME-BACK

Release: 1916, American Film Manufacturing Co.
Description: Silent, 1000 feet
Classification: SF
References: No. 5, p. 149; No. 14, p. 90; No. 50, p. 71; MPN, Vol. 13, p. 3434; MPW, Vol. 28, p. 1751, 1754

Credits

Producer .... Beauty Films

Cast

Professor Peedeegue .... John Steppling
Fuller Speed .... John Sheehan
Claire .... Carol Halloway
Hess E. Tate .... Dick Rosson

Professor Peedeegue is delivering a lecture on the evils of *speed* (i.e., doing everything in a hurry) to a large, partially attentive audience. The professor warns the group that unless it learns to slow down, there will not be a human race by the year 1926.

Fuller Speed, who had accidentally entered the lecture hall as the professor was issuing his warning, became interested in what he had to say but his attention was more drawn to the beautiful young lady seated next to the professor. Fuller's emotions intensify as he dreams of a meeting with the girl, who, he learns, is the professor's daughter Claire.

Immediately after the lecture, the professor and Claire scurry home where they are greeted by Hess E. Tate, Claire's sweetheart. The professor soon leaves the young people and enters his observatory to gaze at the stars. After peering through his telescope into the deep abyss of outer space, he suddenly pulls away from it with a strange look of amazement etched on his face. He then returns to the telescope in an effort to confirm what he has seen--a comet. It seems to be very large and is heading toward earth. Examining his astronomical journals, he discovers that this comet may have been viewed by Hoe Kem, an ancient astronomer in the year 916. Hoe Kem had predicted that the comet's path would allow its return every thousand years. Moreover, he had reported that the tail of the comet contained some unique gases which, when mixed with out atmosphere, might cause all living organisms to slow down.

Meanwhile, Fuller arrives at the Peedeegue residence, indicating that he was at the lecture and wants to learn more about the professor's ideas. After a brief conversation, the professor suggests that the group go to his *oxygen room* (a sealed room with an external supply of oxygen). Once in the room, the professor reveals the impending disaster of the comet. Within moments the group can see the comet through the glass portholes in the chamber. Soon they observe the effects of the comet's gases on the earth's population: all the people appear to have been converted into slow, mechanical-like beings. The animals also appear to move in a mechanical fashion. The professor and the young people are concerned about the fate of their fellow humans, but are relieved that they are safe in the sealed chamber. Unfortunately, their impregnability from the external atmosphere appears to be threatened when the professor reports that his dials indicate they have only enough oxygen for three people. Fuller and Hess decide to draw lots to determine who will be cast out of the chamber. Fuller loses and exits the chamber through what appears to be an airlock. The remaining occupants remorsefully watch the effect the comet's gases have on Fuller as he wanders off in a zombie-like state. The professor, Claire and Hess lean against the chamber walls, pondering their ultimate fate.

The film's story closely resembles the novel *The Poison Belt* (1913) by Arthur Conan Doyle, but the feature's credits give no mention of this parallel. The movie was well made for the 1916 period, and probably produced a great deal of audience excitement.

THE CRIMSON STAIN MYSTERY

Release: 1916, Consolidated Film Corporation
Description: Silent, 16 episode serial; each episode approx. 2000 feet
Classification: SF-H
References: No. 1, p. 511; No. 8, p. 168; No. 14, p. 99; No. 50, p. 80; PHO, Vol. 11, p. 135-38; MPW, Vol. 29, p. 660, 810, 968

Credits

Producer .... Erbograph Company
Director .... T. Hayes Hunter
Screenplay .... Albert Payson Terhune
Camera .... Ludwig G. B. Erb

Cast

Harold Stanley .... Maurice Costello
Florence Montrose .... Ethel Grandin
Dr. Burton Montrose .... Thomas J. McGrane
Vanya Tosca .... Olga Olonova
Robert Clayton .... Eugene Strong
Doctor's Assistant .... William H. Cavanaugh
Layton Parrish .... John Milton
Jim Tanner .... N. J. Thompson

Chapters 1-16 of *The Crimson Stain Mystery*

Chapter 1: The Brand of Satan
References: LC, LP8832; MPW, Vol. 29, p. 1270, 1560, 1604
Chapter 2: In the Demon's Spell
References: LC, LP8838; MPW, Vol. 29, p. 1560, 1604

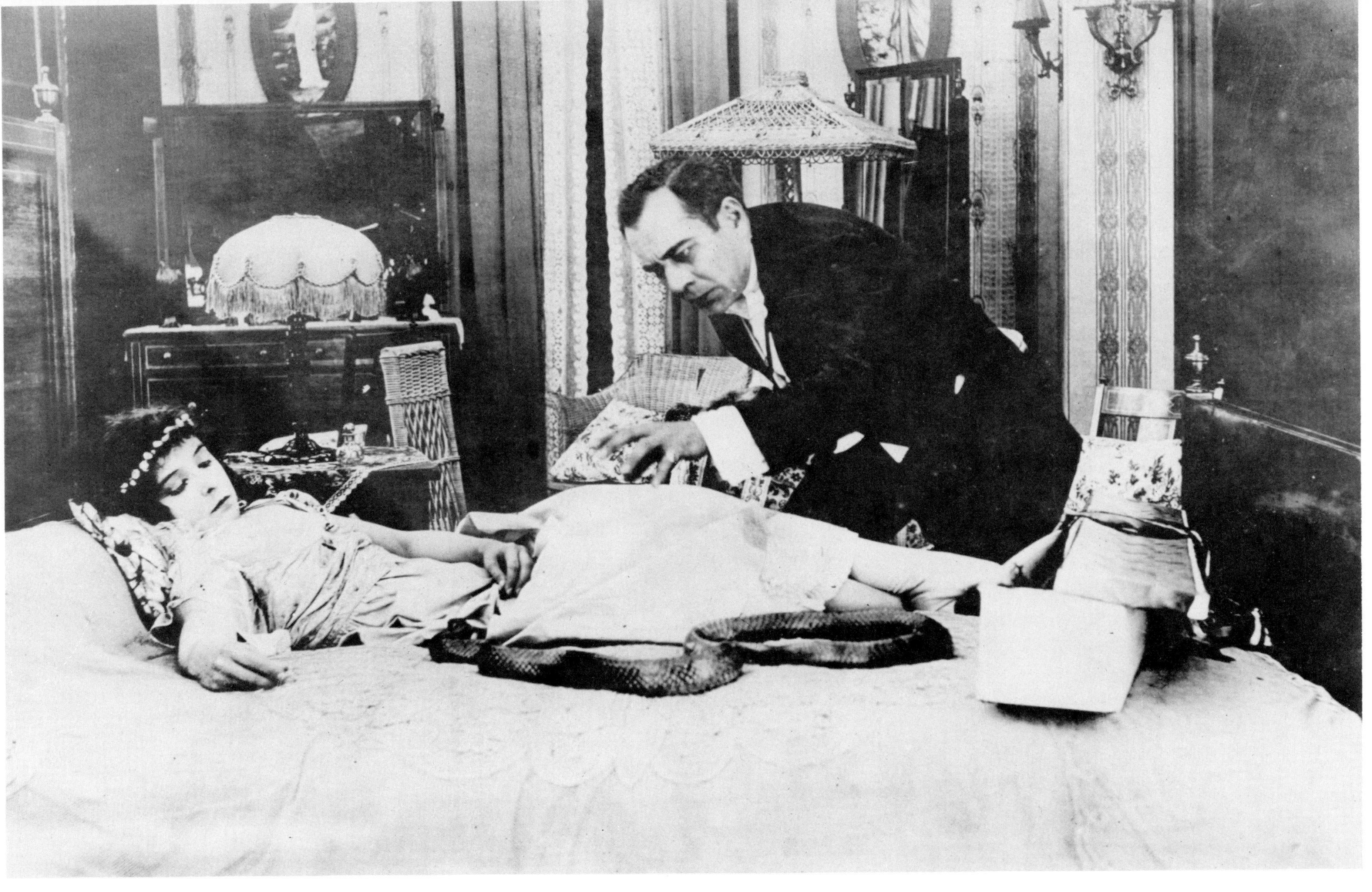

Florence (Ethel Grandin) is nearly killed by a deadly serpent in *The Crimson Stain Mystery* (1916).

Chapter 3: The Broken Spell
References: LC, LP8964; MPW, Vol. 30, p. 133
Chapter 4: The Mysterious Disappearance
References: LC, LP9066; MPW, Vol. 30, p. 133
Chapter 5: The Figure in Black
References: LC, LP9128; MPW, Vol. 30, p. 133, 134
Chapter 6: The Phantom Image
References: LC, LP9206; MPW, Vol. 30, p. 2966
Chapter 7: The Devil's Symphony
References: LC, LP9234; MPW, Vol. 30, p. 296, 297
Chapter 8: In the Shadow of Death
References: LC, LP9303; MPW, Vol. 30, p. 448
Chapter 9: The Haunting Specter
References: LC, LP9356; MPW, Vol. 30, p. 606
Chapter 10: The Infernal Fiend
References: LC, LP9427; MPW, Vol. 30, p. 756
Chapter 11: The Tortured Soul
References: LC, LP9555; MPW, Vol. 30, p. 992
Chapter 12: The Restless Spirit
References: LC, LP9556; MPW, Vol. 30, p. 1224
Chapter 13: Despoiling Brutes
References: LC, LP9664; MPW, Vol. 30, p. 1224, 1225
Chapter 14: The Bloodhound
References: LC, LP9665; MPW, Vol. 30, p. 1551
Chapter 15: The Human Tiger
References: LC, LP9737; MPW, Vol. 30, p. 1697
Chapter 16: The Unmasking
References: LC, LP9738; MPW, Vol. 30, p. 1697, 1698

The Crimson Stain Mystery is a 16 episode serial depicting the bizarre adventures of a set of Frankenstein-like monsters. Doctor Burton Montrose, a famous scientist, discovers an enzyme which he believes will increase the mental prowess of any human. However, his initial tests on human beings seem to go awry as the subjects increase their hostile motivations, becoming quite clever, but savage murderers as well.

As the first chapter begins, we find Jerome Stanley, publisher of the New York *Examiner*, admonishing his reporters about easing up on their relentless attack on the inept New York Police Department. It seems a band of ruthless murderers and robbers have victimized several prominent citizens within the past month. This vicious gang is the by-product of Dr. Burton Montrose's unsuccessful attempts to increase the human brain power, but no one knows of the doctor's connection with the infamous gang, and even he is not positive the gang's members are his former patients.

Jerome Stanley, frustrated by the police's inability to apprehend the gang, asks his son, Harold (a famous detective), to take the case. Agreeing to accept the job, Harold learns the only clue is the crimson stain in the eye of the leader of the criminals. In his quest to locate clues as to the gang's identity, Harold accidently meets Florence Montrose, the doctor's daughter, and the two of them fall madly in love. Florence becomes his constant companion as their sleuthing takes them closer to the gang. Following a set of complicated clues, Harold and Florence soon encounter three culprits in the act of murdering one of New York's most wealthy men. Florence scurries to summon help from the police while Harold confronts the murderers. After a valiant struggle, he is overcome by the trio and would have been killed had it not been for the timely arrival of the police.

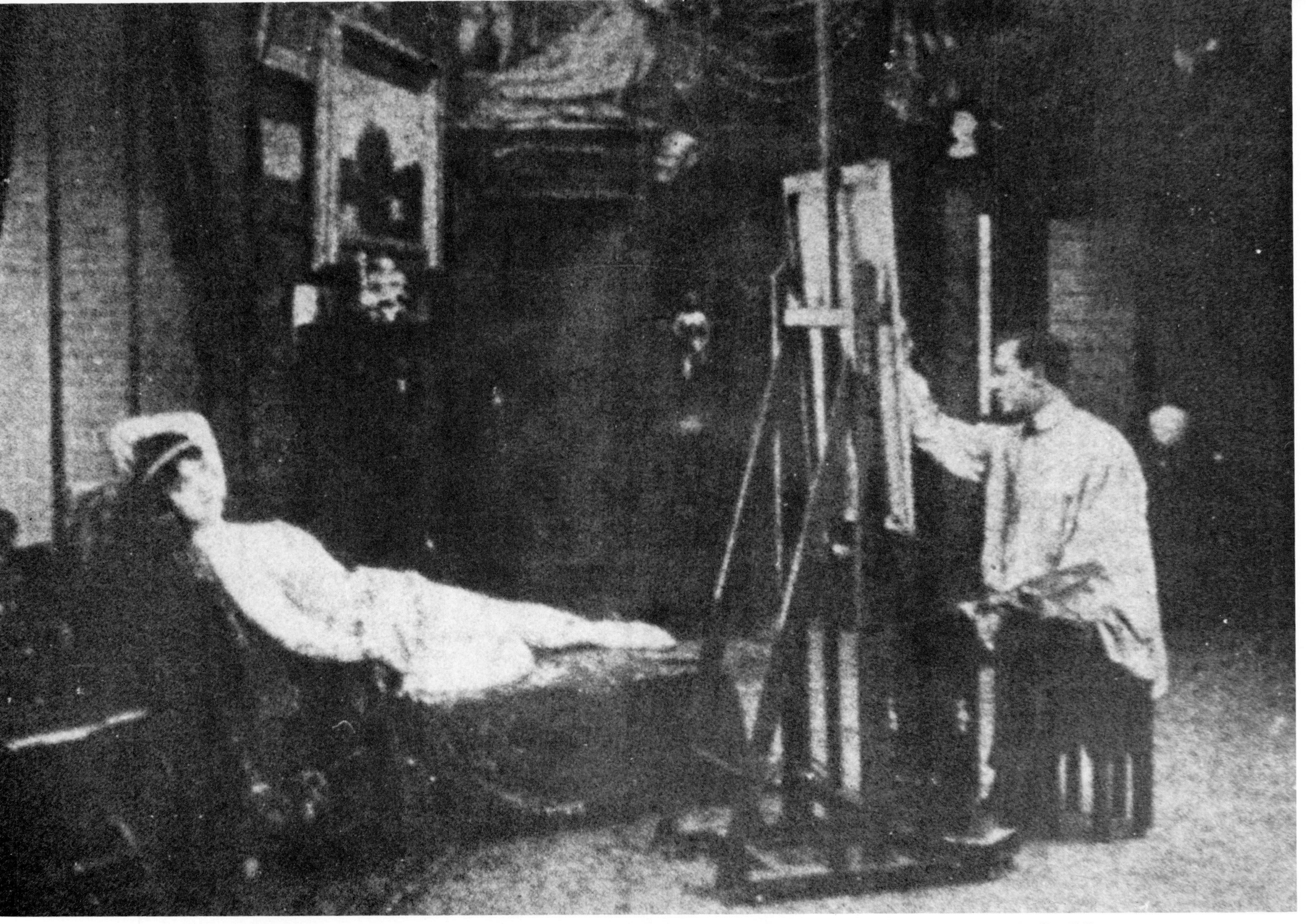

Florence is having her portrait painted when the "Crimson Stain" captures her in Chapter 2, "The Demon's Spell."

In chapter 3, Florence resists the forced consumption of a hypnotic potion while held captive by the "Crimson Stain."

The next evening, Harold, his father, and Robert Clayton, a young artist, are Montrose's dinner guests. During dinner Jerome Stanley is summoned to the library to accept an important call. Once within the room, the *Crimson Stain* (the leader of the gang) attacks him from behind and strangles him to death. Concerned about his father's prolonged absence, Harold enters the library and discovers his father's body. He vows that he will not rest until his father's death has been avenged.

In chapters 2 through 16 Harold Stanley and Florence Montrose inexorably pursue the *Crimson Stain.* In chapter 2 Florence learns that Pierre LaRue, one of her father's subjects, is the *Crimson Stain*, but fear for her life prevents her from revealing this to Harold.

Vanya Tosca, a member of the gang who resembles a vampire with feathers, lures Harold aside while Florence is captured by the others. Harold finally rescues her, but she has been placed in a deep trance and only the person who hypnotized her can release her from it. Harold, frustrated by his earlier attempts to locate the gang's hideout, seeks out the *Crimson Stain* with new resolve.

In chapter 3, *The Broken Spell*, Florence recovers from the hypnotic spell and reveals the truth about the *Crimson Stain.* In the remaining 13 chapters, Harold and Florence encounter many narrow escapes from death, but always manage to eliminate the members of the gang one by one.

Dr. Montrose finally confesses that the members of the gang are his experimental subjects. He further vows to create an antidote to rectify his horrible errors. But his efforts fail, leaving Harold and Florence to battle the gang with whatever means they can devise.

In the final episode Harold finds a secret panel in Dr. Montrose's laboratory behind which he discovers another laboratory and the doctor's diary. He begins to read it and learns of Dr. Montrose's hideous experiments which turned his lab assistant and three other students into savage murderers. While this explains the creation of the force of the gang, it does not explain the identity of Pierre LaRue, the *Crimson Stain.* As Harold finishes reading a passage from the diary, it is suddenly torn from his grasp. He regains consciousness just in time to see Pierre LaRue escape in an automobile. he quickly jumps to his feet and dashes toward his own car to pursue the sinister *Crimson Stain.* Harold pushes the vehicle to its maximum speed, and gains on the criminal's car when it suddenly comes to a halt near a steep cliff. The *Crimson Stain* abandons his car and moves on foot along the narrow edge of the cliff. Within moments Harold moves along the cliff's edge as well. As the *Crimson Stain* turns to catch a glimpse of his pursuer, he trips and accidently plummets to the rocky surface below.

Carefully, Harold makes his way down the cliff's edifice to LaRue's body. As he nears the dying man, LaRue removes what turns out to be a disguise. Harold is shocked to see that it is Dr. Montrose. He pleads with Harold never to reveal the truth to Florence. It seems Dr. Montrose was a victim of his own experiments. He agrees as the doctor dies in his arms.

Harold returns to Florence with her father's body and tells her that he was killed by the *Crimson Stain's* automobile and that their culprit drowned while trying to escape capture.

This is a good SF serial and seems to be a mixture of *Frankenstein* and *Dr. Jekyll and Mr. Hyde*, but does not provide the science fiction flair of *The Exploits of Elaine* (1914), *The New Exploits of Elaine* (1915), or *The Romance of Elaine* (1915).

Only Maurice Costello went on to act in talking films. The other players apparently fell into obscurity soon after this venture. Even Miss Olonova (Vanya Tosca in the movie), who claimed to be a descendant of a race of vampire women, vanished after the feature's release.

DARE DEVILS IN DANGER

Release: 1916, American Film Manufacturing Co.
Description: Silent, 850 feet
Classification: SF-C
References: No. 50, p. p-14; MPN, Vol. 14, p. 792

Credits

Producer .... Beauty Films

Harold Stanley (Maurice Costello), while in the process of cleaning his wound in Dr. Montrose's laboratory, discovers a vital clue to the "Crimson Stain's" identity.

Cast

Art Howell .... John Sheehan
Howell's Fiancee .... Carol Holloway
Secret Agent .... John Steppling

A young ingenious inventor, Art Howell, devises an automatic self-aiming gun for destroying aircraft. But before he can turn over his plans to the United States government, agents of a foreign power steal the valuable plans. Art gives chase in an automobile, a motor cycle, an express train, and then even an airplane. He finally captures the villains and recovers his blueprints. The U.S. government rewards him and states that this new weapon will guarantee peace for years to come.

John Sheehan was the only actor appearing in this feature who went on to act in *talkies*. He acted in over 200 films from 1916 to 1950.

THE FIVE FRANC PIECE

Release: 1916, Selig Polyscope Co.
Description: Silent, 2000 feet
Classification: SF-A
References: No. 14, p. 163; No. 50, p. 140; LC, LP9682; MPW, Vol. 14, p. 4042, 4043

Credits

Producer .... Selig Polyscope Co.
Director .... F. J. Grandon
Screenplay .... Myles d. Savelle

Cast

Margaret .... Edith Johnson
Napoleon Bonaparte .... Lafayette McKees
Jean Villiars .... Charles Wheelock

The feature contains a flashback from 1916 to the era of Napoleon. Napoleon, anxious to promote a new five franc coin, issues an order to Jean Villiars, the treasurer, to produce a million francs of this special issue. Jean saves the order and hides it in a specially constructed five franc piece. He wills the coin to his son, who, in turn, passes it on to his son—each descendant unaware of the coin's secret.

Years later, Jean Villiars' grandson, Jean Villiars III, has invented a wireless torpedo. He has successfully tested this remote controlled weapon, but lacks the money to produce the device. He soon receives an offer for this invention from Green, an unscrupulous promoter. Margaret, Jean's fiancee, urges him not to accept the promoter's unreasonable offer. Jean informs Green that he is rejecting his offer. Later that evening, Green attempts to steal the torpedo model, but is electrocuted in the process. Meanwhile, Margaret uncovers the secret of the five franc piece. She and Jean sell Napoleon's original order, which had been encased inside the inherited coin, and gain sufficient funds to get married and develop the wireless torpedo.

THE FLYING TORPEDO

Release: 1916, Triangle
Description: Silent, 5000 feet
Classification: SF
References: No. 1, p. 141; No. 14, p. 168; No. 20, p. 26, 27, 155; No. 47, p. 121; No. 50, p. 144; COF, Vol. 16, p. 18; FIR, 259, p. 87; LC, LP8297; MPN, Vol. 13, p. 1774; MPW, Vol. 27, p. 1896; PHO, Vol. 17, p. 106

Credits

Producer .... D. W. Griffith and Triangle Film Corp.
Director .... John O'Brien
Screenplay .... Robert M. Baker and John Emerson
Special Effects .... McCarthy Brothers
Camera .... George Hill

Cast

Winthrop Clavering (Novelist) .... John Emerson
Bartholomew Thompson (Inventor) .... Frank Spottiswoode Aitken
Hulda .... Bessie Love
Adelaide E. Thompson .... Viola Barry
William Haverman .... William E. Lawrence
Chief of International Crooks .... Fred J. Butler
Enemy Agent .... Raymond Wells
Enemy Agent .... Lucille Young
Enemy Commander .... Ralph Lewis

A wealthy, but eccentric, novelist decides to back his closest friend in developing a remote controlled flying torpedo. After months of experimentation, the inventor and his assistant create a working model of the wireless flying torpedo. Meanwhile, a group of crooks and enemy agents have been observing the inventor's progress. Realizing that he is about to turn over the invention to the U.S. government, they decide to strike. Late one evening the agents ingeniously murder the inventor with an asphyxiating gas and steal the torpedo model.

Angry, the novelist vows that his friend's work will not go unfinished, nor his death unavenged. He supplies additional funds for the project and urges the slain inventor's assistant to hurry with final production of the unit. While the assistant works feverishly to complete the task, the novelist, aided by his Swedish servant, tracks down the enemy agents. But by the time they locate the hide-out, their government has landed troops in California. The Asian forces become strongly entrenched along the West coast, capturing several large cities in the process. Only the remote controlled flying torpedo can turn the tide and stop the hordes of enemy forces attacking our coastal cities.

Duplicates of the invention are produced with incredible speed and are rushed to the beleaguered forces defending our country. Soon the sky is filled with the torpedos, each precisely programmed toward their designated targets. The Asian forces are routed from our shores and, as the movie ends, are seen sailing their huge vessels homeward. The novelist warns that we should pursue and destroy the enemy, but the government announces that the danger is over.

This is an interesting and prognostic film which closely resembles the *buzz-bomb* used by Germany 28 years after this film. The mysterious Asian invaders are also uncannily like the actual Japanese invaders 24 years later who attacked Pearl Harbor.

Based on a story written by D. W. Griffith, this feature is the first SF film in which the special effects (the *flying torpedo*) can be referenced. Both the photography and the special effects were given much praise by the 1916 critics. Additionally, many of the actors went on to make a number of films, and several became writers and producers of feature films. Truly one of the better SF films of 1916.

THE HALF WIT

Release: 1916, Lubin
Description: Silent, 2000 feet
Classification: SF-A
References: No. 14, p. 205, 206; No. 50, p. 180; LC, LP8629

Credits

Producer .... Sigmund Lubin
Director .... Wilbert Melville and Leon Kent
Screenplay .... Arthur Peterman

Cast

Ned .... L. C. Shumway
Daughter .... Helen Eddy
Gang Member .... George Routh
Gang Member .... Melvin Mayo
Surgeon .... Jay Morely

Ned, a half-witted member of the mafia, endures a marvelous operation by an ingenious surgeon who has perfected a new process for brain restoration. After recovering from the operation, Ned appears to be of normal intelligence.

He decides to save the daughter of a man marked by the mafia for execution. The scenario ends with Ned and the young girl fleeing for their lives.

This is a weak SF film with a plot that closely resembles several films of 1909 and 1910.

THE HAND OF PERIL

Release: 1916, World Film Corporation
Description: Silent, 5000 feet
Classification: SF-A
References: No. 14, p. 207; No. 23, p. 207; No. 50, p. 181; LC, LU7913; MPW, Vol. 27, p. 338, 340, 2033

Credits

Producer .... Paragon Films
Director .... Maurice Tourneur
Screenplay .... Maurice Tourneur

In *The Hand of Peril* (1916), James Kestner's marvelous x-ray machine provides a view of the counterfeiter's lair.

Cast

James Kestner .... House Peters
Maura Lambert .... June Elvidge
Frank Lambert .... Ralph Delmore
Bull's Eye Cherry .... Doris Sawyer
Tony Morello .... Ray Pilcer

This feature is based on the novel *The Hand of Peril*, by Arthur Stringer. Stringer was a popular detective story writer during the period, and this story was among his best works.

James Kestner, a United States government secret agent, is attempting to apprehend a well organized gang of counterfeiters. Kestner seems to have at his command an array of marvelous scientific devices which enable him to circumvent disaster and apprehend criminals (much like Craig Kennedy in *The Exploits of Elaine*).

It seems the counterfeiters also have a few inventions of their own: a tracing disc which can duplicate any form of currency and a device which can reproduce bank cashier's checks.

After many thrilling battles with this adroit gang of criminals, James Kestner employs the use of a secret x-ray device (it makes walls one-way transparent) to identify all the gang's members. In addition, he learns the location of their printing plant. With this new information, he is able to capture the entire gang and halt their nefarious activities.

One of the unique photographic special effects of the film is Tourneur's ingenious division of the screen into nine separate segments so, in effect, the audience was able to see the action in all nine rooms simultaneously.

HER FATHER'S GOLD

Release: 1916, Thanhouser
Description: Silent, 5000 feet
Classification: SF-A
References: No. 14, p. 217; No. 50, p. 190; MPN, Vol. 13, p. 3092

Cast

Young Girl .... Barbara Gilroy
Reporter .... Harris Gordon
Crook .... William Burt
Crook's Wife .... Louise Emerald Bates

Her Father's Gold is definitely a poor SF film. It is about a young girl whose father is killed by a gang of crooks. They were after his fortune in gold bullion. The girl and a young reporter attempt to recover the treasure, and encounter a nondescript monster, *Water Devil*, in the swamps of Florida. The audience never sees the monster, but it supposedly saves the girl's life by overturning the crook's boat. The reporter and young girl recover the gold bullion and never give any more thought to the *Water Devil*.

THE INSURANCE SWINDLERS

Release: 1916, Universal Film Manufacturing Co.
Description: Silent, 2000 feet
Classification: SF-A
References: No. 8, p. 36, p. 163; LC, LP7536; MPW, Vol. 27, p. 979, 1016

Credits

Producer .... Universal Film
Director .... Richard Stanton
Screenplay .... Walter Woods

Cast

Bruce Larnigan .... Hobart Henley
Tom Larnigan .... Harry D. Carey
Mrs. Larnigan .... Nanine Wright
Robert Harding .... Richard Stanton
Dorothy Maxwell .... Jane Novak
Stanford Stone .... Glen White
Roger Maxwell .... Marc Penton
Kitty Rockford .... Mina Cunard
Ben Travers .... Jack Connelly

The Insurance Swindlers is chapter 9 of a 20 episode Universal serial entitled *Graft*, and taken from a story by Hugh C. Weir and Joe Brant. Only episode 9 relates to science fiction. The remaining 19 chapters do not involve any aspect of science fiction.

The Insurance Swindlers focuses on suspended animation as a SF topic. However, the premise is weakly supported within the story.

The *Graft* serial relates the struggles of a young New York attorney, Bruce Larnigan, as he attempts to avenge his father's death and break up the powerful Graft trust. His father, Dudley Larnigan, was the district attorney for New York City, and had uncovered evidence which would expose the corrupt Graft trust. Unfortunately, he was murdered and the evidence stolen before he could make the details public.

By chapter 9, Tom Larnigan has had numerous brushes with death as the powerful coalition seeks to halt his investigation. Tom is about to uncover some damaging evidence on several large insurance companies who have been using policy holders' monies for personal speculation. Larnigan has secured a warrant to inspect the books and vaults of the Providential Insurance Company. While within the enormous vault, the door suddenly slams shut, locking Tom Larnigan inside in an airtight tomb.

After several hours, a group of experts are able to circumvent the time lock on the vault. Meanwhile, Tom has been slowly suffocating. As he passes out, he strikes the back of his head against a sharp projecting handle. Somehow (the incident is never fully explained to the audience), this injury to the base of the skull causes him to fall into a state of suspended animation. When the vault is finally opened, a doctor pronounces Tom dead.

Later he is placed in a coffin for burial. Kitty Rockwell, however, believes Tom is not really dead, and she frantically begins efforts to revive him. She is rewarded by Tom's emergence from the state of suspended animation. He recovers and prevents the insurance companies from halting his investigation of their illegal activities.

This episode is a very weak SF production, but is an interesting adventure serial. Still, there is not a lot here for the serious SF enthusiast.

THE INTRIGUE

Release: 1916, Pallas
Description: Silent, 5000 feet
Classification: SF
References: No. 5, p. 70; No. 14, p. 247; No. 50, p. 219; LC, LP9122; MPN, Vol. 14, p. 2056; MPW, Vol. 29, p. 2101

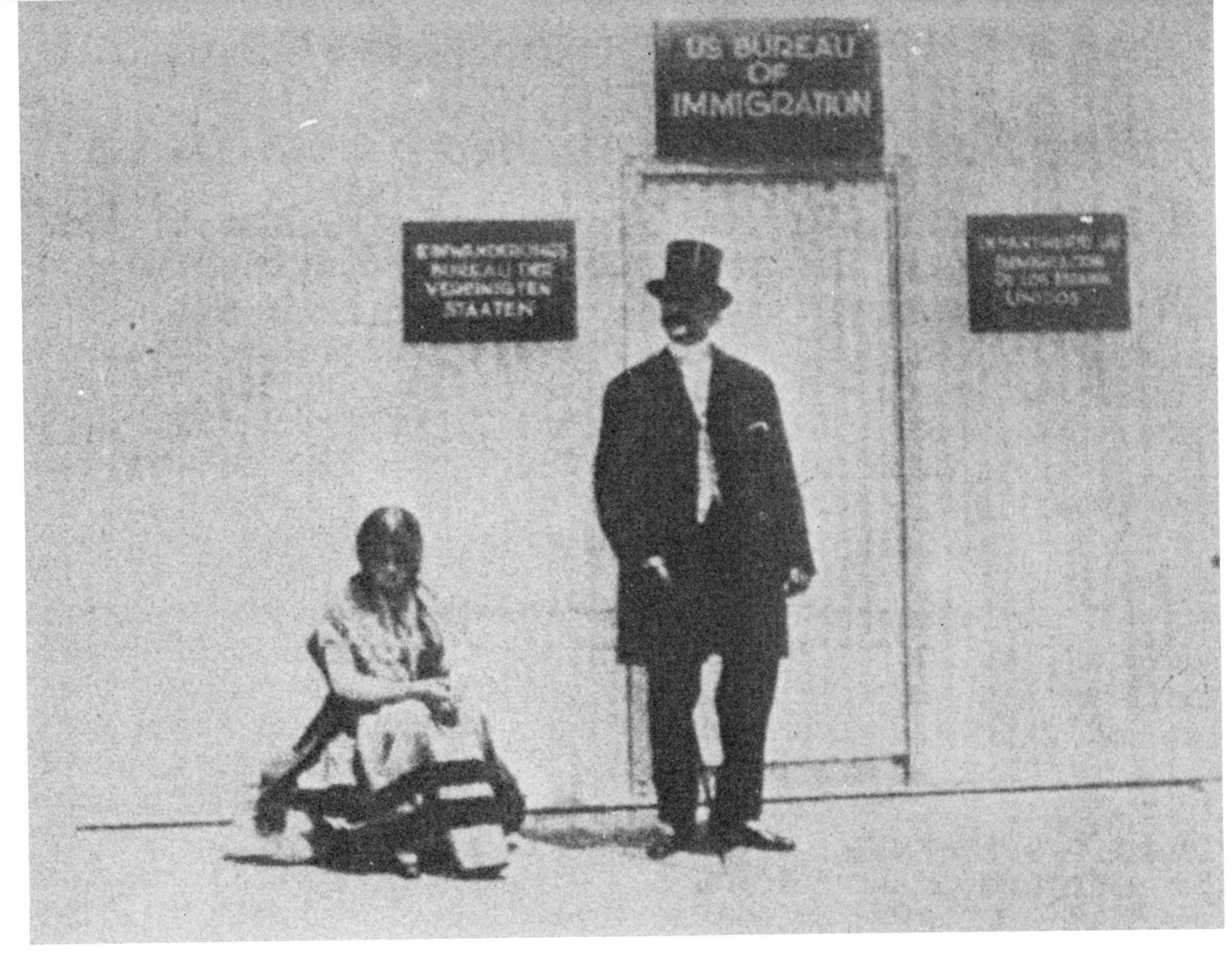

Countess Varnli and Baron Rogniat are waiting for U. S. customs clearance so they can steal the x-ray gun.

Credits

Producer .... Julia Crawford Ivers
Director .... Frank Lloyd
Screenplay .... Julia Crawford Ivers

Cast

Countess Sonia Varnli .... Lenore Ulrich
Guy Longstreet .... Cecil Van Auker
Baron Rogniat .... Howard Davies
Maid .... Florence Vider
King .... Herbert Standing
Emperor .... Paul Weigel

A young American inventor, Guy Longstreet, develops a new weapon which can emit large quantities of electricity. This device is capable of electrocuting people within a wide firing radius. Longstreet attempts to sell his new weapon to the U. S. government, but no one seems to pay any attention, and those that do offer little enthusiasm for his idea. Longstreet decides to sail to Europe and see if one of the European countries would be interested in his new weapon. Almost immediately, the countries of Europe clamor to see his device demonstrated.

Two warring countries send representatives to investigate the potential of this invention: Baron Rogniat is ordered by his emperor to evaluate the weapon and seize it if it can be used by their armed forces. The king of the other warring nation commissions the Countess Sonia Varnli to acquire the weapon or prevent its sale. Guy Longstreet is nearly cheated out of his invention, and twice comes exceedingly close to being killed. The Countess, however, becomes Longstreet's ally against the infamous Baron. Eventually their relationship becomes serious and they disclose their mutual love in the movie's final scene.

The story seems to closely resemble the screenplay for the feature, *Pawns of Mars* (1915). The former film was, however, of much higher quality and more attention was paid to the SF aspects than the adventures of the characters.

THE LION'S BREATH

Release: 1916, Universal Film Manufacturing Co.
Description: Silent, 1000 feet
Classification: SF-C
References: No. 14, p. 280; No. 59, p. 259; LC, LP7710; MPW, Vol. 27, p. 1532

Credits

Producer .... Nestor Films
Director .... Horace Davey
Screenplay .... Al E. Christe

Cast

Clarence .... Neal Burns
Sweetheart .... Billie Rhodes
Mother .... Jean Hathaway
Professor Giblets .... George French
Spike .... Ray Gallagher

Guy Longstreet perfects a powerful "x-ray" weapon in *The Intrigue* (1916).

Professor Giblets, a celebrated physicist and biochemist, has created a revolutionary process for personality transfer. Using the current from a series of highly charged batteries and several ultraviolet lamps, the professor can transform the attributes of one animal to that of another. While he has yet to attempt his process with humans, he readies his apparatus in eager anticipation of such an experiment.

Two young men live near the professor and his careful observations have led him to believe that the pair might serve as his first human subjects. Clarence, a timid young man, can not please his sweetheart's mother, who detests timidity in any man. Spike, the bold, brave sort of man, gains constant praise from the young girl's mother.

The professor seeks to aid Clarence in his quest for boldness. He prepares the experimental apparatus by placing Clarence at one end of a large glass tube and a ferocious lion at the other. Sparks fly; the circuits hum, and the ultraviolet lamp oscillates on and off until a small puff of smoke streams from Clarence's ears. Slowly, he rises and moves toward the lion. He cuffs him on the ears and darts out of the room, roughly pushing the professor aside.

The screenplay, adapted from a story by Ruth Snyder, provides an interesting and entertaining SF comedy format. It is an example of the vast improvements gained in SF comedy from those produced six to eight years before.

ONE THOUSAND MILES AN HOUR

Release: 1916, Universal Film Manufacturing Co.
Description: Silent, 1000 feet
Classification: SF-C
References: No. 50, p. 349; LC, LP9817; MPW, Vol. 31, p. 246, 275

Credits

Producer .... Nestor Films
Director .... Louis William Chaudet
Screenplay .... Bess Meredyth

Cast

Honest Harold .... Eddie Lyons
Dirty Dan .... Lee Moran
Trustful Tillie .... Edythe Roberts
Mike, the murderer .... Harry Nolan

From the title the viewer might think this was a story relating to breaking the sound barrier, or at least traveling very fast. If so, you may be disappointed since the film revolves around the misadventures of the ingenious inventor *Honest* Harold, who has perfected a chemical which can convert water into super automotive fuel. Harold claims that one drop of his wonder brew mixed with two gallons of water will propel his *flivver* machine for a thousand miles. Naturally, such an important discovery could not go unnoticed by the criminal element in our society.

Dirty Dan and Mike the murderer conspire to steal the valuable chemical and the manufacturing process from Harold.

We next see Harold and *Trustful* Tillie in his laboratory preparing a new batch of the chemical for the big cross country auto race—first prize is ten thousand dollars. Harold and Tillie want desperately to win the race so they can get married and begin to manufacture Harold's newest invention. Meanwhile, Dan and Mike have climbed upon the roof of the laboratory and begin to pour chloroform through a hole in the ceiling. Soon Harold and Tillie inhale the fumes and fall to the floor. Moments later Dan and Mike descend and enter the laboratory. They quickly abscond with the precious fluid.

Harold and Tillie awaken and rush to the doorway in time to see the crook's car zoom away down the winding road to the valley below. Suddenly they hear an enormous explosion; Harold and Tillie calmly proclaim, "They should have waited until the liquid had cooled."

The two stars of the feature, Eddie Lyons and Lee Moran, were a famous comedy team from 1914 to 1920, and were billed as *Lyons and Moran*. However, Lee Moran was the only part of the comedy duo who had a superb film career. From 1911 to 1936 he appeared in nearly 500 films. In 1915 alone he made 73 films.

This is an excellent science fiction comedy, even though the title's origin is never explained.

THE SECRET OF THE SUBMARINE

Release: 1916, American Film Manufacturing Co.
Description: Silent, 15 episode serial, each episode approx. 2000 feet
Classification: SF-A
References: No. 8, p. 38, 39, 173; No. 14, p. 421; No. 31, p. 40, 41, 47; No. 50, p. 425; LC, LU7936; NYT, 5-4-16, p. 9

Credits

Producer .... American Film
Director .... George Sargent
Screenplay .... C. C. Hoadley and William Parker

Cast

Cleo Burke .... Juanita Hansen
Lieutenant Jarvis Hope .... Thomas Chatterton
Olga Ivanoff .... Hylda Hollis
Gerald Morton .... Lamar Johnstone
Hook Barnacle .... George Clancy
Satsuma .... William Tedmarsh
Calvin Montgomery .... Joseph Beaudry
Sextus .... Harry Edmondson
Mahlin .... George Webb
Dr. Ralph Burke .... Hugh Bennett

This serial appeared without specific titles for each episode. References for each chapter are, however, listed below.

Chapters 1-15 of *The Secret of the Submarine*

Chapter 1: MPW, Vol. 28, p. 985, 1182, 1220
Chapter 2: MPW, Vol. 28, p. 1220, 1253, 1356
Chapter 3: MPW, Vol. 28, p. 1394, 1537
Chapter 4: MPW, Vol. 28, p. 2014, 2262
Chapter 5: MPW, Vol. 28, p. 2282; Vol. 29, p. 78
Chapter 6: MPW, Vol. 29, p. 268
Chapter 7: MPW, Vol. 29, p. 300, 477

Two crooks attack Lieutenant Hope (Thomas Chatterton) in an attempt to gain *The Secret of the Submarine* (1916).

Chapter 8: MPW, Vol. 29, p. 528, 655
Chapter 9: MPW, Vol. 29, p. 688, 808
Chapter 10: MPW, Vol. 29, p. 839, 946
Chapter 11: MPW, Vol. 29, p. 1104
Chapter 12: MPW, Vol. 29, p. 1153
Chapter 13: MPW, Vol. 29, p. 1418
Chapter 14: MPW, Vol. 29, p. 1443
Chapter 15: MPW, Vol. 29, p. 1558, 1594, 1595

Dr. Ralph Burke, celebrated scientist and inventor, has perfected an apparatus which would enable a submarine to remain submerged indefinitely. Dr. Burke's fantastic submarine mechanism is able to extract oxygen directly from sea water operating on the same principle as a fish's gill. He has invited representatives of the United States Navy to a private demonstration of a submarine outfitted with his invention.

Lieutenant Jarvis Hope has been dispatched by the Secretary of the Navy to inspect and evaluate this new invention. As the Lieutenant arrives in town he encounters an old navy friend, Hook Barnacle, whose life he once saved from a shark attack. They proceed to the laboratory to hear about the invention where they meet Cleo Burke, the professor's daughter. Soon after, Hook excuses himself and returns to town where he becomes inebriated and discloses the nature of Hope's visit. The information is heard by a Russian agent, Sextus, who immediately transmits the details to his superior Olga Ivanoff. Additionally, a Japanese spy, Satsuma, has gained the details of the submarine test and has secretly hidden aboard the experimental craft.

Meanwhile, a wealthy lobbyist, Calvin Montgomery, has dispatched his nephew Gerald Morton to obtain the secret of the underwater apparatus.

Dr. Burke gathers the group together and they board the submarine to begin the demonstration. After several dives and a submerged trip about the bay, the craft returns to the surface to begin the voyage back to the harbor. Dr. Burke invites the party to join him in the galley for lunch. Each of the members soon express their admiration for the professor's achievement in developing such a revolutionary craft. While the group dines in the galley, Satsuma, who has been hiding in the engine room, stealthily crawls forward to examine the mechanism. His presence is discovered by the crew, who open fire on the intruder. During the exchange, the oxygen-gathering device is damaged and in that moment Satsuma leaps up the conning tower ladder and escapes to the open sea. As Satsuma is making his escape, the vessel's dive control lever is hurled forward, sending the submarine into a deep dive. Water starts pouring through the open conning tower hatch. . . .the underwater breathing device is damaged. . . .the submarine is hurled into an uncontrollable dive. . . .the professor and his party battle for their lives in the watery darkness. . . .the words appear on the movie screen, *continued next week.*

Thus, the first episode ends with the audience anticipating the remaining 14 chapters. In the remaining episodes Dr. Burke manages to save the crew and submarine with his quick thinking and sheer genius. Lieutenant Hope informs Dr. Burke that the U. S. Navy will definitely purchase the invention. He returns to Washington to prepare the necessary documents. Dr. Burke becomes the victim of a mysterious murderer, but he leaves clues for Cleo to follow if she is to gain the secret of his marvelous invention.

Chapters 3 through 15 relate to the adventures of Cleo and Lieutenant Hope as they unravel the mystery Professor Burke has left surrounding the *secret of the submarine.* Their progress is often impeded, however, by Satsuma, Sextus, and Calvin Montgomery, all of whom become vicious in their quests for the underwater breathing machine.

The feature introduced a beautiful blonde starlet, Juanita Hansen, who became a silent screen star before disaster struck her life. Thomas Chatterton, already a veteran actor, made a number of films with American Film Manufacturing Company and Kay-Bee Films. Several of the players nearly lost their lives performing stunts in this movie and one unfortunate accident close to the end of the production severely injured Miss Hansen.

"George Sargent, the director in charge of the production, has managed to work into the story some very comprehensive views of a submarine in action, giving both inside and outside scenes."

Moving Picture World, Vol. 28, p. 985

The Secret of the Submarine was an interesting SF adventure serial. The idea of a submarine *gill device* had been proposed a year before by Thomas A. Edison. Interestingly enough, Japan and Russia, villains in this movie, became our allies in World War I.

THROUGH SOLID WALLS

Release: 1916, Universal Film Manufacturing Co.
Description: Silent, 2000 feet
Classification: SF-A
References: No. 5, p. 64; No. 14, p. 484; No. 50, p. 492; MPN, Vol. 14, p. 2714; MPW, Vol. 30, p. 570, 598

Cast

Producer .... Imperial Film Co.
Director .... Walter Morton
Screenplay .... E. J. Clauson

Cast

James Wheelock .... Marc Fenton
Elsie .... Peggy Custer
Parsons .... Tom Jefferson
Dick .... Jay Balasco
Therese .... Irene Hunt
Cummings .... Lou Short

James Wheelock, a wealthy old eccentric, has recently acquired a very large and beautiful diamond. He returns to his mansion and shows the enormous stone to his niece, Elsie, the butler, Parsons, and a young genius, Dick. All admire the gem, but agree that Wheelock should place the valuable stone in a secure place.

Shortly after, Dick announces that his new invention is complete and he would like the group to accompany him to his laboratory for a demonstration. Along the way, Dick explains that his device will allow the operator to see through any opaque substance, and as Wheelock gazes through the x-ray device something in the house across the way catches his attention.

The next morning a young girl appears at the door of the Wheelock mansion and asks for employment. For some mysterious reason, Wheelock employs the woman. This act of charity seems totally out of character for the elderly man. Within a few days Therese, the young girl, has succeeded in having Parsons discharged and disrupting the remainder of the household. She even convinces Wheelock to hire Cummings, her friend, to replace Parsons.

Two days later, Cummings falls on the stairway and an ambulance is summoned to take him to the hospital. As he is leaving, Therese slips him a small black box. Immediately, several policemen, led by Parsons, spring from the bushes at the front of the house and arrest Cummings and Therese: the attempt to steal the Wheelock diamond had been foiled.

James Wheelock then reveals that when he gazed through Dick's x-ray device he saw Therese and Cummings planning the diamond robbery. He and Parsons allowed them to carry out their theft attempt, thus falling into their very clever trap.

TWENTY THOUSAND LEAGUES UNDER THE SEA

Release: 1916, Universal Film Manufacturing Co.
Description: Silent, 8500 feet
Classification: SF
References: No. 14, p. 496; No. 39, p. 236, 237; No. 48, p. 331; No. 50, p. 507; FIR, 9-57, p. 359; LC, LP9183; MPW, Vol. 30, p. 240, 246, 524; NYT, 12-25-16, p. 7; SIS, Vol. 5, p. 43, 44; WID, 1-11-17

Credits

Producer .... Universal Film
Director .... Stuart Paton
Screenplay .... Stuart Paton
Special Effects .... J. Ernest and George M. Williamson
Camera .... Eugene Gaudio

Cast

Captain Nemo .... Allen Hollubar
A Child of Nature .... June Gail
Lieutenant Bond .... Matt Moore
Charles Denver .... William Welsh
Daaker's Daughter .... Lois Alexander
Princess Daaker .... June Gail
Professor Aronnax .... Dan Hamlon
Professor's Daughter .... Edna Pendleton
Ned Land .... Curtis Benton
Cyrus Harding .... Howard Crampton
Pencroft .... Wallace Clark
Herbert Brown .... Martin Murphy
Neb .... Leviticus Jones

The screenplay of this feature is based on the novels *Deux Cent Mille Lieues sous les Mers* [*Twenty Thousand Leagues Under the Sea*] (1870) and *L'lle Mysteriuse* [*Mysterious Island*] (1870), two of Jules Verne's classics. In addition to the amalgamation of these two works, the author of the screenplay, Stuart Paton, introduced Nemo's origin as an Indian prince and the creation of a young girl called *The Child of Nature*. It is never clear, however, whether this girl is his daughter or not, but the final scenes show Captain Nemo leading an attack against a Sudan fort in which the young girl has been imprisoned.

This feature was a true showcase of special effects and was the first film to use real underwater photography. The Williamson brothers pioneered the underwater film industry. They developed special cameras, submarine chambers and special photographic devices. Moreover, they developed and equipped the first underwater film studio located in Nassau, Bahamas. Their sense of realism was evident in the construction of the octopus, which battled Captain Nemo and the Nautilus. The gigantic octopus was manufactured with coil springs and huge rubber arms which could be manipulated by an operator from within the octopus.

This version of *Twenty Thousand Leagues Under the Sea* begins with the Nautilus sailing the seas, attempting to put an end to all warring vessels. The method is to either ram the armored ships, or

Captain Nemo and the crew of the Nautilus prepare for a long sea voyage in *20,000 Leagues Under the Sea* (1916).

The crew of the Nautilus attempts to ward off natives from a hostile island.

a member of the crew plants an underwater mine beneath the vessel's keel. In either case, Captain Nemo has carefully guided the Nautilus in destroying a number of naval vessels from various countries.

Reports of these sinkings have alerted each nation to the danger which awaits their warships. After sinking an American ship, Captain Nemo rescues Professor Aronnax, Miss Aronnax, Ned Land, and Cyrus Harding.

During a discussion with Professor Aronnax, Captain Nemo recalls his youth as a young Indian prince. The professor attempts to learn Nemo's secrets of the sea and soon gains an understanding for his violent actions against the naval vessels of each nation.

Soon they land on a mysterious island where they discover a young girl named *The Child of Nature*. Shortly afterward they depart for the coast of India, where the crew sets out to locate provisions for the crew. *The Child of Nature* and several others are left along the beach with the longboat while the sailors forage for food. Some soldiers of a nearby Sultan capture the young girl and the others as they wait with the boat. As soon as Nemo learns of their capture, he and the remaining crew members engage the Sultan in a fierce battle, eventually recovering the missing members of the Nautilus. The film ends with the group sailing out to sea, leaving the Sultan's fortress ablaze.

> "The most interesting statement in connection with the Universal Film Manufacturing Co.'s eight-reel production of Jules Verne's 'Twenty Thousand Leagues Under the Sea' is that it furnishes novel and engrossing entertainment. Many of the scenes which take place on dry land and on the surface of the water are interesting and out of the beaten track, but it is when the action is transferred to the bottom of the ocean that the picture makes its strongest impression. Here the opportunity for new and startling effects, the almost incredible views of the strange life in the depths of the sea, made possible by the photographic device invented by the Williamson brothers, brings a novel phase to motion picture making."
>
> *Moving Picture World,* 1-13-17, p. 240

> "The submarine episodes are cleverly woven into a tale whose action also passes on a desert island and in an oriental principality, so that there is variety in it. But the undersea pictures furnish its unique note, and these will no doubt win it wide favor."
>
> *New York Times,* 12-25-16, p. 7

> "One of the most remarkable pictures of an educational as well as fictional nature that the season has produced will be found in the adaptation of Jules Verne's novel, 'Twenty Thousand Leagues Under the Sea,' by the Universal Company. The most remarkable point about this eight-reel production is the underwater photography. We peer through the magic window of Captain Nemo's submarine at the wonders of the sea bottom, at the coral beds and wonderful gardens of the ocean, at the various kinds of fish, including the man-eating sharks that inhabit the deep, and at the wreck of an old blockade runner. We watch the hunters of the deep don their undersea garments and wander on the floor of the ocean shooting with guns discharged by compressed air methods at the sea game. We also see them charged by a man-eating shark. This film, which was reviewed in our issue of January 13, is well worth putting forth an effort to see."
>
> *Moving Picture World,* 1-27-17, p. 524

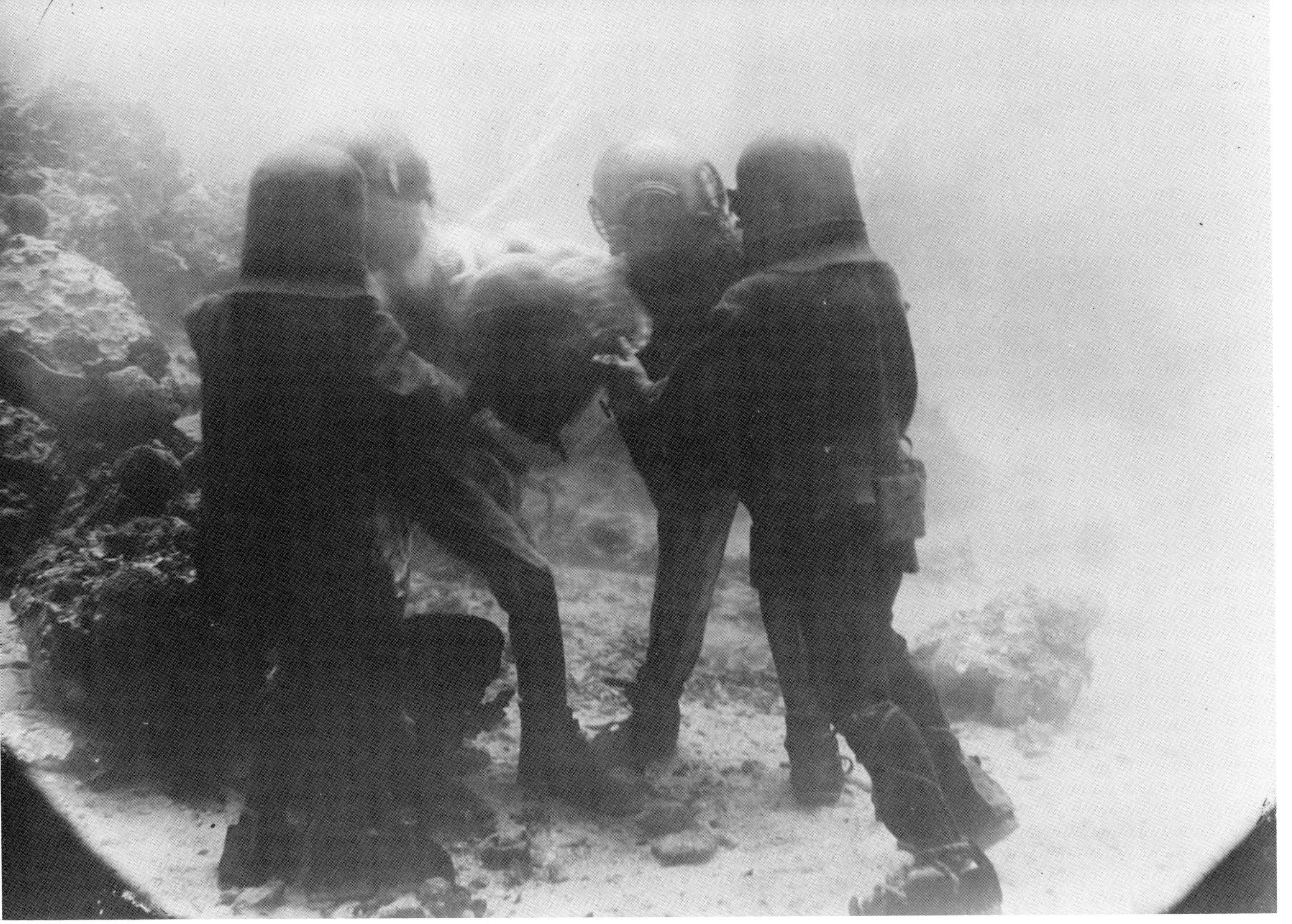

Through some of the finest underwater photography ever filmed, the audience is treated to a ceremonial burial on the ocean floor.

WITHOUT A SOUL

Release: 1916, World Film Corporation
Description: Silent, 5000 feet
Classification: SF
References: No. 14, p. 283; No. 50, p. 545; FIR, 9-16, p. 424; LC, LU9470; MPN, Vol. 14, p. 3171; MPW, Vol. 30, p. 1180, 1181

Credits

Producer .... Young Pictures
Director .... James Young
Screenplay .... James Young

Cast

Lola .... Clara Kimball Young
Lover .... Alec B. Francis
Father .... Edward M. Kimball
Mother .... Irene Tams
Sister .... Mary Moore

This SF film adaptation of the play *Lola*, by Owen Davis, was specially designed by James Young for Clara Kimball Young, his wife. Her father, Edward M. Kimball, portrayed her father in the feature. Both were famous veteran actors of 1916.

As the movie opens, the audience soon realizes that Lola has recently suffered an accident which has taken her life. Her father, a famous scientist and inventor, has created a device which emits an electric ray with the power to restore life. Grief stricken over his daughter's sudden demise, he decides to use the new electric ray to bring his lovely daughter back from the land of the dead. Gently, he places the body on the operating table and begins the intricate adjustments which will result in his daughter's complete recovery. A bright beam of light surrounds the operating table and suddenly Lola's lifeless corpse begins to show slight indications of breath. Within moments the light has disappeared, leaving a young, beautiful Lola to awaken from death's eternal grip.

Her father is overwhelmed by his success in restoring Lola to the world of the living, but after a few days he begins to notice some new idiosyncrasies in her behavior. Mainly, he notices her previous unselfish behavior seems to have been replaced by egotism. Moreover, her relationships with men previously have been platonic and now are more sensual. Her father believes that the electric ray has restored his daughter's life, but it is a life without her original soul.

Within weeks after the restoration process, Lola begins to experience heart abnormalities. She begs her father to recall her life a second time as she dies on his laboratory floor. He vows never to use his electric ray again to restore anyone's life as he proceeds to destroy all his elaborate machinery.

"This picture will almost surely make a tremendous hit. It is unusual and very artistic."

Moving Picture World, Vol. 30, p. 1181

1917

THE DINOSAUR AND THE MISSING LINK

Release: 1917, Edison Film Company
Description: Silent, 850 feet
Classification: SF-C
References: No. 1, p. 221; No. 14, p. 129; No. 46, p. 23; No. 50, p. 103; CNF, 1971, No. 2, p. 9; FAM, No. 12, p. 6; No. 19, p. 36; No. 22, p. 34; No. 63, p. 28; LC, MP893; MPN, Vol. 15, p. 3015

Credits

Producer .... Edison Film Co.
Director .... Willis O'Brien
Special Effects .... Willis O'Brien

This feature was also known under an alternate title, *The Dinosaur and the Baboon*, and was the first of O'Brien's commercially released animated feature films. During his eight year employment with the Edison Film Company, he made a number of similar films. O'Brien's technique was to use clay and wooden prehistoric models, moving their torsos from frame to frame, thus creating the illusion of motion. These unique special effects became extremely significant for the advancement of SF films. Willis O'Brien went on to perfect his techniques, creating the classics, *The Lost World* (1925), and *King Kong* (1933).

O'Brien abandoned the use of clay and wood for this project, developing instead a whole new technique using metal "u-joints" and rubber. The metal, carefully covered with rubber, gave the creatures a life-like appearance. This new process enabled the models to endure long hours under the intense photographic lights. A task which previous models were unable to endure. O'Brien's eight inch prehistoric animals, created for *The Dinosaur and the Missing Link,* were a new milestone in antimated cinematography.

The Dinosaur and the Missing Link was a simple science fiction comedy set in the prehistoric period. The story relates the encounters of early man (although we know creatures similar to man did not exist when the dinosaurs roamed the earth), an ape-like creature (supposedly the *missing link*), and a dinosaur.

The movie barely lasted five minutes, but had much more impact on the future of SF films than many of the efforts which preceded it. The production took nearly two months to complete (an extremely lengthy period for an industry which was expected to complete a new film every three days) and cost approximately $5000.00—expensive, even for a feature with *human* actors.

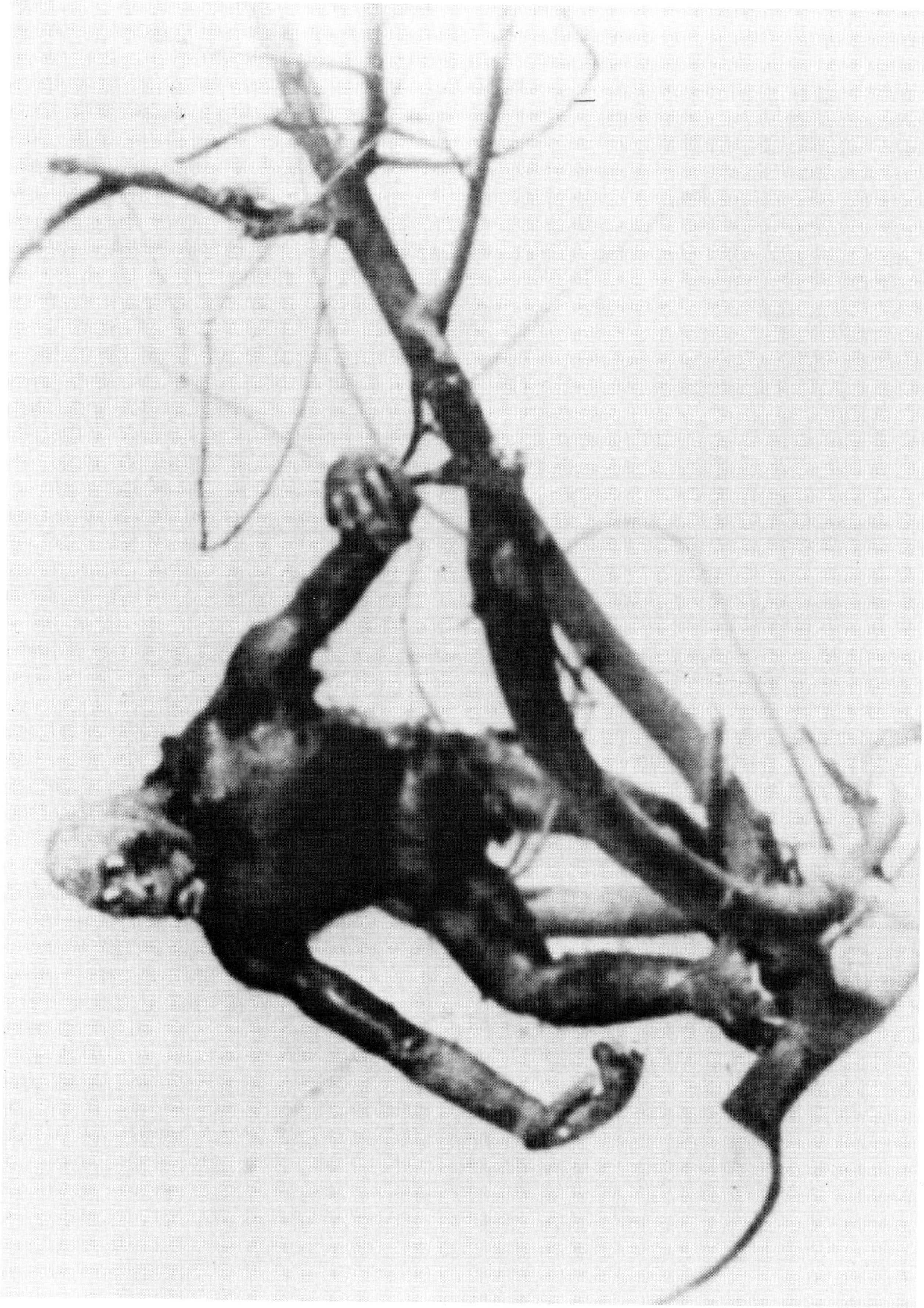

The Missing Link is portrayed by an unknown actor in the Edison animated film, *The Dinosaur And The Missing Link* (1917).

THE HIDDEN HAND

Release: 1917, Pathe
Description: Silent, 15 episode serial, each episode approx. 2000 feet
Classification: SF-A
References: No. 1, p. 140; No. 8, p. 177, 178; No. 14, p. 220; No. 50, p. 193

Credits

Screenplay .... Arthur B. Reeve and Charles Logue

Cast

Doris Whitney .... Doris Kenyon
Doctor Scarley .... Sheldon Lewis
Verda Crane .... Arline Pretty
Jack Ramsey .... Mahlon Hamilton

Chapters 1-15 of *The Hidden Hand*

Chapter 1: The Gauntlet of Death
References: LC, LU11662; MPW, Vol. 34, p. 1333, 1334
Chapter 2: Counterfeit Faces
References: LC, LU11663; MPW, Vol. 34, p. 1486, 1548
Chapter 3: The Island of Dread
References: LC, LU11664; MPW, Vol. 34, p. 1649, 1677
Chapter 4: The False Locket
References: LC, LU11665; MPW, Vol. 34, p. 1808, 1843
Chapter 5: The Air-Lock
References: LC, LU11666; MPW, Vol. 34, p. 1982
Chapter 6: The Flower of Death
References: MPW, Vol. 35, p. 99, 140
Chapter 7: The Fire Trap
References: MPW, Vol. 35, p. 245, 282, 283
Chapter 8: Slide for Life
References: LC, LU12257; MPW, Vol. 35, p. 531, 727
Chapter 9: Jets of Flame
References: LC, LU12258; MPW, Vol. 35, p. 846
Chapter 10: Cogs of Death
References: LC, LU12259; MPW, Vol. 35, p. 932
Chapter 11: Trapped by Treachery
References: MPW, Vol. 35, p. 1006
Chapter 12: Eyes in the Wall
References: LC, LU12260; MPW, Vol. 35, p. 1139
Chapter 13: Jaws of the Tiger
References: MPW, Vol. 35, p. 1270
Chapter 14: The Unmasking
References: MPW, Vol. 35, p. 1412
Chapter 15: The Girl of the Prophecy
References: LC, LU12261; MPW, Vol. 35, p. 1560

The Hidden Hand is an entertaining but rather melodramatic serial which attempts to recreate the excitement of the *Craig Kennedy* episodes made three years earlier. This serial does not seem to contain the intrigue and mystery of the earlier SF adventure epics. The character roles for the secret service agent and the *hidden hand* also seem undeveloped.

The action commences with a flashback to a period 18 years earlier in a small European kingdom. The emperor has received a prophecy from Rascon, the mad monk, declaring that his newborn daughter will bring destruction upon the empire. The emperor, obviously frightened by this prophecy, pleads with a personal friend Judson Whitney, an American millionaire, to take the child to America and raise her as his own daughter, promising never to reveal her true identity.

Eighteen years have passed when the audience next sees the Whitney household and the two young ladies who reside there: Doris Whitney, the daughter, and Verda Crane, Judson Whitney's ward. Next, the Grand Duke arrives intent on claiming the rightful heir to the European kingdom's throne. He carries a special pouch containing the fingerprints of the true daughter of the emperor. As the Grand Duke is about to make his identification, both he and Judson Whitney are fatally wounded by a man cleverly disguised as Jack Ramsey's secretary. Thus, the only two men who could have identified the real princess are dead, and the pouch containing the fingerprints is mysteriously missing.

The *hidden hand* displays his scientific talents in episodes 2 through 15 using specially designed poison gases in his attempt to eliminate the true princess and gain control of her country. His surgical talents also become apparent as he performs plastic surgery which converts one of his henchmen into the likeness of someone known to the Whitney household.

Althought the *hidden hand* provides some chilling moments for Doris, Verda, and Jack, the group manages to capture and unmask Dr. Scarley as the fiendish villain.

While the adventure in this serial is outstanding, the SF aspects are considerably less than earlier SF serialş. Sheldon Lewis played a similar role in *The Iron Claw*, a non-science fiction serial which, however, seemed to expose his varied acting talents to better advantage.

THE INSPIRATIONS OF HARRY LARRABEE

Release: 1917, General Film Company
Description: Silent, 4000 feet
Classification: SF-A
References: No. 14, p. 246; No. 50, p. 219; MPN, Vol. 15, p. 2030

Credits

Producer .... General Film Co.
Director .... Bertram Bracken

Cast

Harry Larrabee .... Clifford Gray
Carolyn Vaughn .... Margaret Landis
Madame Batonyi .... Winifred Greenwood
Dr. Stettina .... William Ehfe
Mr. Batonyi/The Wolf .... Frank Brownlee

Harry Larrabee, a successful and famous playwright, and his sweetheart, Carolyn Vaughn, reside in the same apartment house, and each is being terrorized by a vicious criminal known only as *The Wolf*. It soon becomes apparent that this creature has intimidated every member of the apartment house. Carolyn's good friend, Madame Batonyi, who is in some mysterious way related to Dr. Stettina, reveals the gruesome details of *The Wolf's* nocturnal visits to others.

Unknown to Carolyn, however, he has coerced Madame Batonyi and Dr. Stettina into stealing Carolyn's precious gems. But his well conceived plan goes awry when Carolyn confronts him, forcing him to murder her. He immediately exits by using the dumbwaiter, but as he reaches the ground floor a fierce gun battle ensues with Dr. Stettina which results in both men dying.

Meanwhile, Harry Larrabee has discovered Carolyn's body and he rushes her to the home of a famous research scientist (who is also a close friend). He has created a device called a *pulmoter* which can restore life. The doctor prepares the apparatus for the restoration and is successful in reviving her. He then pleads with Carolyn and Harry to never reveal the miraculous device and the process to anyone.

Back at the apartment house, Madame Batonyi has confessed to the police that the identity of *The Wolf* is that of Mr. Batonyi. They remove the bodies of the two slain men, restoring peace once again to the apartment house.

This is a weak SF film with very little detail or time devoted to the *pulmoter* or the mysterious research scientist. The production is an adaptation of a novelette by Howard Fielding published under the same title.

THE LOVE DOPE

Release: 1917, Metro
Description: Silent, 1000 feet
Classification: SF-C
References: No. 14, p. 287; No. 50, p. 268; LC, LP10557; MPN, Vol. 15, p. 2863

Credits

Producer .... Ralph Hertz

A weak SF film, *The Love Dope* is about a young man who invents a tablet which is able to convert even the coldest of persons into an amorous individual. This feature appears to have a plot similar to films which appeared ten years earlier, and certainly seems rather shallow for 1917.

THE LUST OF THE AGES

Release: 1917, Ogden Independent Productions
Description: Silent, 5000 feet
Classification: SF-A
References: No. 14, p. 290; No. 50, p. 271; MPN, Vol. 16, p. 1665

Credits

Producer .... Ogden Productions
Director .... Harry Revier
Screenplay .... Aaron Hoffman

Cast

Lois Craig .... Lillian Walker
Byron Master .... Jack Mowers

The feature begins with a young college girl, Lois Craig writing a story about lust and eternal love. The unfinished manuscript is read by Byron Masters, her fiance. As he reads, the screen depicts a flashback to ancient times.

Lois and Byron are seen in the garb of shepherds, existing on the simple pleasures of life. Suddenly a horde of invaders begin to savagely plunder their peaceful valley, but Byron manages to protect Lois.

As time advances, Byron is depicted as an army officer working in a secret laboratory. He has just discovered a chemical process which produces a substance called *liquid fire*. This mysterious compound has the capability of melting any known metal. Lois has become a princess in the country where Byron serves as an army officer. She convinces Byron that they should use his *liquid fire* to destroy all the gold in the world, thereby providing a basis for world peace. The princess is sure that gold is the root of all evil. But before she and Byron can complete their plan they are discovered and put to death.

Byron has finished reading Lois' story and remarks on the quality of the writing. He further proclaims that the story has really convinced him that money doesn't bring happiness.

This is an entertaining feature, but rather weak in the science fiction content. Nevertheless, the film produced some interesting special effects.

> "There is a certain grandeur about this exhibition that holds. Some of the best *double exposure* work ever shown on the screen comes to light in the presentment of this product of Ogden Studios. To Harry Revier, the director, is due much of the credit for its entertaining value."
>
> *Motion Picture News*, 9-8-17, p. 1665

THE MAGIC JAZZ BO

Release: 1917, Universal Film Manufacturing Co.
Description: Silent, 1000 feet
Classification: SF-C
References: No. 50, p. 278; LC, LP11513; MPN, Vol. 34, p. 402, 435

Credits

Producer .... Joker
Director .... Alfred A. Santell
Screenplay .... A. F. Statter

Cast

Dave .... Dave Morris
The Ingenue .... Gladys Tennyson

A very funny feature, *The Magic Jazz Bo* is about a young waiter, Dave, who accidently discovers two mysterious men firing pellets at athletes. The *magic jazz bo pellets* have an effect of reducing an individual's physical reactions to a fraction of their previous level. Dave follows the two crooks to their hideout where he manages to steal the container of pellets, but his act of theft is discovered before he can make a clean getaway. He attempts to elude his pursuers but they keep steadfastly on his trail. Finally, Dave uses some of the pellets to slow the crooks. They do their job quickly, and Dave escapes.

As he reaches a nearby river the crooks shoot the bottle containing the *magic jazz bo pellets* out of his hand which causes them to fall into the water. There is a terrible explosion, the force of which causes Dave to tumble into the murky waters. The pellets dissolve quickly, resulting in Dave's being affected by the strange chemicals. Not having the power to stay afloat, poor Dave drowns.

SPEED

Release: 1917, U. S. Motion Picture Corporation
Description: Silent, 850 feet
Classification: SF-C
References: No. 14, p. 448; No. 50, p. 455; LC, LU10467

Credits

Producer .... Black Diamond Films

Cast

Scientist .... James O. Walsh
Lab Assistant .... Rex Taylor
Boss .... Horace G. Plimpton, Jr.
Typist .... William Louis
Typist .... Russell Taylor

Speed is a very weak SF film about a scientist who invents a power which causes acceleration of body movements. An acquaintance steals some of the marvelous power to try on some of his more indolent employees. The two typists who have consumed a small quantity of the powder begin to type with lightening speed. At first, the boss is delighted but becomes a bit angry when their speed nearly melts the typewriters.

10,000 YEARS B. C.

Release: 1917, Conquest Films
Description: Silent, 1000 feet
Classification: SF-F
References: No. 50, p. 482; MPW, Vol. 32, p. 1303

Credits

Producer .... Forum Films
Director .... Willis O'Brien
Special Effects .... Willis O'Brien

This is a short animated feature similar to *The Dinosaur and the Missing Link*. It is another opportunity for Willis O'Brien to experiment with animated movements of prehistoric creatures. The biggest error seems to have been the selection of animals for the 10,000 B.C. period: most of them would have been long since extinct.

Disregarding the time displacement of the prehistoric animals portrayed, the film was another opportunity for O'Bie to experiment with his new technique of metal and rubber construction.

The film appeared in various lengths, ranging from three to ten minutes, and under several alternate titles: RFD 10,000 B.C.; 2,000,000 B.C.; GFD 10,000 YEARS B.C.

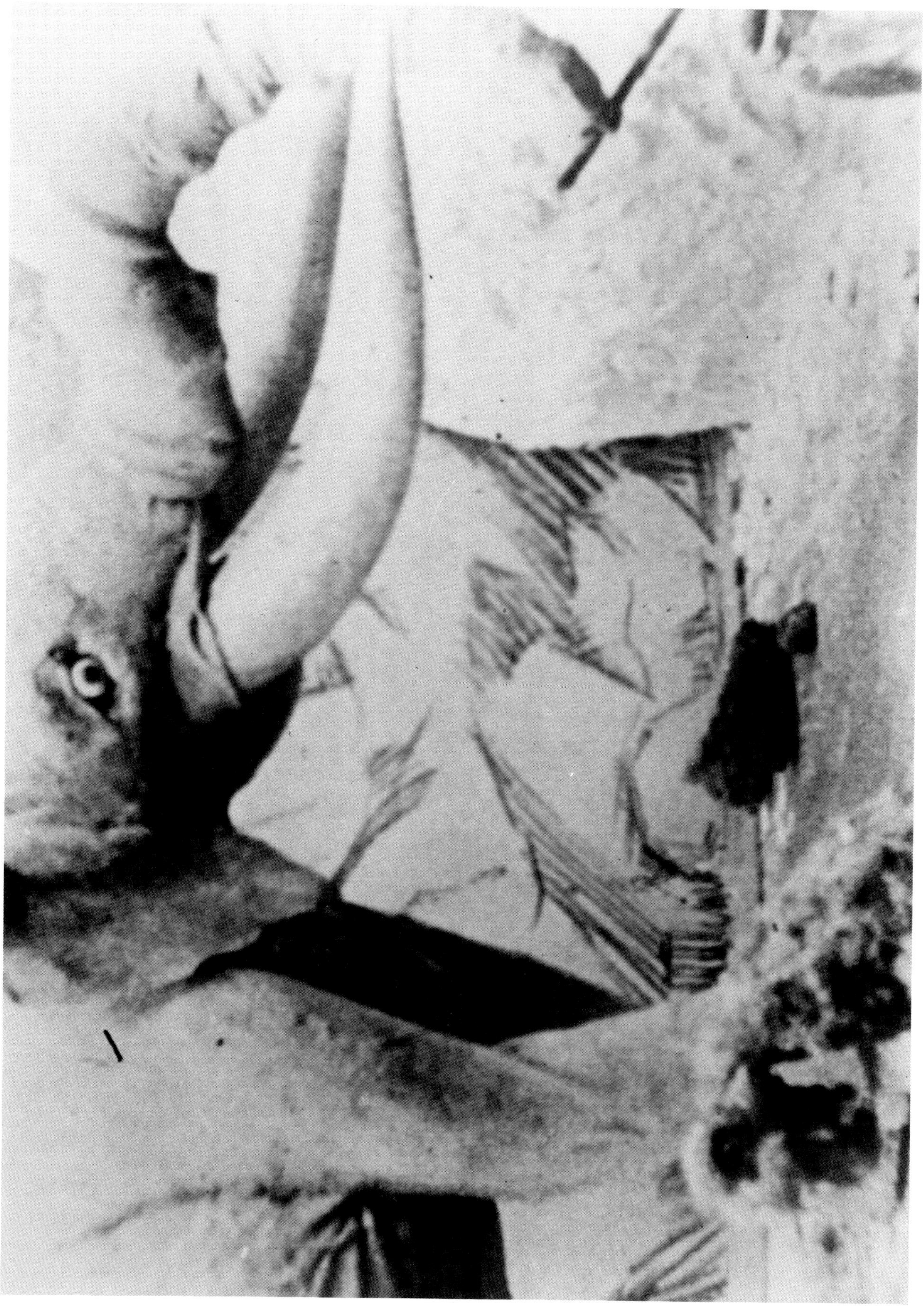

A cleverly animated prehistoric pacaderm in the film *10,000 Years B.C.* (1917).

Even in prehistoric times, the mail must be delivered. This is a scene from Willis O'Brien's silent feature, ***10,000 Years B.C.*** (1917).

The plot of the *10,000 Years B.C.* version revolves around the actions of a jealous Neanderthal postman whose sweetheart has fallen in love with another man. Our intrepid postman delivers his mail (consisting of large stone tablets) in a dinosaur drawn cart. On this particular day, he is delivering stone valentines. While making his deliveries, he discovers a valentine addressed to his sweetheart from the other suitor (or, from the "amorous oaf," in his estimation). He hurles the stone message to the ground, shattering it into hundreds of pieces. He then carefully replaces the shattered valentine with another, but inscribes on it a very insulting message.

Our postman is later obviously deriving great pleasure in the disturbance that his valentine substition has caused. His boasting of this dastardly deed, however, leads the other suitor to his doorstep. Angrily, the wronged man attempts to strangle the letter carrier. The film comes to its final climax with the postman being hotly pursued by the suitor across a far away hill.

Definitely a weak SF film, but a necessary step for the creative work which would lead to *The Lost World* (1925).

WATER ON THE BRAIN

Release: 1917, Universal Fim Manufacturing Co.
Description: Silent, 1000 feet
Classification: SF-C •
References: No. 50, p. 531; LC, LP11721; MPW, Vol. 34, p. 1205, 1546

Credits

Producer .... Nestor Films
Director .... Allen Curtis
Screenplay .... Tom Gibson

Cast

Detective Squibbs .... William Franey
Lucy Lockett .... Gale Henry
Dogfaced Dingbat .... Milburn Morante

Professor Lockett, a famous inventor and chemist, has recently perfected a machine which can control the weather. The professor demonstrates the marvelous machine for his daughter, Lucy: first, he makes it rain, then he brings back the sunshine. Lucy marvels at her father's ingenious device. Soon the butler, Protoplasm, enters the room with a telegram for the professor. After reading it, the professor announces that the government of Bonozaluza has offered one million dollars for his weather machine. Lucy is ecstatic with joy. Meanwhile, the butler, who had remained long enough in the doorway to hear the details of the Bonozaluza offer, rushes off. It seems Protoplasm is really in the employ of Dogfaced Dingbat, the master crook of crookdom. He hurries to tell his employer about the invention and the offer.

Shortly afterwards, Lucy consults her sweetheart, the famous Detective Squibbs, about protecting her father's latest invention. He advises her to remain calm and assures her that he will examine the device later that evening. In the meantime, he dispatches some *Smellodium* (Squibb's latest chemical discovery—it seems he too is a noted inventor) which will lower her anxiety.

Back at the crook's hideout, Dogfaced Dingbat has given each of his men a vial of *Disappearo*, a substance which will allow an individual to remain invisible until *Appearo*, the antidote is taken. With this cloak of invisibility, Dingbat and his gang are able to abscond with the treasured weather machine.

Now the trap is sprung. It seems Detective Squibbs had set up the gang of crooks by implanting a tracking device in the weather machine. Quickly, he follows their trail to their hideout and apprehends the villains, using a substance called *Freezo,* which, as the name implies, freezes its victims until the proper antidote, *Melto,* can be administered.

This is a very entertaining SF comedy featuring the veteran actors William Franey and Milburn Morante. Each played in more than 100 films. Morante appeared in the 1915 SF adventure serial, *Lady Baffles and Detective Duck.*

ZEPPELIN ATTACK ON NEW YORK

Release: 1917, Rothacker
Description: Silent, 660 feet
Classification: SF-A
References: No. 14, p. 541; No. 50, p. 557; MPN, Vol. 55, p. 3474; MPW, Vol. 32, p. 1663

A hair-raising SF adventure, *Zeppelin Attack on New York* depicts the events surrounding an invasion of New York City. A large fleet of the Kaiser's zeppelins (a large dirigible) begins a well planned attack on the Manhattan Island using incendiary and high percussion bombs. The city is set ablaze with only a very few airplanes able to mount a defensive thrust against these denizens of the air. Somehow the airplanes manage to score a direct hit on the command zeppelin, sending it plummeting to the ground below, a cindered mass of molten steel. The remaining ships turn around to escape the attack. We have been victorious—at least, this time.

This is an interesting SF adventure feature. The time was appropriate for serious concerns about the German air threat, and served as a brief warning that the giant oceans would no longer afford us protection from a swift invasion.

1918

THE CRAVING

Release: 1918, Bluebird
Description: Silent, 5000 feet
Classification: SF-A
References: No. 50, p. 77; LC, LP13233; MPN, Vol. 19, p. 448, 456

Credits

Producer .... Bluebird
Director .... Francis and Jack Ford
Screenplay .... Francis Ford

Cast

Carroll Wayles .... Francis Ford
Beulah Grey.. Mae Gaston
Ala Kasarib ....Peter Gerald
Dick Wayles .... Duke Worne
Mrs. Wayles .... Jean Hathaway

A famous scientist, Carroll Wayles, has developed a powerful new explosive which he plans to turn over to the government. But until that time, the explosive's formula is locked in his safe.

Ala Kasarib, a scientist from the East Indies, visits Wayles to learn more about his new explosive. He is accompanied by Beulah Grey, a young English girl whose father was a British army officer. Professor Wayles becomes quite infatuated with Beulah, and Kasarib soon uses this new anxiety to encourage him to relax by having a drink. (It seems Wayles is an alcoholic and had abstained from the spirits for some time.) Kasarib further uses Beulah to get information about the secret formula. After he is successful in obtaining this information, he hastily returns to his homeland.

Meanwhile, Beulah aids Wayles in his fight against alcohol and, after making another recovery, they are married. About the same time Kasarib accidently kills himself when he tries to mix the professor's explosives formula.

When Alfred Nobel (for whom the Nobel Prize is named) discoverd his powerful explosive he probably never dreamed that so many writers of fiction would use this achievement as a basis for their stories, nor that since 1897 explosives would be the subjects of numerous SF films. *The Craving* presents a much smoother plot transition than some of its predecessors, and the acting is equally superb.

Francis Ford (his real name was Francis O'Fearna) became a famous actor, screenwriter, film director, and producer—a true giant in the movie industry. He acted in nearly 150 films from 1909 to 1953.

THE HOUSE OF HATE

Release: 1918, Pathe
Description: Silent, 20 episode serial; each episode approx. 2000 feet
Classification: SF-A
References: No. 8, p. 61, 187; No. 14, p. 230; No. 32, p. 17, 42; No. 50, p. 204; MPW, Vol. 35, p. 1249, 1386, 1685

Credits

Producer .... Astra Films and Louis J. Gasnier
Director .... George Brackett Seitz
Screenplay .... Bertram Millhauser

Cast

Pearl Waldon .... Pearl White
Harvey Gresham .... Antonio Moreno

The Hooded Terror .... Paul Clerget
Winthrop Waldon .... J. H. Gilmour
Haynes Waldon .... John Webb Dillion
Zelda Waldon .... Peggy Shaner

Chapters 1-20 of *The House of Hate*

Chapter 1: The Hooded Terror
References: LC, LU12132; MPW, Vol. 35, p. 533, 1268
Chapter 2: The Tiger's Eye
References: LC, LU12417; MPW, Vol. 35, p. 1706
Chapter 3: A Woman's Perfidy
References: LC, LU12131; MPW, Vol. 35, p. 1867
Chapter 4: The Man from Java
References: LC, LU12230; MPW, Vol. 36, p. 131
Chapter 5: Spies Within
References: LC, LU12231; MPW, Vol. 36, p. 285
Chapter 6: A Living Target
References: LC, LU12232; MPW, Vol. 36, p. 2822
Chapter 7: Germ Menace
References: LC, LU12233; MPW, Vol. 36, p. 434
Chapter 8: The Untold Secret
References: LC, LU12360; MPW, Vol. 36, p. 590
Chapter 9: Poisoned Darts
References: LC, LU12361; MPW, Vol. 36, p. 747
Chapter 10: Double Crossed
References: LC, LU12362; MPW, Vol. 36, p. 897
Chapter 11: Haunts of Evil
References: LC, LU12363; MPW, Vol. 36, p. 1037
Chapter 12: Flashes in the Dark
References: LC, LU12364; MPW, Vol. 36, p. 1188
Chapter 13: Enemy Aliens
References: LC, LU12365; MPW, Vol. 36, p. 1334
Chapter 14: Underworld Allies
References: LC, LU12366; MPW, Vol. 36, p. 1475
Chapter 15: The False Signal
References: LC, LU12566; MPW, Vol. 36, 1758
Chapter 16: The Vial of Death
References: LC, LU12567; MPW, Vol. 38, p. 112
Chapter 17: The Death Switch
References: LC, LU12568; MPW, Vol. 38, p. 250
Chapter 18: At the Pistol's Point
References: LC, LU12569; MPW, Vol. 38, p. 456
Chapter 19: The Hooded Terror Unmasked
References: LC, LU12570; MPW, Vol. 38, p. 590

Chapter 20: Following Old Glory
References: LC, LU12646; MPW, Vol. 38, p. 632

The House of Hate, adapted from a story by Arthur B. Reeve and Charles A. Logue, is a weak SF entry, and certainly not up to the caliber of Pearl White's other serial achievements: *The Exploits of Elaine* (1914), *The New Exploits of Elaine* (1915), and *The Romance of Elaine* (1915). In seven years from 1914 to 1918 the American viewing public paid more than 25 million dollars to see Pearl White appear in her various serial roles. Unfortunately, *The House of Hate* does not measure up to these earlier works. It is supposed to be a Craig Kennedy-type mystery, but the Kennedy character is missing, resulting in a great lessening of the SF impact. Additionally, the action over the 20 episodes seems drawn out and appears as if the producers were purposely attempting to get the maximum mileage out of a poor script and Pearl White's audience appeal.

As the first chapter, *The Hooded Terror*, begins Pearl Waldon is swept up into a romantic struggle between Harvey Gresham (who Pearl truly loves) and Haynes Waldon (her cousin, and the one her father wishes her to marry). Pearl's father is anxious to perpetuate the family name through the union of Pearl and Haynes.

Winthrop Waldon has spent years developing his munitions plant and amassing a great deal of wealth. Recently he has developed a new explosive that is more powerful than any known. In addition, he has perfected a substance called *liquid fire* which has the ability to melt any metal. Winthrop's health, to further complicate matters, is steadily deteriorating and he does not wish to see Pearl left alone to battle the remaining scheming relatives.

As this first chapter draws to a close, a mysterious figure clad in a black robe and mask sculks through the mansion in search of the secret explosive formula. The hooded figure encounters Winthrop in the library and stabs him to death. But before dying, Waldon manages to leave a clue to the identity of his murderer—a clue which Pearl, Harvey and Haynes attempt to pursue in the remaining chapters of the serial.

In a later chapter the hooded figure nearly removes all three when he resorts to "germ warfare", but Harvey quickly supplies an antidote for the deadly bacteria. In the end, Pearl and Harvey are married, and *The Hooded Terror* and Haynes are found to be in league against them.

While Pearl White provided an outstanding performance, the serial never equals the level of entertainment of earlier efforts.

THE MYSTERY SHIP

Release: 1918, Universal Film Manufacturing Co.
Description: Silent, 18 episode serial; each episode approx. 2000 feet
Classification: SF-A
References: No. 8, p. 54, 179, 180; No. 14, p. 346; No. 32, p. 43, 47; No. 50, p. 325; MPW, Vol. 34, p. 885, 1409

Credits

Producer .... Universal
Director .... Francis Ford and Harry Harvey
Screenplay .... William Parker and Elaine Pearson
Special Effects .... Milton Moore

Cast

Miles Gaston, Jr. .... Ben Wilson
Betty Lee .... Neva Gerber
Harry Russell .... Duke Worne

Betty's Aunt .... Elsie Van Name
Jack Fay .... Kingsley Benedict
James Lee .... Nigel De Bruillier

Chapters 1-18 of *The Mystery Ship*

Chapter 1: The Crescent Scar
References: LC, LP11604; MPW, Vol. 34, p. 1038, 1544
Chapter 2: The Grip of Hate
References: LC, LP11605; MPW, Vol. 34, p. 1676
Chapter 3: Adrift
References: LC, LP11629; MPW, Vol. 34, p. 1649, 1841
Chapter 4: The Secret of the Tomb
References: LC, LP11777; MPW, Vol. 34, p. 2000
Chapter 5: The Fire God
References: LC, LP11852; MPW, Vol. 34, p. 1962; Vol. 35, p. 138
Chapter 6: Treachery
References: LC, LP11881; MPW, Vol. 35, p. 99, 281
Chapter 7: One Minute to Live
References: LC, LP11853; MPW, Vol. 35, p. 246, 421
Chapter 8: Hidden Hands
References: LC, LP11854; MPW, Vol. 35, p. 386, 579
Chapter 9: The Black Masks
References: LC, LP11882; MPW, Vol. 35, p. 531, 725
Chapter 10: The Rescue
References: LC, LP11919; MPW, Vol. 35, p. 690, 846
Chapter 11: The Line of Death
References: LC, LP11969; MPW, Vol. 35, p. 868
Chapter 12: The Rain of Fire
References: LC, LP11970; MPW, Vol. 35, p. 988
Chapter 13: The Underground House
References: LC, LP11992; MPW, Vol. 35, p. 1140
Chapter 14: The Masked Riders
References: LC, LP12007; MPW, Vol. 35, p. 1270
Chapter 15: The House of Trickery
References: LC, LP12060; MPW, Vol. 35, p. 1410
Chapter 16: The Forced Marriage
References: LC, LP12084; MPW, Vol. 35, p. 1560
Chapter 17: The Deadly Torpedo
References: LC, LP12106; MPW, Vol. 35, p. 1707
Chapter 18: The Fight in Mid-Air
References: LC, LP12148

The exhilarating first episode of *The Mystery Ship* begins as Betty Lee's father is dying from some respiratory illness. However, he manages enough strength to give Betty an old tattered treasure map and the story of how the map came into his possession. As he begins to relate the sequence of events of nearly 20 years ago, the audience is transported back into time to a remote South Seas island.

Two young explorers, Miles Gaston and Professor Lee, have decided to explore the South Sea islands in search of the hidden treasure of Chang Tuy which had been buried nearly 1,000 years before. After spending many exhausting months on the various islands, they finally stumble upon the remains of a native temple. But as fate would have it, while unearthing the remains an enormous volcano on the north side of the island erupts. The disturbance dislodges some rocks, uncovering the hidden treasure. As the rocks and molten lava endanger the two men, they flee for their lives. Miles Gaston, however, falls into a shallow cave and Professor Lee is unable to rescue him. Desperately, he searches for natives to aid him in the rescue of his friend. While gone, a large piece of rock falls and strikes him on the head causing him to lose consciousness. When he finally awakens, he finds himself at sea in a small boat, totally unaware of how he got there, or what has happened to Gaston. His natural assumption is that Miles was buried by the molten lava and had died. Floating aimlessly in the sea and feeling great remorse, Lee constructs a map of the island, pinpointing the location of the treasure of Chang Tuy.

Professor Lee's last words before dying are to warn Betty that he has heard from Gaston within the past year, and is shocked, to say the least, that he is alive. The letter was extremely bitter and accused Lee of abandoning him in the jungle and fleeing for his own personal safety. Miles' bitterness is apparent in his last statement in the letter. He tells Lee that he can expect a "measure of retribution," that "an eye for an eye would be a fair payment for the misery and pain" that he had endured during the last 15 years. Lee recalls that Gaston had a crescent scar on his right wrist, and he cautions Betty to beware of "the man with the crescent scar," as he can only mean danger and misery for her.

Meanwhile, Miles Gaston hears of Lee's passing; moreover, he learns that Betty has employed several men and has the intention of sailing to the South Sea islands to uncover the treasure. Gaston vows to intercept her. He perpetrates a scam on a group of crooks to gather enough money to buy himself a sailing vessel intent on following Betty's ship. A young reporter, Jack Fay, will acompany Gaston. It seems he admires him for his nerve and wit, while also realizing that he has a certain aura of evil about him. Obviously, Jack, being the good reporter, is more interested in a story than he is in the real character of Gaston.

Betty and her sweetheart, Harry Russell, ready their vessel and begin their long voyage in search of the treasures. Not along out of port they begin to sense that their ship is being followed by another sailing vessel. As night begins to fall, the boat which has been shadowing them during the past few days starts to close the distance. Betty peers through a small telescope at the approaching ship, and the magnification provides the view of a tall, dark complected man standing at the bow, and looking directly at her vessel. On the man's right wrist, Betty observes a crescent scar . . . a cold chill runs through her body. She also observes small cannons along the starboard and port sides of the ship. Her father's warning of danger flashes clearly through her mind. Never had she imagined her quest would be so laddened with peril.

They do not have long to wait for Gaston to make his move, for no sooner had night fallen than Gaston began to fire at their ship with his cannon. Two holes are torn in the railing on the starboard side of the ship. But fortunately for Betty and her crew, a small storm begins to brew which requires all the skill and expertise of each ship's crew to weather the storm. As Betty's ship begins to toss and turn violently in the storm, a large wave passes over the deck, pushing her from the port to the starboard side of the ship. She slides toward the exact spot where the railing had been destroyed...as you would expect, episode one ends at this point and the screen is illuminated with the familiar words, "Continued next week..."

During the remaining 17 weeks, the audience are thrillingly entertained as they are driven to the edges of their seats with anticipation of the next exciting episode. naturally, the public does rush to see if Betty falls over board as it certainly appeared she would in Chapter 1. But Betty is saved at the last minute by Harry Russell. The conflict continues between Betty and Gaston, each attempting to destroy the other's vessel.

In chapter 3 Gaston finally succeeds in sinking Betty's ship, but they rescue both Betty and her crew. Certain that Gaston's motive for the rescue is to gain the treasure map, Betty carefully hides it. However, unknown to her, Harry has observed where she hid the map and his greed begins to show. In the meantime Betty plots to take over Gaston's yacht. But her efforts are thwarted by Gaston who demands the map or he will allow the yacht to drift among the rocks, killing everyone aboard.

Reluctantly, Betty agrees to forfeit the map. However, it is missing from the hiding place, and Gaston believes he has been tricked. The ship draws nearer to the reef laced with razor sharp rocks; Gaston orders the engines started and the course changed to avoid the treacherous reef which guards the narrow channel to the Isle of Hate and the treasure of Chang Tuy. But the engines won't start and disaster seems imminent. Suddenly, a mysterious metallic ship appears alongside and attaches a line which tows the yacht through the channel and to the safe lagoon beyond. Just as suddenly as it appeared, it disappears, leaving Betty, Gaston, and the remainder of the crew completely bewildered.

Betty disembarks the ship to search the island for the ancient ruins. She soon stumbles on Harry and discovers that he had stolen her map. He creates an accident designed to kill Betty, but suddenly a mysterious hand reaches out and grabs her before she plummets from a narrow ledge.

In episodes 5 through 12 Betty learns of Harry's dishonesty and she grows closer to Gaston as she realizes that he is incapable of really hating her father. Several times during these chapters Betty and Gaston are nearly killed by Harry Russell and his evil comrade *The Spider*. Each time they are saved by a mysterious stranger who seems to possess a variety of special powers. This "phantom" is a master scientist who constructed the armour-plated "mystery ship" which saved their lives in the reefs. Additionally, this person seems to have constructed a helmet which intensifies the human senses a 100 times. The "phantom" brandishes several sophisticated weapons. One produces an intense ray of light capable of melting steel or killing any foe (very like a laser); a second weapon showers its victims with a rain of electric sparks which produce a paralyzing effect.

In the remaining 6 episodes the "phantom" aids Betty and Gaston in regaining the treasure of Chang Tuy, which had been stolen by Harry Russell. In the final episode Betty and Gaston realize that they are in love and decide to marry. Harry Russell has been incarcerated and his gang destroyed, thanks to the mysterious good samaritan's efforts. The secret of this person is finally revealed during the closing minutes of episode 18: the "phantom" is James Lee, Betty's father. The serial ends with Betty, Gaston, and Lee rejoicing over their comradeship and newly acquired wealth.

> "A one-man armorclad cruiser is a novel feature of the new mystery serial, 'The Mystery Ship', which is being filmed at Universal City. This craft, which roams the seas alone, is forty feet in length and completely inclosed in armor plate and was built especially for the productions from plans prepared by Milton Moore, technical director of the Universal company. It is propelled by electrical current, and is controlled entirely by a single operator in the observation cupola rising above the deck. The pilot is a mysterious figure whose identity is concealed in a helmet of curious design. His contro station also serves as a turret for a rapid-fire gun. The operator has at his finger tips the steering wheel, motor switches, wireless key, and all the instruments necessary to keep every piece of mechanism in the ship within his command at all times."
>
> Moving Picture World, 11-10-17, p. 885

This is an extremely well executed serial. The *phantom* appears to be a cross between Captain Nemo (*Twenty Thousand Leagues Under the Sea* [1919]) and Craig Kennedy (*The Exploits of Elaine* [1914]). The special effects are very important for 1918, and the weapon suggests a technology decades into the future.

THE REJUVENATORS

Release: 1918, Passing Show Comedies
Description: Silent, 906 feet
Classification: SF-C
References: No. 14, p. 399; No. 50, p. 393; BFI, p. 239

The Rejuvenators is an extremely poor SF comedy. It is about a Dr. Young who develops a rejuvenation process which seems to be effective in converting men physically into young children, but they are mentally still adults. This is very similar to several films which were released in 1908.

1919

A SCREAM IN THE NIGHT

Release: 1919, Select Pictures Corp.
Description: Silent, 6000 feet
Classification: SF-A
References: No. 50, p. 422; LC, LP15701; MPH, Vol. 9, No. 18, p. 74; MPW, Vol. 42, p. 1192: MPN, Vol. 20, p. 3202

Credits

Producer .... A. H. Fischer Features
Director .... Burton King
Assistant Director .... Leander DeCordova
Screenplay .... Charles A. Logue
Camera .... William Reinhart and A. A. Cadwell
Editor .... Ruth Budd

Editor .... John J. Keely

Cast

Darwa .... Ruth Budd
Robert Hunter .... Ralph Kellard
Vaneva Carter .... Edna Britton
Professor Silvio .... John Webb Dillon
Lotec .... Ed Roseman
Senator Newcastle .... Stephen Grattan
Gloris .... Adelbert Hugo

Senator Newcastle lost his infant daughter 18 years ago while exploring the perilous Indian jungle. Even though he scoured the treacherous terrain for several years, no trace of the young girl was found. One of the Senator's college mates, Professor Silvio, had accompanied him on that journey long ago, and has remained in the jungle to carry on research and, at the same time, be able to continue the search for his friend's lost baby. It seems that Professor Silvio believes that he can successfully demonstrate Darwin's theory of evolution; that he can somehow show the evolution of the human species through this untamed jungle environment. Such a person immersed in this foreign element, he hypothesizes, will cause primitive instincts that had been submerged by evolution to stir; they will surface and allow that individual to survive in such a hostile place as this.

His theory is tested when he finds a young white girl scampering about the trees, much like the monkeys. He names this girl Darwa and concludes she is the evidence that will successfully prove his theory and demonstrate his interpretation of the Darwinian theory. Since Silvio is the first white man Darwa has ever seen, she easily becomes attached to him. He proceeds to use this dependence to control her, allowing her only limited freedom in associations with other humans.

However, a young biology student ventures into the jungle in search of Professor Silvio's wisdom. As he nears the camp, he sees the young girl hanging from the enormous deeply foliated trees. He cannot believe this: a white girl in this hostile jungle! Almost immediately Darwa and the student are attracted to each other. And from this point to the end of the movie the interaction between Robert Hunter, the young student, Dr. Silvio, Senator Newcastle, and Darwa becomes very intense: Hunter finds he is in love with Darwa; Professor Silvio claims that she is a by-product of his scientific experiments; and Senator Newcastle is convinced that Darwa is his lost daughter.

A Scream in the Night is a poor SF film, but the events leading up to the discovery of the young girl and the mystery surrounding her identity provide some interesting and very entertaining moments for the audience. Unfortunately the photography was not up to the standards possible in 1919, and this greatly detracted from the film's impact. However, even with the poor camera work, the film was labeled by the reviewers of the time as a "highly entertaining film, presenting unusual aspects of Darwin's theory of evolution." The plot is not much different though than many of the SF films which appeared between 1901 and 1907.

THE CARTER CASE

Release: 1919, Oliver Films, Inc.
Description: Silent, 15 episode serial, each episode approx. 2000 feet
Classification: SF-A
References: No. 8, p. 73, 191; No. 50, p. 57; MPW, Vol. 39, p. 1096, 1097, 1523, 1702, 1703, 1833

Credits

Producer .... Harry Grossman
Director .... Donald Mackenzie
Screenplay .... Arthur B. Reeves and John W. Grey

Cast

Craig Kennedy .... Herbert Rawlinson
Anita Carter .... Margaret Marsh
Cleo Clark .... Ethel Grey Terry
Lester Mason .... Coit Albertson
Walter Jameson .... William Pike
Hugo Geist/Avion .... Joseph Marba
Shelby Carter .... Donald Hall
Rance Dixon .... Kempton Greene
Count von der Witz .... John Reinhart
Alma, The Maid .... Gene Baker
Emanon .... Louis R. Wolheim
Darky Joe .... Leslie Stowe
Bull Rudkin .... Frank Wunderlee

Chapters 1-15 of *The Carter Case*

Chapter 1: The Phosgene Bullet
Chapter 2: The Vacuum Room
Chapter 3: The Air Terror
Chapter 4: The Dungeon
Chapter 5: Title unknown
Chapter 6: The Wireless Detective
Chapter 7: The Nervagraph
Chapter 8: The Silent Shot

Chapter 9: The Camera Trap
Chapter 10: The Moonshiners
Chapter 11: The White Damp
Chapter 12: The X-Ray Detective
Chapter 13: The Ruse
Chapter 14: Title unknown
Chapter 15: Title unknown

The Carter Case is another exciting serial centered around the adventures of Craig Kennedy, the marvelous scientific sleuth. This was Oliver Films' attempt to capitalize on the success that earlier Kennedy serials had enjoyed: *The Exploits of Elaine* (1914), *The New Exploits of Elaine* (1915), and *The Romance of Elaine* (1915). All three had reaped millions in gross sales, and Oliver Films sought to tap into this lucrative market.

This venture, starring Herbert Rawlinson and Margaret Marsh, did not have the impact that the earlier attempts starring Pearl White and Arnold Daly had enjoyed. Certainly part of this is due to the significant difference in the action of the serial, but it seems that neither the acting nor the plot was the major reason for it doing so poorly—it had both a good story line and unique special effects for 1919. In examining the evidence, it appears that it was distributed poorly and did not receive sufficient advertisement to make it a major contribution among the films of 1919.

As the first chapter, *The Phosgene Bullet*, begins, we find Shelby Carter, the president and chief chemist of a large chemical works, terrified over a threat on his life he has just received. Carter had recently developed a secret formula for a very powerful mysterious chemical which has the capability of producing a cloak of invisibility for the user. Before Carter can transfer his formula to a secure hiding place, he is viciously murdered by a villain named *Avion.*

Without moving her father's body, Anita Carter (over the objections of Lester Mason, her fiance) summons Craig Kennedy to the scene of the grotesque murder. While examining the body, Kennedy discovers a *phosgene* bullet, a hollow-type bullet containing a deadly poison within its chamber. Intently examining the bullet, Kennedy, Anita, and Lester fail to notice that they have become surrounded by Avion's henchmen. A fierce battle ensues, during which Anita is nearly strangled to death. But thanks to Craig's resourcefulness, she is pulled away from the crooks' speeding aircraft only moments before it becomes airborne.

Kennedy is quite puzzled by these events and is uncertain what his next course of action should be. He chooses to first investigate Carter's last experiment. Anita shows him about her father's plant and then into the laboratory he used.

In episode two, *The Vacuum Room,* Anita shows Kennedy a specially designed room in which chemicals can be exploded and tested within a complete vacuum and with complete secrecy. As they are about to exit the chamber, the door suddenly slams shut and is locked from the outside. They hear the whirl of the small vacuum pump beginning to remove all the air from the room . . . it will be only a matter of minutes before the air becomes so thin that they will lose consciousness, eventually suffocating. Craig quickly removes a small cylinder from a hidden compartment in his shoe, and attaches it to the door of the room. There is a flash of bright blinding light. When their vision clears they see that the chamber door now has a hole bored through large enough for Kennedy to reach the locking-mechanism and unseal the door.

In chapter 3, *The Terror of the Air*, we learn that Avion's men have created a small airforce of their own, complete with a special device which eliminates the noise of their planes' motors. Additionally, each craft is equipped with missiles that are controlled by a wireless device from within the cockpit.

After Anita's mansion has undergone one attack from Avion's airforce, Craig develops a specially designed air alarm system which warns them well in advance of approaching aircraft.

In the remaining episodes, 4 through 15, Craig and Avion are locked in battle, each time with Craig narrowly escaping death. Only his scientific genius and excellent physical condition save he and Anita from certain doom.

It becomes obvious that Avion has perfected the late Shelby Carter's formula for the invisible fluid as in Chapter 10 Avion and his aircraft become invisible during Craig's pursuit. In the next episode Kennedy devises a special x-ray mechanism which allows him to identify the invisible airplane. Eventually this leads to the capture of Avion and the destruction of his gang.

The Carter Case was launched with a great deal of enthusiasm as evidenced by the following review:

> "At a special showing for the trade on Loew's New York Roof, March 7, *The Carter Case*, produced by Oliver Films, Inc., exhibited a number of startling deviations from the conventional serial photoplay and made a decidely favorable impression on the large number of spectators."
>
> *Moving Picture World*, 3-22-19, p. 1702

Somewhere during the 15 weeks of releasing the serial, Oliver Films must have turned cold on the production. They failed to copyright any of the episodes, and ceased all periodical advertisement after May, 1919.

Four actors in the film continued their careers in movies and achieved prominence. The others appeared to drop out of sight as far as the movie scene was concerned. Herbert Rawlinson, who appeared in the SF adventure film *The Black Box* (1915), appeared in more than 150 films until 1951. Louis Wolheim, Ethel Grey Terry, and Margaret Marsh (the last was the older sister of Mae Marsh, Goldwyn's *Goldwyn Girl*) acted in a number of additional films but failed to continue into the new sound era.

THE GHOST OF SLUMBER MOUNTAIN

Release: 1919, World Film Corporation
Description: Silent, 1000 feet
Classification: SF-F
References: No. 14, p. 186; No. 28, p. 434; No. 50,p. 161; No. 54, p. 12, 13; BIO, Vol. 46, p. 15; CNF, Winter, 1971, p. 9, 10; FAM, No. 12, p. 6; MPH, Vol. 8, p. 43; MPW, Vol. 40, p. 32, 925

Credits

Producer .... Herbert W. Dawley
Director .... Herbert W. Dawley
Special Effects .... Willis O'Brien and Herbert W. Dawley

Cast

Mad Dick .... Willis O'Brien
Uncle Jack .... Herbert W. Dawley

Willis O'Brien, known as "O'Bie" to his friends, had produced two science fiction films in 1917, *The Dinosaur and the Missing Link* and *10,000 Years B.C.* In 1918 he created a wide array of animated features, none of which, however, could be classified as serious sci-fi. Among these masterpieces were *Morpheus Mike, Prehistoric Poultry, Curious Pets of Our Ancestors, Mickey and his Goat, In the Villain's Power, The Sam Lloyd Picture Puzzle,* and a series of short one-reelers called *Nippy's Nightmares.* While all these efforts certainly supplied the money needed to support O'Bie and his family, it also moved him further away from his real ambition of making an animated feature showcasing his work with prehistoric animals.

In early 1918, O'Bie was approached by a New Jersey film producer, Herbert W. Dawley, who was a part-time animator himself though his professional approach differed greatly from O'Brien's.

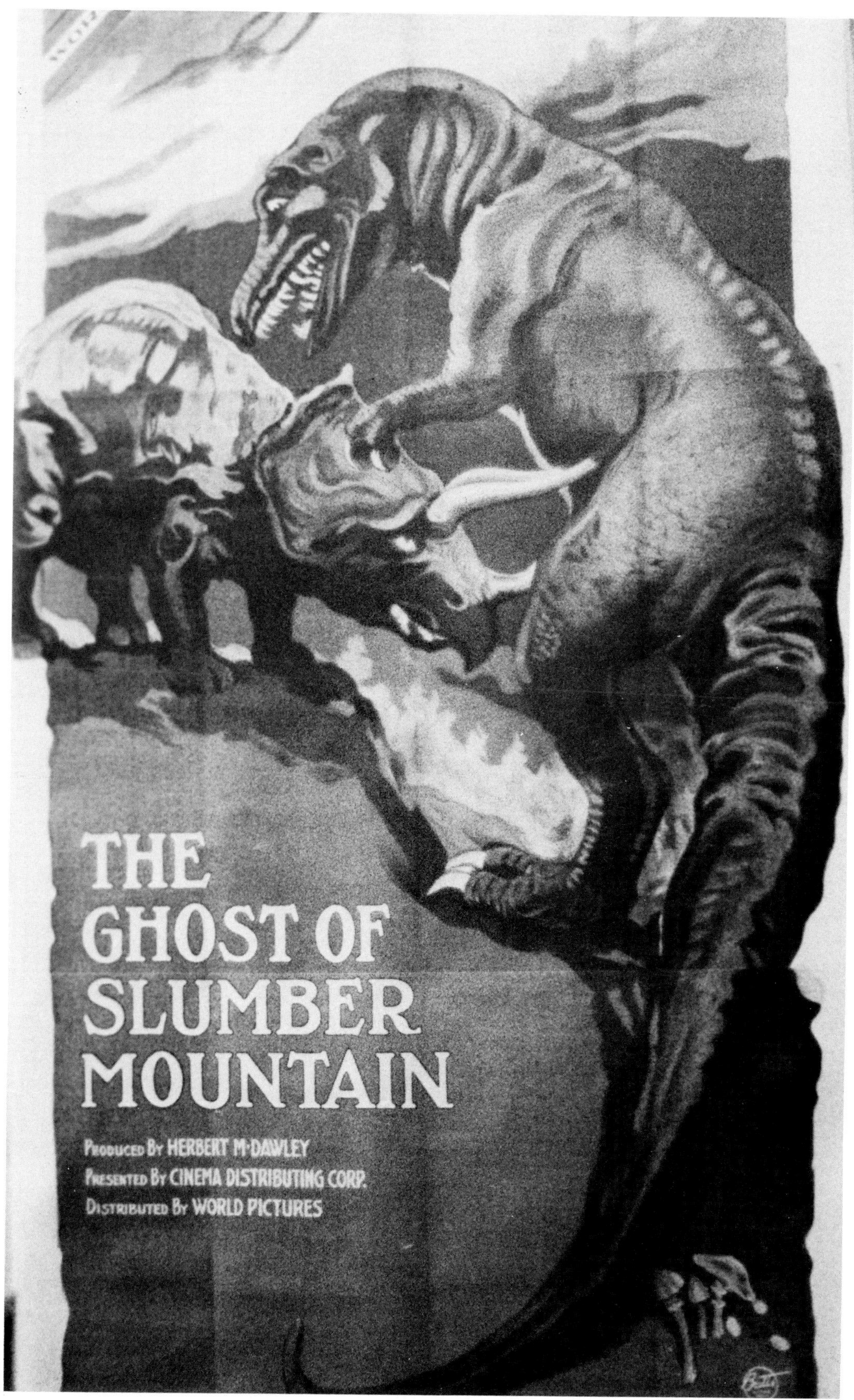

A one-sheet poster advertising the super Willis O'Brien film, *The Ghost of Slumber Mountain* (1919). This rare poster, owned by Forrest J Ackerman, is valued at several thousand dollars.

Dawley offered O'Bie $3,000 to write, direct, and create the special effects for a unique dinosaur film. He obviously leaped at this opportunity to return to his first love--the creation of animated films.

After much labor and considerable battling with Dawley, who seemed to constantly interfere with his work on the project, O'Brien's project resulted in *The Ghost of Slumber Mountain.*

As the film opens, an elderly bearded gentleman is sitting by the fire, surrounded by a group of anxious children. They seem to be clamoring for Uncle Jack (played by Herbert Dawley) to tell them the story of Slumber Mountain.

The tale begins with Jack, his dog, and their faithful guide, Joe embarking on an ardurous ascent up the rocky terrain of Slumber Mountain. Their quest is to reach Dream Valley and River of Peace. It is at Dream Valley that the group hopes to encounter the cabin of the old hermit, Mad Dick. Joe has convinced Jack that Mad Dick has an array of marvelous inventions and artifacts that will astound even the most skeptical of men. Cautiously, the two enter Dream Valley and approach the lonely cabin. With much trepidation Jack timidly knocks at the massive wooden door, but gets no response. They gently push the door ajar and enter the dimly lit room. Even in the faint light provided by a single candle they are able to ascertain that the dwelling is indeed empty.

As Joe wanders about the cabin in search of some unknown treasure, Jack is awed by the fossils and artifacts which litter the cabin floor. Without warning, Joe suddenly leaps into the air, expressing wild joy over some fortuitous discovery of a hidden treasure. He then reveals a precious telescope--one which he claimed earlier to Jack possessed magic powers. It is said, so Joe claims, that anyone gazing through its portal can see the past, revealing such views as no human had ever before seen. He rushes to Jack's side so he might share the wonder of the mad hermit's prized telescope.

No sooner does Jack touch the telescope and attempt to gaze through its rose colored lens than the ghost of Mad Dick (portrayed by Willis O'Brien) appears and leads him out of the cabin to the edge of a nearby cliff. The ghost instructs him to peer through the telescope to the valley below. As if in a trance, Jack responds in a robot-like fashion. He is astonished by the sight of a prehistoric world, seemingly within an arm's length of where he now stands. The images that appear before his eyes are of a world in its prehistoric period (most likely intended to be the Jurassic period).

Within his field of vision appears a dense jungle with a neighboring swamp. (O'Bie had used gelatin to simulate the slimy waters of the swamp.) These prehistoric surroundings appear so real that Jack is convinced he can actually reach out and touch the ancient fauna.

Suddenly there appears a giant bird that swoops down from the sky and perches on the remains of a large dead tree. It appears to be a moa, a species of prehistoric bird generally thought to have lived in the New Zealand region,which grew to heights of twelve feet or more. (In fact, some forms of this beast may have existed as late as 500 years ago.) The moa proceeds to preen its feathers while below it a diplodocus languorously raises its gigantic head from the murky swamp, apparently disturbed by the commotion caused by a brontosaurus feeding near the water's edge.

Jack is truly mesmerized by these prehistoric wonders unveiled before his eyes. He slowly moves the telescope to a nearby meadow (achieved on screen through the use of O'Brien's clever camera technique) where he sees two triceratops engaging in a fierce battle. One of the creatures appears to gain the advantage, spearing its foe with one of its protruding alabaster tusks. No sooner does this confrontation cease than the victorious triceratop is pounced upon by a large allosaurus. The allosaurus wastes little time in defeating its prey as its enormous jaws locate a vital nerve center, mortally wounding the beast.

Meanwhile, Jack's attention is returned to the moa, which has leaped from its perch to pounce upon a prehistoric serpent that was slithering across the marshy grasslands. As the moa feasts upon its prey, Jack is startled by an approaching allosaurus. At this same moment, Mad Dick appears. Jack finds himself confronting the charging reptile helpless until a rifle mysteriously appears by his side. Hurriedly he raises the rifle and fires at the approaching allosaurus. One of the projectiles pierces the creature's neck, but the charging beast is not slowed down. Jack's shots ring out but appear to have little effect on the giant monster. The thrashing jaws and fiery glaze in the attacker's eyes convince Jack that he must be the intended entree for dinner. He hurls the rifle in the direction of the lumbering giant as he turns to run for his life. . . .

As the movie draws to a close, the audience sees Jack stirring as he awakens with a jolt. The children's laughter can be heard clearly now as the confused and still dazed Jack realizes that what he had thought he was experiencing was nothing more than a bad nightmare.

The original footage produced by Willis O'Brien was nearly 45 minutes long, but Dawley, after previewing this lengthy (for that period) animated version, decided that it was much too long for audiences to sit through. Therefore, he cut the film to a mere 16 minutes, leaving many spectacular scenes on the cutting room floor.

Dawley's original investment in the film venture was $3,000.00. Apparently at the time of release he had little expectations of even recovering this $3,000.00. He was astonished, no doubt, when, within a short period of time, he made over $100,000 profit on this small film. The prestige and acclaim that came from the film were widespread across the country. Dawley was, of course, quick to proclaim the responsiblity and receive the resultant fame for having produced such a masterpiece.

Later, he produced several prints without even mentioning O'Brien's name in the credits. Fortunately, however, O'Bie saved much of the film that had been cut from the original version, and a film he produced the following year, *Along the Moon Beam Trail,* contained many monster shots which had been sequences edited out of *The Ghost of Slumber Mountain.*

Dawley's shabby treatment of O'Bie, coupled with his mounting personal problems, made this an extremely dark period in his life. Fortunately for O'Brien, he became involved with Watterson R. Rothacker, a businessman who had established a firm called The Industrial Moving Picture Company. Basically, this was a subsidiary of the old Edison Company, but Rothacker had become an independent producer and had always been intrigued by Willis' work. He immediately hired O'Brien and posted advertisements that the man who had created the effects for *The Ghost of Slumber Mountain* had joined his firm.

After several small animated features, O'Bie and Rothacker began an association which led to the production of the science fiction feature film *The Lost World,* a classic which would once and for all establish Willis O'Brien as the premiere special effects expert of the silver screen.

From *Lost World,* O'Brien went on to even greater achievements in performing the effects for *King Kong* and *Mighty Joe Young.*

> "*The Ghost of Slumber Mountain,* filmed by Willis O'Brien in 1918-19, released by World Films, Inc. When it opened in New York it received praise from G. Clyde Fisher, Ph.D., of the American Museum of Natural History, who said: 'I was greatly pleased. It is astonishing how lifelike those old dinosaurs and the giant bird, Distryma, were." The film contains an impressive scene where the great Distryma consumes a 10′ snake and there is also a battle between a tyrannosaurus and a triceratops. Prof. Fisher concluded: 'The whole thing was extremely well done.'"
>
> *Famous Monsters of Filmland,* No. 63, p. 29, Forrest J Ackerman, Editor.

THE MASTER MYSTERY

Release: 1919, Octagon Films, Inc.
Description: Silent, 15 episode serial, each episode approximately 2000 feet
Classification: SF-A
References: No. 1, p. 137; No. 8, p. 71, 72, 196, 197; No. 14, p. 313; No. 31, p. 94-96; No. 50, p. 294; BIO, Vol. 41, p. 65, 80; FAM, No. 17, p. 7; No. 31, p. 73; FAN, No. 4, p. 63; No. 5, p. 37; MOM, No. 3, p. 21; MPN, Vol. 18, p. 3251; MPW, Vol. 38, p. 856; PHO, 2/1919, p. 101

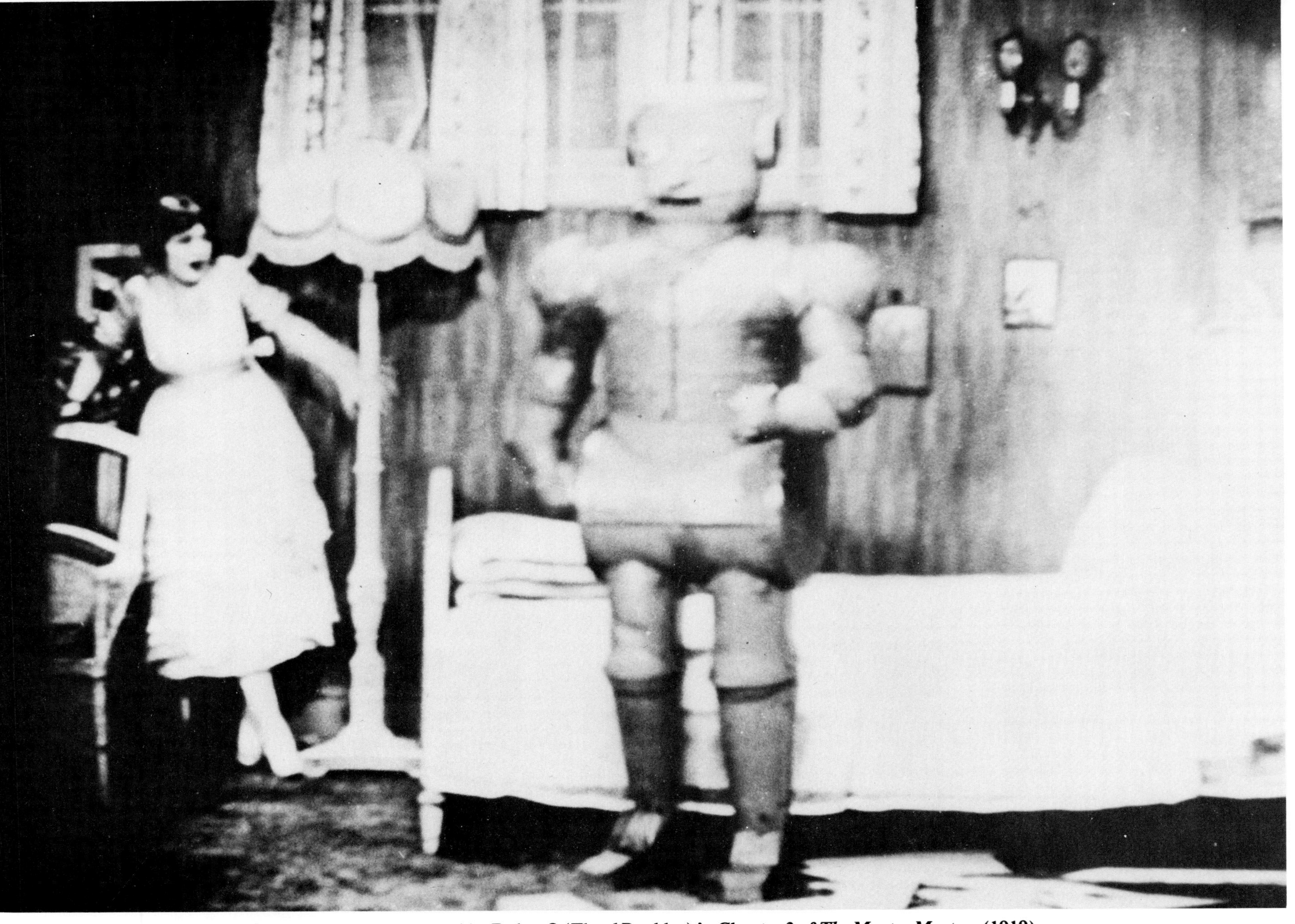

Eva Brent (Marguerite Marsh) is trapped by Robot Q (Floyd Buckley) in Chapter 3 of *The Master Mystery* (1919).

Credits

Producer .... Benjamin A. Rolfe
Director .... Burton King
Assistant Director .... William Haddock
Screenplay .... Arthur B. Reeve and Charles A. Logue

Cast

Quentin Locke .... Harry Houdini
Eva Brent .... Marguerite Marsh
Peter Brent .... William Pike
Deluxe Dora .... Ruth Stonehouse
Madagascar Strangler .... Charles Graham
Robot Q .... Floyd Buckley
Chemist .... Jack Burns
Maid .... Edna Britton

Chapters 1-15 of *The Master Mystery*

Chapter 1: LC, LP13194
Chapter 2: LC, LP13195
Chapter 3: LC, LP13422
Chapter 4: LC, LP13379
Chapter 5: LC, LP13380
Chapter 6: LC, LP13387
Chapter 7: LC, LP13388
Chapter 8: LC, LP13389
Chapter 9: LC, LP13390
Chapter 10: LC, LP13391
Chapter 11: LC, LP13409
Chapter 12: LC, LP13410
Chapter 13: LC, LP13423
Chapter 14: LC, LP13424
Chapter 15: Unmasking of the Automaton
Reference: LC, LP13425

*Chapters 1-14 were copyrighted without their titles listed. Only Chapter 15, *Unmasking of the Automaton,* was copyrighted with title.

The Master Mystery, a 15 episode serial, was designed to showcase Harry Houdini's escapist techniques. It was brilliantly created by Arthur B. Reeve, the creator of the Craig Kennedy mystery series, and Charles A. Logue, with some collaboration from Harry Houdini.

The story involves an evil organization known as International Patents, Inc. This group has been methodically swallowing up the smaller businesses and destroying those that threatened to compete with its own conglomerate. It is headed by the evil but ingenious Peter Brent, a multimillionaire recluse, who somehow feels threatened whenever he must venture from his enormous castle-like retreat. This estate is located some distance from the city, overlooking a large rocky terrain known as the "graveyard of genius." Below this, beneath several feet of solid rock, is housed the secret laboratory where Brent creates his inventions of doom.

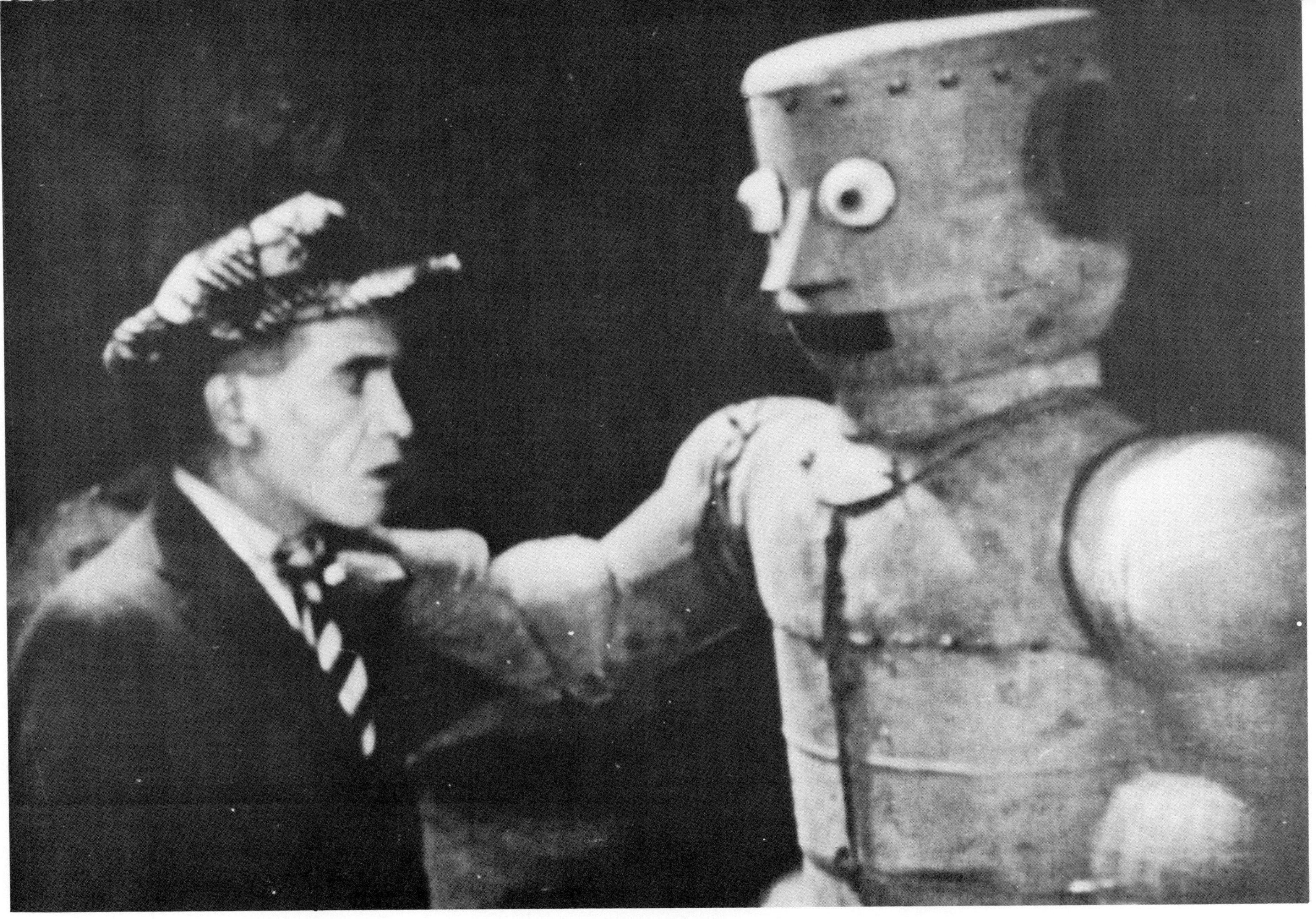

Quentin Locke (Harry Houdini) is snagged by the powerful robot as he attempts to free Eva.

Quentin Locke (portrayed by Houdini), a secret agent for the Department of Justice, has been dispatched to investigate Brent's activities. He must find a way of penetrating the gang's fortress in his quest to eventually bring about International Patent's doom.

As fate would have it, Brent has a beautiful daughter, Eva (exquisitely portrayed by Marguerite Marsh), and Quentin Locke's attention is at first diverted by this beautiful woman.

Suddenly, Brent has an unexplained change of conscious and decides that perhaps what he and his group have been attempting is wrong. He vows to reveal his dastardly deeds to the world by releasing the patents that he has been holding back through his group's exclusive control. That evening however, Brent is visited by his Robot Q, a gigantic automated machine. The robot succeeds in administering a poisonous injection to Brent which renders him physically incapacitated. This "accident" was achieved just before he could give his consent for his daughter to marry one of the younger partners in his organization.

Eva attempts to escape the fortress after her father's attack, but she is pursued by Robot Q. A young chemist who had been working in the laboratory comes to her aid, but, unfortunately, he pays for his intrusion with his life as the robot, obviously impervious to all weapons, crushes his body with his massive arms. Eva is then captured by Robot Q and made a prisoner within her own house.

Not long after this, Locke manages to gain entrance to the castle, but falls into a trap set by the ingenious Robot Q. During the remaining 14 episodes, Locke's attempts to escape the castle and free Eva from Robot Q hold the audience spellbound. Each week he is recaptured and put into impossible situations, bringing him to the brink of death, only to escape miraculously at the beginning of the next episode.

An example of the excellent serial writing can be seen in one of the first episodes when Locke is chained to the large door of a Chinese temple. Huge wheels suddenly begin to slowly reel the chains which bind him, causing their forces to tighten about his body. The episode ends with Locke in this grip of death with no possible means of escape. But in the beginning of the next week's feature, Locke manages to escape before the audience's astounded eyes.

(Unfortunately, these situations may have caused the audience to believe the whole scene was nothing more than camera trickery. However, Houdini later wrote that each and every escape portrayed in the serial was actually done before a rolling camera, and his escapes from each perilous situation were achieved through his own ingeniousness and captured on film without any outside help or mechanical assistance.)

As the story continued to unfold, Locke learns the secret of Robot Q. He and Eva invent a special new bullet which has an explosive device in its center. They carefully plan to ambush the robot in the serial's final episode, "Unmasking the Automaton". The gun is fired and Quinten's specially designed projectile does indeed penetrate the steel armor of the robot. Robot Q slumps to the floor. Suddenly, it is revealed that this had not been an automated creature, but actually encased a human being, who, through some mysterious device, was able to amplify his own muscle power into super-human strength.

Harry Houdini's film career was brief, and this serial and *Terror Island* were probably his two best films, though both still lacked the box office success each of the producers had been assured in using Houdini's name.

Houdini had many problems with *The Master Mystery* and had been promised 50% of the movie's profits. He later had to go to court to obtain these funds, however. In fact the verdict was not given until three years after the film's release and he only received $33,000.00 as his share, not an overwhelming sum compared to his many stage performances which netted him approximately $50,000 per performance. Nevertheless, Houdini continued to seek a film career as he believed that through films he could truly immortalize his escape tricks for posterity, as well as enthrall the audiences who would see him escape nearly impossible situations.

"In *The Master Mystery,* written by Arthur B. Reeve and Charles A. Logue, and produced by B. A. Rolfe, there is every promise that its fifteen episodes will keep the movie fan on the edge of his seat throughout each number and leave him hardly ablt to wait for the time between each installment to pass."

The Moving Picture World, Vol. 38, 11-23-18, p. 856

"To attempt even a summary of the countless thrilling 'stunts' contained in the picture would be a task beyond the strength of the present reviewer. Suffice it to say that every episode is crammed with sensational scenes introducing innumerable original mechanical properties and effects. The photography is notably fine and the settings all that they should be."

Bioscope, Vol. 41, 2-18-19, p. 65

THE POISON PEN

Release: 1919, World Film Corporation
Description: Silent, 5000 feet
Classification: SF-A
References: No. 50, p. 375; BIO, Vol. 45, No. 737, p. 83; LC, LU14428; MPN, Vol. 20, p. 3795

Credits

Producer .... World Film Corp.
Director .... Edwin August
Screenplay .... Edwin August and J. Clarkson Miller

Cast

Allayne Filbert .... June Elvidge
David Alden .... Earl Metcalfe
Bishop Filbert .... Joseph Smiley
Mrs. Filbert .... Marion Barney
Marion Stanley .... Jeanne Loew
Sims .... George Bunny
Johnson .... Irving Brooks
Dr. McKenna .... John M. Sainpolis
Granville Walters .... J. Arthur Young
Dorgan .... Henry West
Morton Wells .... Charles Mackay
Mrs. Wells .... Marguerite Gale
Boy .... Dan Comfort

This is a strange tale of a young girl, Allayne Filbert, who seems to undergo some mysterious transformations while she is sleeping. She is changed from a shy, sweet young girl into a creature whose debased personality seeks pleasure by writing scurrilous attacks on prominent individuals. Even her own meek alter ego is not left unscathed.

Finally, a pair of private detectives catch her during one of her sleep walking (and sleep writing) episodes. When the identity of the infamous *poison pen* is discovered to be Allayne, her fiance seeks special medical help.

An ingenious researcher has created an ultraviolet ray device which he feels will rid Allayne of her dual personality. After many unsuccessful attempts, the process finally works. Allayne is returned to her normal self.

This is a weak SF adventure film, but the mental restoration process makes it a noteworthy film effort.

CLASSIFICATION OF SCIENCE FICTION FILMS FROM 1910 TO 1919

Science Fiction

Comet, The 1910
Frankenstein 1910
Inventor, The 1910
Dr. Growenquick's Feeding Power 1911
Cave Man, The 1912
Dr. Jekyll and Mr. Hyde 1912
Man's Genesis 1912
Navigation By Wireless 1912
Serpents, The 1912
Bolt From The Sky, A 1913
Cave Man's War, The 1913
Cursed Be War 1913
Demonyte 1913
Diamond Makers, The 1913
Doctor Maxwell's Experiment 1913
Dr. Jekyll and Mr. Hyde 1913
Primitive Man 1913
Whirl of Destiny, The 1913
Birth of Emotion, The 1914
Bomb, The 1914
Bully's Doom, The 1914
By Radium Rays 1914
Naidra, The Dream Woman 1914
Surgeon's Experiment, The 1914
Foster Brother, The 1915
Let There Be Light 1915
Mysterious Contragrav, The 1915
Pawns of Mars 1915
Plague Spot, The 1915
Return of Maurice Donnelly, The 1915
Secret Room, The 1915
War O' Dreams, The 1915
Comet's Come-Back, The 1916
Flying Torpedo, The 1916
Intrigue, The 1916
Twenty Thousand Leagues Under the Sea 1916
Without a Soul 1916

Science Fiction - Comedy

A Trip to Mars 1910
Betty's Electric Battery 1910
Electric Insoles, The 1910
Looking Forward 1910
Mechanical Husband, The 1910
Electrified Pig, The 1911
House of Mystery, The 1911
Inventor's Secret, The 1911
Dr. Brompton-Watt's Age Adjuster........ 1912
Hypnotic Chair, The 1912
In the Year 2000 1912
Kissing Pills 1912
Bumble's Diminisher 1913
Bumke Discovers the Turning Microbe 1913
Indestructible Mr. Jenks, The 1913
A Sure Cure 1914
Absent Minded Mother 1914
Blown Upon 1914
Dr. Jekyll and Mr. Hyde 1914
His Prehistoric Past 1914
Miser's Reversion, The 1914
Professor Oldboy's Rejuvenator 1914
Automatic House, The 1915
Hattie, the Hair Heiress 1915
Jack Spratt and the Scales of Love 1915
Mechanical Man, The 1915
Mr. Jarr's Magnetic Friend 1915
Dare Devils in Danger 1916
Lion's Breath, The 1916
One Thousand Miles an Hour 1916
Dinosaur and the Missing Link, The 1917
Love Dope, The 1917
Magic Jazz Bo, The 1917
Speed 1917
Water on the Brain 1917
Rejuvenators, The 1918

Science Fiction - Adventure

Theft of the Secret Code 1912
Diamond Maker, The 1914
Exploits of Elaine, The 1914
Reader of Minds, The 1914
Silent Peril, The 1914

Won in the Clouds 1914
Beneath the Sea 1915
Black Box, The 1915
Diamond from the Sky, The 1915
Electric Alarm, The 1915
Inventor's Peril, The 1915
Jungle Lovers, The 1915
Kite, The 1915
Lady Baffles and Detective Duck, The 1915
Monopolist, The 1915
New Exploits of Elaine, The 1915
Romance of Elaine, The 1915
Ventures of Marguerite, The 1915
When the Mind Sleeps 1915
Beggar King, The 1916
Five Franc Piece, The 1916
Half Wit, The 1916
Hand of Peril, The 1916
Her Father's Gold 1916
Insurance Swindlers, The 1916
Secret of the Submarine, The 1916
Through Solid Walls 1916
Hidden Hand, The 1917
Inspirations of Harry Larrabee, The 1917
Lust of the Ages, The 1917
Zeppelin Attack on New York 1917
Craving, The 1918
House of Hate 1918
Mystery Ship, The 1918
A Scream in the Night 1919
Carter Case, The 1919
Master Mystery, The 1919
Poison Pen, The 1919

Science Fiction - Horror

Life Without Soul 1915
Crimson Stain Mystery, The 1916

Science Fiction - Fantasy

Dances of the Ages 1913
10,000 Years B.C. 1917
Ghost of Slumber Mountain, The 1919

Companies Releasing Films from 1910 to 1919

Alhambra - Kriterion

Birth of Emotion, The 1914

American Film Manufacturing Co.

Let There Be Light 1915
Comet's Come-Back, The 1916
Dare Devils in Danger 1916
Secret of the Submarine, The 1916

Biograph Company

Inventor's Secret, The 1911
Man's Genesis 1912
Primitive Man 1913

Bison

Silent Peril, The 1914

Bluebird

Craving, The 1918

Conquest Films

10,000 Years B.C. 1917

Consolidated Film Company

Crimson Stain Mystery, The 1916

Cosmopolitan

Electrified Pig, The 1911

Crystal

A Sure Cure 1914

Danube

Navigation by Wireless 1912

Eclair

Diamond Maker, The 1914

Edison Film Company

A Trip to Mars 1910
Frankenstein 1910
Dr. Brompton-Watt's Age Adjuster 1912
Dances of the Ages 1913
Absent Minded Mother 1914
Dinosaur and the Missing Link, The 1917

Elite Film Company

Bumke Discovers the Turning Microbe 1913

Empress Film Company

Automatic House, The 1915

Essanay Film Manufacturing Co.

Electric Insoles, The 1910
Jack Spratt and the Scales of Love 1915

Falstaff

Hattie, The Hair Heiress 1915

Film Releases of America

Demonyte 1913

Fine Arts

Flying Torpedo, The 1916

General Film Company

Inspirations of Harry Larrabee, The 1917

Gold Seal

By Radium Rays 1914

Independent Moving Picture Company

Dr. Jekyll and Mr. Hyde 1913

Kalem Company

Comet, The 1910
Bolt from the Sky, A 1913
Cave Man's War, The 1913
Indestructible Mr. Jenks, The 1913
Professor Oldboy's Rejuvenator 1914
Ventures of Marguerite, The 1915
When the Mind Sleeps 1915

Kay-Bee

Kite, The 1915

Keystone

His Prehistoric Past 1914

Kriterion

Blown Upon 1914

LCC

Mechanical Husband, The 1910

Lubin

Kissing Pills 1912
Doctor Maxwell's Experiment 1913
Bomb, The 1914
Bully's Doom, The 1914
Beneath the Sea 1915
Inventor's Peril, The 1915
Beggar King, The 1916
Half Wit, The 1916

Majestic

Hypnotic Chair, The 1912
Surgeon's Experiment, The 1914
Electric Alarm, The 1915

Metro Pictures Corp.

Love Dope, The 1917

Mica Film Corporation

Foster Brother, The 1915

Mundstuk Features

Whirl of Destiny, The 1913

North American Film Company

Diamond from the Sky, The 1915

Ocean

Life Without Soul 1915

Octagon Films, Inc.

Master Mystery, The 1919

Ogden Independent Productions

Lust of the Ages, The 1917

Oliver Films, Inc.

Carter Case, The 1919

Pallas

Intrigue, The 1916

Passing Show Comedies

Rejuvenators, The 1918

Pathe

Betty's Electric Battery 1910
Inventor, The 1910
House of Mystery, The 1911
Exploits of Elaine, The 1914
Monopolist, The 1915
New Exploits of Elaine, The 1915
Romance of Elaine, The 1915
Secret Room, The 1915
Hidden Hand, The 1917
House of Hate 1918

Rex Motion Picture Company

Diamond Makers, The 1913

Rothacker

Zeppelin Attack on New York 1917

Select Pictures Corp.

A Scream in the Night 1919

Selig Polyscope Co.

Jungle Lovers, The 1915
War O'Dreams, The 1916
Five Franc Piece, The 1916

Solax

In the Year 2000 1912

Starlight

Dr. Jekyll and Mr. Hyde 1914

Thanhouser

Looking Forward	1910
Dr. Jekyll and Mr. Hyde	1912
Miser's Reversion, The	1914
Naidra, The Dream Woman	1914
Reader of Minds, The	1914
Her Father's Gold	1916

Universal Film Manufacturing Co.

Bumble's Diminisher	1913
Won in the Clouds	1914
Black Box, The	1915
Lady Baffles and Detective Duck, The	1915
Mechanical Man, The	1915
Mysterious Contragrav, The	1915
Insurance Swindlers, The	1916
Lion's Breath, The	1916
One Thousand Miles an Hour	1916
Twenty Thousand Leagues Under the Sea	1916
Magic Jazz Bo, The	1917
Water on the Brain	1917
Mystery Ship, The	1918

Vitagraph Company of America

Cave Man, The	1912
Serpents, The	1912
Mr. Jarr's Magnetic Friend	1915
Pawns of Mars	1915
Plague Spot, The	1915
Return of Maurice Donnelly, The	1915

Vitascope Company

Theft of the Secret Code	1912

Walterdaw

Dr. Growenquick's Feeding Power	1911

World Film Corporation

Hand of Peril, The 1916
Without a Soul 1916
Ghost of Slumber Mountain 1919
Poison Pen, The 1919

U.S. Motion Pictures Corporation

Speed 1917

Unknown*

Cursed Be War 1913

*No evidence available to determine releasing company.

1920 – 1929

AN OVERVIEW OF 1920 - 1929

The 1920-29 decade was one of great change for the film industry. The aftermath of World War I produced an accelerated technological revolution which was coupled with a political and economic climate that saw great vascillation from the beginning of the 1920's through the end of the decade.

The cinematic isolation created during World War I provided a false sense of security for the American film industry, virtually removing all foreign competition, and, thus, providing a sterile laboratory in which to develop its own techniques. As film makers refined their skills, their creative efforts seemed to gravitate toward a "true art" form.

By 1921 this incubation period was over, and foreign films once again descended on the United States. The result was an inevitable comparison between American and foreign cinema efforts--an analysis which revealed vast differences in artistic perception and detail. Generally, Europeans seemed to be concerned with plot detail, right down to the most minute, while domestic films exhibited a stronger emphasis on action and the development of the "star" image.

In 1921, *The Cabinet of Dr. Caligari,* a 1919 German science fiction film, found its way into American theaters. The public's acclaim for it was soon so overwhelming that many American film producers revamped their cinemagraphic offerings by concentrating more on plot development while still attempting to maintain the intensity of action that had become the hallmark of their films. Meanwhile another German film, *Metropolis,* appeared in the theaters reaffirming again the competence of the Germans to produce dramatic, entertaining, and artistic offerings.

All of this infusion of European films spawned an impetus for American producers to strive for better and more artistic works. As the decade marched forward, their efforts to reach a parity with their foreign counterparts were fulfilled by such great science fiction offerings as *The Lost World* (1925) and *Mysterious Island* (1929).

The technological revolution during the 1920's resulted in vast changes for our country and in particular for American cinema. In only a matter of a few years engineering advances in transportation had converted the American population into a society on the move. The media also made great strides in giving this mobile population a reason for getting in their new cars and going out for the evening as a plethora of new movie theaters sprang into existence. They began to draw thousands of new fans and competition was soon keen to create the most ornate settings for these valued patrons. A favorite decoration theme was that of an outdoor play production with castle-like walls and balconies on either side of the screen. Invariably the ceilings were dotted with "stars" and painted clouds. All designed, of course, to lure the "at homers" into the theaters to see the heroes and heroines wrestle the powers of evil.

Advertising through the various media also increased the proliferation of theaters throughout the country as the Hollywood image was born. Numerous movie stars began to endorse a variety of products on radio, screen, and through the newspaper and magazine pages. Naturally, the public clamored to try these products since their favorite screen idols were obviously using them.

The 1920's was a period when the general public was in a state of political and economic confusion. The post-war period gave birth to a new morality and many of the leaders of the day attempted to cleanse the nation by "drying it out." Thus, the 18th amendment which instituted prohibition passed Congress with ease. It was not amazing that the passage of this drastic law ushered in the era which we have come to label as the "Roaring Twenties."

These times also brought on the Women's Suffrage Movement and its campaign for women's rights. Thus, women became not only a force in the political arena, but a very vocal presence in the social climate. One of the results of this new feminine power was the advent of the female heroine in science fiction with such stars as Pearl White echoing the cause in her many roles on the screen.

The economic oscillations of this time eventually plummeted the nation to its rock bottom as the stock market crashed and the great depression was upon us. Stocks that had been selling for $10 during the early part of the decade had, by the middle years, reached prices of $500-600 per share, only to drop to the unbelievable price of less than a penny a share by 1929. People who had heard the promise of prosperity voiced by their leaders now had their dreams suddenly dashed to despair by the advent of the depression.

The film industry showed a similar economic rollercoaster trend and those movies which enjoyed moderate success during this time echoed the fears and anxieties of a troubled nation. Many of the established movie makers vanished from the scene while others banded together to form new companies. Carl Laemmle, who had established Universal Studios in 1912, spent years vying for power and growth with a variety of partners. Finally, with the creation of his California based film company, Universal became one of the strongest of the 1920's—and continues to be so today.

Adolph Zukor, who had established his own company in 1914, joined with Famous Players Lasky to form a studio which eventually became known as Paramount Pictures. Likewise, Louis Mayer of Metro Pictures and Sam Goldwyn of Goldwyn Company joined to form Metro-Goldwyn-Mayer. William Fox also merged his efforts to become known as Fox Film Company. In fact, Fox was one of the few independent film companies during the previous decade which posed a substantial threat to the old Film Patents Company, eventually helping to break it.

During this time many of the studios that had developed great power under the original Patents Act saw the industry slip from their ironclad grasp. Edison, Kalem, Lubin, Biograph, Thanhouser, and many others simply faded away giving rise to the new independents.

These new studios also ushered in a new attitude toward the production of films as more money and time were spent on each. For example, *Tarzan and the Apes* became an extravagant production costing more than one million dollars to make. Of course, it returned a phenomenal amount of capital to its producers and led the industry to believe that spending sufficient time and money could be financially rewarding at the box office.

Likewise, many actors became real"stars" with salaries equivalent to their positions and power in box office appeal. By 1921, Pearl White was demanding--and getting--$250,000 per picture, plus an array of fringe benefits. Moreover, she was hardly, if ever, out of work during these years.

The 1920's had been ushered in by three remakes of *Dr. Jekyll and Mr. Hyde,* which may have been a bit too much even for the most ardent science fiction fan. Two of these productions were serious dramatic offerings and one was billed as a comedy. The Paramount version was by far the most outstanding of the two dramatic productions with John Barrymore's performance as the infamous Jekyll/Hyde character. This portrayal has stood through the years as a glowing illustration of his great acting ability and talents. As you might have guessed, the comedic production of this great favorite was a miserable disaster. In fact, it was only shown in a few of the major theater houses before being removed from the film circuit.

Science fiction serials which had enjoyed unprecedented popularity during the early part of the previous decade seemed to lose momentum as that period drew to a close. However, 1920 saw a resurgence of the SF serial popularity as *The Branded Four, The Flaming Disk, The Hidden Code, The Mystery Mind,* and *The Screaming Shadow* were released. Each offered weeks of spine-tingling adventure, leaving the audience on the edges of their seats, gnawing at their fingernails as they saw their heroes and heroines held at the brink of disaster until the following week's episode.

During the next three years, theaters across America were treated to a cornucopia of science fiction feature films and serials. *The Isle of Lost Ships* was one of these and shines as an outstanding film. At the same time, audiences were being lured back to the movie houses each week by the action filled serials of *The Radio King* (1922) and *Around the World in Eighteen Days* (1923).

Each of the above merely set the stage for the best science fiction feature of the decade, *The Lost World.* Based on a 1912 novel of the same name, the film version set a new plateau for SF cinematic art and became one of the classic films ever produced and, even when compared with today's technology, it is amazing how realistic the various prehistoric animals appeared to be throughout the jungle sequences. The story, created by Arthur Conan Doyle, and the special effects, ingeniously created by

Willis O'Brien, became the basis for additional films such as *King Kong* (1933, 1979), *Son of Kong* (1933), *Mighty Joe Young* (1949), and, of course, the 1960 remake of *The Lost World*. O'Brien's outstanding animation achievements (utilizing over 45 separate models of prehistoric animals) gave the SF genre its note of continued distinction—special effects!

The decade drew to a close with the 1929 production of *Mysterious Island.* While the film only loosely followed Jules Verne's classic tale, it excelled in cinematography. The underwater sequences showed the precision and skill of master craftsmen at work. In fact, the film, 90 percent of which was shot in color, gave the viewing public some of its first glimpses of the undersea kingdom as it really is. Unfortunately this film took so long to complete that it was a late arrival into an emerging sound era. But a last minute sound track was hastily added to the film release to make it competitive with the contemporary features of 1929, which, luckily, didn't seem to detract from its superb quality and cast.

The Roaring Twenties spawned a wealth of new cinema talent which guaranteed the continued success of motion pictures. The age of infancy was over for the film industry; there had been growing pains and numerous mistakes, but these had been overcome as new and better productions for the American theatergoers were promised in the decades to follow.

1920

ALONG THE MOON BEAM TRAIL

Release: 1920, Dawley
Description: Silent, one real
Classification: SF-F
References: No. 50, p. 10; CNF, Winter 1971, p. 9; FAM, No. 63, p. 28; SFD, 5/33, p. 7

Credits

Producer .... Herbert W. Dawley
Director .... Willis O'Brien
Special Effects .... Willis O'Brien

As the story begins, two small children are transported to the moon via a "magically enchanted" airplane. As soon as they disembark from their craft, they are viciously pursued by an enormous pterodactyl, which chases them down a ravine. The pair finally come upon a thick grassy swamp bordered by jungle-like vegetation, a scene resembling the earth's own prehistoric era. Somehow the two manage to escape the gigantic creature.

Tired from their ordeal, they seek shelter in a small cave located in the high rocks. After having an opportunity to catch their breath and relax, they take full notice of their strange surroundings and are truly amazed: a swamplike area, dense jungle forests, and prehistoric animals are not what they had expected to find on the moon.

As they scan the scene more fully, a variety of prehistoric creatures begin to parade across the marshy swamp. A trachodon lumbers near the edge of the marsh, stirring up its murky waters, and from the nearby jungle a loud roar is heard (via the silent movie's subtitles, of course), apparently coming from deep within the thick foliage.

Suddenly a tyrannosaurus emerges in search of food. It wastes no time in pursuing and attacking the trachodon. The two beasts commence a fierce battle, clawing and tearing each other's thick hide. Within a few moments, the battling duo is joined by a stegosaurus. This adds even more to the bloody scene. The combat seems to last an eternity, but finally the fighting subsides as each of the great beasts fall to the ground, suffering immensely from their many wounds.

The children take this opportunity to leap from their cave and scurry back to their enchanted craft and make their retreat along the moon beam trail back to the safe haven of earth.

Along the Moon Beam Trail was a short feature which Willis O'Brien managed to put together from footage cut out of *The Ghost of Slumber Mountain.* It was produced, as a result, at a phenomenally low cost, yet its returns resulted in significant sums of money for both O'Brien and Dawley.

This also served to reinforce O'Brien's belief that the public certainly craved animated features, and that his expertise in creating them would be greatly rewarded in the future.

Many of the films O'Brien produced did achieve such lifelike effects that even naturalists of the time were truly amazed at their authenticity. Even the movements of the beasts on the screen appeared real. O'Brien soon became the acclaimed expert of all the special effects industry and was sought by the most prestigious producers to work miracles. His greatest triumphs, however, still lay ahead with the *The Lost World* (1925) and *King Kong* (1933).

> "*Along the Moon Beam Trail,* a fantascifilm produced by Major Herbert Dawley. The opening scenes were negligible in its content, but after the two small children, the characters of the story, arrived on the Moon via enchanted aeroplane, the picture became most interesting."
>
> *Science Fiction Digest,* May, 1933, p. 7.

THE BRANDED FOUR

Release: 1920, Select Pictures Corp.
Description: Silent, 15 episode serial, each episode approx. 2000 feet
Classification: SF-A
References: No. 5, p. 72; No. 8, p. 83, 201; No. 14, p. 64; No. 32, p. 43; No. 50, p. 46; BIO, Vol. 57, 12-6-23, p. 51

Credits

Director .... Duke Worne
Screenplay .... Hope Loring and George W. Pyper

Cast

A. B. C. Drake .... Ben Wilson
Marion Leonard .... Neva Gerber
Dr. Horatio Sciaggs .... Joseph Girard
The Lawyer .... William Dyer
Mr. Leonard .... Ashton Dearholt
Second Daughter .... Pansy Porter
Jason (the servant) .... William Carroll

Chapters 1-15 of *The Branded Four*

Chapter 1: A Strange Legacy
References: LC, LP15382
Chapter 2: The Devil's Trap
References: LC, LP15385
Chapter 3: Flames of Revenge
References: LC, LP15810
Chapter 4: The Blade of Death
References: LC, LP15478
Chapter 5: Fate's Pawn
References: LC, LP15515
Chapter 6: The Hidden Cave
References: LC, LP15479
Chapter 7: Shanghaied
References: LC, LP15506
Chapter 8: Mutiny
References: LC, LP15526
Chapter 9: The House of Doom
References: LC, LP15607
Chapter 10: Ray of Destruction
References: LC, LP15679
Chapter 11: Buried Alive
References: LC, LP15977
Chapter 12: Lost to the World
References: LC, LP15738

In the final episode, "Sands of Torment," from the serial *The Branded Four* (1920), A. B. C. Drake reveals to the two orphaned girls that their father had a secret diary.

Chapter 13: Valley of Death
References: LC, LP15758
Chapter 14: From the Sky
References: LC, LP15739
Chapter 15: Sands of Torment
References: LC, LP15759

The Branded Four begins with a flashback to a period 18 years earlier. Dr. Horatio Scraggs has converted his immense fortune into pure gold; then carefully stored the ingots within a secret chamber, and concealed the chamber's entrance.

Dr. Scraggs is the father and sole parent of four infant daughters: his wife had recently passed away while giving birth to their fourth child.

The doctor created an unusual process by which he was able to brand each of the four babies with a mysterious mark, a mark that will not appear visible to the naked eye until each one reaches 21 years of age. Scraggs writes in his diary that upon the day that each of the daughters reaches womanhood a clue to his fortune will appear, and if they possess the ingenuity to assemble the various clues, the fortune in gold will be theirs. He carefully places this diary in an envelope and sends his servant to place it in his vault with the instructions that it not be opened until after his death.

Within a few days an unfortunate accident occurs: the good doctor is struck by lightning and killed. During the subsequent settlement of Scraggs' estate, his faithful friend and attorney is dismayed to find the coffers empty. He is also distraught and angry that Scraggs failed to mention him in his will.

Later, quite by accident, he stumbles upon Scraggs' diary and notices the mentioned fortune the daughters will inherit when they reach their twenty-first birthdays. The Scraggs' servant discovers him examining the diary and, during the ensuing scuffle between them, the family dog wanders off with the book and buries it.

The young girls, now penniless, must be put up for adoption. Each is placed in a suitable foster home, with Marion (the oldest daughter) being adopted by a wealthy family named Leonard. On the very day she reaches 21 years of age, the evil lawyer attempts to kidnap her but his effort fails. This incident leads to Marion's introduction to the famous *alphabet* criminologist, better known as *Alphabet Drake*. With Drake's assistance they seek to unravel the clues surrounding Marion's father's death and seek the fortune that has been hidden.

Meanwhile the lawyer has gone to great expense to attempt to thwart their efforts in recovering this treasure. In episode 10, he and his scientist friend create a hideous device called the *ray of destruction* which has the capability of destroying the entire human race if it gets into the wrong hands. Fortunately, Drake manages to rewire the device which causes it to overload and self-destruct.

It is not until the final chapter of the serial that all the clues become obvious and thus reveal the cache of gold's resting place. Almost simultaneously, the lawyer and Drake reach the solution through these branded clues. The lawyer reaches the cavern where the gold is hidden just before Drake and the four sisters, but greed has taken hold of his judgment and, as he tries to store the gold in his car, the car rolls back and crushes him to death. Drake and Marion transport the gold to the old Scraggs mansion where it is equally divided among the four sisters. It is at this time that Marion and Drake realize they are attracted to each other, and indicate in the final episode that they can now marry in peace since the secret of *The Branded Four* has been resolved by the famous criminologist, A. B. C. Drake.

Ben Wilson, who portrayed Drake, and Neva Gerber, who portrayed Marion, appeared in many serials as a team between 1919 and 1921; *The Trail of the Octopus* (1919), *The Screaming Shadow* (1920), *The Branded Four* (1920), and *The Mysterious Pearl* (1921). In 1925 and 1926 they were again teamed and appeared in three more serials: *The Power of God* (1925), *The Mystery Box* (1925), and *Officer 444* (1926). Thus, the Wilson/Gerber combination seemed to be a highly successful box office attraction as the seven serials they starred in grossed nearly 17 million dollars.

Wilson's career spanned the silent period, while Gerber's was limited to the seven serials in which she appeared alongside Wilson.

THE DEVIL TO PAY

Release: 1920, Pathe
Description: Silent, 6000 feet
Classification: SF-H
References: No. 50, p. 97; LC, LP1888; MPN, Vol. 22, p. 4347; VAW, Vol. 61, No. 3 p. 35

Credits

Producer .... Brunton Films
Director .... Ernest C. Warde
Screenplay .... Jack Cunningham and Frances Nimmo Green

Cast

Cullen Grant .... Roy Stewart
Brent Warren .... Robert McKim
Dare Keeling .... Fritzi Brunette
Larry Keeling .... George Fisher
Mrs. Roan .... Evelyn Selbie
George Roan .... Joseph J. Dowling
Dick Roan .... Richard Lapan
Dr. Jernigan .... Mark Fenton
Detective Potter .... William Marion

The Devil to Pay is an entertaining film, but an impuissant entry into the science fiction-horror category.

The story centers on a young man who is sentenced to be hanged for a crime he didn't commit; it seems a wealthy banker and politician have convincingly framed him. Sometimes, however, the innocent have a way of revealing the truth. As Cullen Grant is hanged and pronounced dead, a young physician asks to use his body in an experiment. Since there is no next of kin, the warden grants permission for Dr. Jernigan to claim the body.

Dr. Jernigan has created a mysterious device which may be able to resuscitate individuals who have been dead for sometime. He rushes Grant's body to his laboratory where he begins his unique experiment. It is successful and Grant is brought back to life. When he relates to Dr. Jernigan the details of his frame, he convinces the doctor to aid him in his quest to prove his innocence.

Dr. Jernigan contacts the district attorney, who is indeed amazed that Jernigan's process was successful. At the same time he is uneasy about having originally convicted Grant. He agrees to join in the gathering of criminal evidence against the banker.

The film reaches a climax during the banker's trial when the presumed dead Grant appears as a special prosecution witness. In fact, the banker falls apart and confesses his hideous crimes and political corruptions. Grant is declared innocent and a free man as the banker is led away for a date with the hangman (presumably with no chance for a resuscitation attempt).

A number of the actors in this feature were very experienced. This depth of experience added a great deal to the continuity of the feature. Moreover, the story and the scenario blended together more successfully than many other productions which preceded it.

Several earlier films used the reviving of criminals sentenced to death as the theme for their action; *The Surgeon's Experiment* (1914) is just one example which closely paralleled *The Devil to Pay.*

DR. JEKYLL AND MR. HYDE

Release: 1920, Paramount Pictures Corp.
Description: Silent, 103 minutes
Classification: SF
References: No. 1, p. 119; No. 7, p. 45; No. 14, p. 132; No. 23, p. 370, 371, 442, 451, 471; No. 26, p. 31; No. 45, p. 24; No. 47, p. 104, 127, 150, 220; No. 49, p. 85-87; No. 50, p. 106; BIO, Vol. 43, No. 710, p. 50, 51; FAN, No. 2, p. 15, 16; LC, LP14921; MPW, Vol. 44, p. 239, 300, 599, 1672; NYR, 3-29-20, Vol. 18, No. 1; PHO, July, 1920, p. 107; SCL, 3-18-20; STR, No. 18, p. 44-47

Credits

Producer .... Famous Players Lasky Corp.
Associate Producer .... Adolph Zukor
Director .... John S. Robertson
Screenplay .... Clara S. Beranger
Camera .... Karl Struss
Cinematographer .... Roy Overbough

Cast

Dr. Jekyll/Mr. Hyde .... John Barrymore
Millicent Carew .... Martha Mansfield
Sir George Carew .... Brandon Hurst
Dr. Richard Lanyon .... Charles Lane
John Utterson .... J. Malcolm Dunn
Edward Enfield .... Cecil Clovelly
Therese .... Nita Naldi
Poole .... George Stevens
Servant .... Louis Wolheim

The Strange Case of Dr. Jekyll and Mr. Hyde, by Robert Louis Stevenson (published in 1888), had been the basis for four previous American SF film attempts. The attempt by Selig Polyscope Company in 1908 was the first of the four based on Stevenson's novel. It was presented in a play format with four different *acts*, and as a result the continuity of the effort was impaired by these various segmented parts of the feature. The next *Dr. Jekyll and Mr. Hyde* was released by Thanhouser in 1912 and starred James Cruze as the Jekyll/Hyde character. This version attempted to follow the book very closely and resulted in an extremely entertaining film and brought the realism to the screen that had been lacking in the 1908 version. However, neither of these productions showed the transformation of Mr. Hyde back into Dr. Jekyll upon his death.

The 1913 *Dr. Jekyll and Mr. Hyde*, by Independent Moving Picture Company, featured King Baggot as the infamous Dr. Jekyll. An elaborate makeup system was used to create the character of Hyde. This movie however attempted too many alterations of the original novel, a mistake which became all too apparent on the screen. However, it did end with Dr. Lanyon finding the hideous Mr. Hyde dead in the laboratory, and the audience actually glimpses the change from Hyde to Jekyll as he dies. He covers the body with a cloak thus preventing the police and Alice from seeing that the villain was really Dr. Jekyll. Instead, he offers the explanation that Mr. Hyde had killed Dr. Jekyll and, furthermore, that Jekyll was a noble martyr to medical science.

John Barrymore realistically portrayed the sinister character of Mr. Hyde in Paramount's version of *Dr. Jekyll and Mr. Hyde* (1920).

Sir George Carew (Brandon Hurst) provides the impetus for Mr. Hyde's evil and wicked ways.

The 1914 *Dr. Jekyll and Mr. Hyde*, produced by Starlight, was a poor attempt to make the novel into a comedy. The film was so poor in fact that it was only shown twice before it was withdrawn from the market.

This 1920 version, produced by Paramount, has become a classic reproduction of the Robert Louis Stevenson novel. John Barrymore's characterization of Dr. Jekyll/Mr. Hyde stands as one of the most creative achievements of his illustrious acting career. His pantomime and facial expressions during the film add seriousness and a sense of deprivation to the plight of Dr. Jekyll, as well as a sense of savage ruthlessness to the character of Hyde.

The film is set in the 19th century during the time period in which Stevenson had originally written the novel. Its attempt to depict the grand and debonaire mood in England at this time (about the turn of the century) adds an air of realism to the film even before the action begins. The screenplay was written by Clara S. Beranger, and is a combination of Stevenson's work and a play by Mansfield which was written in 1897. Beranger went one step further, however, by using a character from Oscar Wilde's *The Picture of Dorian Gray*, the sinister Lord Henry, who, in the film, is Sir George Carew, Jekyll's evil mentor. As can be seen early in this film, it is Carew who suggests after dinner that every man has two selves and that temptation must be yielded to in order to be removed from one's constant thought. He urges Jekyll to continue with his experimentation with human cells, an experiment which will prove to be the bane of Jekyll's creative work.

As the movie opens, Dr. Henry Jekyll, a philanthropist physician, is visiting the St. Anthony Hospital, a place where he is well known for his work with charity cases. Dr. Jekyll's friend, Dr. Richard Lanyon, has just discovered that Dr. Jekyll has been conducting experiments on human cells, and even with human beings. Later at Jekyll's house, he protests this practice, but the pair is suddenly interrupted when Dr. Jekyll's servant announces that it is time for him to visit the clinic, followed by dinner at the home of Sir George Carew. It seems that Millicent Carew, the young attractive daughter of Sir George, has been enamored of Dr. Jekyll for many months, and the dinner is her ploy to gain his attention and reciprocal affection. She succeeds admirably in this task and, in time, she and Jekyll become engaged.

Meanwhile, Jekyll, with prodding from Sir George, continues to experiment with human beings (despite Lanyon's strong objections), attempting to eliminate the evil in mankind. After many months of labor, he is finally successful in producing a mixture which he believes will separate the good and evil. At first he is reluctant, however, to experiment with the strange mixture, but one evening Sir George and a group of friends lure him to a debased music hall where he finds himself attracted by a dancer named Therese. After this incident, during which Jekyll manages to restrain his temptations to become involved with the dancer, he feels that the power of good and evil in each man is too strong to fight together. Therefore, he decides to use the elixir to separate the two forces, producing two characters--one good and one evil. He even decides he will refer to this evil side as Mr. Hyde.

Dr. Jekyll takes a minuscule sip of the powerful mixture. The fluid immediately takes effect, causing convulsive movement in his arms and legs; his vision blurs, and his head spins. He now realizes that he is no longer himself, but rather has undergone the transformation to the evil Mr. Hyde. As he looks in the mirror, the full realization of the grotesqueness of his evil side jars him back to reality. Quickly, and with some degree of panic, he mixes the compound which will return him to his true self. After this he instructs his servant that a "Mr. Hyde may frequent the house from time to time," and further that he "should have complete liberty to go wherever he wishes on the premises." The servant is puzzled by the need for such a request, but still abides by his wish.

The story continues with Mr. Hyde going out frequently to the poorest quarters of London, becoming involved with Therese until he finally so degrades her that she becomes a poor miserable wreck which he then casts aside, leaving her to die in the gutter. During this time, Dr. Jekyll becomes more deeply involved with Millicent and they make plans for marriage. However, he realizes that unless he can rid himself of Mr. Hyde, this marriage is impossible. Unfortunately, he finds Hyde is beginning to dominate his personality. Even more amazingly, the transformations from Jekyll to Hyde now take place without the fluid's injection. He finds himself needing greater quantities of the antidote to return to his former self.

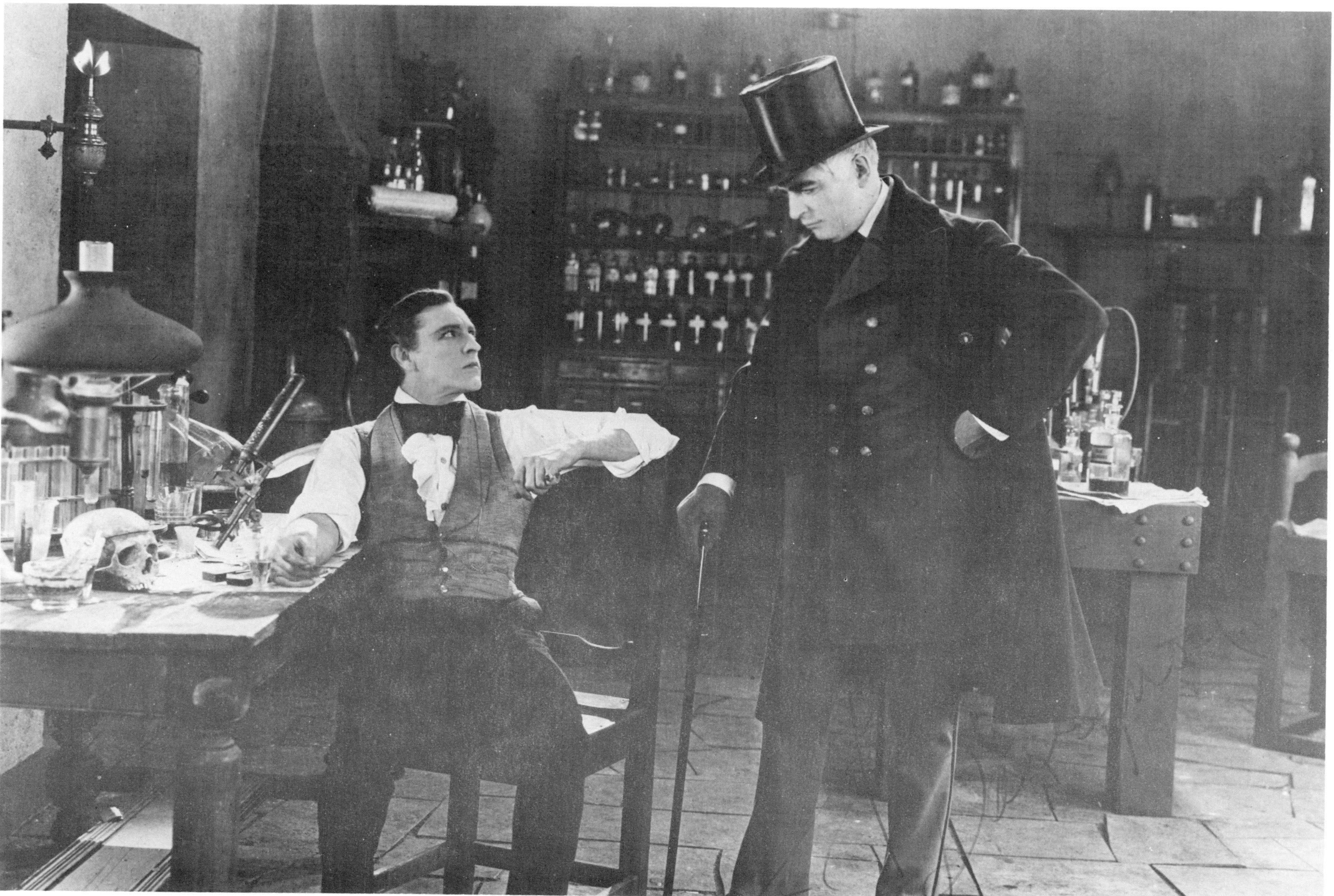

Dr. Jekyll (John Barrymore) relates the nature of his experiments with human cells to Dr. Lanyon (Charles Lane).

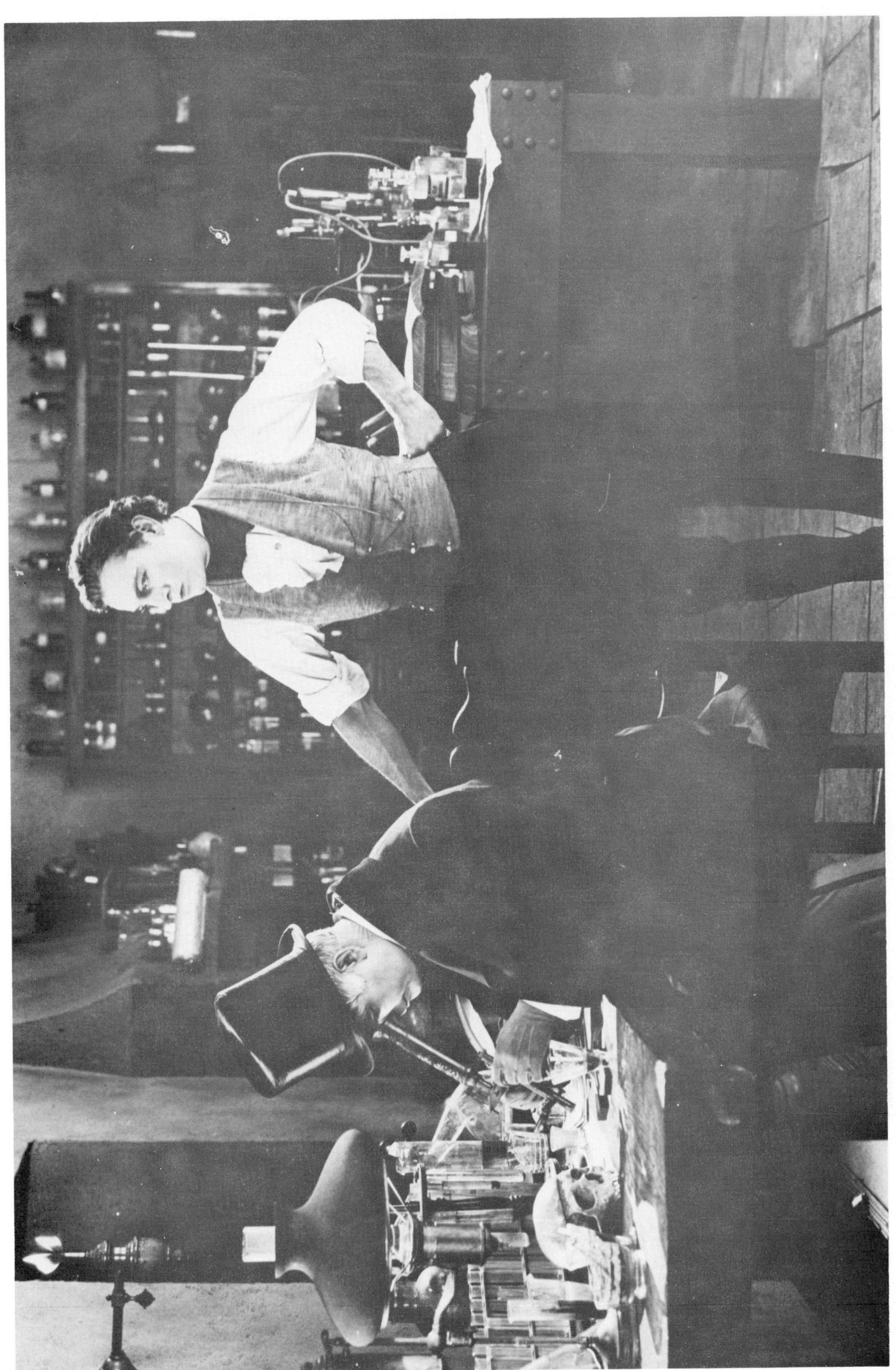

Dr. Lanyon examines the evidence of Jekyll's research in the laboratory.

Converted from the brilliant Dr. Jekyll into the hideous Mr. Hyde, the creature frequents the lower side of London to participate in the night life of the music halls.

Finally, he realizes that the only escape from the hideous Hyde is to mix a poison which will end the dual personality. He locks himself in his laboratory while Dr. Lanyon and Millicent plead for him to open the door. He quickly mixes the poison, but as he does so he begins to transform into Hyde. At first, Hyde's personality will not allow him to take the poison, but as Millicent gains entrance to the room and Hyde tries to kill her, something inside the tormented mind of Jekyll/Hyde reaches out for the poison and it is quickly consumed. Falling to the floor, he looks up and gazes into Millicent's eyes as if to plead for forgiveness. At the same time, his body begins to transform from Hyde back into Jekyll. Millicent is startled by this transformtion from one human body into another and faints as Jekyll begins to replace Hyde. Dr. Lanyon, who had suspected the secret of Jekyll's dual personality for sometime, is equally horrified by the events which he has witnessed. He quickly recovers sufficiently to place his cloak on the body, hiding it from further view. He then revives Millicent and they both vow that Dr. Jekyll's name will not be soiled. Thus, they report to the authorities that the hideous Hyde has killed Dr. Jekyll and escaped into the gutters of lower London.

John Barrymore's performance in this film was heralded by the critics:

> "John Barrymore's conception of Dr. Jekyll adds a romantic combination of youth and picturesque personality not suggested by Stevenson. Wearing the ruffled shirt, sweeping cloak and bell shaped hat of early Victorian times he has more the air of a gay young blade than that of a studious and deep thinking scientist. The classic contour of his face and the grace of his movements recall a member of his own profession . . . As Hyde, the actor is the incarnation of mental and physical deformity. Deprived of the blood curdling effect achieved by Richard Mansfield with the fiendish tones of his voice, Mr. Barrymore justifies the terrible repulsiveness of the character by the truth and power of his impersonation. It is worthy to rank along side the Mephistopheles of Harry Irving and The Bertuccio of Edwin Booth. The screen has never before known such great acting."
>
> *Moving Picture World*, 4-10-20, p. 239

DR. JEKYLL AND MR. HYDE

Release: 1920, Arrow
Description: Silent
Classification: SF-C
References: No. 14, p. 132; No. 50, p. 106; MPW, Vol. 44, p. 1672; FAM, Vol. 34, p. 55

Cast

Dr. Jekyll/Mr. Hyde .... Hank Mann

Starlight attempted in 1914 to make a comedy version of *Dr. Jekyll and Mr. Hyde*. Needless to say, they failed miserably. Arrow's efforts in 1920 were equally dismal. In fact, this attempt was only shown three times before the audiences' reactions forced them to permanently withdraw the film from the theaters. A factor which I'm sure highlighted this failure was the sudden appearance of three versions of the Stevenson book in 1920. The other two endeavors were vastly superior to the Arrow offering.

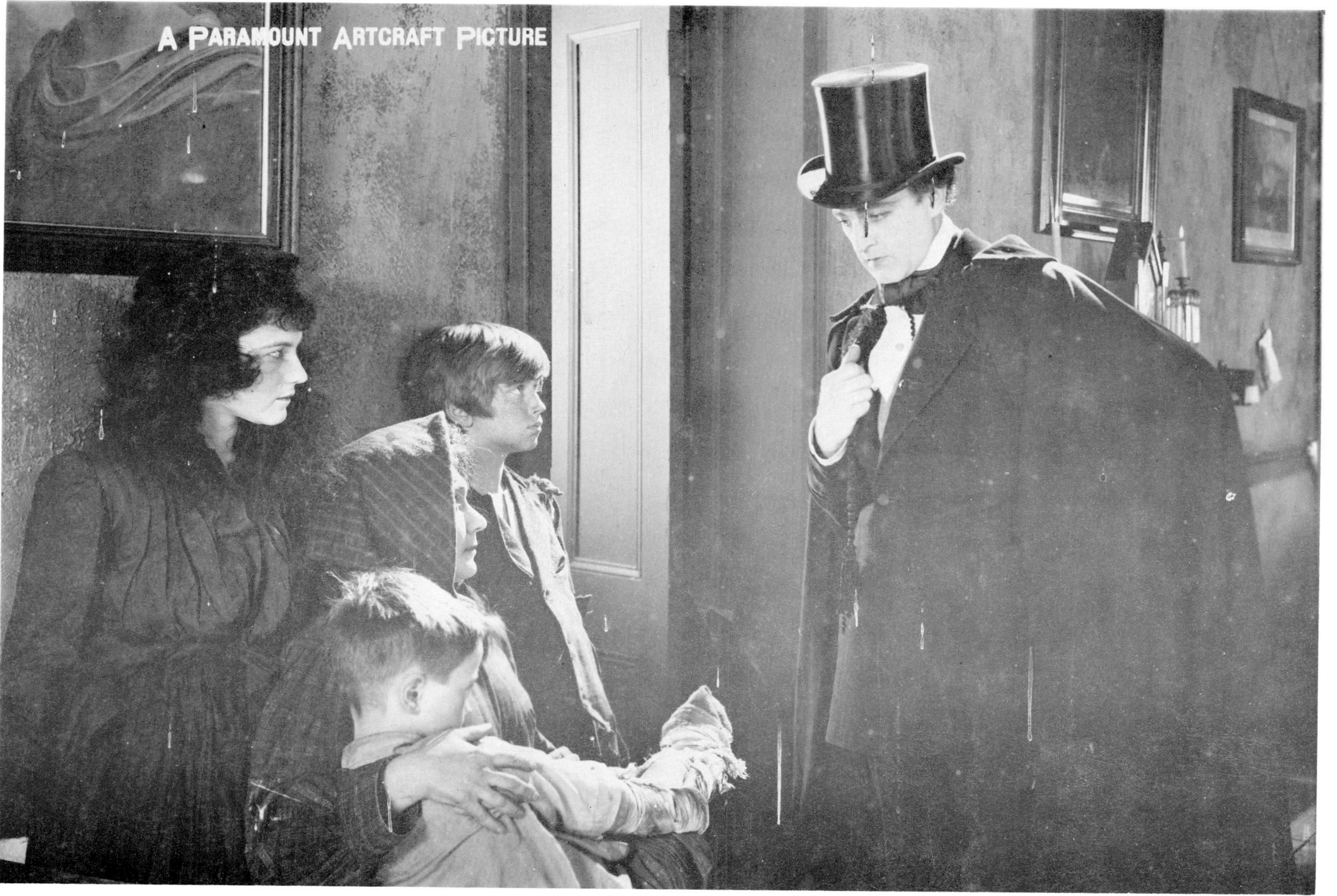

Dr. Jekyll's experiments leave little time for his former medical practices.

DR. JEKYLL AND MR. HYDE

Release: 1920, Pioneer Film Corp.
Description: Silent, 40 minutes
Classification: SF
References: No. 14, p. 132; No. 22, p. 41; No. 49, p. 88, 89; No. 50, p. 106; FAN, No. 2, p. 15; LC, LU15033; MPW, Vol. 44, p. 599; PHO, July, 1920, p. 107

Credits

Producer .... Louis Mayer

Cast

Dr. Jekyll/Mr. Hyde .... Sheldon Lewis
Dr. Lanyon .... Alexander Shannon
Mrs. Lanyon .... Dora Mills Adams
Bernice Lanyon .... Gladys Field
Edward Utterson .... Harold Forshay
Danvers Carew .... Leslie Austin

The Pioneer version of *Dr. Jekyll and Mr. Hyde* was well received by the viewing public despite the poor production quality. Louis Mayer, in order to avoid a copyright infringement claim by Paramount and Adolph Zukor, carefully altered the Robert Louis Stevenson story by placing the action in contemporary New York City. Additionally, they made the character of Mr. Hyde a figment of Dr. Jekyll's dream world from which he awakens at the end of the feature. After Dr. Jekyll's horrible nightmare, he vows never to return to his research of attempting to separate good and evil. This would have been a unique twist on the original if the production had not been so cheaply done and technically poor. The claim has been made that this poor quality and insufficient funding of the venture were the reasons the director failed to add his name to the published credits.

In spite of the above, the acting was well above the average for films of this era. Unfortunately, it could not compare with the Paramount version of 1920 which starred John Barrymore. Sheldon Lewis played Dr. Jekyll and Mr. Hyde in the Pioneer issue. His transition into Hyde's character produced a hideous creature labeled "an apostle of hell." This depiction resembled a vampirish type creature, dressed in tattered inexpensive cutaway, with long protruding fangs, dark bushy hair, and a disheveled top hat. Obviously this makeup enabled Lewis to portray the ghoul he was intended to be, a role which had striking similarity to his earlier portrayals of the Clutching Hand in *The Exploits of Elaine.* Lewis also created the villainous characters in *The Iron Claw* (1916) and *The Hidden Hand* (1917). He went on to duplicate his role of Dr. Jekyll/Mr. Hyde in a sound *short* version in 1929.

> "The Pioneer version of Robert Louis Stevenson's great story of man's dual nature, *Dr. Jekyll and Mr. Hyde*, shows that Sheldon Lewis has made a careful and intelligent study of his dual role. In his portrayal there is displayed an ability to get at the essence of nobility in Jekyll quite as well as the hideous perversion of Hyde. Most emotional actors are fascinated by the idea of interpreting the tragic side of human nature, even in its lowest manifestations, but they are apt to carry it too far for these times. Keenest appreciation of tragic roles is apt to come from those who have tragedy in their hearts. Hence an actor who carries his interpretation beyond the needs of contrast into an overdose of the hideous is liable to revolt his audience. The wisest thing Sheldon Lewis has done is to attempt to strike a balance."
>
> *Moving Picture World*, Vol. 44, p. 599

THE EMPIRE OF DIAMONDS

Release: 1920, Pathe
Description: Silent, 6000 feet
Classification: SF-A
References: No. 14, p. 146, 147; No. 50, p. 122; BIO, Vol. 46, p. 65; MPN, Vol. 23, p. 256

Credits

Producer .... Leonce Perret
Director .... Leonce Perret
Screenplay .... Leonce Perret

Cast

Matthew Versigny .... Robert Elliott
Marguerite Versigny .... Lucy Fox
Paul Bernac .... Henry G. Sell
Arthur Graves .... Leon Mathot
Trazi d'Aricola .... Jacques Volnys
Andre Zarnoff .... L. Morlas
Baron de Lambri .... M. Mailly
Esther Taylor .... Ruth Hunter

The Empire of Diamonds reactivates an old SF theme which appeared in the early 1900's: the creation of diamonds by artificial means.

Two ingenious scientists, Andre Zarnoff and Baron de Lambri, have created a unique process for producing artificial diamonds. During the past two years this pair of clever crooks has been distributing the stones as though they were genuine diamonds.

During this same time, the pair has been relentlessly pursued by the famous French detective, Matthew Versigny, accompanied by his sister Marguerite, and his fiancee Esther Taylor. The trio has traveled thousands of miles, crossed two continents, and the Atlantic Ocean but seems to have finally caught up with the manufacturers of these fake stones in Paris. As they get even closer to the Baron and Zarnoff, the chase leads them through some very scenic and historic French sites: the Champs Elysee, the Arc de Triomphe de l'Etoile, the Eiffel Tower, and the Quai Notre Dame.

The scenery is probably the best part of the feature as the plot wears very thin after the first reel. There are, however, some excellent stunts which occur at the various famous sites. A frightening scene atop the Quai Notre Dame is especially suspenseful as the villain plummets 80 feet to the pavement below.

> "From a production standpoint, *The Empire of Diamonds* is one of the best pictures we have ever seen. Excluding the story, which is one of the average mystery variety, the feature is a combination of wonderful shots which begin in London, take in Paris and its suburbs and then jump to Monte Carlo."
>
> *Motion Picture News,* 12-25-20, p. 26

THE FLAMING DISK

Release: 1920, Universal Film Manufacturing Co.
Description: Silent, 18 episode serial, each episode approximately 2000 feet
Classification: SF
References: No. 5, p. 72; No. 88, p. 204, 205; No. 14, p. 162; No. 31, p. 124; No. 50, p. 141; MPW, Vol. 46, p. 392

Credits

Producer .... Great Western Producing Co.
Director .... Arthur Henry Gooden and Jerry Ash

Credits

Producer .... Great Western Producing Co.
Director .... Robert F. Hill
Screenplay .... Arthur Henry Gooden and Jerry Ash

Cast

Professor Wade .... Lee Kohlmar
Helen .... Louise Lorraine
Rodney Stanton .... Roy Watson
Elmo Gray .... Elmo Lincoln
Jim Gray .... Elmo Lincoln
Briggs .... Fred Hamar
Stanley W. Barrows .... George Williams
Bat .... Monte Montague
Con .... Jenks Harris

Chapters 1-18 of *The Flaming Disk*

Chapter 1: The Rails of Death
References: LC, LP15580
Chapter 2: The Span of Life
References: LC, LP15605
Chapter 3: The Perilous Leap
References: LC, LP15655
Chapter 4: Fires of Hate
References: LC, LP15685
Chapter 5: The Vanishing Floor
References: LC, LP15714
Chapter 6: The Pool of Mystery
References: LC, LP15742
Chapter 7: The Circle of Fire
References: LC, LP15770
Chapter 8: Through Walls of Steel
References: LC, LP15802

Chapter 9: The Floating Mine
References: LC, LP15822
Chapter 10: Spiked Death
References: LC, LP15841
Chapter 11: The Dynamite Trail
References: LC, LP15871
Chapter 12: The Tunnel of Flames
References: LC, LP15915
Chapter 13: Caged In
References: LC, LP15940
Chapter 14: The Purple Rays
References: LC, LP15966
Chapter 15: Poisoned Waters
References: LC, LP15992
Chapter 16: Running Wild
References: LC, LP16008
Chapter 17: Rails of Destruction
References: LC, LP16027
Chapter 18: The End of the Trail
References: LC, LP16043

The Flaming Disk is an imaginative SF serial which centers around the development of a very large double convex lens, a lens powerful enough to focus the sun's rays into a narrow beam which has the intensity to reduce iron and steel into vapor. The secret service is assigned to protect the ingenuous inventor who developed this incredible optical weapon. They have been instructed that, upon completion of the project, both the professor and the new weapon are to be escorted to Washington, D.C. where a special demonstration will be held. The military leaders of the country wait in the meantime with eager anticipation of this fantastic new optical defense.

As the first episode, *The Rails of Death*, begins to unfold, we find Professor Wade busily working on the experiment to perfect the optical lens—the ultimate scientific dream of harnassing the sun's energy. The professor doesn't see so much the *weapon* in his device as he does the usefulness of the intense energy from the sun as a blessing for mankind. He feels that if properly controlled, this energy could produce new compounds and alloys that would serve the industrial expansion of the country. However, he has resigned himself to serve the interests of the government in developing his device as a weapon and accepts the protection of the secret service.

Later that day, Elmo Gray, chief secret service agent, is dispatched from Washington and arrives at the Wade mansion where he is greeted by Wade and his daughter, Helen. Elmo outlines for the professor the nature of his protective duties and establishes a mild set of rules each of them must follow for their own safety, and they quietly agree. Then the professor shows Elmo to his room.

Meanwhile, some very clever crooks enter the laboratory through a rear door which they have forced open. The group is led by Rodney Stanton, an infamous and particularly evil individual. Stanton has enlisted Jim Gray, Elmo's brother, as one of his henchmen. However, as we shall later learn as the serial progresses, this has not been done with Jim's consent—he is under a powerful hypnotic state induced and controlled by Stanton. Helen hears a noise emanating from the laboratory and cautiously investigates the source. When she observes the crooks dismantling the optical lens, she rushes to summon Elmo and her father. Elmo leaps across the laboratory table, landing in the midst of the criminals, and in the process sends several of them cascading unconscious to the floor. His immense size and tremendous power soon overwhelm the fiendish villains as the others scurry through the half-open doorway to escape. Suddenly, Elmo hears a noise behind him; quickly, he turns as if he were a cat preparing to leap on his prey. But his eyes lock tight on the face of Professor Wade—the criminals were gone. As they face each other, they realize that this battle has only been a glimpse of the danger to come.

In episodes 2 through 6 Elmo continues to battle the crooks who seem to be attacking the mansion with increased frequency. Each time Elmo is about to apprehend Stanton, his efforts are diverted by his brother. Elmo is embarrassed when he realizes that his own brother is an ally of Stanton's. Because of this, he fails to report this facet of the case to his superiors. He does mention the difficulty involving his brother to Helen, telling her that he doesn't understand why his brother would be part of this gang. She attempts to comfort him, but the shame continues to nag at his every thought.

In episode seven, *Circle of Fire*, Stanton and his gang are finally successful in securing the large disk. Additionally, Stanton manages to kidnap Helen and holds her as hostage should Elmo and the other secret service agents attempt to retaliate, which, he threatens, would result in Helen's death. Stanton begins to employ the use of the weapon and wreaks havoc on nearby towns, and in particular their banks where he carefully bores through their vaults and absconds with the bank funds. Stanton's avarice is rampant and he demands a ransom from the government—or he will destroy the entire population of a large metropolitan city. The pressure on the secret service (especially on Elmo Gray) is enormous . . . they must find Stanton and the flaming disk before the deadline or millions of innocent people will perish.

In episode 17, *Rails of Destruction*, Elmo encounters his brother Jim as he engages the Stanton gang aboard a speeding locomotive. During this encounter, the spell on Jim is somehow broken . . . he awakens to find himself in Elmo's grip, and is ignorant of what he has done, where he has been, or who he has been associated with. Elmo attempts to bring him up-to-date on the mysterious events which have transpired during the past several weeks. The two then vow that they will rescue Helen and recover the flaming disk in order to clear Jim's name and save the millions of lives in jeopardy.

In chapter 18, *End of the Trail*, Stanton's hideout is finally discovered by Elmo. He and Jim manage to gain entrance and a fierce hand-to-hand battle ensues. During this struggle, Stanton inadvertedly opens a portal in the roof which exposes the disk's mirror to the radiant sunlight. The lens focuses a thin beam of this intense solar energy and it moves across the length of the room, boring a hole through the thin metal walls. Stanton swings a large axe at Elmo, which he miraculously manages to avoid. He responds with a strong right fist to the fragile jaw of Stanton, hurling him backward across the room. As he does so, his body intercepts the path of the intense sunlight: Stanton's heart is pierced by the golden beam, sending his lifeless body to the cold laboratory floor. Afterwards, Elmo, Jim, and Helen secure the disk and return to the Wade mansion where they are greeted as heroes by Professor Wade and the other secret service agents.

The Flaming Disk is truly an exciting SF adventure film. However, it sometimes lacks the continuity that earlier serials, such as *The Exploits of Elaine* (1914) and *The Hidden Hand* (1917), had obtained. The real asset of the serial has to be Elmo Lincoln, a truly outstanding actor who brought a physical presence to the screen that was unequaled for many years.

Lincoln's fame had preceeded this project when he appeared in *Tarzan and the Apes* (1918) and again in *The Romance of Tarzan* (1918). Both of these pictures resulted in his acceleration to the top of Hollywood's list of *players in demand.* His first appearance in film was in *The Birth of a Nation* (1915). It seems his enormous size attracted the attention of D. W. Griffith, who asked him to change his name from Otto Elmo Linkenhelt to Elmo Lincoln. From that time on, Griffith personally groomed Lincoln for the various parts he played. His role in *Tarzan and the Apes* was so outstanding that it was one of the first half-dozen pictures to gross over a million dollars. Needless to say, the advertisements for *The Flaming Disk* started by saying, "Elmo Lincoln, appearing in *The Flaming Disk*," in very large letters. This produced long lines outside the theaters as eager patrons waited to see the new Lincoln epic.

Additionally, Louise Lorraine, who appeared as Lincoln's costar (Helen) in *The Flaming Disk*, appeared a year later in the serial *The Adventures of Tarzan* (1921) as Jane, Tarzan's mate. This 1921 production was recut and released with sound in 1928, one of the first *talkies* released in America.

The reviewers of 1920 were caught by the excitement and aura of Elmo Lincoln as much as the audiences:

"Film fans who know and appreciate the good work of Elmo Lincoln in previous serials are going to have the time of their lives watching this new continued yarn . . . This serial is well constructed, starts a simple, interesting story and fairly pulls the spectator along by its breathless action."

Moving Picture World, Vol. 46, p. 392

THE HIDDEN CODE

Release: 1920, Pioneer Film Corp.
Description: Silent, 5000 feet
Classification: SF-F
References: No. 14, p. 220; No. 50, p. 193; LC, LU14938; LC, LU14938; MPH, Vol. 11, p. 88; MPN, Vol. 22, p. 1009; MPW, Vol. 45, p. 640

Credits

Producer .... Sulmac Production Co.
Associate Producer .... Norman Harsell
Director .... Richard Lestrange
Screenplay .... Norman Harsell
Camera .... Harry Fischbed

Cast

Grace Lamont .... Grace Davison
Eben Lamont .... Ralph Osborne
Richard Leslie .... Richard Lestrange
August Mason .... Clayton Davis

The Hidden Code, a science fiction fantasy film, starts with Grace Davison, a very comely heroine, in the act of reading a melodramatic novel entitled *The Hidden Code*. As Miss Davison reads she begins to imagine herself playing the leading role and, thus, chapter by chapter, the audience is led through this SF melodrama.

The story begins with a famous chemist, Professor Eben Lamont, having recently discovered a new explosive. As he continues to perfect and refine his process, his work is betrayed by a greedy laboratory assistant. The assistant has transmitted a portion of the results of the professor's experiments to Richard Leslie, president of a large explosives company. At first, Leslie offers Professor Lamont a handsome sum for the new explosive's formula, but the professor intends to turn over his discovery to the government. Leslie now realizes that the process is vastly superior to anything he contains in his arsenal, but there is no way to acquire the complete process for the new invention.

Professor Lamont, fearing that his new research may be in jeopardy, inscribes the formula on his daughter's shoulder. This inscription is done with special ink that is invisible to the naked eye. He gives Grace a small vial of chemicals and informs her that when her shoulder is rubbed with the mixture the formula will reappear. Even though both Grace and her father are in fear for their lives, each sets out in separate directions to try and reach the government offices where they and the precious formula will be secure.

Meanwhile, a band of criminals is conspiring to gain control of the treasured explosive process and begins to pursue the Lamonts. The gang leader is the infamous sinister Stella. One of her henchmen, August Mason, a once famous hypnotist, accidently observed the professor inscribing the formula on Grace's shoulder and takes this information to Stella. Later he tries to gain information about the formula and in the process kills Professor Lamont. He then hypnotizes Grace in order to control her mind and thus gain the formula. While Grace is in Mason's control, she encounters a young rather innocent member of the gang named Tony. Tony finds himself extremely attracted to Grace and eventually the two of them express their feelings for each other. He then aids her in her escape from Mason and helps her reach the governmental office. The formula is now secure and, as the movie ends, Tony and Grace are headed toward matrimony.

The viewer is left to wonder what will happen to Richard Leslie, the crooked explosives manufacturer; August Mason, the murderer; and Stella, leader of the gang of criminals. It is left to the audience to assume that they are captured and receive their just rewards.

The Hidden Code appears to be a very weak science fiction fantasy film. What science there is, is certainly masked by the interaction of the players. As one reviewer noted, the film appears to be a mini-serial within a film. The only difference is the continuity is lost and one gets the feeling of a syncopated type of action. Additionally, similar plots have been used at least five times during the period from 1897 to 1909, and another six times between 1910 and 1919. Little or nothing was added to make it a unique contribution. One reviewer made the following comments which clearly illustrate the poor quality of the production.

> "There is plenty of plot in this story, but if suffers from overacting and a general lack of reality. The attention is held quite firmly at times by the intensity of the melodramatic incidents, some of which contain genuine thrills, but on the whole the action is too uncertain to make a very successful production. It moves like a serial in which convincing effect has been sacrificed for the sake of melodrama."
>
> *Moving Picture World*, 7-31-20, p. 640

THE INVISIBLE RAY

Release: 1920, Frohman Amusement Corp.
Description: Silent, 15 episode serial, each episode approx. 2000 feet
Classification: SF-A
References: No. 8, p. 83, 84, 206; No. 14, p. 253; No. 50, p. 222; MPH, Vol. 10, p. 103 MPN, Vol. 22, p. 1746; MPW, Vol. 42, p. 120, 427

Credits

Producer .... Jesse J. Goldburg and Joan Film Sales Co.
Director .... Harry Pollard
Screenplay .... Guy McConnell

Cast

Jack Stone .... Jack Sherrill
Mystery .... Ruth Clifford
Jean Deaux .... Sidney Bracy
John Haldane .... Ed Davis
Crystal Gazer .... Corrine Uzzell
Gang Member .... W. H. Tooker

The Invisible Ray did not have chapter titles. In addition individual episodes were not copyrighted, and, according to the Library of Congress, the serial itself was not even copyrighted.

The Invisible Ray unfolds its adventure laden episodes by transporting the audience back through time in a cinema technique often used by producers called a flashback. The time is 15 years earlier when a young mineralogist is scouring the rocky countryside of Persia. He accidently exposes a strange new substance which seems to possess an unusual *ray* power that can have a fatal effect on humans. Luckily the mineralogist has enough time to realize the danger of this unique mineral and he hurriedly secures enough samples of the rock and places them in a sealed lead box. The box has two specially fashioned locks, each requiring a separate key to unlock it. The scientist puts one of the keys around his infant daughter's neck. (It seems his wife's recent death required that, for the first time, someone—namely his orphaned daughter—accompany him on this expedition.) The second key is sent to an old friend in the U.S., Professor Stone, a famous mineralogist in his own right. Accompanying this second key is a note which outlines the circumstances of his discovery and tells him briefly of the force it has.

The young explorer is soon convinced that he is slowly dying and dispatches his daughter back to England to live with an elderly aunt. Somehow the baby never arrives at the aunt's; instead she is put in a foundling home. Additionally, her name is, for some reason, unknown and while at the home she is known as Miss Mystery. Throughout her time here, the young girl continues to wear the key about her neck—even though she is unaware of its purpose or the danger attached to it.

As she reaches womanhood, by chance she comes in contact with Professor Stone who informs her that she is the lost daughter of his friend and further relates the story behind the key she wears.

Jack Stone, the professor's son soon becomes enamored of Mystery as the two of them listen to the professor read from a note written by Mystery's father many years ago. As we know, the note relates her father's discovery of the meteorite and the material's ability to produce rays of light energy. They now realize the seriousness of the situation the family is in. However, after several weeks of getting to know each other, Jack and Mystery seem able to only concentrate on their feelings. Then one evening, in the process of eloping, Mystery is kidnapped and taken to an underground chamber where she is tortured into giving up her key. Unfortunately for her captors, during the process of seizing her, the key fell from her neck and is back at the Stone mansion.

Jack and his friend, John Haldane, are very distraught over Mystery's disappearance and visit a star gazer who has in the past been able to foretell the future. In this instance, they ask the star gazer the whereabouts of Mystery. She responds by providing the location of the kidnappers' hideout.

Jack and John are now able to rescue Mystery. But in their attempt to escape through the myriad of underground passages, Mystery again falls into the hands of the notorious gang known as *The Crime Creators.* (Later we learn that John is a member of this gang, and his deceit continues to throw danger and peril into the path of Jack and Mystery as they search for the mysterious mineral.)

Finally, Jack is successful in rescuing Mystery from the chamber. The two visit the star gazer once more to learn what they can about Mystery's father and the secret of the powerful atomic rays, and she does indeed provide sufficient clues to lead the pair in their quest for this treasured box.

Continually, as Mystery is about to be done in by The Crime Creators, a mysterious figure named Deaux manages to arrive just in time to save her from certain death.

In the final episode, we learn that Jack Deaux is really Mystery's father. He had not died earlier, but had instead disappeared as The Crime Creators were on his trail and wanted the mysterious mineral to create a weapon to terrorize the world. Additionally, in this final chapter, it is revealed that the star gazer is Mystery's mother. She had been presumed dead during a steamship accident some 16 years before.

In any event, in the final two episodes, Jack and Mystery, with the aid of her parents, are able to overcome The Crime Creators and secure, once and for all, the atomic weapon which is contained in the secret box. It is then stored in a deep well where no man will ever be able to use its power to destroy people.

For the 1920's this serial contains a lot of scientific information and data of the future, making it an excellent entry into the science fiction productions of this period. It is our loss that there has not been more written concerning this serial, and that the reviewers sought to overlook it during its release period. This was primarily because it was an independent production, and was not in league with the major producers of the 1920's. And not being among this elite group meant it would not be afforded the opportunity to display the feature in many of the theatrical houses of the country.

To make matters worse, there is no copy of this film in existence, since it was destroyed prior to the conversion from nitrate to acetate film. From the evidence that has been gathered, however, it does appear that *The Invisible Ray* was surely one of the more noteworthy serials in the SF category of the 1920's.

THE MYSTERY MIND

Release: 1920, Pioneer Film Corp.
Description: Silent, 15 episode serial, each episode approx. 2000 feet
Classification: SF-A
References: No. 8, p. 87, 88, 208; No. 14, p. 344; No. 50, p. 324; BIO, Vol. 46, 1-13-21, p. 58, 59; LC, LU15877; MPW, Vol. 43, p. 428, 926

Credits

Producer .... Supreme Pictures
Director .... Fred W. Sittenham and William S. Davis
Screenplay .... Arthur B. Reeve and John W. Grey
Camera .... David Calcagini

Cast

Violet Bronson .... Violet MacMillian
Dr. Robert Dupont .... Dr. J. Robert Pauline
Vera Collins .... Peggy Shanor
Dr. Sutton .... Paul Panzer
Carl Canfield .... Ed Rogers
The Phantom Face .... De Sacia Saville

Chapters 1-15 of *The Mystery Mind*

Chapter 1: The Hypnotic Clue
Chapter 2: The Fires of Fury
Chapter 3: The War of Wills
Chapter 4: The Fumes of Fear
Chapter 5: Thought Waves
Chapter 6: A Halo of Help
Chapter 7: The Nether World
Chapter 8: The Mystery Mind
Chapter 9: Dual Personality
Chapter 10: Hounds of Hate
Chapter 11: The Sleepwalker
Chapter 12: The Temple of the Occult
Chapter 13: The Binding Ray
Chapter 14: The Water Cure
Chapter 15: The Gold of the Gods

This serial probably received more advanced publicity than any other serial of 1920. From June of 1920 to January 1, 1921 more than 150 advertisements appeared in *Variety*. In addition, some 40 ads during the same interval of time were placed in *Moving Picture World*, while *Bioscope* contained 18, and *Motion Picture Herald*, 16 ads. The producer's rationale for this tremendous publicity that preceded the effort was to build up the leading character played by Dr. J. Robert Pauline. Dr. Pauline, a well known hypnotist and vaudeville star, was given the title "They Mystifier of the Multitudes." He professed that hypnotism was not a black art and stressed that at least 80% of all human beings could be influenced by some form of hypnosis. Dr. Pauline further expressed the belief that one day hypnosis could be used to perform minor surgery on patients. To augment the advertising campaign by Pioneer Film Corporation, he went from one end of the country to another (literally, coast to coast) making a whistle-stop tour of the major metropolitan motion picture areas in hopes that when the film was released it would gather a tremendous following of fans who would recognize his name on the marquee.

As the first episode, *The Hypnotic Clue*, unfolds the audience soon learns that this is no ordinary serial, but one which will entice them with each episode. It begins with a flashback (a common technique for many serials) to a period 15 years earlier. Carno, a priest of the Black Band of Devil Worshippers of Orinoco (on the island of Orinoco), betrays the whereabouts of his cult's cave of hidden treasure to a young American sailor named Richard Bronson. Bronson's companion, Stuart Steel (who secretly covets Bronson's wife), seizes this opportunity to eliminate Bronson by telling the chief priest of the Devil Worshippers, Evil Eye, that he will surrender Bronson's body if he can avert the consequences for the betrayal of their secret cave. Somehow while this bartering between Steele and Evil Eye is taking place, Bronson manages to slip away and avoid his capture and certain murder by Steele and the Devil Worshippers. When Evil Eye learns of this, he becomes furious and immediately invokes all his power to turn Steele, Carno, and two other tribal members from human beings into a phantom face, a wolf, a fox, and a snake, respectively. And, upon Bronson's infant daughter Violet, he invokes the most horrible death curse ever rendered by any chief of the Devil Worshippers. With Bronson gone, his young daughter is left alone. A friend, Dr. Sutton, takes her in and raises the girl as though she were his own daughter.

Fifteen years later, Violet Bronson has matured into a beautiful young woman. Unaware of the curse that lies in her past and now hangs heavy over her head, she proceeds to make plans to go away to school. But Dr. Sutton, who is aware of the curse, must relate to her the nature of this curse and what it holds for her future. At the same time, four American criminals known as Phantom Face, Carl Canfield, Vera Collins, and Reynard appear. They are the reincarnation of Evil Eye's transmuted creatures. They begin to set forth an evil and sinister plan which will work the secret of the cave's treasure from Violet's lips and then they will murder her as prescribed by Evil Eye, the ancient priest of the Devil Worshippers.

A young physician and hypnotist, Dr. Robert Dupont, calls upon the Sutton mansion. The beauty of Violet immediately attracts his attention, and it isn't long before they fall in love. Dr. Dupont vows to aid her in fighting the evil powers. He devises a plan by which he will fully and regularly hypnotize Violet and bring out of her subconscious the seeds of the past which will lead them to the secret cave of treasure.

In this first episode, Violet also suffers an injury and Dr. Dupont hypnotizes her and performs minor surgery without the use of any anesthetic, and yet, Violet feels no pain at all (a truly prognostic medical event for 1920).

In episodes two through ten, Dr. Dupont and Violet continually trace down the clues, one by one, which eventually lead them to the cave. Each step of the way they are pursued and attacked by the four avengers of the Devil Worshippers.

In chapters 10 through 12, they actually uncover the entrance to the cave and begin to find a collection of unusual paraphernalia which lies deep within the cave. Chapter 12, entitled *The Temple of the Occult*, is a visionary delight of ornaments and artifacts dating back to the time of the ancient Babylonia. A sect of the Babylonian culture believed in devil worship and practiced it as an ardent religion. Within the cave, Dr. Dupont and Violet discover a strange type of weapon as well, which, when exposed to the sun, seems to emit a strong ray of light. This ray has the power to fuse metals and vaporize rocks. And it is this device which enables them to uncover the hidden chamber of the Temple of the Occult—a chamber which is a cornucopia of jewels, gold, and artifacts. It also helps them destroy their four ardent pursuers.

In the final episode, *The Gold of the Gods*, Violet and Dupont are seen rejoicing in their new found wealth and the happiness which surely awaits them as they again profess their love for each other.

The depiction of hypnotism far outsteps its conceived use during the period in which this film was released. There is even a suggestion in chapter five of telepathy between Violet and Dr. Dupont. These ideas and their portrayal make *The Mystery Mind* a unique science fiction entry.

THE SCREAMING SHADOW

Release: 1920, Hallmark Pictures Corp.
Description: Silent, 15 episode serial, each episode approx. 2000 feet
Classification: SF-A
References: No. 8, p. 83, 210, 211; No. 14, p. 417, 418; No. 50, p. 442; MPH, Vol. 10, p. 56; MPW, Vol. 43, p. 30, 31, 45, 82

Credits

Producer .... Hallmark
Director .... Duke Worne
Screenplay .... J. Grubb Alexander and Harvey Gates

Cast

John Rand .... Ben Wilson
Mary Landers .... Neva Gerber
J. W. Russell .... Howard Crampton
Jake Williams .... William Dyer
Harry Malone .... William Carroll
Fred Wilson .... Fred Gamble
Baron Velska .... Joseph Girard
Nadia .... Frances Terry
Young Maiden .... Pancy Porter
Young Maiden .... Claire Mille
Butler .... Joseph Manning

Chapters 1-15 of *The Screaming Shadow*

Chapter 1: A Cry in the Dark
References: LC, LP14674
Chapter 2: The Virgin of Death
References: LC, LP14675
Chapter 3: The Fang of the Beast
References: LC, LP14690
Chapter 4: The Black Seven
References: LC, LP14845

Chapter 5: The Vapor of Death
References: LC, LP14842
Chapter 6: The Hidden Menace
References: LC, LP14915
Chapter 7: Into the Depths
References: LC, LP14940
Chapter 8: The White Terror
References: LC, LP15116
Chapter 9: The Sleeping Death
References: LC, LP15008
Chapter 10: The Prey of Mong
References: LC, LP15031
Chapter 11: Liquid Fire
References: LC, LP15055
Chapter 12: Cold Steel
References: LC, LP15165
Chapter 13: The Fourth Symbol
References: LC, LP15117
Chapter 14: Entombed Alive
References: LC, LP15141
Chapter 15: Unmasked
References: LC, LP15166

The Screaming Shadow is based upon the theory that transplantation of animal glands into the human body can provide the recipient with eternal youth. It seems about the time that Alexander and Gates were creating the screenplay, the newspapers were publishing details of a prisoner who was being held in San Quentin Prison. He had undergone an experimental operation to transplant a goat's gland into his body. Previous to this experiment the prisoner had been dull and lacked the aggressive qualities normally attributed to the hardened criminal, while after the patient had sufficiently recovered from the experimental surgery, he began to take on new characteristics--becoming more aggressive and having a great deal more vigor than had been previously noted during his years of incarceration. This medical phenomenon--the transplantation of animal glands into the human body--was the basis for *The Screaming Shadow* serial.

As the action begins, John Rand, a famous scientist and archeologist, has uncovered a tribe in the remote jungles of Africa that performs a ritual using monkey's glands inserted into a liquid mixture and then consumed orally. Somehow this nauseating concoction provides them with immunities to various diseases and seems to cause increased longevity.

Upon returning to the U. S., Professor Rand begins a series of experiments which will eventually allow him to test the theory of whether man's life can be prolonged by the insertion of various glands transplanted from other primates. Rand's experiments center on using glands coming from orangutans, as their longevity seems to be the source of the strange power of the African tribe he had observed.

While on his mission, it seems Rand had also learned that other strangers had recently visited the African tribe—a group of physicians from a country called Burgonia. As Rand begins the serious work of screening the animals and providing proper medical testing procedures, he decides to investigate the use of the knowledge that the Burgonians had taken back to their own country in hopes of advancing his research.

In episodes two through 14, Rand and Mary Landers, a young newspaper woman and heiress to millions of dollars, begin to investigate the mysterious experiments being conducted by Baron Velska, prime minister of Burgonia. It seems that Velska has been experimenting with human beings and animals, not following the proper research techniques that would require extensive animal research before the transfer of animal glands to humans could be carried out. The Baron has elected instead to jump dangerously ahead and use the humans as guinea pigs. During these episodes, Rand and Landers encounter Nadia, the high priestess of the *virgins of eternal youth*. These young women seem to be the successful byproducts of Baron Velska's gruesome experiments. Each of them remains a radiant young beauty and it is theorized that they will stay that way for the rest of their lives.

Meanwhile, J. R. Russell, millionaire and head of the mysterious Eternal Light syndicate, has also uncovered the youth experiments which are transpiring in Velska's laboratory. Russell's insatiable desire to prolong his own life makes him a staunch ally of the Baron. Russell and several of his trusted employees, Jake Williams, Harry Malone, and Fred Wilson, continually try to thwart John and Mary's efforts in securing the secret of Baron Velska's experiments. Eventually, John and Mary succeed in exposing the hideous experiments and destroy the Baron's experimental laboratory.

While *The Screaming Shadow* is an exciting serial and certainly another tribute to the Wilson/Gerber duo, it lacks the intrigue and scientific paraphernalia that had been exhibited in earlier works. It almost appears that the producer of the feature skimped on the scenery and the creation of the screenplay.

The idea of eternal youth is not a new one; obviously it has existed for eons of time. The most lavish expedition ever mounted to acquire eternal youth probably can be attributed to Ponce de Leon, who, in 1513, sought the Fountain of Youth within the flowered gardens of Florida. Many of the early films from 1897 to 1909 dealt with the issue of eternal youth, or turning back time to one's youth. This concept will probably always be a viable plot as everyone feels the need to recapture life and youth.

The Screaming Shadow appears to be a very weak SF adventure film, although it does have merit in the medical and scientific detail to which the glandular transplantations were to take place. Moreover, Wilson and Gerber continued to produce exciting serials with science fiction interest.

TERROR ISLAND

Release: 1920, Paramount Pictures Corp.
Description: Silent, 5813 feet
Classification: SF-A
References: No. 1, p. 137; No. 50, p. 484; BIO, Vol. 44, No. 717, p. 41, 42; LC, LP14920; MPH, Vol. 10, p. 70; MPN, Vol. 21, p. 4069, MPW, Vol. 42, p. 676; Vol. 44, p. 861; VAW, 4-30-20, p. 43

Credits

Producer .... Famous—Lasky Players
Director .... James Cruze
Screenplay .... John W. Grew, Arthur B. Reeve, and Walter Woods
Camera .... William Marshall

Cast

Harry Harper .... Houdini
Starkey .... Jack Brammall
Beverly West .... Lila Lee
Stella Mordaunt .... Rosemary Theby
Job Mordaunt .... Wilton Taylor

An attempt is made to destroy the model of Harry Harper's (Houdini) fantastic submersible in *Terror Island* (1920).

Guy Mordaunt .... Eugene Pallette
Captain Black .... Edward Brady
Chief Bakaida .... Frank Bonner
First Officer Murphy .... Captain Ted E. Duncan
Mr. West .... Fred Turner

Terror Island was Houdini's third appearance on the silver screen. His first, entitled *The Master Mystery* (1919) and produced by Octagon Films, displayed his remarkable ability to escape near impossible situations. The next two films he made for Paramount release: *The Grim Game* (1919) and *Terror Island* (1920). They also sought to display the amazing abilities which Houdini possessed in the art of escape. While *Grim Game* was not an overwhelming success at the box office, it did indicate that a large portion of the population wished to see Houdini's escape tricks, even if they were less convincing on the screen than in his live performances on stage. Thus, *Terror Island* was designed especially to showcase his unique escape abilities and magical talents.

In the previous adventures, Houdini had portrayed a more villainous type of character, whereas in this production he is clearly the hero. The original title for this work was *Salvage*, but the powers of Paramount felt it did not indicate enough mystery and gruesomeness to the public; thus, the reason for renaming it *Terror Island.* The screenplay, which was a combination of the work of John Grew, Arthur Reeves, and Walter Woods, gave an air of reminiscence to the Craig Kennedy type serials in that the character Houdini played, Harry Harper, was depicted as a scientific type detective and inventor.

The film was not an inexpensive production, with the cost of the actual filming, script, and rewrites of the scenarios running about $14,000, and that figure did not include any salaries to the principal players. It is estimated that the total cost of the film was something on the order of $600,000 to complete, making it a very expensive undertaking indeed for 1920. To make matters worse box office receipts indicate that Paramount barely broke even on the venture. Afterwards the decision was made by the studio that they would not subsidize or release any more of the Houdini pictures.

As the story begins, we find Harry Harper, a young philanthropist and successful scientific detective, in his laboratory experimenting with a new device—a deep sea submersible craft. Harry believes that he can invent a craft to go far below the depths submarines could currently descend.

Later that afternoon, Harry intercepts a wireless report concerning the news of a vessel, *The Hawk*, being sunk by a German u-boat very near a South Sea island. While this information doesn't have any particular meaning to Harry at the moment, it is somehow subconsciously retained in the depths of his mind and (as we will later see) will play an integral part in Harry's struggle for survival.

From time to time Harry has been known about town as an intelligent scientific detective who can take the most difficult of circumstances and find a resolution to nearly any situation. It is for that precise reason that young beautiful Beverly West finds herself at his doorstep.

As she enters the Harper mansion she relates to Harry a fantastic tale about her father, who is being held captive on a South Sea island by a native chief. She then shows him a letter from her father indicating that he has been able to stall the chief from killing him only because he has promised to deliver as a sacred pearl which he gave to his daughter many years ago. Beverly pleads with Harry to take her to the South Sea island and aid in her father's rescue.

Suddenly a thought flashes through Harry's mind: the South Sea island on which Beverly's father is being held prisoner is only a few miles from the point at which *The Hawk* was sunk by a German u-boat. Harry now recalls a newspaper report that *The Hawk* had a treasure of diamonds aboard. Immediately, he seizes this opportunity to test his new submersible vessel and at the same time aid Beverly West in securing her father's release. He makes the necessary arrangements and the two of them are off in his submersible craft to the island for an adventure which neither of them will soon forget.

There is one minor detail Beverly forgot to mention to Harry: The Mordaunts—Stella, Job, and Guy (Job is Beverly's uncle, Guy her cousin, and Stella is Guy's wife.)—have received a letter from Beverly's father pleading for their help, in which he also mentioned the sacred pearl Beverly possesses.

The Mordaunts scheme and plan to steal the pearl from Beverly, and when she manages to talk Harry into taking her to the South Sea island, they naturally have no choice but to pursue the pair. While on the voyage, the three scheming relatives try every unscrupulous trick to steal the pearl and stop their mission. Job even attempts to damage the submersible craft that Harry had spent hours constructing. Luckily, he discovers the damage and repairs it just before they are ready to submerge.

When the Mordaunt crew lands on the island, Stella and Guy, who had somehow during the trip been able to steal the precious stone, agree that Stella should pose as Beverly and give the treasured pearl to the chief. She does so and the chief responds by giving her the booty from a ship that had recently sunk near a reef off their island. In addition, the cheif immediately releases West. But then Stella is somewhat dismayed as the chief begins to stare at her as though she were his next victim. The chief and his natives do, in fact, seize her and decide that she should be sacrificed in place of West. Within moments, Beverly and Harry arrive and, unaware of the turn of events, claim that she is West's daughter. The chief, at first confused, quickly makes the decision to release Stella and capture instead Beverly. She is then tied to a stake and readied for the sacrifice.

Naturally, Harry doesn't just stand around watching all this. He attempts to repel the natives' efforts to capture Beverly, but is quickly overcome and bound with chains and large hemp ropes. Once bound, Harry is thrust into a safe which is locked and cast into the deep murky waters off the island's reef (The safe was conveniently salvaged from the sunken ship—no doubt just in time for this great escape scene!). The audience is now led to believe that Harry is surely going to die. But we all know that Harry not only possesses great physical strength, but also has strange mystical powers. Needless to say he employs all his resources to escape the fate which he has been dealt.

Upon his escape, he returns to the island's shore and quickly hurries to the site where Beverly is about to be sacrificed. The natives and their chief are panicked by his presence and think he must certainly be a ghost returned from the *Isle of Death*. They scurry from the sacrificial altar in utter horror. Harry thus saves Beverly and they return to their submersible craft.

As they reach the craft, Harry notices a small explosion near the reef. He realizes there must be some divers below the surface near what Harry determines is the site of the sunken *Hawk*. As Harry and Beverly carefully maneuver the vessel to the sight where *The Hawk* is sunk, he observes two divers on the ocean floor placing a large metal box into a basket which is about to be hauled to the water's surface. His craft dives to the level of the divers and using a special type of underwater gear, he exits through a pressure chamber in the craft and battles the divers. They successfully retrieve the diamond treasure, but the Mordaunts are not through; they retaliate by capturing West again and then hold him as ransom for the treasure. As part of the deal, they agree to meet Harry and Beverly on the south beach of the island.

The evil Mordaunts arrive first and are immediately forced into battle with the natives who are still upset by Harry's reappearance and Beverly's escape. During this fierce fight, Job is fatally slain. Beverly and Harry arrive in the midst of the melee. Of course, his sudden reappearance seems to change the fighting mood of the natives, who cautiously back away still believing that he is a demon returned from the dead. This shock allows he and Beverly an opportunity to free West. Carefully, they make their way back to the submarine, but as they reach the shore Harry sees his submarine making its way out to sea. Evidently, Stella and Guy had slipped aboard while the others were battling the natives' attack. Harry hopes his valiant crew member, Starkey, will manage to overcome the pair and return to the shore to rescue them all. Then he spies a longboat that the Mordaunts must have used to reach the shore. Quickly, he and the Wests board the boat and Harry, using his great physical strength, manages to overtake the submarine.

He leaps over the side and enters the craft through a secret underwater door. Meanwhile, Stella has shot and wounded Starkey which causes the ship to move erratically. Harry's entrance goes undetected and he cautiously creeps forward and surprises Guy and Stella. They then battle for the ship. During the struggle, Guy accidently shoots and kills Stella. He also strikes Harry with a large steel wrench and is about to finish the job when he is shot by Starkey, who then helps Harry regain consciousness and the pair return to the longboat and rescue Beverly and her father. Afterward, they all return to San Francisco in the submarine, where he and Beverly are married. A large portion of the salvaged treasure is used to aid the poor children of the city.

This film has a weak SF plot, but the submarine, which is described as being able to submerge to great depths, is noteworthy in its resemblance to the Nautilus in *20,000 Leagues Under the Sea.* Its power source, though unexplained to the audience, is still a true SF element in a submersible craft of this period. In addition, Harry's possession of an inordinate amount of physical strength and other mystical powers which enable him to make unbelievable escapes from perilous situations, add a unique dimension to the science fiction aspect of the film. And the coalition of these factors make it a credible entry into the SF adventure category.

> "*Terror Island* is too well constructed as a story to be classed as a vehicle, but it suits the peculiar qualifications of Houdini as if it was made expressly for him. The authors have done their part with skill and good taste. A vast amount of capable effort has been made by the director to give the voyage to a treasure island the force and charm of realism."
>
> *Moving Picture World*, Vol. 44, p. 861

1921

THE DIAMOND QUEEN

Release: 1921, Universal
Description: Silent, 18 episode serial; each episode approx. 2000 feet
Classification: SF-A
References: No. 8, p. 149, 218, 219; No. 14, p. 127; No. 50, p. 101; BIO, Vol. 49, No. 782, p. 55, 56; MPH, Vol. 12, p. 78; MPN, Vol. 22, p. 3217, 3235

Credits

Producer .... Universal
Director .... Edward Kull
Screenplay .... Robert F. Roden and George W. Pyer

Cast

Doris Harvey .... Eileen Sedgwick
Mark Allen .... George Chesebro
Professor Jason Ramsey .... Al Smith
Frank Wilson.................... Frank Clarke
Mr. Harvey .... Lou Short
Louise .... Josephine Scott

Chapters 1-18 of *The Diamond Queen*

Chapter 1: The Vow of Vengeance
References: LC, LP16045
Chapter 2: The Plunge of Doom
References: LC, LP16072
Chapter 3: Perils of the Jungle
References: LC, LP16073
Chapter 4: Fires of Hate
References: LC, LP16121
Chapter 5: The Tide of Destiny
References: LC, LP16157

Chapter 6: The Colossal Game
References: LC, LP16189
Chapter 7: An Amazing Ultimatum
References: LC, LP16259
Chapter 8: In Merciless Clutches
References: LC, LP16277
Chapter 9: A Race with Rogues
References: LC, LP16294
Chapter 10: The Betrayal
References: LC, LP16331
Chapter 11: In Torture's Grip
References: LC, LP16344
Chapter 12: The Kidnapping
References: LC, LP16375
Chapter 13: Weird Walls
References: LC, LP16404
Chapter 14: The Plunge
References: LC, LP16421
Chapter 15: The Decoy
References: LC, LP166440
Chapter 16: The Dip of Death
References: LC, LP16496
Chapter 17: The Hand of Hate
References: LC, LP16553
Chapter 18: The Hour of Reckoning
References: LC, LP16571

The serial *The Diamond Queen* with its 18 episodes focuses on the development of a device which is capable of artificially synthesizing diamonds. The production of artificial diamonds was not a unique plot for the year 1921. On three previous occasions films had centered on the development, a device, or chemists with the expertise to form artificial diamonds. The first of these productions, *The Diamond Maker* released by Vitagraph Company of America in 1909, was a short film in which the inventor of the stones sought to get back at the large diamond conglomerate.

In 1913 Rex Motion Picture Company produced a film entitled *The Diamond Makers.* Again a chemist was employed to find a process by which artificial diamonds could be produced in order to break the diamond cartel.

In 1914, Eclair produced a film entitled *The Diamond Maker.* This plot very closely resembles the plot for *The Diamond Queen:* a young girl's father, pressured by diamond moguls, is virtually on the brink of bankruptcy and commits suicide. The daughter vows to ruin her father's enemies by creating an artificial diamond and then flooding the market with these gems so as to lower the price of the true diamonds. Obviously, this plot had some merit as Universal's offering of *The Diamond Queen* focuses on such a theme. Moreover, Universal saw fit in 1929 to remake *The Diamond Queen* and entitle it *The Diamond Masters.* The 1929 version proved to be substantially more popular than the 1921 serial.

As the story unfolds through the first episode, *The Vow of Vengeance,* a young girl, Doris Harvey, is being pursued by her father's financial enemies. She and her father ascend to the top of an enormous sky scraper in downtown Manhattan. In their possession are incriminating documents which will link the diamond cartel's members to corrupt dealings in various bribes and swindles in some very large European countries.

Both Doris and her father attempt to escape the villains by crossing a narrow plank from one building to another. Doris safely traverses the board high above the city's streets, but her father fails to keep his balance and falls to his death. The viewer is led to believe at this point that her father has committed suicide. Doris, now alone, is the sole guardian of the precious evidence. Somehow she manages to escape the pursuing criminals, but as she creeps along the edge of the building she suddenly slips from it and falls into the darkness. . . .the screen grows dim and then a sudden burst of light proclaims the familiar words, "Continued next week!"

In episode two, Doris is not only miraculously rescued from her perilous fall that ended chapter one, but begins a pattern of misadventures which leave her life in jeopardy all the way to episode 15.

Early in the serial, Doris is locked in a safe but somehow manages to escape this steel tomb. Then, only a few episodes later, she makes her way to the Kimberly mines in the deepest part of Africa. There she looks for two members of the cartel who helped hasten her father's death.

While on this particularly dangerous adventure, Doris is captured by a band of cannibals. It seems they are dominated by women, and Doris, with her amazing beauty, has obviously attracted their attention. The natives vow she is to be spared and perhaps will even be made a ruler in the tribe. First, however, she must undergo grueling tests to measure her strength and endurance.

These episodes, during which Doris pits herself against other members of the tribe and meets the challenge of almost superhuman tasks, are certainly hair-raising and nail-biting times for the audience. The outcome of these tests is that Doris is made queen of the cannibals, who, by matter of coincidence, just happen to control the richest diamond mine in darkest Africa.

At this point Doris comes into contact with an ingenious inventor, Professor Jason Ramsey. Ramsey has been studying and searching for deposits of diamonds within the African jungles for some time. He thinks he has devised a process by which the precious stones can be produced artificially by simulating nature's extremely high temperatures and the enormous pressures needed to create the real thing. Doris urges him to continue his experiments, and even sponsors the research by giving him financial support.

When the professor is finally able to make the breakthrough and produce the artificial stones, Doris sees her path of vengeance clearly as she floods the market with these fake gems.

Not long after these events, Doris encounters a young millionaire, Mark Allen, while he is on an African safari. They become very attached and, as the serial draws to a close, we find Doris and Mark heading toward matrimony (the usual ending for serials of this period).

Obviously, *The Diamond Queen* is a thrilling and exciting serial. But despite this, it still comes across as a very weak science fiction adventure work, offering little new in science or technology from its three predecessors. For some strange reason, there was a definite trend by the film companies of the 1920's to produce movies about breaking the diamond trust that had been established in south Africa. Perhaps this was simply a mirror for the disdain the general public held for the cartel.

This serial was adapted from a novel, *The Diamond Master,* by Jacques Futrelle, a book which proved to be the basis for many screenplays about artificial diamonds.

Eileen Sedgwick, the daughter of Edward and Josephine Sedgwick, was part of the vaudeville team called The Five Sedgwicks, a tumbling and acrobatic group. This probably accounts for the many death-defying scenes which are portrayed in the tale--all stunts were performed by Eileen since doubles were seldom used in the early 1920's.

George Chesebro had been in films only since 1918, but already had starred or costarred in four other serials. This was still the beginning of his career; a career which lasted until 1954. During this time period he appeared in nearly 300 film works. Few of the other actors of the 1920's ever made it to sound films.

Calthrope Masters spys on Darmond in *The Hell Diggers* (1921).

THE HELL DIGGERS

Release: 1921, Paramount Pictures Corp.
Description: Silent, 4277 feet
Classification: SF-A
References: No. 50, p. 189; AFI, F2.2404, p. 336; LC, LP16896; MPH, Vol. 13, p. 57; MPW, Vol. 52, p. 95, 273; Vol. 61, p. 439, 546; SEP, Vol. 193, p. 8, 9; VAW, Vol. 64, 8-26-21, p. 36

Credits

Producer. . . . . Famous Players-Lasky
Director . . . . Frank Urson
Screenplay . . . . Byron Morgan
Camera . . . . C. E. Schoenbaum

Cast

Teddy Darman . . . . Wallace Reid
Dora Wade . . . . Lois Wilson
John Wade. . . . . Alexander Broun
Calthrope Masters . . . . Frank Leigh
Silas Hoskins . . . . Lucien Littlefield
Silverby Rennie . . . . Clarence Goldart
Fat Farmer . . . . Bud Post

The Hell Diggers is a unique science fiction melodrama that offered the 1921 viewing public the first glimpse of ecological problems which can occur in large mining and logging operations. Similar environmental problems would take 50 years before the American public would consider them serious enough to do anything to remedy the situation.

In this particular story, the Continental Gold Dredging Company has instructed its superintendent Teddy Darman to surface mine an area called Cherry Valley--the new location of the Continental Gold Dredging Company's recent mineralogical find. Darman has instructions to buy the mineral rights to the land and use the newest dredging machines to mine the whole area.

The farmers, led by John Wade, resist Continental's move into their area, proclaiming that everytime a dredging company or logging operation comes into their valley the land is so decimated that it remains useless for farming purposes. At first, Teddy Darman resists their claims, but as he begins to become more acquainted with Dora Wade, John's daughter, some of his rigid views begin to vacillate. He begins to understand the true meaning of caring for land. Dora's explanations of the farmer's beliefs as the two of them walk in the lush forests and look at the abundant beauty of the land help further persuade him that his company's machines would destroy the environment. She pleads with him to find a way to leave the valley the placid and tranquil place it is.

Reluctantly, Darman agrees to postpone the dredging company's mandate and in the interim finally decides to leave the company and design a machine of his own--one which will still be able to dredge for gold but will restore the land to its original beauty as it digs trenches searching for the valuable metal. The farmers support this idea and some even mortgage their farms to help him in the construction of this miraculous device.

Calthrope Masters, agent for Continental Gold Dredging Company, originally lent the money for the Continental dredging operation. He now plots and schemes to undermine Darman's efforts. He succeeds when Darman's newly completed machine is destroyed by a dynamite charge placed under it.

A battle between Master's men and the farmers commences with Darman and the farmers winning. The sheriff arrives and arrests Masters who finally agrees to pay for any machine that can leave the valley unmolested. He further declares that the dredging of the valley will be left in Darman and the farmers' hands. The farmers and Teddy agree to establish a new company with him and Dora as officers--as well as partners in marriage.

While this particular film is weak in science fiction content, the idea of a machine that can reconstitute the land as it reaped minerals from its depths is certainly a unique idea for the 1920's. Unfortunately, this was indeed still science fiction during this era. It would not be until the 1970's that such machines would become a reality, and not because of the desire of the companies behind the dredging operations, but because of the fierce pressure exerted by the public.

NAN OF THE NORTH

Release: 1921, Arrow
Description: Silent, 15 episode serial, each episode approx. 2000 feet
Classification: SF-A
References: No. 88, p. 100, 101, 229; No. 14, p. 348; No. 50, p. 328

Credits

Producer .... Ben Wilson
Director .... Duke Worne
Screenplay .... Karl R. Coolidge

Cast

Nan .... Ann Little
Sergeant Colby .... Leonard Clapham
Gang Leader .... Joseph W. Girard
Mounted Policeman .... Hal Wilson
Store Owner .... Howard Crampton
Henchman .... J. Morris Foster
Gang Leader's Mistress .... Edith Stoyart

Chapters 1-15 of *Nan of the North*

Chapter 1: The Missil from Mars
References: LC, LP17216
Chapter 2: Fountain of Fury
References: LC, LP17217
Chapter 3: The Brink of Despair
References: LC, LP17218
Chapter 4: In Cruel Clutches
References: LC, LP17276
Chapter 5: On Terror's Trail
References: LC, LP17352
Chapter 6: The Cards of Chance
References: LC, LP17379
Chapter 7: Into the Depths
References: LC, LP17399
Chapter 8: Burning Sands
References: LC, LPi7400

Chapter 9: The Power of Titano
References: LC, LP17401
Chapter 10: A Bolt from the Sky
References: LC, LP17402
Chapter 11: The Ride for a Life
References: LC, LP17476
Chapter 12: Adrift
References: LC, LP17477
Chapter 13: Facing Death at Sea
References: LC, LP17478
Chapter 14: The Volcano
References: LC, LP17511
Chapter 15: Consequences
References: LC, LP17512

The focus of *Nan of the North,* a science fiction epic serial, produced by Ben Wilson, is clearly identified in the very first chapter entitled *Missil from Mars.* A small meteor enters the earth's atmosphere and strikes its surface in the Yukon area. This meteorite (the word change indicates that the meteor has struck the earth) is said to contain a powerful substance known as "titano".

A young scientist discovers the meteorite and refines this valuable material. In a written report he claims that the substance has unlimited energy and estimates that it could be more powerful than electricity, or steam, or gas, or all three combined. Having written his report, he seals it in a pouch and starts off toward the nearest city. Before departing he carefully hides the metal container of titano and makes a duplicate copy of his report, leaving it, too, in his cabin in what he assumes is a secure place. However, while gone, a stranger enters his cabin and makes himself at home. It isn't long before he discovers the report left by the scientist. He too realizes the value of what he has found and, seeking to make his fortune, locates the leader of a notorious gang of crooks which has operated for some time in the Yukon.

Meanwhile, our scientist encounters a storm that brings his journey to a grinding halt. The bitter cold and chilling winds are merciless and he finally succumbs to the intense cold and dies a lone bitter death.

A day or so later, Nan, with her dogsled, moves across the snowy area on her way to Dawson and discovers the stranger's body. She searches through his belongings to try and identify him and uncovers the report. Realizing the seriousness of this discovery and the value of such a report, she loads his lifeless body on her dogsled and proceeds to Dawson. Upon arriving, she seeks out Sergeant Colby, the constable in charge of Dawson and the surrounding area.

Colby immediately senses the grave danger that could result from having such a valuable energy tool, and cautions Nan not to mention the report. He then solicits her help in trying to locate the cabin the dead scientist was coming from in the hope of finding the titano that he had discovered.

The remainder of the serial is devoted to the interaction between Nan, Sergeant Colby, and the gang of Yukon thieves. Each is trying to find the hidden box of titano, the rare mineral which holds more energy potential than any other substance on earth. In the end, Sergeant Colby manages to destroy the box before the thieves can acquire it, and he and Nan round up all the gang members and cart them off to jail.

While *Nan of the North* is an interesting SF adventure serial, the science fiction aspect of the production is weak, at best. This is the eighth film since 1897 to focus on meteors from outer space bringing rich gifts of minerals to the earth's population; definitely an interesting prospect, but one that as yet has not been fully developed from a scientific point of view in any of the films reviewed.

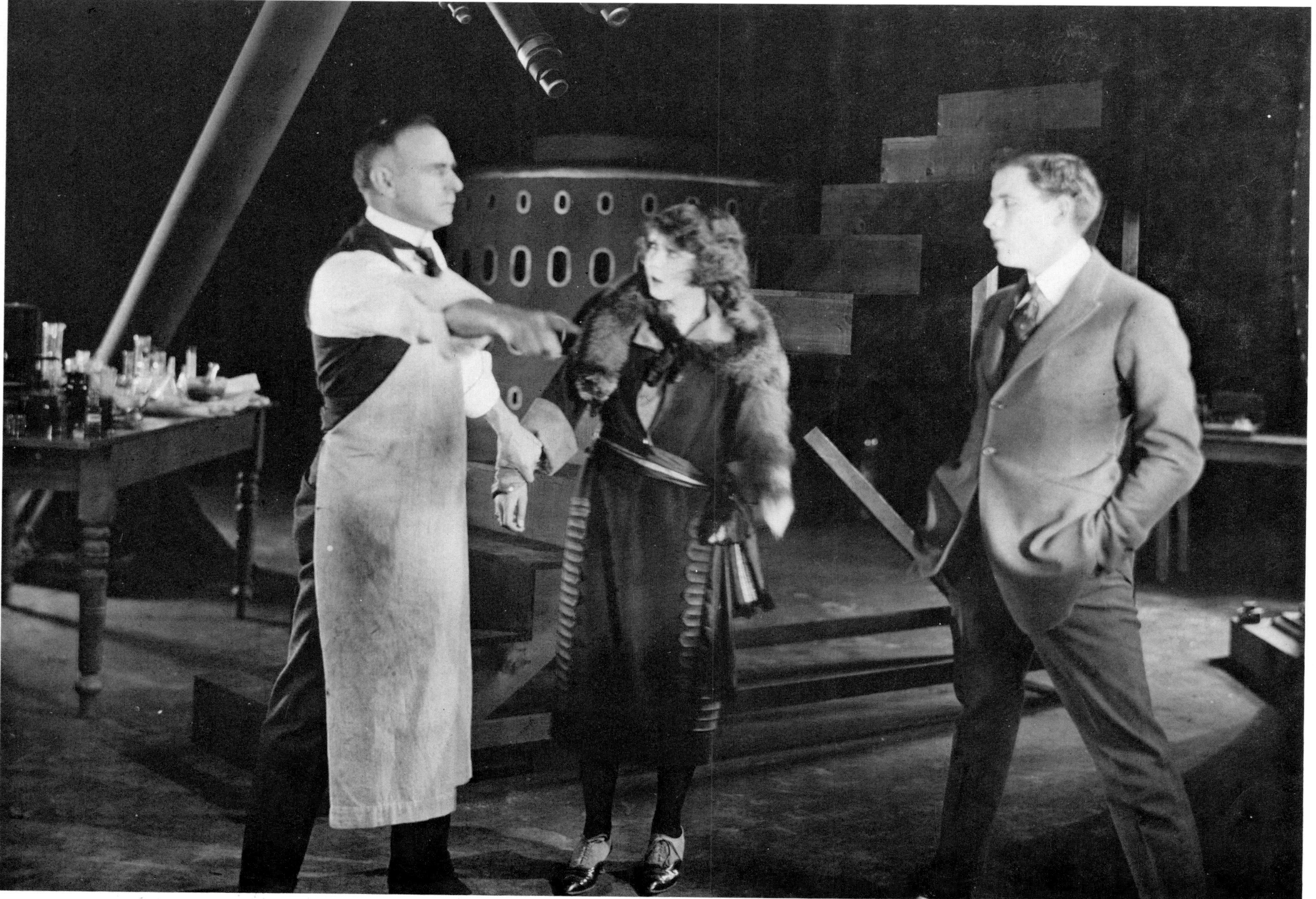

Professor Elliot (Frank Redman) orders George Rockwell (George B. Seitz) from his astronomical laboratory.

THE SKY RANGER

Release: 1921, Pathe
Description: Silent, 15 episode serial, each episode approx. 2000 feet
Classification: SF
References: No. 8, p. 94, 95, 224; No. 14, p. 438; No. 50, p. 444; BIO, Vol. 49, No. 778, p. 36; MPW, Vol. 49, p. 993; VAW, Vol. 12, No. 17, p. 61

Credits

Producer.. George B. Seitz
Director.. George B. Seitz

Cast

June Elliot.. June Caprice
George Rockwell.. George B. Seitz
Dr. Santro.. Harry Semels
Peggy Santro.. Peggy Shanor
Professor Elliot.. Frank Redman
Joe Bentley.. Joe Cuny

Chapters 1-15 of *The Sky Ranger*

Chapter 1: Out of the Clouds
References: LC, LU16357
Chapter 2: The Sinister Signal
References: LC, LU16358
Chapter 3: In Hostile Hands
References: LC, LU16359
Chapter 4: Desert Law
References: LC, LU16360
Chapter 5: Mid-Air
References: LC, LU16361
Chapter 6: The Crystal Prism
References: LC, LU16362
Chapter 7: Danger's Doorway
References: LC, LU16526
Chapter 8: Dropped from the Clouds
References: LC, LU16527
Chapter 9: The House on the Roof
References: LC, LU16528
Chapter 10: Trapped
References: LC, LU16529
Chapter 11: The Seething Pool
References: LC, LU16530
Chapter 12: The Whirling Menace
References: LC, LU16531

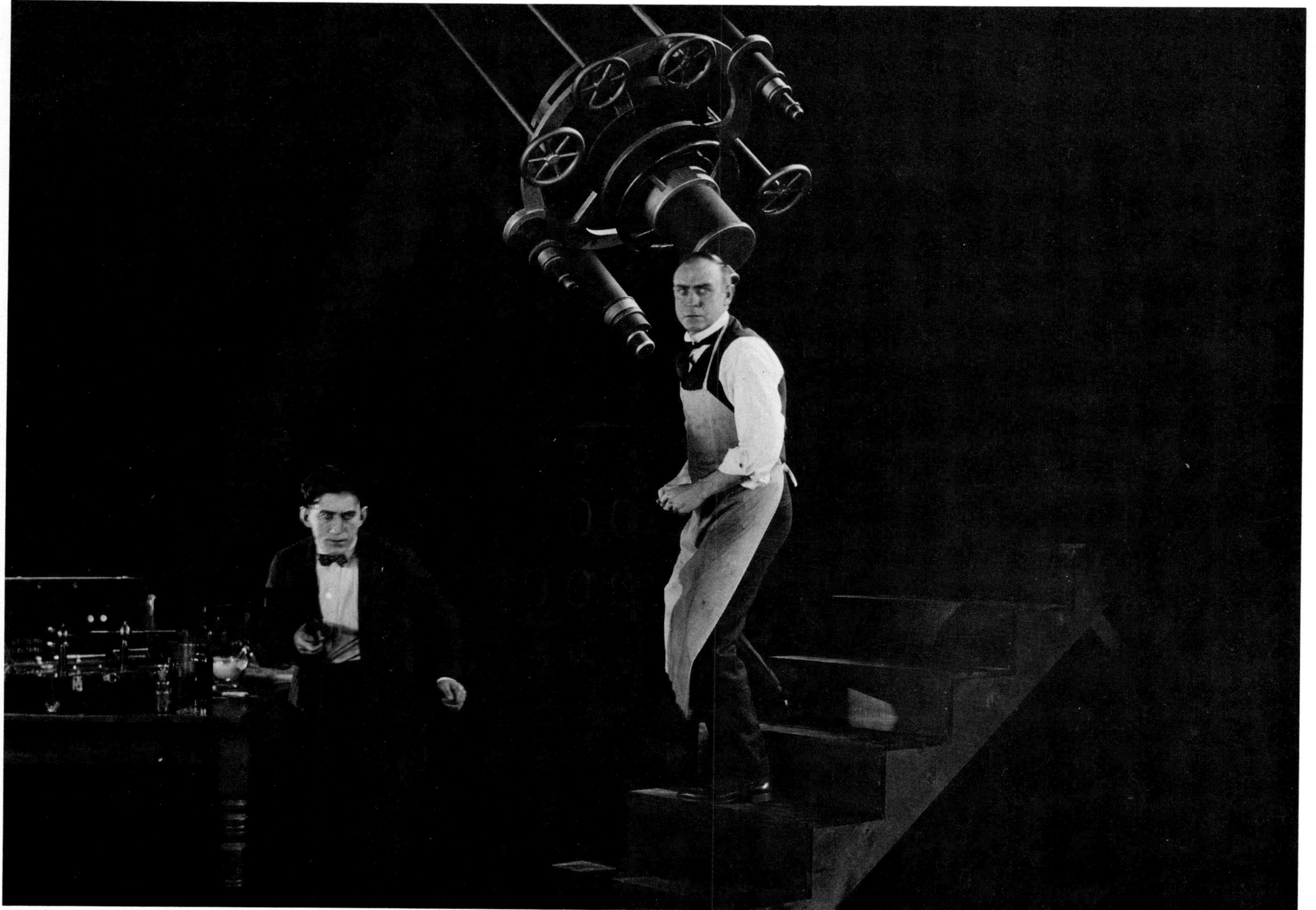

The secret astronomical work is discovered in *The Sky Ranger* (1921).

Dr. Sandro continually tries to destroy Professor Elliot's research work in *The Sky Ranger* (1921).

Chapter 13: At the Last Minute
References: LC, LU16649
Chapter 14: Liquid Fire
References: LC, LU16650
Chapter 15: The Last Raid
References: LC, LU16648

The Sky Ranger is a serial based on the work by Frank Leon Smith. The epic was originally titled *The Man Who Stole the Earth* and the leading characters were intended to be Martians. But Pathe wasn't ready apparently for this extreme degree of science fiction. So, the work was rewritten resulting in *The Sky Ranger*, a toned down version of the original story.

The serial focuses on the conflict between two inventors: Dr. Santro has perfected an airplane with extraordinary speed (It is inferred that it is powered by jet engines.) that can travel around the world in a matter of a few hours and ascend to any height in a matter of seconds, all without producing any sound. Professor Elliot, the other inventor, has developed a powerful searchlight that is capable of sending signals as far away as the planet Mars. This light can detect objects in the sky regardless of how high they may be. Somehow Dr. Santro interprets the searchlight's existence as a threat to his flying machine and seeks to destroy the professor's work.

Meanwhile, on the other side of town, George Rockwell innocently visits a fortune teller who foresees Mary, a beautiful blond woman--a description which just happens to fit that of June, Professor Elliot's daughter. It isn't long afterward that George meets Mary Elliot, and the two are instantly attracted to each other. As a result of this involvement George is caught up in the conflict between the two inventors.

Santro continually tries to destroy the searchlight and the professor's ongoing research efforts, and begins to reveal some of his more sinister nature and the power it can invoke. It seems he is an expert hypnotist who uses this power to coerce others into performing his more malicious work.

In episode three, George and June are trapped aboard one of Santro's flying vessels and are transported to a remote region of Asia. Once in this desolate land their plight seems almost hopeless as the barrenness of the area provides little means for their survival. But within hours, they are rescued by Peggy Santro, the doctor's niece. She arrives in a second aircraft she had commandeered and relates to them her desire to thwart her uncle's aggressive tendencies. Immediately, June and George become her allies in this common mission.

The serial provides some truly thrilling moments for the audience, and the suggestion of an aircraft that is either rocket or jet propelled is certainly conceptually advanced for this period. Professor Elliot's powerful searchlight was more than a step ahead of 1921 in its depiction of a laser-type light. The beam is described as a narrow beam of coherent light capable of traveling great distances without any appreciable dispersion.

In the final episode, Dr. Santro's aircraft plummets toward earth and crashes in a flaming ball of gases, thus ending the conflict between Professor Elliot and himself. Unfortunately, the doctor's secret for the marvelous flying invention was lost as well, and the audience is reminded that his evil designs and sinister nature finally overcame his scientifically creative genius.

George and June are seen entwined in a romance that will surely lead toward marriage. They have also acquired a lifelong friend in Peggy Santro, the ally to whom they owe their lives.

> "Judged by the opening episodes, the new Pathe serial, 'The Sky Ranger', starring June Caprice and George E. Seitz, will prove a winner."
>
> *Moving Picture World,* Vol. 49, p. 993

In Chapter 15, George Rockwell foils his mysterious captors which eventually leads to the demise of the sinister Dr. Santo (*The Sky Ranger*, 1921).

THE WITCHING HOUR

Release: 1921, Paramount Pictures Corp.
Description: Silent, 5240 feet
Classification: SF
References: No. 14, p.532; No. 50, p. 545; BIO, Vol. 48, No. 777, p. 48; LC, LP16139; MPW, Vol. 49, p. 193

Credits

Producer.......................................Famous Players-Lasky
Director.......................................William D. Taylor
Screenplay.......................Julia Crawford Ivers and Augustus Thomas
Camera.......................................James Van Trees

Cast

Jack Brookfield.......................................Elliott Dexter
Judge Prentice.......................................Winter Hall
Viola Campbell.......................................Ruth Renick
Frank Hardmuth.......................................Robert Cain
Clay Whipple.......................................Edward Sutherland
Helen Whipple.......................................Mary Alden
Lew Ellinger.......................................Fred Turner
Mrs. Campbell.......................................Genevieve Blirn
Tom Denning.......................................Charles West
Judge Henderson.......................................L. M. Wells
Colonel Bailey.......................................Clarence Geldart
Harvey.......................................Jim Blackwell

The Witching Hour is a unique film involving hypnotism, telepathy, and mental suggestion, all of which are entwined about a rather unusual murder that takes place at a dinner party. The story revolves around a gem called the "cat's eye". It seems that young Clay Whipple has some sort of fear regarding the jewel, and as we shall see, this phobia that he harbors will be his undoing before the night is over.

The party is held at Jack Brookfield's gambling house. This night he has closed the house to the public and is having a private gathering for some friends. Actually, his real intention is to woo his old sweetheart back, the recently widowed Helen Whipple (Clay's mother).

During the evening's festivities, Harvey, an uninvited guest, begins to torment Clay Whipple by showing him his cat's eye and causing young Whipple to become more anxiety-ridden as the evening wears on. Finally, as the night draws to a close, Harvey thrusts the evil gem in Clay's direction once too often. The young boy slaps the jewel from his hand and the two begin to fight. During this struggle, Harvey is accidently hit on the head with a heavy ivory paper cutter. The result is as suspected--Harvey lies dead upon the floor. Immediately, Clay is taken into custody and charged by the district attorney, who secretly hates Clay as he is in competition with him for the attention of Viola Campbell. The district attorney leaves no stone unturned in order to prosecute Clay to the fullest extent of the law. The result is that Clay is found guilty of murder and sentenced to die.

Jack Brookfield and Helen, however, work in harmony with each other and launch a prodigious effort to obtain a retrial for the young lad. Jack also calls on some friends who have hypnotic and telepathic powers to help convince Justice Prentice of the Supreme Court to grant a retrial for Clay. Obviously, their diligent efforts are rewarded as Clay is given a second trial.

Brookfield also has succeeded in exposing the injustice and greed of the present district attorney and has had him removed from office while a new one is appointed. Public sentiment moves toward Clay's side and, as the new trial begins, the powers that Brookfield seems to possess lie just below the surface of the action of the film. The jury vacillates and then suddenly seems to be grabbed by the truth of the matter as though their very minds had become united and some hidden power had caused them to coalesce in a single cause. They render a "not guilty" verdict, and young Clay is freed.

As a result of the hypnotic power, Clay's phobia surrounding the cat's eye jewel is removed, and Brookfield and Helen are engaged and heading for matrimony as Clay and Viola express their affection for each other.

The Witching Hour has some weak science fiction moments, but still offers some interesting applications for hypnotism, telepathy, and mental suggestion. The part of the film that seems to focus on telepathy is really many years ahead of the time when ESP would become a commonly studied subject at many psychological institutions and universities throughout the country. Certainly, extrasensory perception and telepathic powers were very much SF phenomena in the 1920's, especially as far as the general public was concerned.

1922

A BLIND BARGAIN

Release: 1922, Goldwyn Pictures Corp.
Description: Silent, 4473 feet
Classification: SF-H
References: No. 1, p. 419; No. 6, p. 100, 101; No. 10, p. 231; No. 14, p. 54; No. 50, p. 39; AFI, F2.0464, p. 67; BIO, Vol. 55, No. 871, p. 65; LC, LP18423; MPH, Vol. 16, p.56, 128, 130; MPN, Vol. 26, p. 2798; MPW, Vol. 59, p. 667, 668; Vol. 61, p. 77, 152, 319, 338, 438, 841; NYR, 12-4-22; VAW, Vol. 69, No. 3, 12-8-22, p. 33

Credits

Producer .... Samuel Goldwyn
Director .... Wallace Worsley
Screenplay .... J. G. Hawks
Camera .... Norbert Brodin

Cast

Dr. Lamb/Hunchback .... Lon Chaney
Robert .... Raymond McKee
Angela .... Jacqueline Logan
Mrs. Lamb .... Fontaine LaRue
Robert's Mother .... Virginia True Boardman
Bessie .... Aggie Herring
Angela's Mother .... Virginia Madison

A Blind Bargain is an extraordinary film based on the original story by Barry Bain entitled *The Octave of Claudius.* Lon Chaney gives an unmatched performance as both the creature and the scientist, Dr. Lamb. The film focuses on the theory of extending the longevity of man's life by the transplantation of

Lon Chaney as the hunchback in *Blind Bargain* (1922).

animal parts to replace various vital organs in man, perpetuating the basic premise that if one can replace the spare parts then perhaps one can live longer. This theme, in fact, was the focus of the 1920 serial *The Screaming Shadow*, but the effort put forth by Lon Chaney, Sr. and his supporting cast in this film is vastly superior to that of the actors in *The Screaming Shadow*.

As the story begins, we find that Dr. Lamb has been conducting experiments, much against his wife's wishes, on several poor victims. A hunchback is the most notable byproduct of his experiments. Once a handsome, completely normal human being, he is now a gruesome, terrifying creature controlled by the fear that Dr. Lamb will continue to use him in future experiments.

One evening when the doctor is returning from the theater, he is assaulted by a young desparate ex-soldier, Robert. Somehow the doctor manages to overpower the youth who then starts begging the doctor not to turn him over to the police. He explains that all he really wanted was enough money for his mother's operation; it seems she will die without it. Dr. Lamb strikes a bargain with the young man: he will perform the operation on his mother if the young man will consent to be a subject in his experiments even though it may mean the young man's death. Hesitantly, Robert agrees, and thus gives us the foundation for the title as "a blind bargain" is struck.

The die has been cast as Dr. Lamb performs the needed surgery on Robert's mother, and the youth returns to the Lamb house for the experiments, even though he is not sure what the outcome will be. As he enters the house and follows the doctor to his basement laboratory, he is horrified by the sight of an ape-like hunchback creature. He learns that this is a byproduct of the doctor's sinister experiments. The hunchback is a repulsive and pathetic beast and Robert cannot bear the sight of him. Soon, however, he learns that the creature only wants to communicate and desires to spare Robert the same ordeal to which he had been subjected. Mrs. Lamb even pleads with the doctor not to use the young soldier in his experiments, but he rebukes his wife and tells her to keep quiet, that the experiments must continue for the benefit of mankind. Meanwhile, the hunchback has succeeded in showing Robert the results of previous experiments. He now wishes he could renege on his promise, but the doctor will not allow such a bargain to be dissolved.

A fierce battle takes place between the doctor, Robert and the hunchback. During this, the hunchback releases several of the other misshapen creatures that had been locked in cages. Each of them takes their vengeance upon Dr. Lamb and Robert escapes during the confusion. Needless to say, Dr. Lamb does not survive the ordeal. The laboratory and the creatures are, in fact, all destroyed in the battle, and his research and chamber of horrors are finally erased.

As the movie ends, we see Robert and his mother returning to their home to live a happy life. But Robert will certainly always remember the blind bargain that nearly cost him his life.

Lon Chaney's performance in this picture is at least equal to the performance by John Barrymore in *Dr. Jekyll and Mr. Hyde* (1920). These two features probably marked a new era for science fiction motion pictures in America. They both were such outstanding dramatic presentations that their successors surely found it difficult to equal them for some time.

Lon Chaney, Sr. had played in nearly 200 films prior to the production of *A Blind Bargain*, but this was his finest performance thus far in his career and remained so until his starring role in *The Hunchback of Notre Dame*.

> "Lon Chaney's fine work in two widely divergent roles is the outstanding feature of the Goldwyn production 'A Blind Bargain' in which he appears both as an eminent surgeon with strange theories, and as an ape-like hunchback.
>
> The picture itself is sensational and gruesome, dealing with the attempts of a half-mad scientist to prolong human life by transplanting into human beings vital substances taken from animals, and in the manner of handling this subject it would seem to be a slap at the monkey gland theory."
>
> *Moving Picture World*, Vol. 59, p. 667

THE ELECTRIC HOUSE

Release: 1922, First National
Description: Silent, 2231 feet
Classification: SF-C
References: No. 50, p. 120; BIO, Vol. 59, p. 37; LC, LP18329; MPN, Vol. 26, p. 2316; MPW, Vol. 58, p. 804; Vol. 61, p. 754, 845

Credits

Producer .... Buster Keaton and Joseph M. Schenck
Director.................................... Buster Keaton and Eddie Cline
Screenplay .... Buster Keaton and Eddie Cline

Cast

Buster Keaton .... Buster Keaton

The Electric House is a Buster Keaton comedy which centers around a mistake that happens to Buster upon his graduation from college. He has spent the last four years studying botany and is, therefore, more than a little surprised when he receives his diploma and it lists him as a construction engineer. While he attempts to correct the college's mistake, they unequivocally deny that such an error could have been made. Frustrated by his inability to alter the diploma, Buster decides to look for employment in this strange new field.

He immediately starts getting offers from companies who are seeking his supposed talents as a construction engineer. His first job is to wire a house with all the latest modern electrical conveniences. In doing so, he not only wires them to operate, but they almost seem to do so independently from the owner's wishes. There are doors that open and close for no apparent reason; stoves and numerous other appliances that also turn on and off without anyone's command. The whole sequence of events surrounding this construction job produces an extremely amusing film.

Many of the labor saving conveniences displayed are very advanced for this time period, but *The Electric House,* an amusing and entertaining film, is still a weak science fiction entry. Only the ultramodern devices that are displayed in the house permit it to be considered as a SF comedy work.

GAMBLING WITH THE GULF STREAM

Release: 1922, Hodkinson
Description: Silent, 967 feet
Classification: SF-F
References: No. 14, p. 177; No. 50, p. 155; LC, MP2281; MPN, Vol. 26, p. 3003; MPW, Vol. 60, p. 596

Credits

Producer... John R. Bray

Gambling with the Gulf Stream is a film that blends the use of animated diagrams to fantasize what would happen to Great Britain should the path of the Gulf Stream be altered. The proposal is to investigate the resultant temperature change in Great Britain by building a wall on the banks of Newfoundland, thus directing the Gulf Stream's current an additional four miles out to sea. This is theorized on the screen through a graphic representation of the movement of the warm waters of the stream as it moves farther away from the isle of Britain. The result is a thick layer of ice which covers the nation.

Gambling with the Gulf Stream is a unique concept in animation showing through a set of drawings a projection of what the possible consequences in altering the environment would be. The length of the feature (967 feet) indicates the shallowness with which the issue was approached.

THE JUNGLE GODDESS

Release: 1922, Export-Import Film Company
Description: Silent, 15 episode serial, each episode approx. 3000 feet
Classification: SF-A
References: No. 8, p. 102, 103, 228, 229; No. 50, p. 236; BIO, Vol. 51, p. 57; MPH, Vol. 14, p. 69; MPW, Vol. 54, p. 16, 17, 427

Credits

Producer .... Colonel William N. Selig
Director .... James Conway
Screenplay .... Agnes Johnston and Frank Dazey

Cast

Betty Castleton/Jungle Goddess .... Elinor Field
Ralph Dean .... Truman VanDyke
Rajah .... Lafe McKee
Guardian of the Temple .... Vonda Phelps
Leopard Woman .... Marie Pavis
High Priest .... Olin Francis
Constable .... William Platt
Lord Castleton .... H.G. Wells
Native Guide .... George Reed

Chapters 1-15 of *The Jungle Goddess*

Chapter 1: Sacrificed to the Lions
Reference: LC,LP17618
Chapter 2: The City of Blind Waters
Reference: LC, LP17619
Chapter 3: Saved by the Great Ape
Reference: LC, LP17620
Chapter 4: The Hell Ship
Reference: LC, LP17621
Chapter 5: Wild Beasts in Command
Reference: LC, LP17622
Chapter 6: Sky High with a Leopard
Reference: LC,LP17712
Chapter 7: The Rajah's Revenge
Reference: LC, LP17713
Chapter 8: The Alligator's Victim
Reference: LC, LP17714

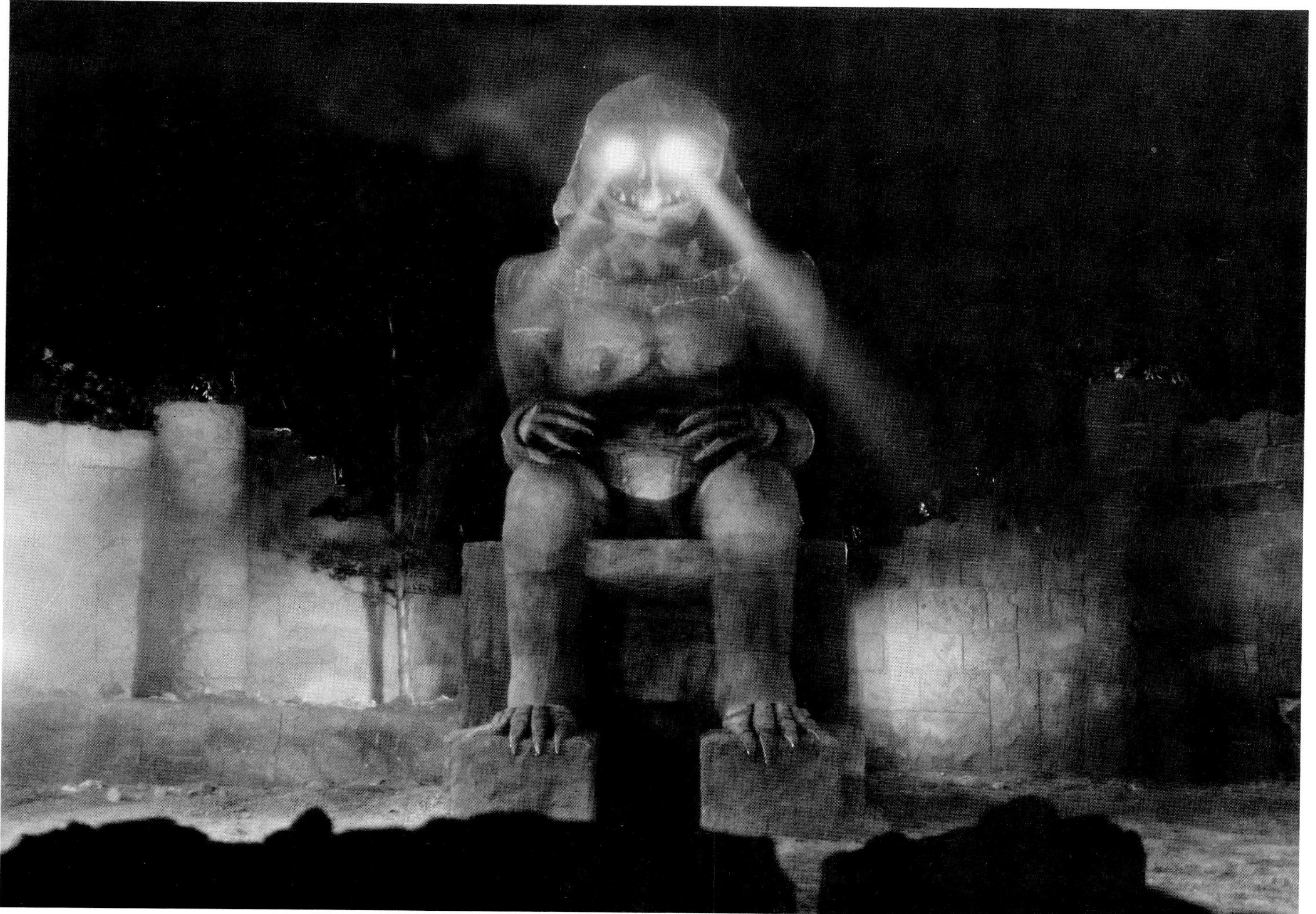

The mysterious eyes of the idol in *The Jungle Goddess* (1922) destroy its victims almost instantly.

Chapter 9: At Grips with Death
Reference: LC, LP17715
Chapter 10: The Leopard Woman
Reference: LC, LP17716
Chapter 11: The Soul of Buddha
Reference: LC, LP17771
Chapter 12: The Jaws of Death
Reference: LC, LP17772
Chapter 13: The Cave of Beasts
Reference: LC, LP17773
Chapter 14: Jungle Terrors
Reference: LC, LP17774
Chapter 15: The Mad Lion
Reference: LC, LP17775

Colonel William Selig's *The Jungle Goddess* of 1922 is but another jungle feature among the many that appeared in the early 1920's. His earlier film, *The Lost City,* was a movie with the jungle theme that received great praise by an enthusiastic public. *The Jungle Goddess* was so well performed that it resulted in a new plateau for serials. Not only did it feature an array of varied animals (more than 470 wild creatures were used), but it contained three villains who provided constant thrills and suspense for movie fans.

The serial opens with Betty Castleton, the young daughter of Lord Castleton, being kidnapped by an unidentified criminal. She is thrust by the assailant into the basket of a balloon, which suddenly works free from its moorings. Ascending high over the English Isle, it drifts for days, carrying its small passenger finally to deep, dark Africa.

Betty is found by natives who worship a giant stone god with eyes that gleam during certain times of the year. This entrances the natives who believe it has mysterious power. Within the structure are subterranean chambers where more than 40 lions are housed. Every previous sacrificial victim has obviously met a horrible end as these fierce cats' dinner. Somehow, Betty, who is immediately offered to the stone god by the natives as their sacrifice, survives the ordeal.

It is not quite clear how the young girl escapes, but it is believed that the Guardian of the Temple finds her attractive and saves her just before she is to be plunged into the jaws of certain death. When she reappears, unscathed by the god's terror, the high priest and his natives perceive it as a sign that she possesses greatness. They adopt her as a member of their tribe, a true child of their jungle god.

Throughout the remaining episodes of the serial, Betty is constantly beseiged and threatened by all kinds of villains. The high priest is the first to try and do away with their goddess, but at each turn he is somehow foiled as she manages to escape each of his cleverly designed traps.

Finally, Betty encounters a powerful rajah who feels that her power over the natives has somehow undermined his rule, and so he seeks to destroy her. It is he, however, who ends up plunging into an alligator-filled pit to meet death.

Our heroine next encounters a treacherous leopard woman, leader of a tribe of natives who practice cannibalism. She, too, is eventually killed in her quest to rid the jungle of Miss Castleton.

In the last episodes, Ralph Dean, a former playmate of Betty's, makes the arduous trip to the continent of Africa to try and locate poor lost Betty. With the entire jungle before him, he miraculously stumbles on the very village in which Betty is the jungle goddess. At first, she doesn't recognize him, but as he begins to relate stories from her childhood, including the tale about her kidnapping and journey by balloon to this place, she realizes that he must be the young lad of long ago with whom she shared so many happy hours.

They begin their treacherous trip across the continent, through Africa, China, and India, in the hope of reaching civilization. Each step is filled with pitfalls and dangers and time after time Ralph and Betty escape death only through their ingenuity and courage.

The Jungle Goddess did an admirable job of exciting its audiences, resulting in a handsome profit for the tireless Colonel Selig.

> "For genuine, honest-to-goodness thrills this serial is hard to beat. Once your patrons see one episode they will flock to your house to see the serial through to its finish. The acting is splendid, particularly that of Elinor Field and Truman Van Dyke. The savages look dangerous enough to keep any one from wanting to penetrate the interior of Darkest Africa. But if your patrons like serials or want thrills that will knock them out of their seats you cannot afford to overlook booking this one. The photography is excellent, as is also the direction. If you liked Col. Selig's *The Lost City* or *Miracles of the Jungle,* you'll go wild over *The Jungle Goddess.*"
>
> *Moving Picture World,* Vol. 54, 1-28-22, p. 427

> "The plot of this really remarkable series of pictures is in every way equal to that of its predecessors, which in many ways it closely resembles, but the film certainly derives more than ordinary interest from the ingenious way in which Colonel William N. Selig has utilized the services of the magnificent collection of wild animals which he has at his disposal. The human participators in these wonderful adventures are well known and highly skilled artists who know exactly how to get full value out of the situations in which they find themselves, and they are ably assisted by vast crowds of intelligent and admirably handled supers."
>
> *Bioscope,* Vol. 51, 6-15-22, p. 57

MINNIE

Release: 1922 First National Pictures
Description: Silent, 6696 feet
Classification: SF-C
References: No. 1, p. 507; No. 50, p. 303; AFI, F2.3636, p. 515, 516; BIO, Vol. 55, No. 863, p. 60; LC, LP18404; MPH, Vol. 16, p. 52, 55; MPW, Vol. 59, p. 575; Vol. 61, p. 342

Credits

Producer .... Marshall Neilan
Director .... Marshall Neilan and Frank Urson
Assistant Director.......... Thomas Held
Screenplay.......... George Patullo and Marshall Neilan
Camera.......... David Kesson and Karl Struss
Editor.......... Daniel J. Gray
Titles.......... Frances Marion

Cast

Minnie .... Leatrice Joy
Newspaper Man .... Matt Moore
Minnie's Father.......... George Barnum
Stepmother .... Josephine Crowell
Stepsister.......... Helen Lynch
Chewing Gum Salesman .... Raymond Griffith

Minnie's father questions her about her mysterious dead lover as she grieves her loss. Courtesy of The Museum of Modern Art Film Stills Archives. (*Minnie*, 1922)

Young Doctor .... Dick Wayne
Boarding House Janitor .... Tom Wilson
Local "Cutup" .... George Dromgold

Minnie is the story of a young girl whose homely appearance and constant snubbing by her peers cause her to create a make-believe lover. She even begins to send presents to herself to keep up the rumor that she has a suitor.

This fantasy is fostered by the pressure felt in Minnie's household. It seems her father, portrayed by George Barnum, is laboring feverishly to perfect a wireless machine which can transmit power over great distances. The whole town is waiting in eager anticipation for this invention to hit the market as every resident believes it will bring fame and fortune to all the town's people.

Meanwhile, Minnie's deception is getting more and more out of hand. Her suspicious stepsister is about to expose her fantasy when fortunately (at least for Minnie it seems fortunate) there is discovered a body of a young man at the edge of town. Minnie travels to the morgue and identifies the unclaimed body as that of her secret lover. Each of her friends soon offer their condolences in her time of grief. Later, a newspaper man, played by Matt Moore, manages through his careful questioning to trip Minnie up in her tale and finally gets the truth from her. Minnie breaks down and tells of the hardships she has suffered and that this is the reason for her deception. Further, she tells him she is relieved it is finally over. During this tearful outpouring of Minnie's, the man sees an inner beauty in her and soon becomes quite attracted to her.

He offers a solution if she truly believes her physical appearance is so detracting. He suggests they visit his friend in a nearby town who performs experimental plastic surgery. She agrees to undergo this surgery, and after recovering sufficiently from the operation she and the reporter return to her hometown. In fact they return on the very day her father's wireless transmitter has been perfected. The town's excitement is without equal and Minnie and her friend find themselves caught up in it, too. At first, no one recognizes her, but then her father realizes her voice and basic facial features are unchanged and embraces her as he remarks about her exquisite beauty. She soon attracts the eye of every young man in town, but finds that she is in love with the newspaper man. People who would not even turn their heads previously now offer her their complete attention. Minnie finds happiness with her reporter and begins a life which holds new challenges and rewards for her in another town.

This is an extremely weak science fiction comedy. The wireless transmitter which seems to gather a great deal of attention during the feature and the extraordinary plastic surgery that is performed on Minnie provide the basis for the movie's classification in the SF comedy category.

THE RADIO KING

Release: 1922, Universal
Description: Silent, 10 episode serial, each episode approx. 2000 feet
Classification: SF-A
References: No. 8, p. 103, 104, 230; No. 14, p. 395; No. 50, p. 390; BIO, Vol. 54, No. 854, p. 78, 79; MPH, Vol. 17, p. 88; MPW, Vol. 58, p. 401, 803; Vol. 61, p. 342

Credits

Producer .... Universal
Director .... Robert F. Hill
Screenplay .... Robert Dillon

Minnie, after surgery, and Matt Moore, her newspaperman in *Minnie* (1922). Courtesy of The Museum of Modern Art Film Stills Archives.

Cast

Brad Lane .... Roy Stewart
Mary Harden.. Louise Lorraine
John Leyden .... Al Smith
Marnee .... Sidney Bracey
Commander Nelson.................................... Clark Comstock
Jake .... Ernest Butterworth, Jr.

Chapters 1-10 of *The Radio King*

Chapter 1: A Cry for Help
References: LC, LP18215
Chapter 2: The Secret of the Air
References: LC, LP18233
Chapter 3: A Battle of Wits
References: LC, LP18240
Chapter 4: Warned by Radio
References: LC, LP18269
Chapter 5: Ship of Doom
References: LC, LP18294
Chapter 6: S. O. S.
References: LC, LP18323
Chapter 7: Saved by Wireless
References: LC, LP18338
Chapter 8: The Master Wave
References: LC, LP18357
Chapter 9: The Trail of Vengeance
References: LC, LP18372
Chapter 10: Saved by Science
References: LC, LP18381

The Radio King, released in October, was one of the shortest serials of 1922. The action focuses on the development of a powerful radio transmitter device which is capable of providing instantaneous worldwide communication.

The heroes of the serial, Brad Lane and John Leyden, have invented an ingenious electronic system which will enable the United States to be in communication with any country of the world almost immediately. Moreover, it allows the United States to be in touch with any of its military bases throughout the world. The conflict begins when Marnee, an electronic genius and sinister leader of a group of international criminals, seeks to steal the invention from Brad and John. Marnee plans to utilize this communication tool to eventually overthrow the U. S. government.

In episode 2 Brad encounters an attractive young newspaper reporter, Mary Harden, who wants to write a story about the transmitter. Brad and Mary soon are attracted to each other and this relationship continues through the end of the serial.

John, Brad, and Mary travel throughout the U. S. testing their wireless device, while being constantly pursued by Marnee and his gang. During the remaining eight chapters, Marnee brandishes many electronic devices which are used in an effort to snare the radio transmitter from the clutches of its inventors. Somehow the trio manages to escape each time from the peril that Marnee plans for them. In the final episode, Brad creates a marvelous wireless door-closing mechanism which finally traps Marnee and his gang. Once and for all the powerful radio transmitter is protected and can now provide a worldwide communication network for the military services.

The Radio King is filled with electronic gadgetry and scientific paraphernalia and, yet, its basic plot seems to be extremely weak in comparison with other serials of this period. The action that transports the audience from one episode to the next is lethargic and lacks the continuity of a polished production. Moreover, Roy Stewart doesn't seem to fit the role of Brad Lane, a scientific inventor and radio expert. The majority of his roles previous to this serial were as western heroes, and throughout the feature he seems to resemble a transplanted cowboy.

> "The idea of detectives and criminals employing science against each other is not new, but the introduction of radio, the use of the latest developments along this line and the utilization of the possibilities of the subject which are still speculative, multiply and hold the interest."
>
> *Moving Picture World*, Vol. 58, p. 401

THE SKY SPLITTER

Release: 1922, Hodkinson
Description: Silent, 970 feet
Classification: SF-C
References: No. 14, p. 438; No. 45, p. 26; No. 50, p. 444; No. 51, p. 27; LC, MP2221; MPN, Vol. 26, p. 2735; MPW, Vol. 59, p. 364

Credits

Producer . . . . John R. Bray
Director . . . . Ashley Miller and J. A. Norling
Screenplay . . . . J. A. Norling

Cast

Adam Cooley . . . . Actor unknown

The Sky Splitter is a short, one reel feature which centers around Adam Cooley's invention of an engine which is capable of traveling at speeds equal to that of light (186,000 miles per second, or 299,793 kilometers per second).

In the first part of the film, Adam is seen tinkering with his automobile engine, attempting to modify the engine with his acceleration invention so that he can produce speeds equal to light. He decides to take his car for a test run with the newly installed engine firmly mounted to its frame. After only a few short yards, the car goes out of control and Adam is sped upward into the stratosphere and finally out of the earth's gravitational field. As he moves faster and faster through space, he realizes the sensation of approaching the speed of light. Suddenly, the vehicle begins to decelerate and he brings his car (or his pseudo-spaceship) to a firm landing on the surface of a mysterious planet.

While rummaging about the planet, he discovers a huge telescope through which he gets a clear view of earth, but much to his surprise, he is able to see the earth not as it is but rather as it was. Because he has traveled at the speed of light, or greater, he is able to see the past rather than the present. In using this very powerful telescope, he is able to focus on his hometown and miraculously sees himself as he was 50 years ago. As he watches these 50 years of his life pass before his very eyes, he realizes there were some serious changes that he should have made in his social behavior and his interactions with other people. He vows that if he ever returns to earth, he will institute those changes.

Suddenly Adam is shaken by someone's hand on his shoulder and a voice beckoning him to awaken. As he emerges from what appears to have only been a few moments of unconsciousness, he realizes that his automobile had been involved in an accident, and that he had never traveled faster than the speed of light, nor ever visited a far off planet. Instead, he had been lying unconscious in a grassy knoll beside the road. But as he arises from his stupored state, he remembers the vow made regarding his social behavior and silently commits himself to carrying out that promise.

The Sky Splitter is an interesting SF comedy which reveals a strange space vehicle and a lucid examination of the concept of time travel. It is the first SF film to convey the idea of speeds equal to or greater than that of light, and introduces the conceptualization of Albert Einstein and his theory of relativity. Although they are treated in a semi-humorous manner, one cannot help but get the feeling that there was a degree of seriousness being attempted by the producer.

THE YOUNG DIANA

Release: 1922, Paramount Pictures Corp.
Description: Silent, 6744 feet
Classification: SF-F
References: No. 14, p. 540; No. 50, p. 555; AFI, F2.6584, p. 933; LC, LP18021; MPN, Vol. 26, p. 304, 305; MPW, Vol. 57, p. 530, 629, 631; Vol. 60, p. 688; Vol. 61, p. 340; Vol. 62, p. 322; VAW, Vol. 68, 9-1-22, p. 41

Credits

Producer .... Marion Davis and Cosmopolitan Films
Director.............................. Albert Capellani and Robert G. Vignola
Screenplay .... Luther Reed
Art Director .... Joseph Urban
Camera.. Harold Wenstrom

Cast

Diana May .... Marion Davies
James P. May.. Maclyn Arbuckle
Richard Cleeve .... Forest Stanley
Lady Anne .... Gypsy O'Brien
Dr. Dimitrius... Pedro de Cordoba

This is the story of a young maiden, Diana May, who is forced by her socially ambitious father, James P. May, into a marriage with Lord Richard Cleeve. But the night before the proposed wedding, Lord Cleeve gets a strange sensation to withdraw from the impending ceremony scheduled to take place the next day. Unknown to Lord Cleeve and the rest of the players in this drama, Dr. Dimitrius, a metaphysical and powerful scientist, has used his mental telepathy to suggest to Cleeve that he should quickly flee before this marriage can take place.

Lord Cleeve, accompanied by Lady Anne (Diana's best friend), boards one of his ships and plans for them to be married at sea. Needless to say, Diana is heartbroken over the sudden withdrawal of her fiance and angered by the fact that he has run off with her friend. Naturally, Dr. Dimitrius appears on the scene to comfort her.

While dozing, Diana dreams that she has aged terribly and her father is about to cast her out, but Dr. Dimitrius comes to her rescue. By utilizing a unique device in his secret laboratory, he is able to re-establish her youth and beauty. She then envisions that she and Dr. Dimitrius are wandering through the countryside visiting the various winter festivals that take place everywhere. Finally, she awakens from this dream and by her side is the enamored Dr. Dimitrius. She relates her dream to him and he abates her fears by telling her that he does have such an elixir that will provide her with youth and eternal life.

Diana, fearing the future her dream has foretold, concludes that she has nothing to lose by taking the mixture, even though Dr. Dimitrius warns her that if the experiment goes awry it will mean her death. Quickly, she consumes the volatile liquid and her body immediately begins to feel the warmth of the fluid

Diana is crowned queen of the ice carnival in *The Young Diana* (1922).

as it flows through her body. As she turns and peers into the mirror, she finds herself the radiant beauty of her earlier youth. Her skin is soft and rose colored and her hair is once again pure gold. While under the influence of the substance, she visits the magnificent ice carnival in Montreux and is eventually crowned queen of the carnival. As time passes those about her age, but Diana is secure in the resolve of Dr. Dimitrius' promise that she will remain young forever.

One day, while attending an opera in Paris, she encounters Lord Cleeve, her former suitor. She finds him a decrepit, wrinkled, old man while she has not aged a day since their last meeting. He fails to recognize her and she finds herself uninterested in the revenge that had gnawed at her soul these many years. As the opera draws to a close, Diana begins to die. It seems Dr. Dimitrius (who had died some time ago) had miscalculated: while Diana's body always displayed the appearance of youth, her heart remained unaltered by the magic mixture and finally ruptured due to the strain of old age.

While *The Young Diana* (based on the novel written by Marie Corelli) is a weak science fiction fantasy entry, it does display magnificent scenery produced by Joseph Urban. The ice carnival scenes with its radiant ice dancers in the background, provided an opportunity to showcase many of the motion picture industry's beauties of the day. Additionally, the concept of a chemical in which the aging process would be halted or reversed provides a new adaptation to some of the older rejuvenation plots displayed in SF feature films of 1910 through 1919.

> "With customary lavishness in mounting and costuming, Cosmopolitan Productions furnishes the Paramount release schedule with a Marion Davies starring vehicle that is based on a story which has already received wide publicity in having been published in Hearst's magazine and is now being run serially in many papers throughout the country."
>
> *Moving Picture World*, Vol. 59, p. 530

1923

AROUND THE WORLD IN EIGHTEEN DAYS

Release: 1923, Universal
Description: Silent, 12 episode serial, each episode approx. 2000 feet
Classification: SF-A
References: No. 88, p. 109, 232; No. 31, p. 322, 323; No. 50, p. p-3; BIO, Vol. 54, No. 855, p. 62; LC, LP18412; MPW, Vol. 60, p. 63; Vol. 62, p. 324

Credits

Producer .... Universal
Director .... Reeves Eason and Robert F. Hill
Screenplay .. George Bronson, H. Howard, Robert Dillion, and Frank H. Clark

Cast

Phileas Fogg, Jr. .... William Desmond
Martha Harlow .... Laura LaPlante
Jiggs .... William P. DeVaul
Wallace J. Brenton .... Wade Boteler
Matthew Harlow .... William Welsh
Rand .... Percy Challenger
Smith .... Hamilton Morse
Davis .... Tom S. Guise
White .... Gordon Sackville

Phileas Fogg, Sr. .... Alfred Hollingsworth
First Detective .... L. J. O'Connor
Second Detective .... Arthur Millett
Harlow's Butler .... Pat Calhoun
Man Who Makes Bet .... Harry DeVere
Piggott .... Spottiswoode Atkins
Munfare .... Boyd Irwin
Hippolyte Darcy .... Sidney DeGrey
Desplayer .... Jean DeBrine

Chapters 1-12 of *Around the World in Eighteen Days*

Chapter 1: The Wager
References: LC, LP18412
Chapter 2: Wanted by the Police
References: LC, LP18427
Chapter 3: The Apaches of Paris
References: LC, LP18461
Chapter 4: The Man Who Broke the Bank at Monte Carlo
References: LC, LP18455
Chapter 5: Sands of Doom
References: LC, LP18474
Chapter 6: The Living Sacrifice
References: LC, LP18528
Chapter 7: The Dragon's Claws
References: LC, LP18536
Chapter 8: A Nation's Peril
References: LC, LP18560
Chapter 9: Trapped in the Clouds
References: LC, LP18576
Chapter 10: The Brink of Eternity
References: LC, LP18594
Chapter 11: The Path of Peril
References: LC, LP18620
Chapter 12: The Last Race
References: LC, LP18639

Around the World in Eighteen Days is a serial based on the novel *Around the World in Eighty Days* (1872), by Jules Verne. It is the first adaptation of the famous Verne novel; however, the movie attempts to modernize the book by having the son of Phileas Fogg travel about the earth using ultramodern transportation devices. He employs the use of a super high-speed airplane, an express train, an inboard speed boat, and a specially constructed submarine.

The story centers on a wager which evolves out of an argument that takes place during the first episode entitled *The Wager*. Wallace J. Brenton and Matthew Harlow are officers of a large energy producing company. Harlow is up for re-election as president of the company and wishes to develop a new synthetic fuel that will provide energy that is economically feasible for the poor. The senior vice-president (Brenton) is opposed to this idea and has challenged Harlow for the presidency of the

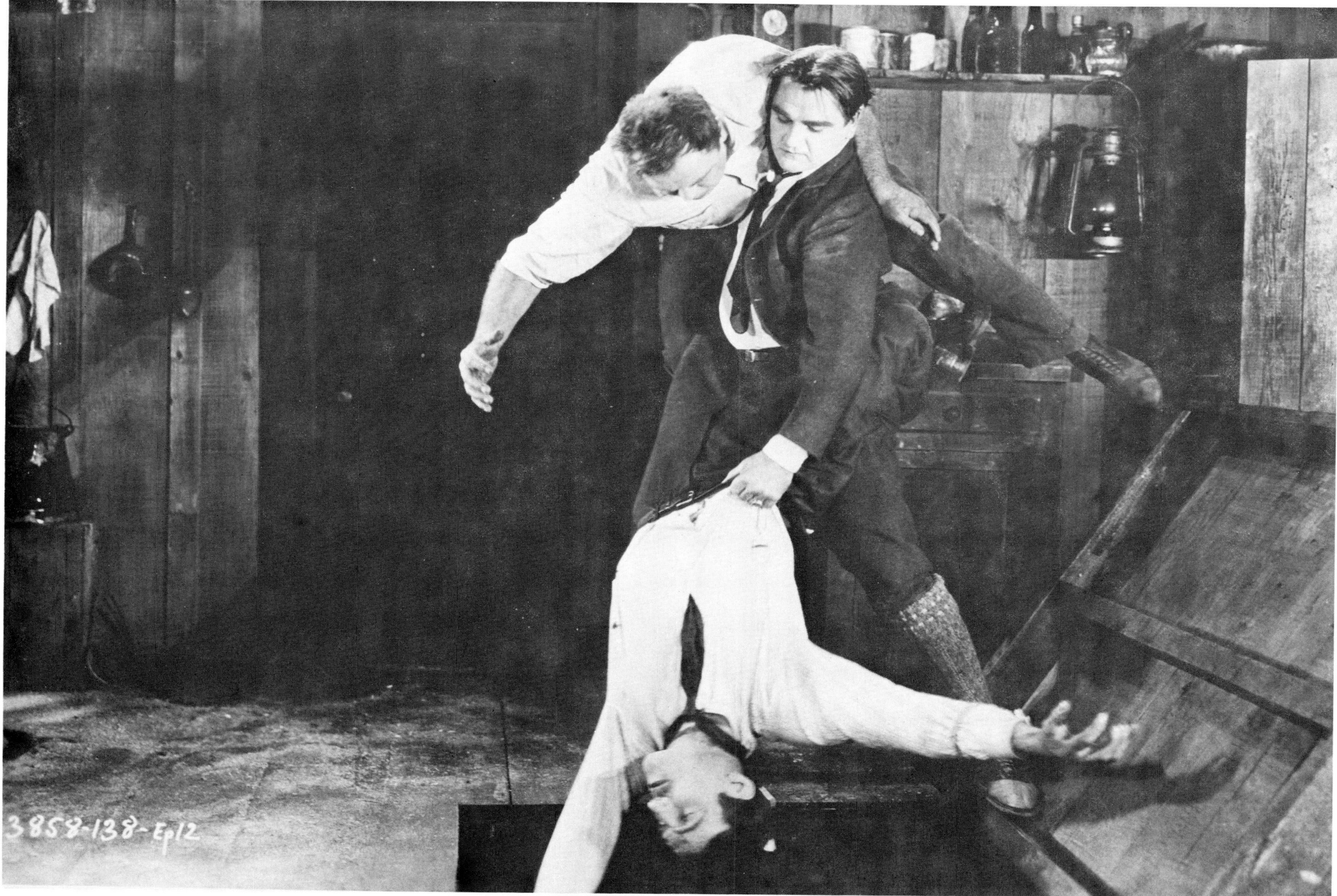

Phineas Fogg and faithful Jiggs are in peril once again on their journey *Around the World in Eighteen Days* (1923).

company. Harlow now realizes that his only hope of retaining the presidency is to quickly gather the needed proxies of the stockholders. However, these various people are scattered throughout the world, and he has only 19 days in which to get them. Naturally, he becomes quite discouraged because of the hopelessness of the task.

Martha Harlow, Matthew's daughter, is engaged to Phileas Fogg, Jr., an adventurer and son of the famous Phileas Fogg, Sr., who traveled around the world in 80 days. Martha relates her father's plight to Phileas during dinner that evening. The idea of traveling around the world in only 18 days immediately pops into Phileas' head as well as the fact (obviously with some suggestion and coaxing from Martha) that he might be able to acquire the needed proxies for his future father-in-law by traveling through the world using various high speed vehicles.

Wallace Brenton scoffs at this idea and wagers an enormous sum of money that it will be impossible for him to return to New York within the 18 day period, much less acquire any of the needed proxies. Harlow decides, with Phileas' approval, to accept this wager and the scene is set for a fantastic scientific adventure serial that carries the audience around the world in a mere 18 days.

Fogg is accompanied by his faithful companion, Jiggs, played by William P. DeVaul. They begin by wiring the various places that Fogg plans to travel so that the needed proxies will be signed and ready for his pickup. In addition, Fogg carefully lays out the route that will take them on their 18 day journey. His father, Phileas Fogg, Sr., provides some logistic help by using some old friends that were acquired during his 80 day jaunt. Needless to say, the task will not be as simple as it appears on the surface. Wallace is not just going to sit back and see his wager or the future presidency jeopardized by this buffoon Fogg. He sends out a collection of thugs and detectives to impede Phileas' travel wherever they can.

Using a specially designed airplane, Fogg travels from the United States to England via Greenland. Upon his arrival, and while trying to acquire the proxy from the London stockholder, he is pursued by a hoard of police. It seems poor Fogg has been identified by an anonymous accuser as the prime figure in a large jewelry robbery that occurred that very afternoon. Miraculously Fogg and Jiggs manage to board their aircraft and make it across the English Channel just before the police nab them. Arriving in Paris only moments ahead of Wallace's thugs, Fogg is able to secure the pledges from the pair of stockholders and leaps aboard the high speed express train to Monte Carlo. While aboard, he and Jiggs are twice nearly pushed from the speeding train, but Fogg has an ingenious knack for escaping difficult situations, as well as possessing a great deal of luck. It isn't long before Fogg and Jiggs find themselves in Monte Carlo where they scurry to secure the needed proxies. They next board a speedboat to transport them to Constantinople. Once there, the fearless pair make their cautious way to Bombay, India via a speeding locomotive. Once in Bombay, having survived several attempts to derail the train, they charter a high speed aircraft to Shanghai, but the aircraft is nearly forced down over the jungles when the engines catch fire. Only Fogg's quick thinking saves the airplane and the stalwart crew.

Arriving to a tumultuous greeting in Tokyo, Fogg shares the limelight with the gallant submarine commander who provided their safe passage from Shanghi. While there, they secure the valuable proxies and begin their preparations for travel to San Francisco, and board a specially designed airclipper that will take them. Twice during this part of their journey they are nearly shot down by unidentified fighter planes. But they arrive safely on the western shores of the United States, collect the last needed proxy, and board a high speed nonstop passenger train to New York.

The last two episodes focus on the final jaunt across the country in which Brenton marshalls all of his financial resources in a feeble effort to impede Fogg's journey back to New York. But time after time, Phileas and Jiggs manage to escape the perilous jaws of death and the treacherous obstacles Brenton has placed in their way.

The triumphant duo returns to New York within the 18 day time period and Fogg not only delivers the needed proxies to Harlow, but collects for himself the largest portion of the wager which totals several hundred thousand dollars, a sum which will provide security for him and Martha the rest of the days of their lives.

Around the World in Eighteen Days is a cleverly portrayed adventure serial in which the most modern transportation devices are showcased. Several vehicles were even more advanced than the theoretical technology of the period. The uniquely designed aircraft which could travel several times the speed of conventional airplanes at the time, and the submarines and surface vessels vastly exceeded the speed of other designs of 1923 and provided moments of excitement for the audience. The reviewers of the day heralded the serial as unique entertainment for the audience of 1923:

> "Universal's new chapter play is entertainment that should appeal not only to serial fans but to anyone who likes thrilling action and romance. The first three episodes pass the supreme test. Each one leaves the spectator keyed up and eager for the subsequent number."
>
> *Moving Picture World*, Vol. 60, p. 63

> "The speed with which this thrilling story races from climax to climax is admirably sustained, and really does succeed in creating a breathless interest in what is to follow. The immensity of the theme is only rivalled by the elaborate scale upon which it it carried out."
>
> *Bioscope*, Vol. 54, No. 855, p. 62

BACK TO EARTH

Release: 1923, Universal
Description: Silent, 1525 feet
Classification: SF-C
References: No. 14, p. 34; No. 50, p. 23; LC, LP19283; MPW, Vol. 28, p. 1363; MPW, Vol. 64, p. 281

Credits

Producer .... Century Films
Director .... Albert Herman
Screenplay .... Albert Herman

Back to Earth is an extremely short science fiction comedy. The feature revolves about a group of clandestine real estate agents who have manufactured a flying house. They place the house on a vacant lot and then round up a poor fool to purchase it, but while they are consummating the deal at a nearby bank, the house flies away to a new location.

The house is also equipped with a myriad of electronic gadgets that are supposed to attract buyers. It's even outfitted with an electronic device which changes the color of the entire house.

The feature does fulfill its main purpose--to entertain--but in the process results in a shallow science fiction effort.

BLOW YOUR OWN HORN

Release: 1923, F. B. O.
Description: Silent, 6315 feet
Classification: SF-A
References: No. 14, p. 66; No. 50, p. 42; AFI, F2.0486, p. 70; MPW, Vol. 65, p. 238, 623

Credits

Producer .... R. C. Pictures
Director .... James W. Horne
Screenplay .... Rex Taylor
Camera .... Joseph Dubray

Cast

Jack Dunbar .... Warner Baxter
Nicholas Small .... Ralph Lewis
Ann Small .... Derelyn Perdue
Augustus Jolyon .... Eugenie Acker
Dinsmore Bevan .... William H. Turner
Gillen Jolyon .... Ernest C. Warde
"Buddy" Dunbar .... John Fox, Jr.
Julie Yates .... Mary Jane Sanderson
Mrs. Jolyon .... Eugenie Forde
Mrs. Gilroy Yates .... Dell Boone
Percy Yates .... Billy Osborne
Timothy Cole .... Stanhope Wheatcroft

Blow Your Own Horn is a rather weak SF adventure film. Nevertheless, it offers some entertaining moments and a glimpse of a device which could easily be the forerunner of large microwave transmitters.

As the story begins, Jack Dunbar, a young communications officer who has just been discharged from the army after completing his tour of duty during World War I, is sitting along a remote country road discouraged about his re-entering society and how he might fit into some large industrial company. Jack has several keen ideas on how he might be able to transmit energy by use of a large wireless transmission device, but so far his ideas have fallen on deaf ears. As he sits along the road, a speeding automobile whirls by him and then comes to a sudden stop only a few hundred yards farther on. As Jack continues his slow dawdling pace, he soon is alongside the car and discovers that the auto has a flat. He offers to lend a hand in changing the tire. The driver, Nicholas Small, a wealthy munitions millionaire, eagerly accepts Jack's assistance. Small then notices Dunbar's despondent nature and encourages him by saying that the way to succeed in the world is by blowing your own horn and letting people know how good you are; the key to success is not what you know, but what people think you know. He then offers Jack a ride toward the next town.

After a short while, Small stops at a large mansion which is the site of an enormous party that he had been invited to. He asks Jack to accompany him saying, "I will show you what I mean about blowing your own horn," and he introduces Jack as a millionaire. Jack continues the ruse by talking about his inventions to which he seems to get a responsive ear from many of the people. Small realizes that his ploy has gotten a little out of hand, but is not sure how to stop it. Eventually, some of the entrepreneurs at the party decide to support his ideas and give him sufficient funds to begin construction on a powerful wireless device that will transmit electrical energy across the country.

Nicholas Small, who has holdings in other energy companies, is very much against this and makes several attempts to undermine Dunbar's project. But he is outfoxed in his diabolical maneuvers by his own daughter, Ann, who has fallen in love with Jack. By the end of the feature, Jack creates a wireless device to transmit electrical energy and Nicholas graciously welcomes him into the family as his future son-in-law.

This feature is based on a play with the same title and created by Owen Davis, although it wasn't seen on stage until 1926.

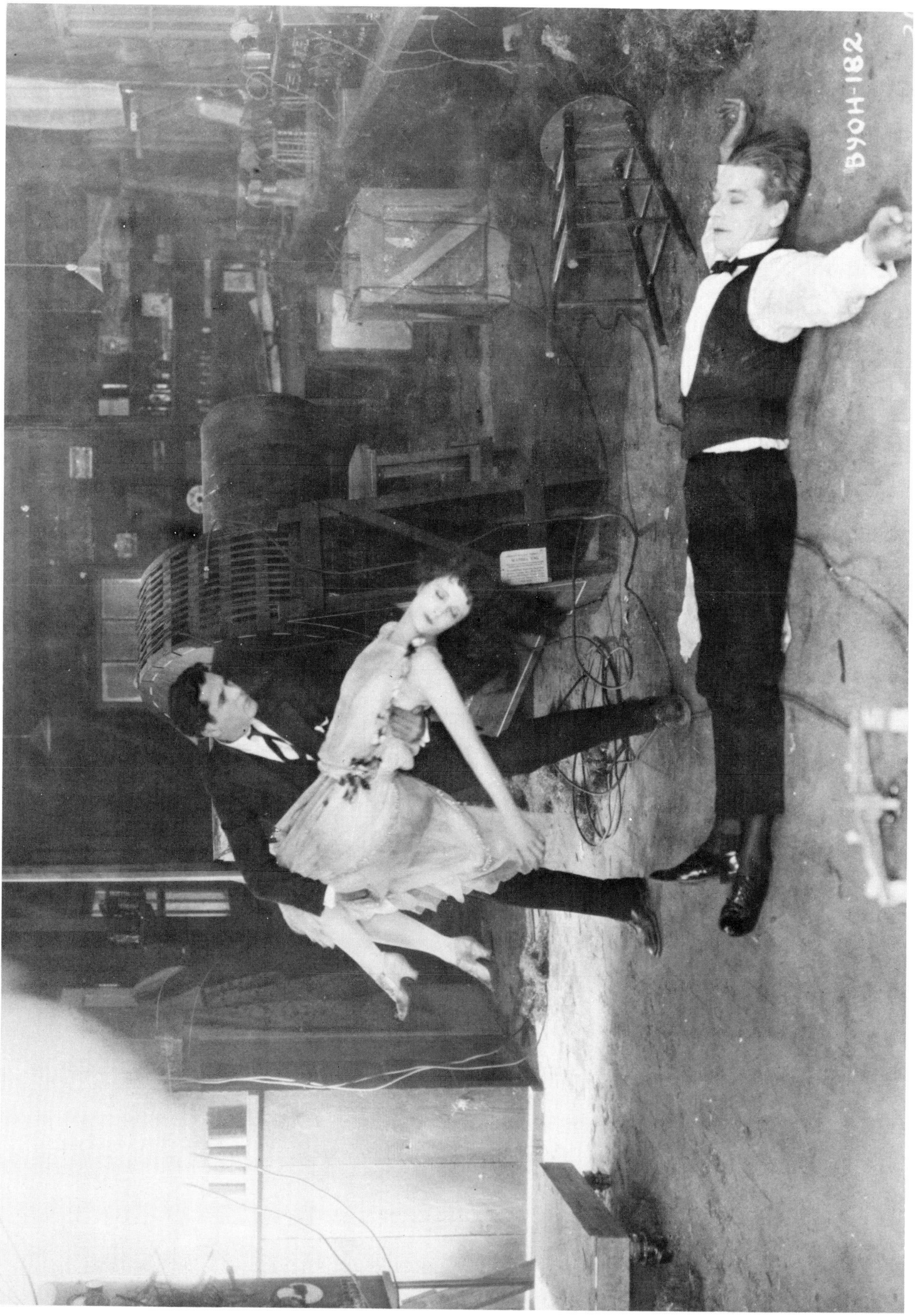

Jack Dunbar rescues his beloved Anne as her father lies unconscious on the floor in ***Blow Your Own Horn*** (1923).

The wireless device which is described in this particular film resembles the microwave devices which appeared some 20 years later for the transmission of electrical energy across our great nation. Such inventions currently dot our landscape for not only the transmission of electricity, but the transmission of television and radio signals which provide an extensive communication network through the country. It has even been recently suggested that such a microwave transmitter could be located in space which would beam back to earth electrical energy from a satellite that had converted the solar energy into electrical power.

> "The picture has been produced in a peppy manner with plenty of action and should provide satisfactory entertainment for the average patron even though the working out of plot introduces situations which test the credulity of the spectator and seem at times rather far-fetched. It belongs to the type of productions that are built to entertain and whose themes will not bear too critical analysis along the lines of probability."
>
> *Moving Picture World*, Vol. 65, p. 238

THE ELEVENTH HOUR

Release: 1923, Fox Film Corp.
Description: Silent, 6819 feet
Classification: SF-A
References: No. 14, p. 145, 146; No. 50, p. 121; AFI, F2.1516, p. 212; LC, LP19412; MPH, Vol. 16, p. 48, 50; MPN, Vol. 28, p. 563; MPW, Vol. 63, p. 405; Vol. 67, p. 309; NYR, 8-23-23, p. 161

Credits

Producer .... William Fox
Director .... Bernard J. Durning
Screenplay .... Lincoln J. Carter and Louis Sherwin
Camera .... Don Short

Cast

Barbara Hackett .... Shirley Mason
Brick McDonald .... Charles Jones
Herbert Glenville .... Richard Tucker
Prince Stefan de Bernie .... Alan Hale
Dick Manley .... Walter McGrall
Estelle Hackett .... June Elvidge
Submarine Commander .... Fred Kelsey
Mordecai Newman .... Nigel De Brulier
Foreman .... Fred Kohler
Barbara's Uncle .... Edward Martindel

As the feature begins, the viewer is immediately caught up in the action and held until the final frame as we learn that Prince Stefan de Bernie, the dictator of a small country, has been trying to acquire a new explosive that is being developed at a munitions plant located just inside his country's border.

A young chemist, Herbert Glenville, has successfully developed a new explosive that is more powerful than anything previously developed by any other company in the world. Shortly after he perfects the explosive, he is mysteriously murdered. Barbara Hackett, the owner of the plant, starts to fear for her own life and takes the small vial containing the explosives formula and attempts to leave the country.

By now the repugnant nature of Prince Stefan has the audience hissing and booing each time he appears on the screen--he is truly the epitome of villainy. One of the Prince's employees, Brick McDonald, seeks out Barbara, and it isn't long before the two are attracted to each other as Brick attempts to help her escape the country and travel to the United States.

From this point in the movie the action appears almost like a serial within a film as Barbara and Brick go through some of the most unbelievable perilous escapes that any serial could dare. They survive a leap off a high cliff; an escape in a speedboat; having their airplane shot down and their parachutes snagged by an aircraft diving at high speeds; and, finally, they are trapped inside the torpedo room of a submarine and are shot from its torpedo tubes.

In the last few minutes of the film, Barbara is rescued from a precarious perch above a vat of molten metal by Brick's death-defying swing on a cable over her. Needless to say, Prince Stefan does not succeed in getting the new explosive. In fact, no one gets it—it's accidently dropped into the molten metal which causes a tremendous explosion only moments after Barbara and Brick's escape from the building.

As they approach the United States, Brick reveals to Barbara that he is an employee of the U. S. secret service and was sent to this small country to make sure the new explosion didn't fall into the hands of some corrupt, evil, diabolical individual.

The Eleventh Hour is an exciting science fiction adventure and provides thrilling scenes throughout its 6819 feet of film—a truly worthwhile effort. Although the idea of new and more powerful explosives is certainly not unique, this production does a marvelous job of developing an action packed plot that won strong audience and critic approval.

> "Thrills, thrills and more thrills characterize the Fox special for the new season, *The Eleventh Hour.* Announced in the opening subtitle as an honest melodrama built solely to entertain, it would appear to have been the idea of those responsible for this production to provide a maximum of excitement, and they have certainly succeeded, for there are enough thrills and stunts in this picture to supply a serial. They follow each other in such rapid succession that hardly is one over before another flashes on the screen and they follow each other smoothly."
>
> *Moving Picture World*, Vo. 63, p. 405
>
> "*The Eleventh Hour* is straight melodrama and is offered as such. It is daring and mystifying in theme, keeping up a rapid fire succession of thrilling events that intrigue and never allow the interest to lag."
>
> *Motion Picture Herald*, Vol. 16, p. 50

EVOLUTION

Release: 1923, Red Seal Pictures Corp
Description: Silent, 4200 feet
Classification: SF
References: No. 14, p. 150; No. 50, p. 127; AFI, F2, 1572; BIO, Vol. 56 No. 877, p. 57; FID, 4-19-25; MPW, Vol. 75, 432

Credits

Producer .... Max Fleischer

Special Effects .... Willis O'Brien

The film *Evolution* attempts to trace man's evolution to early primatial stages as the characters go through the process of reconstructing the fossil remains of various prehistoric men such as Java and Neanderthal, thus showing the resemblance of each to its theorized predecessor, the primate ape. The feature traces the history of man in a unique way by going from the present back to the past after first highlighting the technological advancements of the modern society of 1923. Each of the segments tears away a little of the social and physical structure of mankind until we reach the primeval state of man.

The SF nature of this particular film is probably contained in the filming of the topic of evolution by treating it as reality when in 1923 it was considered by the general public to be a very far out theory. The movie also emerged at a timely moment: the release was during the very month the famous Scopes trial (a trial which attempted to convict a young man for teaching the theory of evolution) was in progress. The trial centered on whether or not the theory of evolution was anti-Christian or anti-moral and further if teaching such an idea undermined the basic precepts on which our country was founded.

Evolution is a compact version of the history of mankind as seen through the eyes of a Darwinian follower, and makes for an interesting film for 1923.

The prehistoric animal scenes pictured in *Evolution* were stock footage from *The Ghost of Slumber Mountain* (1916). Obviously, O'Brien's early work had been so precise and expertly performed that Max Fleischer saw no reason to produce new prehistoric animal scenes.

THE ISLE OF LOST SHIPS

Release: 1923, First National Pictures
Description: Silent, 7425 feet
Classification: SF-A
References: No. 50, p. 224; AFI, F2.2757, p. 387; BIO, Vol. 57, 11-29-23, p. 60; LC, LP18766; MPH, Vol. 16, p. 50, 51; MPN, Vol. 27, p. 1454; MPW, Vol. 61, p. 443; Vol. 62, p. 234, 406; NYR, 5-14-23; VAW, Vol. 70, 5-17-23, p. 22

Credits

Producer.......... M. C. Levee and Ned Martin
Director.......... Maurice Tourneur
Assistant Director.......... Scott B. Beal
Screenplay.......... Charles Maigne
Art Director.......... Milton Monasco
Camera.......... Arthur L. Todd
Editor.......... Frank Lawrence

Cast

Dorothy Fairfax.......... Anna Q. Nilsson
Frank Howard.......... Milton Sills
Detective Jackson.......... Frank Campeau
Peter Forbes.......... Walter Long
Patrick Joyce.......... Bert Woodruff
Mother Joyce.......... Aggie Herring
Captain Clark.......... Hershall Mavall

The Isle of Lost Ships is a science fiction adventure melodrama which takes place in a mysterious ocean region known as the Sargasso Sea.

As the story begins we find Dorothy Fairfax, the young daughter of a wealthy New York industrialist, aboard the ship Tibouron which is traveling from New York to New Orleans by way of the straits of Florida. As it nears the region near the Bahamas, sometimes referred to as the Sargasso Sea, the ship enters a violent storm. During the onslaught of high winds and huge rolling waves, the passengers of the ship are gathered together in the dining room for their own safety, and all are requested to wear life perservers and be prepared in case the ship suffers damage or begins to take on water during the storm.

It is in the dining room that Dorothy first encounters Frank Howard, a navy officer who has been charged with the misappropriation of naval funds. He is handcuffed to Detective Jackson, a large burly man in his mid-thirties, who is escorting Frank back to a naval review board due to be held in two weeks in New Orleans. About the time they all become acquainted and are getting used to the tossing and turning, a crackling sound eminates from the hall below--like the shifting of steel plates. It begins to grind and make the eerie sounds of a creaking door. Frank comments that the ship seems to be in trouble from the storm, and it doesn't take Detective Jackson a second clue to make his move. He tells Dorothy that she is to accompany the two of them and they quickly move to a position closer to the life boats.

No sooner have they begun to make their move, than the ship starts to break apart. The steel plates make death-defying sounds over the roar of the ocean and the thunder of the storm. Somehow the three passengers manage to get into a life boat and steer it away from the Tibouron as the massive ship slowly sinks deep into the lashing waves. Even more amazing is that the three are able to keep the small boat afloat the remainder of the night. But as dawn approaches, the storm abates, and the waters are once again placid.

Before long the three encounter a large clump of seaweed which seems to stretch for miles. They decide that since the seaweed is in their way they will try and pull their boat across it. At about 70-85 yards inside, they come upon the remnants of a spanish galleon somehow being buoyed up by the seaweed. The vessel lies on the surface as though it were a ghost ship waiting for a new crew to arrive and sail it away. The three survivors don't have time to enjoy this unusual sight as a long-boat headed by a stocky man (Captain Forbes) approaches. It seems that the crew, numbering nearly 50 men and two women, have dwelt in the Sargasso Sea area most of their lives, part of a culture going back 150 years or more. They know little or nothing of the outside world and have survived on ships that became stranded in the sea, picking them clean and gaining wares and other essentials from them. They are led by Captain Forbes.

The captain, having recently lost his wife, has eagerly anticipated the arrival of the next female and Dorothy appears to be in line for the horrible position as Forbes' new mate. The pressure of his men, love-starved themselves, is too great for him to chance claiming her immediately; a contest must be devised, one in which the victor would receive the female as the prize. The contest decided on is a fist fight, and the one who is left standing will claim Dorothy as his bride.

Frank enters the arena, not only to win Dorothy, but essentially to save his life and that of Jackson's as well, as two more mouths to feed without proving their physical prowess is more than Forbes and his crew would allow. As it turns out, Frank beats Forbes for Dorothy's hand, and they are married by the captain. Frank assures Dorothy later that it is not a binding marriage ceremony, but a way of protecting her for the time being. Dorothy, however, is not distraught about the situation and seems undisturbed about whether it is for real or not. In any case, there is little time for speculation as they realize their lives hang by a slim thread; sooner or later, Forbes will retaliate for the beating Frank has given him.

They secretly watch the Sargasso Sea for a vessel that can possibly rescue them from this time-locked place. Finally, Jackson spots the conning tower of what appears to be a submarine. He and Frank investigate and find that it is a World War I German submarine. Frank believes he can sail it under the sea and escape the seaweed that permeates the surface of the water.

There is time for a last battle scene as Frank, Dorothy, and Jackson try to hold off the grizzly henchmen and their captain. They quickly board the submarine and lock the hatch. Only after they are submerged, however, does Frank realize that a good portion of the instruments are malfunctioning. Nevertheless, he manages to get the craft to move forward, but as they near the edge of the sea they are forced to surface. Fortunately, a United States naval cruiser arrives as they emerge and brings them aboard. Once safe, they relate their tale of adventure and horror.

The captain of the cruiser also has good news for Frank: the charges of embezzlement were dropped a week ago when an ensign aboard his ship confessed to the crime. Each of the three vow that some day

Dorothy (Anna Nilsson) feeds a friendly monkey aboard the Tibouron as it nears the Sargasso Sea.

Frank battles Captain Forbes for Dorothy's hand in marriage in *The Isle of Lost Ships* (1923).

they will return to the Isle of Lost Ships in hopes of helping those poor beings still living in the dark ages of feudalism under the tyranny of Captain Forbes.

The Isle of Lost Ships is based on a novel entitled *The Isle of Dead Ships,* by Crittendon Marriott (1909). It is an exciting tale filled with mystery and intrigue on a subject that even as early as 1923 had captured the imagination of the American people. The unexplained phenomenon of the Sargasso Sea has mystified sailors and scientists alike for more than 500 years. Many science fiction stories have used the Sea and the Bermuda Triangle legends as their focal points for yarns that have been spinning for the last 50 years.

This film would have to be classified as a weak SF adventure production, but there is no doubt that it is filled with adventure and intrigue which surely left the 1923 audience sitting on the edges of their seats throughout the movie.

LEGALLY DEAD

Release: 1923, Universal
Description: Silent, 6076 feet
Classification: SF-A
References: No. 14, p. 278; No. 50, p. 254; AFI, F2.3029, p. 428; BIO, Vol. 57, 10-11-23, p. 64; LC, LP19191; MPH, Vol. 16, 8-18-23, p. 54; MPW, Vol. 65, p. 626; PHO, 10-23, p. 106; VAW, Vol. 71, 8-2-23, p. 23

Credits

Producer .... Universal
Director .... William Park
Screenplay .... Harvey Gates
Camera .... Richard Fryer

Cast

Will Campbell .... Milton Sills
Mrs. Campbell .... Margaret Campbell
Minnie O'Reilly .... Claire Adams
Jack Dorr .... Edwin Sturgis
Jake's Sweetheart .... Faye O'Neill
Malcolm Steel .... Charles A. Stevenson
District Attorney .... Joseph Girard
The Anarchist .... Albert Prisco
The Judge .... Herbert Fortier
The Governor .... Charles Wellesley
Detective Powell .... Robert Homans
Dr. Gelzer .... Brandon Hurst

Legally Dead is a weakly constructed science fiction adventure film which focuses on a young physician's ability to restore life to a criminal who has been executed. He performs this miraculous feat by creating a chemical called *adrenalin* which, when injected directly into the heart, has the ability to restore life.

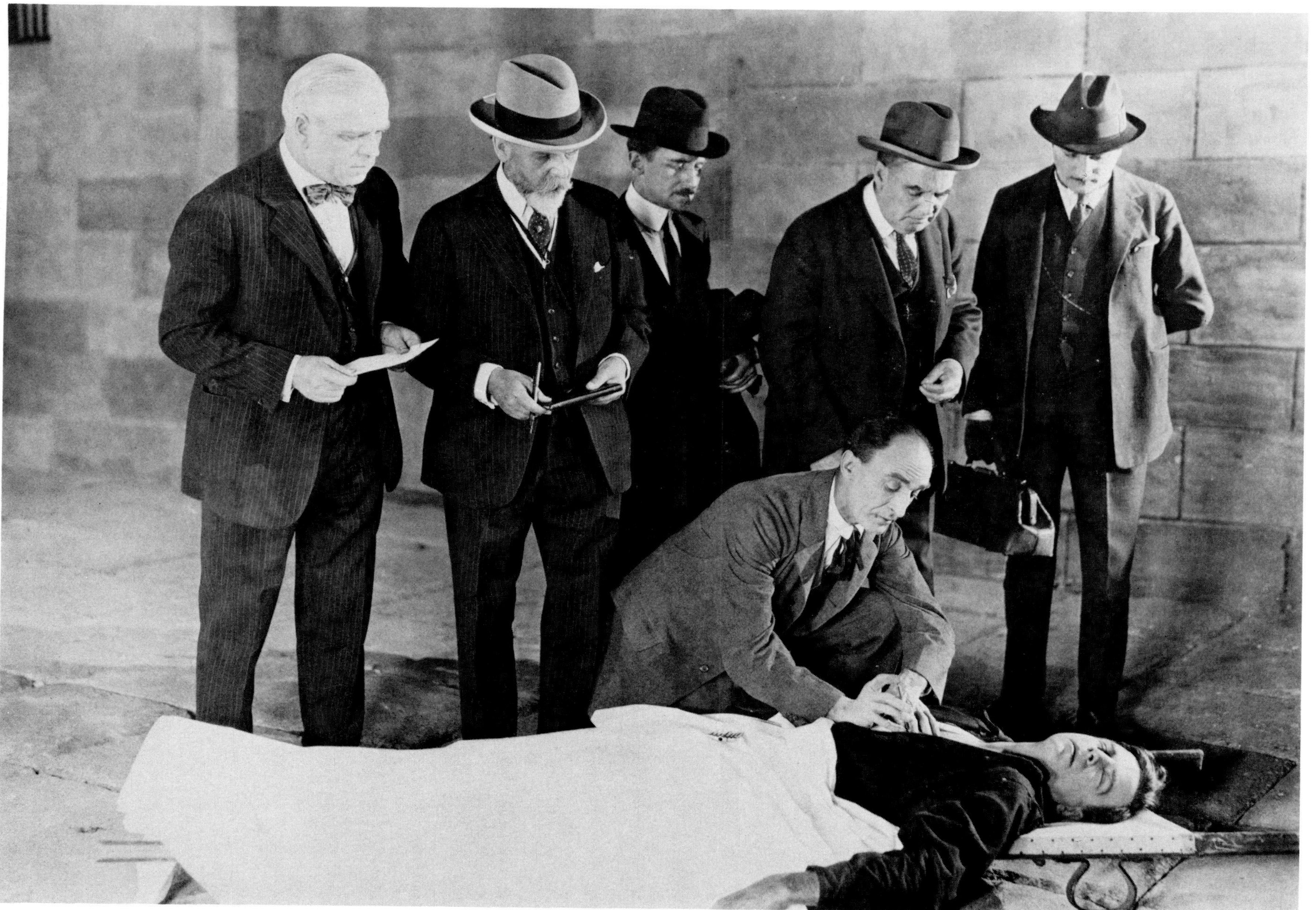

Dr. Gelzer injects the adrenalin into Will in an effort to restore his life. (*Legally Dead*, 1923).

As the story begins we find an investigative reporter, Will Campbell, who, while investigating a bizarre robbery and murder news story, is having a difficult time getting all the facts. He finally decides to get himself arrested on a minor charge in order to gain admittance into the prison where he hopes to continue his investigation.

Once inside, Campbell comes in contact with Minnie O'Reilly who has been incarcerated for slaying her boyfriend after the bank robbery. He gains her confidence so that he might learn all the true details of the robbery. But as the two begin to have frequent and more lengthy encounters, a bond of sincere affection grows between them. Soon Will forgets about his investigation—and his wife and family. (Meanwhile, Mrs. Campbell, unaware of her husband's original intent, is totally confused about why Will is in prison since she doesn't believe he is a true criminal.)

It isn't long after Will and Minnie become enamored of each other that a massive jail break is attempted in one of the cell blocks. The warden is in great danger and Will and Minnie manage to save his life while thwarting the efforts of the other prisoners to escape. As a result of their heroism, the warden requests a pardon for both of them, which the governor grants.

Once free, Will secures a divorce from his wife and he and Minnie move to a small town in an effort to rebuild their lives. He has discarded his newspaper story and further vows never to return to journalism. However, they are pursued by a greedy detective who recognizes them as former criminals. His zeal leads to open persecution of the pair and, not long after a public confrontation between the detective and Will, he is found murdered. Needless to say, Will is the obvious suspect. The prosecutor builds an infallible case out of the circumstantial evidence, and Will is convicted of murder and sentenced to hang.

On the very morning of his execution, the dead detective's fiancee confesses to his murder. The frantic, last-minute call to the warden to stop the hanging is five minutes too late—Will is already dead. However, Dr. Gelzer, a brilliant chemist and physician, has acquired permission from the governor to attempt to restore Will's life. He injects a large syringe of the adrenalin directly into Will's heart. His experiment is successful and Will makes a complete recovery. When he is well enough, he and Minnie once again make a new life in a different part of the country, far from the scene of their unhappiness.

> "With its strong human interest, dramatic action and novel climax, *Legally Dead* should prove a real success at almost any middle-class or popular house. The execution scenes, which include a detailed study of the grim march to the scaffold, may seem a trifle gruesome to some audiences, but it would be a simple matter to make a slight cut here without damage to the story."
>
> *Bioscope*, 10-11-23, p. 64

> "Milton Sills is about the only thing that is connected with this picture that will mean anything. It is intended as a melodramtic thriller. It could have easily been switched into a melodramatic farce, for the greater part of it is exactly that, at least as far as the story is concerned."
>
> *Variety Weekly,* 8-2-23, p. 23

> "The success of *Legally Dead*, which is sad in tone, dealing with prisons, court rooms and hospitals, in which an innocent man falls victim of circumstances, depends on just how far the sympathies of an audience are awakened."
>
> *Motion Picture Herald*, 8-18-23, p. 56

The strange creatures of Mars examine the earthling, who is equally strange to them, in *Radio-Mania* (1923).

RADIO-MANIA

Release: 1923, Hodkinson
Description: Silent, 5400 feet
Classification: SF-F
References: No. 14, p. 395; No. 50, p. 390; No. 51, p. 27; AFI, F2.4418, p. 628-29; MPH, Vol. 16, 8-18-23, p. 54, 56; MPN, Vol. 28, p. 588; MPW, Vol. 63, p. 313; PHO, 3-23, p. 70; PHO, 10-23, p. 106; VAW, Vol. 69, 1-5-23, p. 42

Credits

Producer .... Herman Holland and Teleview Corporation
Director.. R. William Neill
Assistant Director .... Charles Van Arsdale
Screenplay .... Lewis Allen Browne
Camera.. George Folsey
Titles.. Joseph W. Farnham

Cast

Arthur Wyman .... Grant Mitchell
Mary Langdon.. Margaret Irving
Mrs. Langdon... Gertrude Hillman
Mr. Sterling.. W. H. Burton
Landlady.. Isabelle Vernon
Buz Buz .... J. D. Walsh
Gin Gin... J. Burke
Pux Pux .... Peggy Smith
Tuz Tuz .... Betty Borders
Martian Flapper .... Alice Effinger and Peggy Williams

Radio-Mania was originally presented by the Teleview Corporation as a three-dimensional film for which the audience was required to wear special teleview glasses and, thus, had the thrill of seeing the character and the action in perspective. This was the first science fiction film to ever be photographed in three dimensions. Unfortunately, the film was not an overwhelming success, and was reprocessed and reissued under several different titles--*M.A.R.S., Mars Calling,* and *The Man from Mars* were all alternate titles attached to the film during its reissue period from 1923-1924.

The story centers around a scientific inventor named Arthur Wyman. Arthur has received funds to develop a powerful radio apparatus in order to communicate with the planet Mars. During this scientific task, Arthur becomes enamored of Mary Langdon, his landlady's daughter. Soon his work begins to take second place to Mary, but one evening, while asleep, he begins to dream about the successful completion of his project. A project that will allow two-way communication between Earth and Mars.

In Arthur's dream he is not only able to talk with the Martians, but has created a communication device that will allow video and audio transmission from Earth to Mars and back.

The Martians begin to reveal their secrets to Arthur. First, they give him a process by which he can turn coal into diamonds as large as hen eggs. In addition, the Martians reveal to him the method by which clay can be converted to gold. He is obviously excited about these new transmissions from Mars and his ability to change common ordinary materials into rare diamonds and precious gold, but he is even more excited about the contact he has with the Martians themselves.

Mary Langdon (Margaret Irving) attempts to prevent an officer from destroying Professor Wyman's work.

A series of mysterious experiments lead to a visit to the red planet Mars in the feature *Radio-Mania* (1923).

The character he identifies with and has conversations with is Buz Buz, a semi-grotesque individual with an extremely large head--obviously for the purpose of housing his oversized brain. He soon learns that most of the Martians have dual names and seem to all have oversized heads.

Arthur meets other inhabitants: Gin Gin, Pux Pux and Tuz Tuz. There are also Martian dancers who look like the flappers of Earth's 1920's era.

These Martians, for all their enormous brain power housed in their egg-shaped heads, don't seem to be very advanced socially, or at least no more advanced than the Earthlings.

It isn't long after this dream encounter that Arthur wakes up. He realizes that his entire communication process with Mars has been nothing more than a dream sequence and naturally feels discouraged, in fact, ready to give up the whole idea of inventing.

While he had been sleeping, however, Mary Langdon had taken one of his inventions--a remarkable noiseless clock--to several manufacturing firms and managed to sell it for a fortune. She has just returned to tell him of the good news.

This immediately lifts his spirits, and he is ready once again to continue his grind of experimentation and work on the radio communication device with the planet Mars in the hope that his dream was perhaps merely an indication of the reality to come.

Radio-Mania appears to have been a very significant SF film. It deals with telecommunication devices which possess both audio and video capabilities. It talks, for the first time, about creatures on Mars being of humanoid form, and deals with them in more of a real than fantasy sense.

The special effects in this feature should not go unnoticed, nor the costume designs for the Martian creatures. Their large heads and enormous ears were created to show features thought to be necessary for Martians with extraordinary mental abilities.

Finally, *Radio-Mania* deserves a great deal of credit for attempting to expose to the public a new cinema phenomena–the illusion of three-dimensions on screen, something that did not reappear until the mid-1950's.

> "Highly imaginative is the newest Hodkinson feature, 'Radio-Mania', which stars Grant Mitchell, a Broadway stage star who makes his screen debut in this picture. As indicated by the title, radio plays an important part in this production, for it furnishes the link by which the hero believes he is in communication with the planet Mars."
>
> *Moving Picture World,* Vol. 63, 7-28-23, p. 313

> "The odd scenes of life on Mars with the inhabitants pictured with huge heads and ears, whose mentality is a thousand years in advance of the earth beings, are especially well done."
>
> *Motion Picture Herald,* 8-18-23, p. 56

RED LIGHTS

Release: 1923, Goldwyn Pictures Corp.
Description: Silent, 6841 feet
Classification: SF-A
References: No. 14, p. 398; No. 50, p. 395; AFI, F2.4506, BIO, Vol. 57, 10-18-23, p. 72; LC, LP19342; MPH, Vol. 16, p. 60, 61, 84; MPN, Vol. 28, p. 782, 1446; MPW, Vol. 64, p. 354; NYT, 9-10-23; PHO, 11-19-23, p. 100, 133; VAW, 9-13-23

Credits

Producer.. Cosmopolitan
Director.. Clarence G. Badger
Screenplay........................ Carey E. Wilson and Alice D. G. Miller
Camera.. R. J. Bergquist
Editor.. June Mathis

Cast

Ruth Carson	Marie Prevost
Sheridan Scott	Raymond Griffith
Blake	Johnnie Walker
Norah O'Neill	Alice Lake
Roxy	Dagmar Godowsky
Luke Carson	William Worthington
Kirk Allen	Frank Elliott
Alden Murray	Lionel Belmore
Ezra	Jean Hersholt
Porter	George Reed
Henchman	Charles B. Murphy
Conductor	Charles H. West

This is an entertaining science fiction mystery production. The story focuses on Luke Carson, a famous railroad magnate who has been searching for his lost daughter. It seems that when Ruth was a child she was kidnapped from their home, and there hasn't been a trace of her since that day.

Through some friends in the railroad business, Luke gains information which leads him to believe his daughter has been seen in Los Angeles, and sends his attorney to escort her back to Chicago.

The lawyer arrives in Los Angeles aboard a private pullman furnished by Mr. Carson and finds Ruth has been subjected to strange mysterious warnings of death accompanied by intense flashing red lights. (Unknown to him for the moment, all these devices have been created by an eccentric scientist who is determined to frighten the girl and prevent her return to Chicago.) The attorney immediately employs the services of the famous crime deflector (a person who prevents crimes before they occur), Sheridan Scott, to accompany them on their trip back to Chicago to assure Ruth's safety.

The group aboard the pullman bound for Chicago is a strange one. The crime deflector has disguised himself as a millionaire, while the sinister scientist who is frightening Ruth has disguised himself as a railroad reporter. Then there is Ruth, her fiance John Blake, and a second attorney and his girl friend Norah O'Neill. There is also a second detective aboard who has disguised himself as Charlie Chaplin. Not only does the trip back provide peril for Ruth, but the 1923 audience surely found themselves in a state of confusion trying to keep track of the passengers on the pullman, who all seemed to enter rooms through trap doors, windows, and secret passages in the walls. And everytime Sheridan appears (always mysteriously emerging from one of his secret hiding places) he has a cigarette in his mouth and asks, "Do you have a light?" But even when he gets the light he never appears to smoke the cigarette!

Even with all this frivolity, Sheridan finally uncovers the true criminal. It turns out that Ruth had a half-brother who did not wish her to return to Chicago because of the probability that she would eventually inherit her father's millions. This half-brother, Kirk Allen, had hired the scientist to frighten Ruth in the hope that she would remain on the West Coast. Before the end of their trip and Kirk's capture, there are many vicious schemes thwarted through Sheridan Scott's remarkable sleuthing.

The science fiction comedy melodrama, *Red Lights,* is based on a stage play entitled *The Rear Car,* by Edward E. Rose. The adaptation provided the audience with a great deal of enjoyment and laughter. The SF aspects of the movie center around the scientist's mysterious machine which uses bright red lights to aid in introducing a telepathic suggestion into the mind of the intended victim. The red lights supposedly direct as well as project the human voice over great distances so the mental suggestion can be induced.

> "Red Lights just misses being a wow of a comedy mystery melodrama. The fault is with the script, the direction, and finally the cutting. The script did not handle the story clearly; the direction was given to decidedly middle length shots, so that the audience failed to get the drift of what was going on on the screen, a fault likewise present in the showing of writing and telegrams in the feature."
>
> *Variety,* 9-13-24

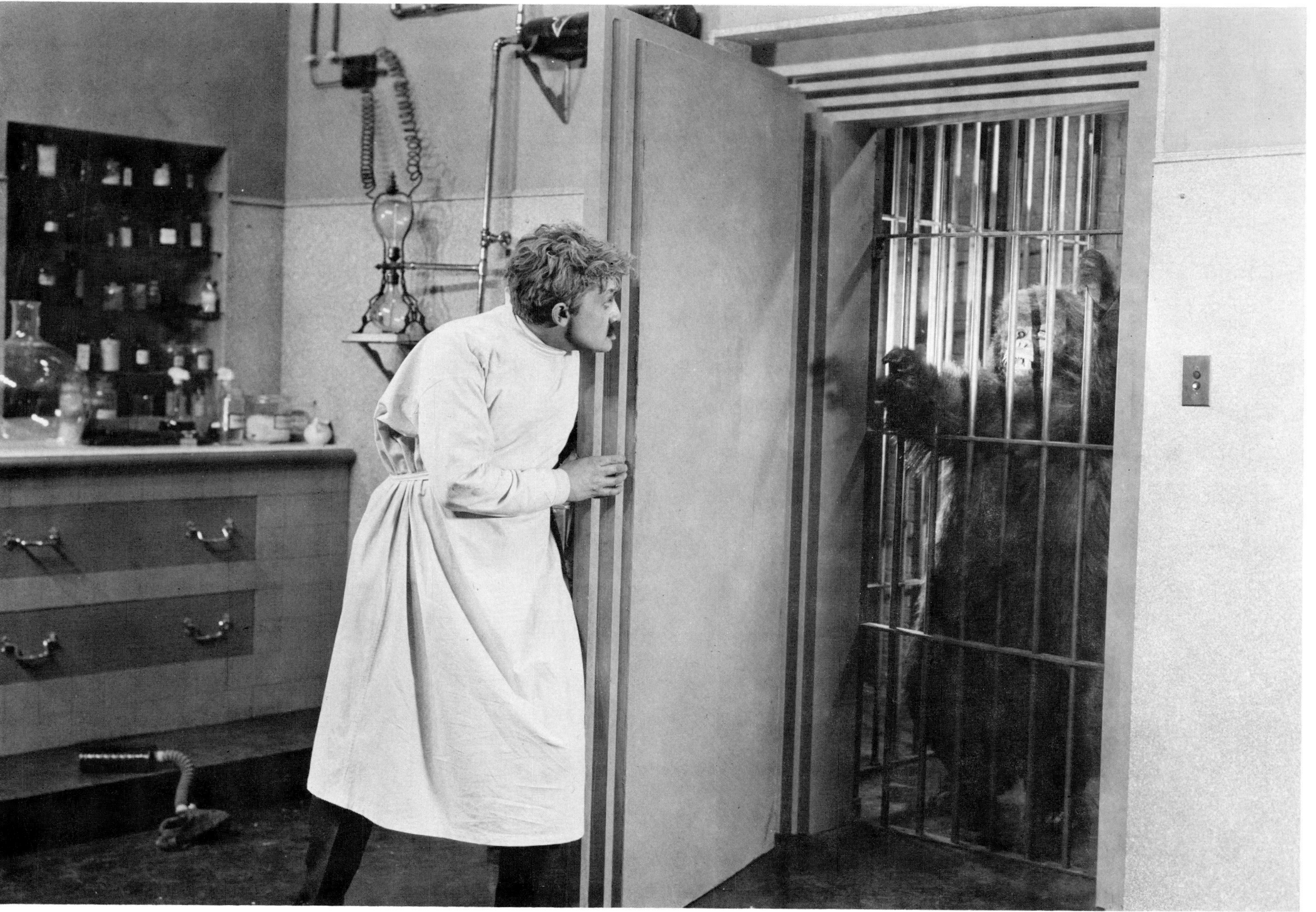

The mysterious red lights in the 1923 feature *Red Lights* transmit telepathic messages to a killer ape.

"Probably the biggest thrill comes when a private car and train are racing madly into an obvious collision, which is avoided through the timely pulling of a switch. The lone car, however, proceeds to the edge of a cliff, where it all but hangs in the balance."

Motion Picture Herald, 9-1-23, p. 61

"A delightful jumble of all the elements that go to make the complete mystery play. Not too skillfully (sic) done, perhaps, but so amusing that one scarcely notices the rough edges. The daughter of a railroad president, kidnapped in infancy, learns of her parentage, and is immediately menaced by a mysterious force that threatens her life--and comes in the form of a talking red light. The mystery is finally solved by one Sheridan Scott, a crime 'deflector', played charmingly by Raymond Griffith. Good entertainment."

Photoplay, 11-1923, p. 100

THE UNKNOWN PURPLE

Release: 1923, Truart Film Company
Description: Silent, 6950 feet
Classification: SF-H
References: No. 14, p. 503; No. 50, p. 514; AFI F2.5974, p. 848; LC, LP19682; MPH, Vol. 16, p. 44, 45; MPN, Vol. 28, p. 2324, 2454, Vol. 29, p. 233, 234; MPW, Vol. 65, p. 565; NYR, 3-24-24, p. 190; VAW, 3-26-24

Credits

Director .... Roland West
Screenplay .... Roland West and Paul Schofield
Set Director .... Horace Jackson
Camera .... Oliver T. Marsh
Editor .... Alfred A. Cohn

Cast

Peter Marchmont .... Henry B. Walthall
Jewel Marchmont .... Alice Lake
James Dawson .... Stuart Holmes
Ruth Marsh .... Helen Ferguson
Bobbie .... Frankie Lee
Mrs. Freddie Goodlittle .... Ethel Grey Terry
Leslie Bradbury .... James Morrison
Freddie Goodlittle .... Johnnie Arthur
George Allison .... Richard Wayne
Hawkins .... Brinsley Shaw
Burton .... Mike Donlin

The Unknown Purple's intriguing plot has a scientist, Peter Marchmont, concluding many months labor toward inventing a process which produces a brilliant purple light while rendering its human subject invisible. But Marchmont's work into the wee hours of the morning, day after day, constructing his incredible invisible ray has proven to be very costly for him. He has neglected his family to the point that his wife has become seriously involved with another man, James Dawson. Dawson plots to remove Marchmont from the marriage by devising an elaborate scheme in which

Marchmont will be accused of committing a large robbery. Dawson is indeed successful in framing him and Marchmont is sent to prison. While incarcerated, his wife divorces him and marries the scheming Dawson.

Eight years later, Peter Marchmont is released from prison. The secret of the purple light has still not been revealed to the public as his notes evidently were not discovered by Dawson and his ex-wife during his absence. Marchmont dons a clever disguise and calls himself Victor Cromport, a character accepted by society as a delicate, intelligent and handsome Frenchman. It isn't long before he becomes quite the social figure and moves through the same circles as Mr. and Mrs. Dawson. Marchmont (as Cromport) is very interested in seeing his son Bobby and begins to spend time with him, although the boy doesn't know that Cromport is really his father. Ruth Marsh, the child's governess soon becomes infatuated with Victor, and before long he is equally enchanted by her. However, he cannot involve himself in a love affair until his mission is completed.

Victor schedules an elaborate dinner party, making sure every detail is rehearsed to perfection by his servants and himself. After all the guests are assembled a messenger arrives and hands a note to Mrs. Dawson. The note announces that at the stroke of midnight she will lose her valuable pearl necklace from around her neck. Victor, seemingly appalled at such a threat, immediately summons two detectives who come and join the dinner party. The note is mysteriously signed by the "Unknown Purple". The enigma boasts in the letter of how he will foil any effort to stop him from obtaining the valuable pearl necklace. As the night progresses, constant close ups are shown of the clock and the Dawsons' anxiety increases as the appointed hour approaches. At a few minutes before twelve, the detectives scoff that any attempt will not materialize this evening, and further there is no need for concern by any of the guests--especially the Dawsons. But as the clock strikes twelve, an eerie purple glow fills the ornate dining room. (The film was actually tinted purple at this point to provide the special effects necessary for the purple scene.) Suddenly a mysterious hand emerges from the deep purple light and snatches the necklace from around Mrs. Dawson's neck. Within moments the light is gone. All the guests are still at the table and the detectives are clearly puzzled by this strange turn of events.

A few evenings later, the Dawsons are seen in the comfort of their Long Island home when, through an open window, the cone of purple light begins to appear in their drawing room. Again a hand emerges from the light and this time writes a scathing note on the drawing room table. The writer boasts that he will rob the safe in their home that very evening. As with the first experience, the note is signed by the curious "Unknown Purple". The Dawsons summon the detectives to guard their home and especially their safe. Sand is spread in front of the safe in the hope that they will get an imprint of the robber's feet. But the purple shadow decides not to break open the safe. Instead he enters and moves to the basement which once contained Peter Marchmont's secret laboratory. Behind a secret panel in the room he uncovers his valuable laboratory notes and log book. He then returns to the mansion of Victor Cromport.

With the pearl necklace that he has stolen and the return of his log book, Marchmont now feels he has secured the proper vengeance upon his wife and the scheming James Dawson. His power as the Unknown Purple, however, provides one more element of surprise for the Dawsons: he cleverly creates a frame involving both his faithless wife and her new husband in a robbery attempt which eventually leads to their conviction.

Afterwards, he reveals that he is Peter Marchmont as he discards the disguise of Victor Cromport. Being the only surviving relative of Bobby's, the boy joins Peter at the Cromport mansion. And as the film draws to an end, Bobby, Ruth, and Peter are presumed to live happily ever after, comforted in the knowledge that the true criminals have been put in prison--the revenge of the Unknown Purple is complete.

This science fiction horror film was adapted from a play by Roland West, which appeared in New York theaters in 1918. The movie offers many exciting moments for the audience as well as fascination in the disguises created as Marchmont becomes Cromport and then the Unknown Purple. The critics of 1923 praised the actors for admirable jobs in portraying their appointed parts.

Peter Marchmont as Victor Cromport confronts Mr. and Mrs. Dawson in *The Unknown Purple* (1923).

"As a melodrama with a fair element of mystery, the picturization of 'The Unknown Purple,' which is the chief film feature at the Capitol this week, is in many respects a vehicle well suited to the screen. It seems, however, that with more adroit handling and less attention to some sequences the actual dencuement could have been better concealed."

New York Review, 3-24-24

"A sensational melodrama, which features Henry Walthall to the best advantage, this Truart picture should have a strong boxoffice appeal. The story is entertaining and mysterious but is without the superabundance of tricks that make some such attractions too baffling for general enjoyment."

Moving Picture World, Vol 65, p. 565

WASTED LIVES

Release: 1923, Second National Film Corp.
Description: Silent, 4874 feet
Classification: SF-A
References: No. 14, p. 519; No. 50, p. 531; AFI, F2.6110, p. 867; LC, LP18843; MPH, Vol. 16, p. 58, 60

Credits

Producer .... Mission Film Corp.
Director .... Clarence Geldert

Cast

Randolph Adams .... Richard Wayne
Dorothy Richards.. Catherine Murphy
Dr. Wentworth .... Winter Hall
Mrs. Johathan Adams ....Lillian Leighton
Madge Richards .... Margaret Loomis
Ned Hastings..Arthus Osborne
Noah Redstone ....Walt Whitman
Bobby Adams .... Phillippe DeLacy
Mrs. Hastings .... Fannie Midgley

Wasted Lives is a weak science fiction adventure melodrama. The story centers on Randolf Adams, a rich playboy in his second year of medical school. Unfortunately, he sees little purpose in continuing his medical degree and drops out of school. Afterwards, while on a hunting trip, he comes upon a cabin where a child is gravely ill. His medical knowledge enables him to save the child's life, and the experience so deeply affects him that he immediately returns to medical school to devote all his attention to his studies.

Upon graduation, he opens a children's hospital (with his mother's very generious financial backing) and devotes his time to healing children. He has also married Madge Richards in a perfect ceremony with his best friend, Ned Hastings as best man.

Ned, the audience soon learns, is somewhat miffed about Madge marrying Randolph since he was also in love with her. This jealousy continues to eat away at him until he finally plots to remove Randolph from Madge's life. But even while he is scheming, there appears to be little competition since Randolph devotes all his waking hours to the hospital. Madge is left alone and this affords Ned ample opportunities to shower attention on her.

It isn't long after these events that World War I breaks out and Randolph enlists to serve in the medical corp. Ned, on the other hand, elects to remain in the United States as a civilian.

Randolph is sent to the front lines and soon Madge receives word that he has been killed. Upon hearing this news, Ned intensifies his pursuit of Madge, but she stalls for time.

Meanwhile, Mrs. Adams has become so distraught over her son's death that she stops all funding for the hospital and the facility must close its doors. Several days later she is severely injured in an automobile accident. As Madge stands vigil by her bedside, there seems little anyone can do for the poor woman; her heart is slowly failing. But, as can only happen in the movies, when all seems lost, our hero (Randolph) appears. It seems he wasn't killed but had instead been missing.

While on the front lines, he invented a marvelous new device called a "Vibrameter" which has the capacity to strengthen one's heart and, thus, give it new life. He uses the Vibrameter on his mother and her life is spared. While at war Randolph also realized his mistakes and vows now to devote his energies to the hospital, but without neglecting his wife and family.

> "While getting over the message Clarence Geldert, who directed, did not fail to take into consideration the box office values, and the picture, besides having many touches which bring the heart throb, also has a good holding love story and plenty of dramatic appeal. The picture should prove a good attraction."
>
> *Motion Picture Herald,* 1-6-23, p. 60

1924

ALL ABOARD FOR THE MOON

Release: 1924, Bray
Description: Silent, 780 feet
Classification: SF-F
References: No. 50, p. 9, LC, MP2664

Credits

Producer .... J. R. Bray
Animation .... Max Fleischer

All Aboard for the Moon is an animated short movie detailing a rocket trip to the lunar surface. Surprisingly, the feature uses chemical rockets as the means of transportation. This is an interesting feature, but apparently never received widespread circulation.

BLACK OXEN

Release: 1924, First National
Description: Silent, 7937 feet
Classification: SF-A
References: No. 14, p. 52; No. 49, p. 243; No. 50, p. 38; AFI, F2.0444, p. 64; BIO, Vol. 58, 2-28-24, p. 53; LC, LP19700; MPH, Vol. 16, p. 42, 43; MPW, Vol. 67, p. 388; NYR, 1-7-24; VAW, 1-20-24

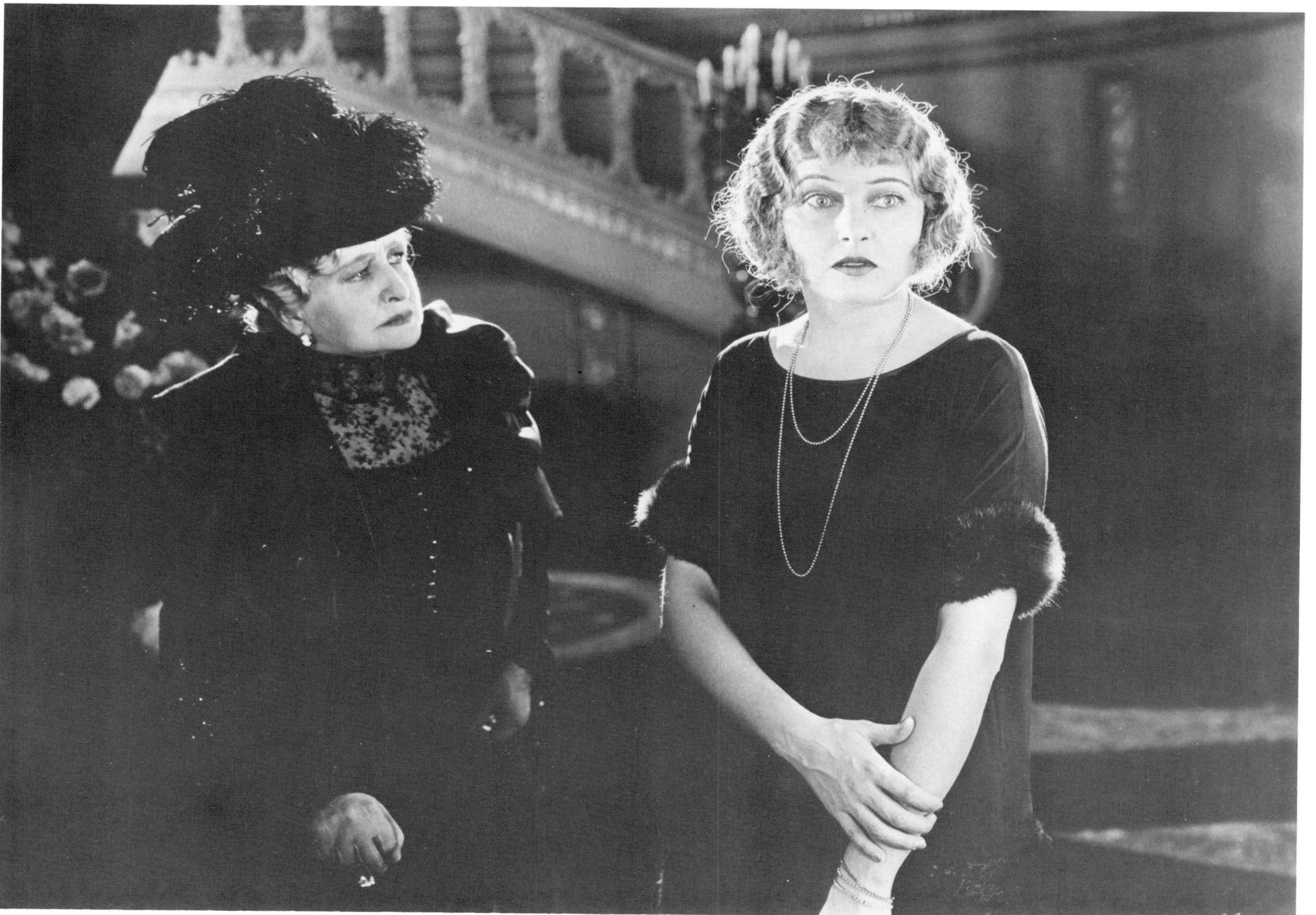

Mrs. Oglethorpe confronts the youthful Mary in *The Black Oxen* (1923).

Credits

Producer.......................................Frank Lloyd Productions
Director.......................................Frank Lloyd
Screenplay.....................................Mary O'Hara
Camera...Norbert F. Brodine

Cast

Madame Zattiany/Mary Ogden.......................Corinne Griffith
Lee Clavering....................................Conway Tearle
Charles Dinwiddie................................Thomas Ricketts
Judge Gavin......................................Thomas Guise
Janet Oglethorpe.................................Clara Bow
Jane Oglethorpe..................................Kate Lester
James Oglethorpe.................................Harry Mestayer
Donnie Ferris....................................Lincoln Stedman
Agnes Trevor.....................................Claire McDowell
Prince Rohenhauer................................Alan Hale
Gora Dwight......................................Clarissa Selwynne
Oglethorpe butler................................Fred Gambold
Ogden butler.....................................Percy Williams
Dr. Steinbach....................................Otto Nelson
Chancellor.......................................Eric Mayne
Austrian advisor.................................Otto Lederer
Anna Goodrich....................................Carmelita Geraghty
Flappers...............Ione Atkinson, Mila Constantin and Hortense O'Brien

The film *Black Oxen* is a screen adaptation of Gertrude Atherton's popular novel of the same title. The theme of the film is rejuvenation--a popular science fiction theme from the beginning of the industry, that reached its height during the 1920's. Many of the movies from 1897 to 1909 dealt with rejuvenation in a comedic manner, but it became less humorous in the next decade and in the period from 1920-1929, rejuvenation was treated very seriously. The *Black Oxen* is certainly one of these serious dramatic presentations, and Corinne Griffith's dual portrayal of Madame Zattiany and Mary Ogden is certainly a noteworthy achievement.

The story begins with a short flashback to the time when a young girl of 28 years, Mary Ogden, meets a handsome dashing Austrian nobleman. A whirlwind romance follows and they are soon wed. They return to his native country of Austria, and during the next 30 years enjoy much happiness.

But, alas, a war suddenly breaks out; their country is ravaged, their economy is near collapse, and, worst of all, Count Zattiany is killed. After peace is restored, Madame Zattiany returns to the United States determined to resolve her personal financial problems and raise sufficient funds to aid her war-torn Austria.

While in New York, Madame Zattiany encounters an unusual scientist, Dr. Steinbach, who uses an x-ray operation to create a process for rejuvenation. He convinces Madame Zattiany, who is 58 years old, that this process can convert the faded and wrinkled Madame into the beautiful woman of her former youth. Madame Zattiany agrees to the operation, and after a few short weeks is seen fully recovered. Gazing in the mirror, the Madame--now Mary Ogden--is amazed at her radiant beauty. She believes that she is even more attractive than when she was younger. Certainly, she is more intelligent and emotionally mature.

The costume worn by Madame Zattiany (Corinne Griffith) in the film *Black Oxen* (1924) cost over $5,000.

Madame Zattiany and Lee Clavering (Conway Tearle) chat about her resemblance to a former acquaintance, Mary Ogden.

The Black Oxen (1924).

She enters the elite society of New York through an attorney whose aid she has sought in solving her financial problems. Almost immediately, she comes in contact with Lee Clavering, a dramatic critic and playwright. He becomes enamored with Mary and they begin to move together in the New York society circles.

Before long, Mary and Lee attend a party which is given by the venerable Mrs. Oglethorpe. Mary had forgotten until now that Mrs. Oglethorpe had been a friend during their younger days. Mrs. Oglethorpe is taken aback by the sight of Mary as she recalls a young girl she new 30 years ago who was identical in appearance to Mary. Since there is strong suspicion among the society ladies that Madame Zattiany had no children, and yet Mary Ogden resembles her in every detail, a great mystery and much confusion results. In fact, Mrs. Oglethorpe, with the aid of her two daughters, Janet and Jane, and her son, James, seeks to uncover the mystery of Madame Zattiany and Mary Ogden.

Soon Mary is cornered and finally must reveal the truth of her identity. At first, Lee Clavering is shocked and the society ladies are unable to believe that her youth has been restored. It isn't long before their jealousy surfaces and they openly ridicule her, even accusing her of unladylike behavior.

In the final scenes of the film, Mary, though in love with Lee, leaves him to the young Janet and Jane Oglethorpe who both profess to have great affection for the playwright. She then returns to Austria where she later meets a young prince and they vow to restore Austria to its once great power among the European nations.

The cast of *Black Oxen* was an experienced one. Most of them had already appeared in more than 30 productions. One of the players, Clara Bow, featured in this particular movie had a relatively minor part, but went on to become known as the "It Girl" during the mid-1920's. It seems the *Black Oxen* was a platform from which many actors sprung to stardom since many went on to even greater productions after this venture. The film was reviewed as one of the better efforts of this period, which certainly must have aided them in their career efforts as well.

THE LAST MAN ON EARTH

Release: 1924, Fox Film Corp.
Description: Silent, 6637 feet
Classification: SF-C
References: No. 14, p. 276; No. 20, p. 32, 48; No. 45, p. 54; No. 50, p. 252; AFI, F2.2975, p. 421; FID, 12-28-24; MPH, Vol. 20, p. 52; MPN, Vol. 30, p. 3893-3896, 3365; NYR, 12-13-24, p. 223, 224; PHO, 2-1925

Credits

Producer .... Jack G. Blystone
Director .... Jack G. Blystone
Screenplay .... Donald W. Lee
Camera .... Allen Davey

Cast

Hattie (age 6) .... Jean Johnson
Elmer (age 8) .... Buck Black
Elmer's Pal .... Maurice Murphy
Hattie's Father .... William Steele
Hattie's Mother .... Jean Dumas
Elmer's Father .... Harry Dunkinson
Elmer's Mother .... Fay Holderness
Elmer Smith .... Earle Foxe

Gertie	Grace Cunard
Frisco Kate	Gladys Tennyson
Hattie	Derelys Perdue
Red Sal	Maryon Aye
Dr. Prodwell	Clarissa Selwynne
Furlong	Pauline French
Paula Prodwell	Marie Astaire

The Last Man on Earth is a unique screen adaptation by John D. Swain. Its basic theme is very similar to *The Poison Belt* (1913), a novel by Arthur Conan Doyle. Despite this similarity of plot (One man is left on earth after a disease has wiped out the remainder of the male population), the film and novel still retain distinct differences.

As the movie begins, we find three children, Hattie, Elmer, and Elmer's pal playing in Elmer's back yard. Time passes and we next see these three as young adults. In fact, Elmer has reached the point where he proposes to Hattie, his longtime childhood sweetheart. But she doesn't feel the same way and reluctantly turns him down, stating that she is interested in a career first. Humiliated and discouraged by this turn of events, Elmer decides to wander off to the forest—far from civilization and its disappointments—and become a hermit living at peace with nature.

About ten years later a strange plague spreads over the entire earth, attacking all males over the age of 14 years. They become violently ill and eventually suffer a terrible death. The women of the world, though grief stricken and frightened, are also determined to carry on. Eventually the power and responsibility is readily assumed by the females as they govern and manage the world's nations.

The Presidentess (female President) of the United States is portrayed as a rather peculiar woman. The While House grounds have become overgrown with weeds and grass, and black cats, the Presidentess' favorite pet, roam the mansion without supervision or confinement. But it seems women in general have changed as evidenced by their penchant for transparent dresses and other revealing fashions.

Meanwhile, a female criminal named Gertie is trying to elude capture by a pursuing policewoman. She hides in the forest and after several days of aimless wandering comes upon Elmer. She is both surprised and frightened at the sight of the only man left on earth. Elmer, thickly bearded, bushy haired and dressed in old clothes, under normal circumstances would not be considered attractive to any female, but the absence of men in the female society makes him very appealing.

After a period of time, Gertie sees more in Elmer than just his masculine appeal, she sees the chance to use him as a pawn for fame and fortune. She sends a message to the Presidentess at the White House asking for 10 million dollars in exchange for Elmer's delivery to her. As they arrive in Washington it seems plans have already been made for a contest with Elmer as the prize. The Senatoress from Massachusetts and the one from California resort to a boxing match with the victor claiming Elmer. As fate would have it, Hattie attends this most exciting event and Elmer catches a glimpse of her in the seats. He quickly rushes to her side and claims that he belongs to her. The scene fades as the two childhood sweethearts make their wedding plans.

As time passes, Elmer's body fluids are discovered to contain a natural serum against the dreaded male-killing disease that plagued the world and within a year after their marriage Hattie gives birth to twins: the human race is saved and will continue to prosper.

This feature is an interesting concept which provides amusement for the audience, but also offers a glimpse into the future possibility of germ warfare—one that is barely science fiction today.

> "*The Last Man on Earth* is a forgotten little comedy that concerns a world of the future that is now behind us (1950), when all the men have been eliminated by a strange disease called *masculitis*, and the women run everything, including the Congress of the United States. Women's liberationists and misogynists alike should find it amusing."
>
> Eileen B. Bower, 7-15-74

LAUGHING AT DANGER

Release: 1924, F. B. O.
Description: Silent, 5254 feet
Classification: SF-A
References: No. 14, p. 277; No. 50, p. 253; AFI, F2.2991, p. 423; LC, LP20939; MPH, Vol. 20, p. 52, 53; MPN, Vol. 30, p. 3185; MPW, Vol. 71, p. 725

Credits

Producer .... Carlos Productions
Director .... James W. Horne
Screenplay .... Frank Howard Clark
Camera .... William Marshall

Cast

Alan Remington .... Richard Talmadge
Cyrus Remington .... Joe Girard
Professor Leo Hollister .... Joe Harrington
Carolyn Hollister .... Eva Novak
Darwin Kershaw .... Stanhope Wheatcroft

Laughing at Danger is a thrilling science fiction comedy which gave Richard Talmadge a chance not only to display his stunt and acrobatic capabilities, but also provided evidence of his acting ability.

The story itself is not unique when compared with others from this same 20 year period. Briefly, it involves an ingenious professor, his daughter who falls in love with a rich sponsor, and, of course, an extraordinary weapon--the death ray. Since ships were easier to mock-up and then blow up for special effects purposes than were buildings the target for such a device was a naval vessel.

As the feature begins, we find Alan Remington quite despondent after a shattered love affair. Cyrus, Alan's father, attempts to encourage Alan and remove his thoughts from the girl he has just lost. He offers Alan a chance to work with the eminent Professor Leo Hollister on a grand scientific project. The elder Remington describes the project in such grandiose terms that Alan is immediately buoyed up by the thought of working on the new weapon system for the navy. Cyrus therefore immediately tells the professor he will sponsor his work on the condition that Alan becomes his assistant.

The project begins and as time passes, Alan also begins to notice Carolyn (the professor's daughter), an attractive young lady who occasionally visits the laboratory. As the completion of their work draws near, Alan and Carolyn strike up a relationship that is surely destined for matrimony. Both the professor and Cyrus are delighted over these events. But this bliss is soon shattered as crooks, led by Darwin Kershaw, receive information about the marvelous weapon that has been invented. They move to capture the weapon and succeed not only in gaining the death ray, but also kidnap the professor and Carolyn.

Alan pursues the criminals with the utmost vigor. It seems Kershaw left a message behind revealing that the United States naval vessels in the harbor would be his first targets. Upon hearing this the naval intelligence forces assist Alan in tracking this madman.

Through a careful bit of sleuthing and several fights along the way, Alan finally finds the hideout situated on a high bluff overlooking the harbor. As he sneaks up on the building, Alan clearly sees Carolyn standing next to a window. He runs toward it; Carolyn sees him and lowers herself to the ground as Alan springs through the door into the room. A fierce battle with the crooks is on. By this time the naval intelligence group has signaled the death ray's location to the ships in the harbor who immediately train their guns on the crooks' hut. Alan, sensing impending danger, grabs Carolyn's hand and they escape just as three large shells strike the hideout, completely destroying it and the death ray.

Later, Alan and Carolyn find her father tied up next to some bushes along a path leading to where the hideout had been. They free him and all three quickly return to the shores at the base of the cliff where they are greeted by the naval officers. Alan is immediately proclaimed a hero. Needless to say, as the movie ends, it is expected that Alan and Carolyn will make final plans for their wedding after having shared so much danger together.

Interesting enough, the death ray device depicted here very closely resembles a large microwave transmitter—a device which in 1924 was being espoused by a bright and ingenious physicist, Tesla. He proposed as early as 1917 that large quantities of electricity could be directed by such a device. Unfortunately, few of the leading electric companies listened to him. He also believed that large quantities of such electricity would make an excellent weapons system—something which is being considered very seriously today.

> "This stunt thriller has a pippin of a story, something not always found in Talmadge pictures, and is very highly and satisfyingly disturbing to the nervous system. It opens with definite characterization of the leading character, tinged with bits of effective humor, develops a real plot logically and then, with ever increasing suspense, moves on to a thrilling conclusion."
>
> *Moving Picture World*, Vol. 71, p. 725

ON TIME

Release: 1924, Truart Film Company
Description: Silent, 6030 feet
Classification: SF-H
References: No. 14, p. 364; No. 50, p. 347; AFI, F2.3978, p. 565; LC, LP20000; MPN, Vol. 29, p. 1920; MPW, Vol. 67, p. 215

Credits

Producer	Carlos Productions
Director	Henry Lehrman
Screenplay	Garrett Fort
Camera	William Marshall
Editor	Ralph Spence
Titles	Ralph Spence

Cast

Harry Willis	Richard Talmadge
Helen Hendon	Billie Dove
Richard Drake	Stuart Holmes
Wang Wu	George Selgman
Casanova	Tom Wilson
Horace Hendon	Charles Clary
Mr. Black	Douglas Gerard
Dr. Spinks	Fred Kirby
Mrs. Spinks	Frankie Mann

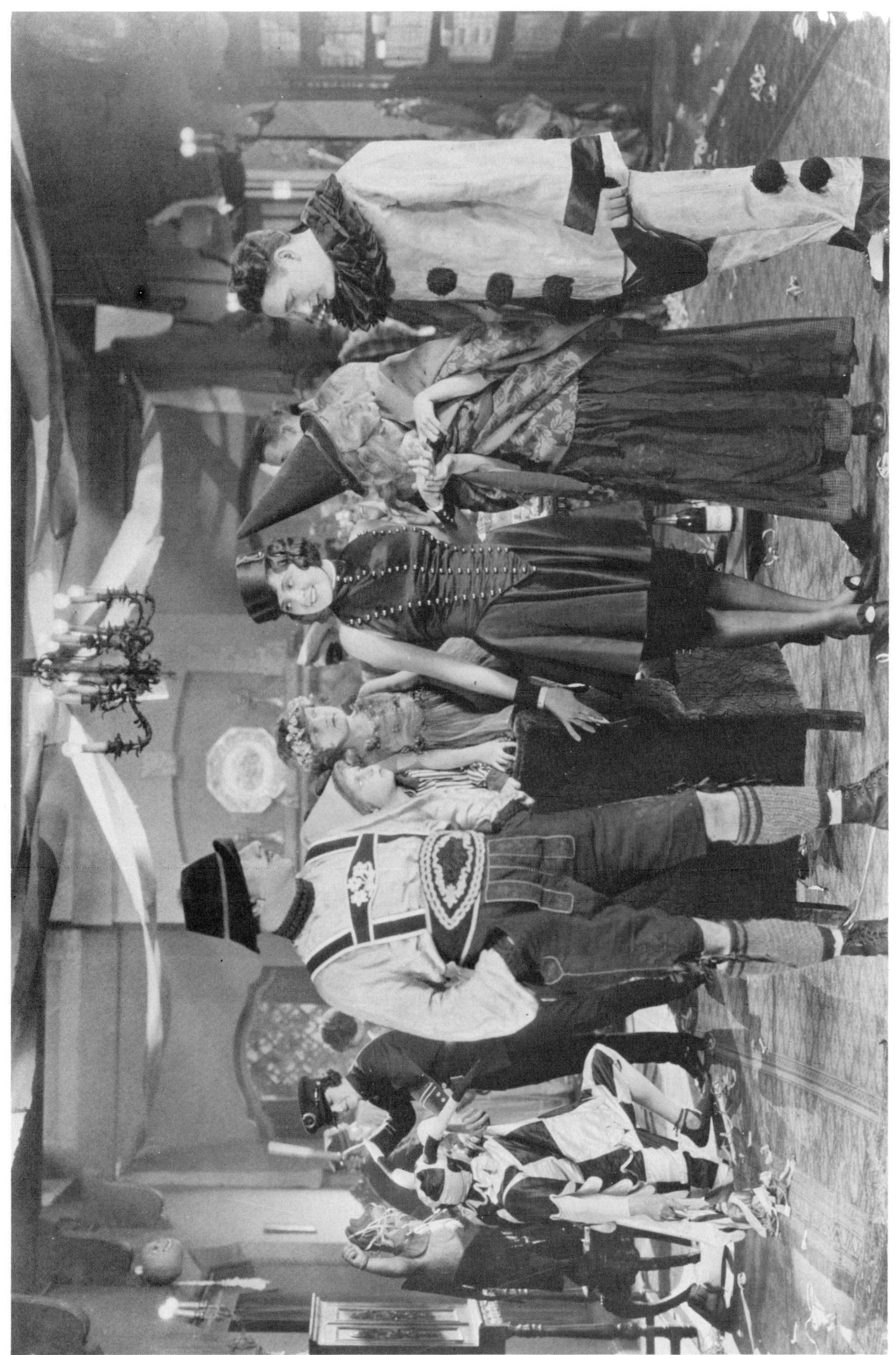

Harry finds life more hazardous than he expected in the feature *On Time* (1924).

A weakly conceived science fiction horror feature, *On Time* leaves the viewer not only bewildered by the characters' actions, but in many scenes throughout the film bored as well.

The story features a young man, Harry Willis, who is trying to seek his fortune in six months so that he can marry his sweetheart, Helen Hendon. Helen gives him a Chinese idol for luck. Immediately, events begin to happen that stagger the imagination.

Harry is contacted by a mysterious gentleman who offers him $10,000 for one day's hazardous work. As he begins his day, Harry finds that the word *hazardous* was an inaccurate description when compared to the events encountered during the 24 hour period. Several times Harry is nearly killed while attempting to perform the tasks laid out by the mysterious Chinaman. In addition, there is a hoard of thugs intent on capturing him for the purpose of replacing his brain with that of a gorilla's. Obviously, the idea of a transplant spurs Harry to try everything to avoid capture.

As the 24 hour day reaches a close, Harry is faced with a very unusual turn of events. It seems the whole day had been a masquerade. He learns from a movie agent that this entire fiasco was designed to see whether or not he would be an adequate motion picture actor for a new feature that was scheduled to go into production.

Having met the challenge, Harry receives the $10,000 he was promised and is also offered a sizeable contract to appear in several upcoming motion picture ventures. As the movie draws to a close, he and Helen are shown in a state of total euphoria.

> "So bewildered does the spectator become wondering what it is all about that he is apt to lose interest and be entirely befuddled before he finds that these sequences are part of a frame-up to determine whether he would be a suitable motion picture star . . ."
>
> *Moving Picture World*, Vol. 67, p. 215

THE PERILS OF PARIS

Release: 1924, F. B. O.
Description: Silent, 5264 feet
Classification: SF-A
References: No. 14, p. 374; No. 50, p. 363; LC, LP20785; MPN, Vol. 30, p. 2491

Credits

Producer . . . . Fordy's Film Company
Director . . . . Edward Jose
Screenplay . . . . Gerard Bourgeois

Cast

Helen Aldrich . . . . Pearl White
Roger Durant . . . . Robert Lee
Professor Aldrich . . . . Henry Bandin
Mrs. Gauthier . . . . Arlette Marchal
Paul Peret . . . . Martin Mitchell
Erdman . . . . George Vermoyal

The Perils of Paris is a weak science fiction adventure film, in which many of the exploits that Pearl White had made famous in her various serial roles were thrown together and then a plot loosely designed around these stunts to hold the viewer's interest.

The feature's premise is the development of a secret power ray, a device which has the capability of transmitting large quantities of electricity in a single narrow beam. When the beam strikes individuals, the result is instantaneous death.

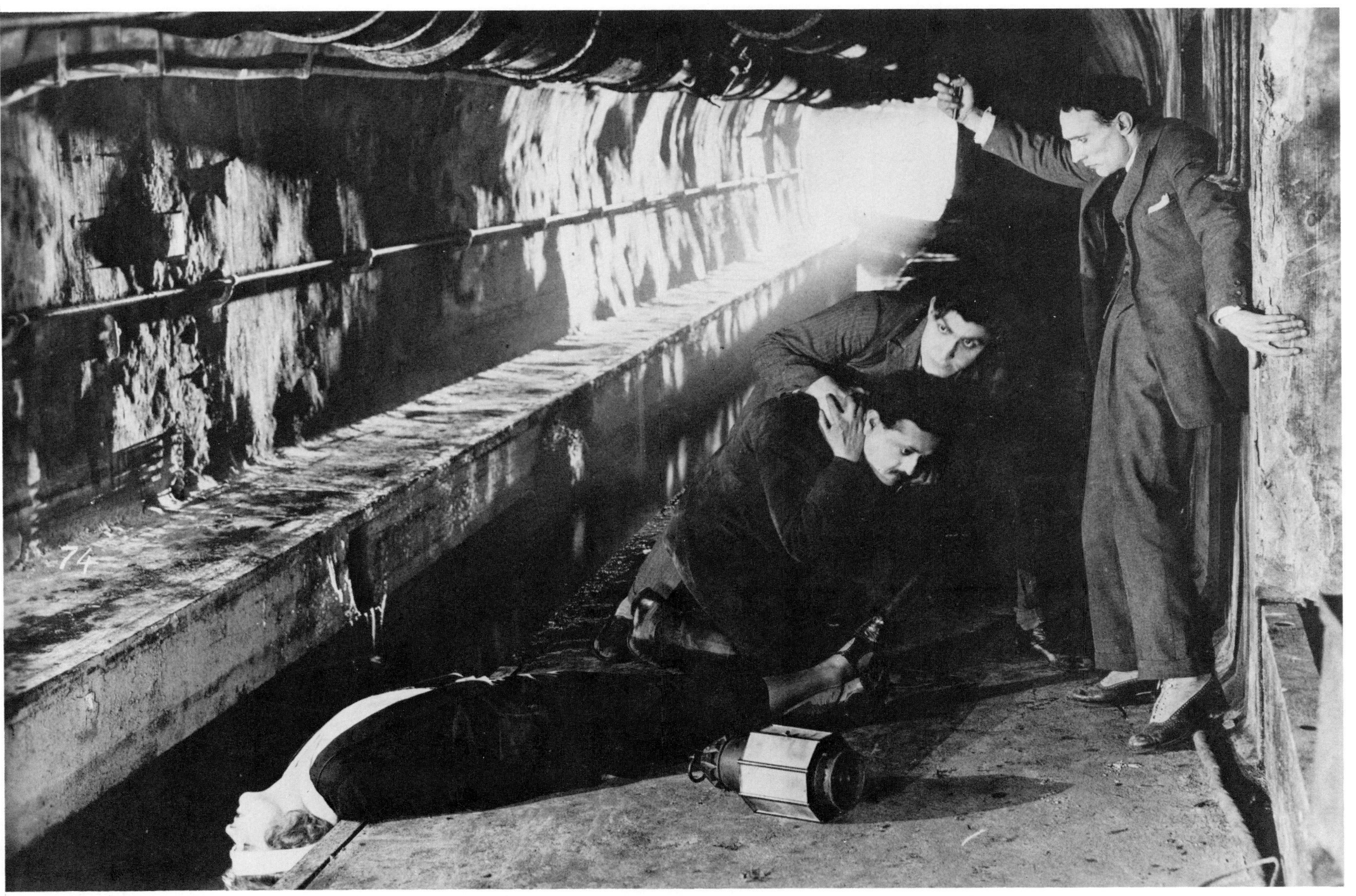

Pearl White as Helen Aldrich faces another dilemma in *The Perils of Paris* (1924).

The movie opens with Professor Aldrich in the middle of developing a successful model of the power ray. For its first official test, the professor has invited a great many of the government officials to witness his creation's awesomeness. Later that evening, Professor Aldrich is murdered and the powerful ray stolen. The bullet riddled body is discovered by his daughter, Helen.

Helen Aldrich, played by Pearl White, spends the rest of the feature trying to recover the power ray and avenge her father's death. It is believed that her lover is the primary suspect for the theft, but this charge proves to be erroneous, as revealed near the close of the film. In the final scenes, Helen vindicates her father's death and recovers the mysterious ray.

The most satisfying part of this film is obviously the many stunts for which Pearl White had gained fame throughout the world.

There is some question as to whether *The Perils of Paris* is American in origin since the entire cast, save Pearl White, is foreign. However, there is strong evidence to support the premise that the film was produced by an American company and merely filmed in Paris.

> "The cast is made up of continental players, aside from the star,--and none of them are known on this side of the Atlantic. These thespians seem to move about the stagey sets like so many mannikins on strings. In fact much of the action is taken up in meaningless groupings of the personnel.
>
> The one bright spot of this offering is Pearl White who works hard and bravely to put the story over but it is a losing fight. The popularity of Pearl, however, in many of the 'Main Streets' of the country, may help you do some business on this one. It will also do as an attraction for the smaller houses that play westerns, etc."
>
> *Motion Picture News,* 12-13-24, p. 3074

SINNERS IN SILK

Release: 1924, Metro-Goldwyn-Mayer Corp.
Description: Silent, 5150 feet
Classification: SF-C
References: No. 14, p. 435; No. 50, p. 441; AFI, F2.5110, p. 726; LC, LP20688; MPH, Vol. 19, p. 52; MPW, Vol. 69, p. 732, 733; NYR, 9-10-24

Credits

Producer .... MGM
Director .... Hobart Henley
Screenplay .... Carey Wilson
Art Director .... Richard Day
Camera .... John Arnold
Editor .... Frank Davis

Cast

Arthur Merrill .... Adolphe Menjou
Penelope Stevens .... Eleanor Boardmar
Brock Farley .... Conrad Nagel
Dr. Eustace .... Jean Hersholt
Bates .... Edward Connelly
Jerry Hall .... Jerome Patrick
Powers .... John Patrick
Mrs. Stevens .... Hedda Hopper

Ynez .... Miss DuPont
Flapper .... Virginia Lee Corbin
Ted .... Bradley Ward
Rita .... Dorothy Dwan
Sir Doanld Ramsey .... Frank Elliott
Mimi .... Ann Luther
Estelle .... Peggy Elinor
Cherie .... Eugenie Gilbert
Peggy .... Mary Akin
Carmelita .... Estelle Clark

Sinners in Silk resembles the film *Black Oxen* in that both features focused on rejuvenation. *Black Oxen* emphasized the rejuvenation of a female (an Austrian countess), while *Sinners in Silk* that of a man (Arthur Merrill). This latter movie, like many others that appeared in the 1923-1924 period, had a slight resemblance to Arthur Wilde's novel, *The Picture of Dorian Gray*. The power in each of these films seemed to be controlled by some mysterious physician who possessed the surgical skills to reclaim a patient's youth.

As the scene opens, we find Arthur Merrill, a middle-aged man, undergoing an operation by Dr. Eustace in a remote European country. Merrill is preceived to possess a great deal of wealth, and following his recovery from the operation, suddenly appears 20 years younger: he has successfully recaptured his lost youth. He soon boards the ocean liner Majestic for his return to the United States.

While aboard, Merrill is constantly pursued by young women who are interested in his wealth as much as his handsomeness. One of the young ladies who is enamored by his charm and appearance is Penelope Stevens, a young society debutante. She attempts to use her beauty to entrap Arthur, who, however, sees through her facade.

Upon arriving in New York, Merrill invites Penelope to his palatial roof garden apartment in an attempt to foil her amorous advances by showing her the error of her ways. Once there, Penelope's flirtations result in Merrill purposely placing her in a very compromising situation. At this point, after sufficiently scaring her, he gives her a stern lecture on her unbecoming behavior. He tells her she should put her petty flirtations aside and concentrate on someone she really cares about.

As it turns out, she does have a young man for whom she has sincere affection, Brock Farley. As the story becomes more involved, it seems that Brock is actually Merrill's son from a marriage that failed some 25 years ago. Realizing that he has a grown son, Arthur is awakened to the folly of his own behavior and casts aside his attempt to recapture his lost youth. He begins assuming some of the responsibilities a middle-aged father should. As the film draws to a close Arthur developes a warm relationship with his son.

Throughout the feature, the mysterious shroud of medical magic that has enveloped Dr. Eustace remains unexplained. And even as he departs for his home in Europe, leaving Merrill with a youthful physique but the wisdom of his years, the mystery still pervades.

While the film *Sinners in Silk* is a weak science fiction comedy, it echoes the interest the American public had in rejuvenation as a viable medical alternative to aging. The movie was also endowed with a large selection of outstanding players, many of whom went on to greater heights after this MGM production.

Adolph Menjou (Arthur Merrill) had an illustrious career on both the screen and television. Menjou began appearing in films in 1916 and participated in more than 100 features during his career, which ended in 1960.

Another famous actor who appeared in this film was Jean Hersholt, a two-time Academy Award winner, who had gained fame in 1921 by his outstanding performance in the *Four Horsemen of the Apocalypse*. Eventually the American Academy of Motion Picture Arts and Sciences created a special humanitarian award in his name to honor persons who have unselfishly devoted their lives to working

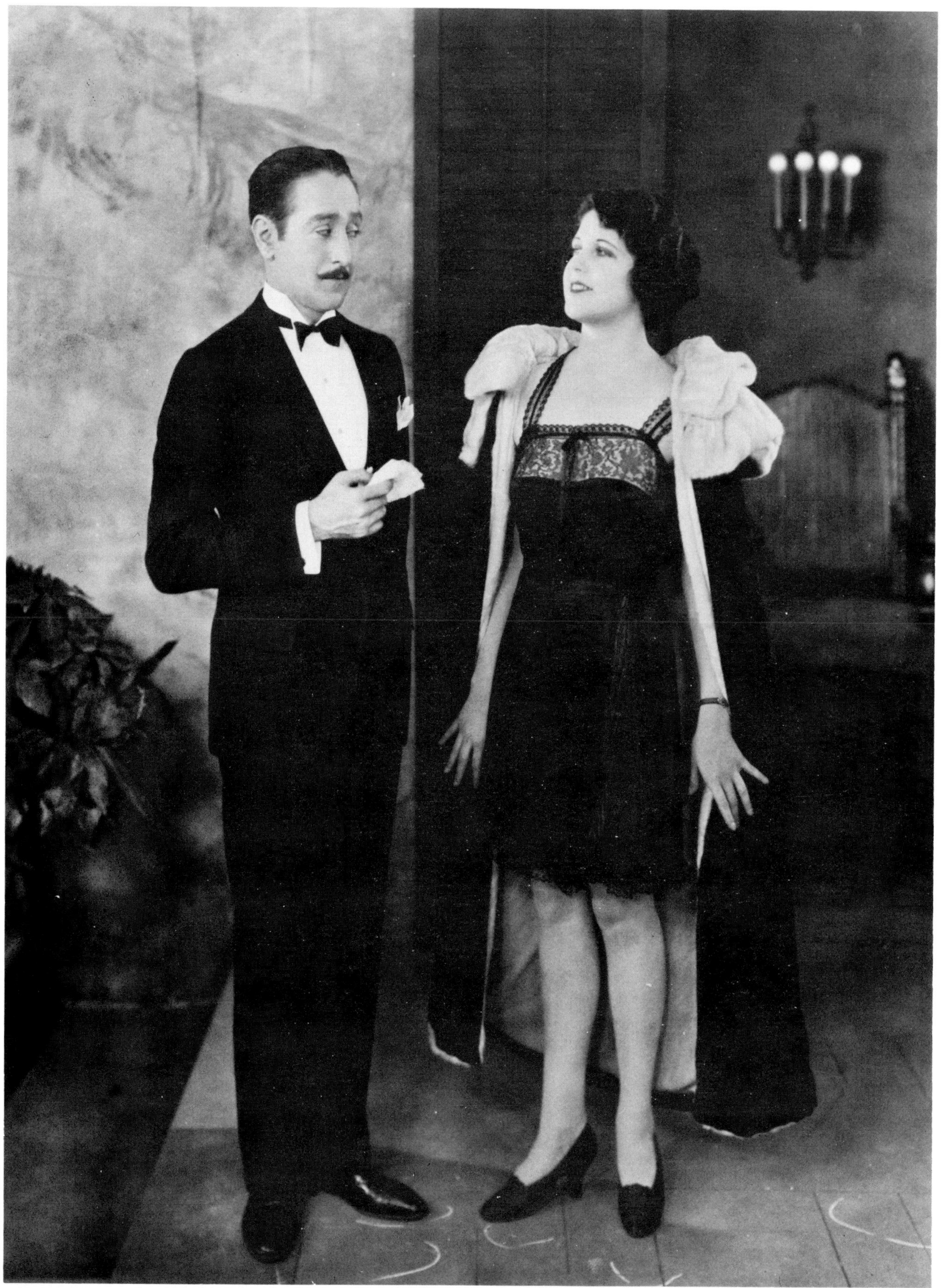

Arthur Merrill and Penelope in his New York apartment in *Sinners in Silk* (1924).

for the humane efforts of others. It is given in those rare instances when the Academy finds a person they deem worthy of such a high honor.

Sinners in Silk also featured another Academy Award winner, Conrad Nagel. He appeared in over 100 films during his career and was featured in another SF effort, *One Million B.C. (1940),* in which he provided the narration.

Penelope's mother in *Sinners in Silk* was played by Hedda Hopper, who also played in more than 100 films. She is, however, probably more renowned as an outstanding Hollywood columnist.

> "There is no denying the entertainment value of this picture, as it is equipped with lavish settings, excellent photography, novel and amusing situations and the excellent acting of Adolphe Menjou.
>
> Mr. Menjou is as efficient in his expressive pantomines in this picture as in any we have seen him. It is worth going to the Capital just to see this capable player in this picture, even if the narrative is light and impossible."
>
> *The New York Times,* 9-10-24

> "Although *Sinners in Silk* is snappy and jazzy neither of those qualities is exaggerated. There brilliance is natural and at time roams close to the border of the salacious, but never too close or across that line. Under less skillful hands than those of Director Hobart Henley this Horizon of discrimination could easily have been made too prominent or too vague. Henley treats risque conditions which arise with such refinement that the crass and the brusque are skillfully avoided, making the spiciness of the production intelligently delightful."
>
> *Moving Picture World,* Vol. 69, p. 732

THE STORY WITHOUT A NAME

Release: 1924, Paramount Pictures Corp.
Description: Silent, 5912 feet
Classification: SF
References: No. 14, p. 455; No. 50, p. 463; AFI, F2.5417, p. 769; FID, 10-26-24; FIR, 3-72; LC, LP20645; MPH, Vol. 19, p. 59; MPW, Vol. 70, p. 1625; NYR, 10-6-24; VAW, 10-8-24, p. 30

Credits

Producer.......... Famous Players-Lasky
Director.......... Irvin Willat
Screenplay.......... Victor Irvin
Camera.......... Hal Rosson
Editor.......... Victor Irvin

Cast

Mary Walsworth.......... Agnes Ayres
Alan Holt.......... Antonio Moreno
Drakma.......... Tyrone Power
Kurder.......... Louis Wolheim
Claire.......... Dagmar Godowaky
Don Powell.......... Jack Bohn
Cripple.......... Maurice Costello
Admiral Wadsworth.......... Frank Currier
Laboratory Assistant.......... Ivan Linow

The Story Without a Name is an exciting science fiction film which displays an ultraviolet device whose rays are projected by an immense radio transmitter. The creative inventor of this radio death ray, Alan Holt, soon finds himself the object of an attack by the infamous Drakma and Kurder, two notorious international spys. These foes of the United States kidnap Alan Holt and his fiancee, Mary Walsworth (who happens to be the daughter of Admiral Walsworth, the head of the U.S. Navy). Needless to say, their kidnapping causes great concern among both the military and government leaders. An all out search is conducted by the various intelligence agencies, but they are unable to find a single clue to the whereabouts of Alan and Mary.

Meanwhile, Drakma and Kurder, unbeknownst to Alan, have disposed of Mary by giving her to a rum smuggler who will either sell her in the slave market of India or dispose of her on his sea voyage. They place Alan on an island in the Bahamas and tell him they will kill Mary unless he reproduces the ray transmitter. (It seems that in the struggle to capture Alan and the device Mary managed to render the working model of the ray useless.) The captors then decided to abscond all the laboratory equipment as well as Alan's laboratory assistant and a cripple who is an electronics advisor.

Alan, instead of working on the death ray, however, manages to ingeniously create a transmitter which sends out a signal to the Navy, who, in turn, dispatches a fleet of vessels to the Bahama Islands. The ship containing the spies is immediately sunk by a large naval destroyer which arrived on the scene firing its guns at the fleeing vessel.

Meanwhile, Mary has offered sufficient resistance by hitting the rum smuggler and his crew with oars and pieces of wood to ward them off. She then escapes on a life raft and is drifting not far from the island on which Alan has been imprisoned.

One of the naval vessels rushing to the islands sees the lonely raft and rescues Mary. In the end, Alan is returned to his laboratory in the United States and he and Mary are wed.

The device displayed in this film is unique. It resembles a modern day microwave generator which transmits ultraviolet rays, killing large numbers of people while giving little or no detection of the impending danger.

The Story Without a Name was adapted from a story by Arthur Stringer which appeared in *Photoplay* in 1923. An intense publicity campaign was launched to provide an alternate title for the feature with ads appearing in *Photoplay* that offered $5,000 for the winning entry. The title selected was *Without Warning.* As a result, this feature may appear in some reviews under this alternate title.

Agnes Ayres played the year before in the famous silent epic *The Ten Commandments.* Her appearance in this film and in *The Story Without a Name* aided her in her quest for fame. Moreno, on the other hand, was a veteran serial actor, having appeared in films as early as 1912. Previously, he had been cast in the role of villains and his performance in *The Story Without a Name* was his first heroic part.

The film was carried, however, by the performance of the supporting actors rather than the stars. Tyrone Power, Sr. gave an outstanding performance as Drakma, sinister villain who sought to destroy the U.S. with the ultraviolet weapon. An equally extraordinary performance was delivered by Louis Wolheim in the role of Kurder, Drakma's partner in crime. Wolheim appeared in the earlier SF film *Dr. Jekyll and Mr. Hyde* (Paramount, 1920) and continued to play villainous types the remainder of his career. Maurice Costello's performance as the cripple was clearly the most powerful. Costello was also the star of the science fiction adventure serial, *The Crimson Stain* (1916).

Story Without a Name produced a great deal of attention due to the contest over its title. It produced even greater attention, however, due to the intensity of the action contained in it and the timeliness of the invention which was so realistically displayed. A great many of the viewers actually came to believe that there was such a device available in the United States' arsenal of weaponry.

> "Paramount in *The Story Without a Name,* adapted from a prize title story by Arthur Stringer that was published in a popular fan magazine, has a production that should certainly satisfy all who crave excitement, for it is just chock full of thrills and adventure.
>
> Obviously a melodrama, Director Irvin Willat has succeeded in getting every possible ounce of thrills and punch out of the story, sacrificing plausibility at times when it will add to this effect."
>
> *Moving Picture World,* Vol. 70, p. 625

"Some of the sea shots are great, although miniatures of vessels are used. The action stuff, too, is smeared on heavy.

Because it is so very melodramatic the impression is given that the big cities won't take so kindly to it, but in the wheat and corn belts they will probably sit in open mouthed amazement and applaud at the proper time."

Variety Weekly, 10-8-24, p. 30

VANITY'S PRICE

Release: 1924, F.B.O.
Description: Silent, 6124 feet
Classification: SF-A
References: No. 14, p. 511; No. 50, p. 520; AFI, F2.6024, p. 855; LC, LP20647; MPH, Vol. 19, p. 22; MPN, Vol. 30, p. 1525; MPW, Vol. 70, p. 246, 247; NYR, 10-8-24; VAW, 10-15-24, p, 32

Credits

Producer .... Gothic Pictures
Director .... R. William Neill
Screenplay .... Paul Bern
Music .... Edward Turk
Camera .... Hal Mohr
Editor .... Paul Bern

Cast

Vanna Du Maurier .... Anna Q. Nilsson
Henri De Greve .... Stuart Holmes
Richard Dowling .... Wyndham Standing
Teddy, Vanna's son .... Arthur Rankin
Sylvia, Teddy's fiancee .... Lucille Bickson
Bill Connors .... Robert Bolder
Mrs. Connors .... Cissy Fitzgerald
Katherine, Vanna's maid .... Dot Farley
Butler .... Charles Newton

Vanity's Price is a weak science fiction film which reiterates the popular theme of the 1920's--rejuvenation. It is the third film in 1924 which emphasized this process of renewal. The movie also closely parallels Gertrude Atherton's novel *Black Oxen* (also the title of a film based on her novel), as the heroine of the film undergoes the famous Steinbach operation which results in her regaining her lost youth. The feature does not compare favorably, however, with either *Black Oxen* (1924) or *Sinners in Silk* (1924). Both of these productions were better directed and had a wider array of talented players. Nevertheless, *Vanity's Price* was quite successful at the box office and provided average entertainment for the viewer.

As the story begins we find that Vanna Du Maurier, a famous actress, has reached the frustrating age of 40 and finds her theater popularity waning. Not wishing to see her career dissipate and having ambitions of owning her own theater, Vanna travels to Vienna to undergo the Steinbach treatment in the hope of restoring her youth. After some time, she recovers from the operation, which has been a

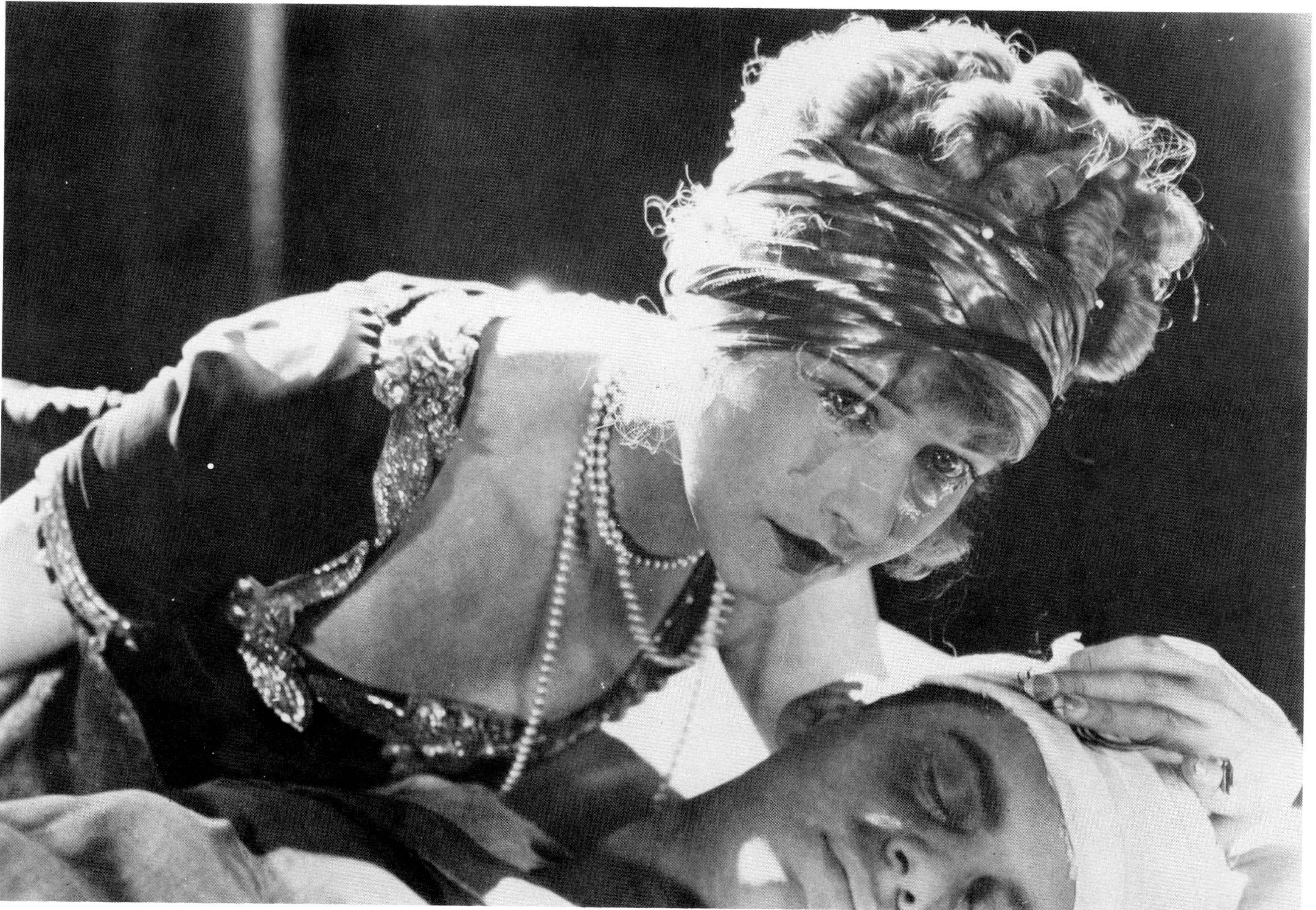

Vanna DuMaurier (Anna Q. Nilssen) in *Vanity's Price* (1924).

great success. However, the process did leave a certain amount of amnesia regarding the events which occurred the weeks before she embarked on her voyage to Vienna. This may not seem important, but during that period of time a playwright and longtime friend, Richard Dowling, proposed to Vanna. He had loved her for years, and Vanna had left promising an answer to his proposal upon her return. In addition, while she has been under treatment, her former husband, Henri De Greve, drove her son's fiancee, Sylvia, away after trying to seduce her.

The action becomes rather torrid upon Vanna's return to the States. She doesn't seem to recall Henri De Greve at all, and introduces him as a prominent millionaire of the New York society circles. He agrees to fund her operation to develop a theater of her own as he is entranced by her amnesia and beauty.

The relationship between Richard Dowling and Henri over Vanna's affections becomes strained, to say the least, as Dowling feels he has a prior commitment from Vanna and is frustrated by her inability to recall the promise made on the eve of her voyage. The rivalry reaches an apex as De Greve forces his way into Vanna's boudoir revealing that he is her former husband and the father of Teddy, her son. Vanna becomes enraged and begins to strike De Greve. As this happens, her son enters the room and joins in the battle. In the struggle a blow is delivered to Teddy which renders him unconscious and later he suffers from a severe concussion. As Vanna appears about to receive the beating of her life, Richard enters and continues the struggle with Henri, who is severely thrashed by Dowling. He tries to escape and finally withdraws from the room having been solidly beaten. Dowling then attends to Vanna, who appears to have aged during the fight.

It seems that the height of emotions caused by the conflict sent a large portion of adrenalin through her body and thus started to reverse the process. While she does not appear the age she was prior to the operation, she is obviously not the young girl present only moments before.

Her appearance does not diminish Dowling's affection for her as he once again expresses his desire to marry her. Vanna apparently now remembers her promise to him and responds with an affectionate yes. In the end Vanna and Richard are married, and Teddy and Sylvia are reunited with the anticipation of their own wedding in the near future.

The film is quite involved in the conflict between the players and becomes one in which the viewer finds it impossible not to take sides.

The two stars, Anna Q. Nilsson and Stuart Holmes, were experienced actors. Anna began her career in 1911 and appeared in well over 100 films. Stuart Holmes appeared in nearly 75 films, having begun in 1914. Both of their careers spanned the silent era and they continued to appear in films through the mid-1950's.

> "*Vanity's Price* an original story by Paul Bern, filmed by F.B.O. is a great box office bet for the flappers who like a sensationally treated romance. Lavishly produced and excellently acted, it nears technical perfection."
>
> *Moving Picture World*, Vol. 70, p. 246

> "A likeable screen yarn, somewhat overdressed, perhaps, but nevertheless an interest sustainer and superior to many of the features that have edged their way into the major first-run houses.
>
> Judicious picking by the casting director is an outstanding note, while Neill has slipped in a few novel touches that will surely be repeated by others who serve the silent art in like capacity. The error is in the settings, which illusion as being too gaudy to be reasonable. Such furnishings may awe the intermediate theatre clientele, but it is hardly to be supposed that the magnitudinous display was ever concocted in the most regal of genuine homes."
>
> *Variety*, 10-15-24, p. 32

> "While this is not a film that is going to set the world on fire, it is an entertainment which is not badly done. The story was written by the imaginative Paul Bern, and it would have been a superior effort if he had directed it."
>
> *The New York Times*, 8-1924

1925

DR. PYCKLE AND MR. PRIDE

Release: 1925, F. B. O.
Description: Silent, 1470 feet
Classification: SF-C
References: No. 14, p. 134; No. 50, p. 107; FAM, Vol. 34, p. 55; LC, LP21889; MPW, Vol. 75, p. 647

Credits

Producer .... Standard Films

Cast

Dr. Pyckle/Mr. Pride .... Stan Laurel

Dr. Pyckle and Mr. Pride is a short science fiction comedy, featuring one of the outstanding comedians of this era, Stan Laurel. The film was made only a year before the famous duo of Laurel and Hardy became a household word, but Laurel's great talents were already obvious in this particular effort.

The movie attempts to burlesque the Robert Louis Stevenson novel, *Dr. Jekyll and Mr. Hyde,* and achieved both with finesse and care.

The character of Dr. Pyckle is a very straight-laced, staunch individual, while Mr. Pride, instead of cruel and fiendish, is more mischievous and childlike.

The set used for the feature was that used in 1923 for the film *The Hunchback of Notre Dame* (Universal), obviously an attempt to cut expenses on the film. But the producers, who thought this would be a short inexpensive film that would receive little attention from the general public, were mistaken. *Dr. Pyckle and Mr. Pride,* along with two other films produced in 1925, gave Stan Laurel the attention that brought him to the forefront of the industry and resulted in his teaming with a comic of equal talent and genius, Oliver Hardy.

Stan Laurel started his career in 1917 and played in more than 50 features prior to his attachment with Hardy. Similarly, Oliver Hardy began his career in 1913 and appeared in nearly 100 films before the partnership with Laurel. The pair then went on to win the 1933 Academy Award for the best short subject called *The Music Box,* a comedy short of great merit.

> "There are several amusing moments and while not as uproarous as some of this star's previous burlesques and lacking in the more subtle touches it nevertheless should prove entertaining especially to patrons who like to see burlesque of familiar stories."
> *Moving Picture World,* 8-8-25, p. 647

FROM MARS TO MUNICH

Release: 1925, Fox Film Corp.
Description: Silent, 1 reel
Classification: SF-C
References: No. 14, p. 175; No. 50, p. 152; MPN, Vol. 31, p. 1514

From Mars to Munich is an unusual science fiction comedy about an invisible alien from Mars who visits a brewery in Munich. The Martian decides to partake of the aromatic brew and his unrestrained consumption leads to an enebriated condition. While in this stupified state the Martian provides many amusing scenes for the audience.

This was definitely an entertaining, though shallow, short film. It almost ends up depicting a semi-documentary on the beer industry of the period.

THE LOST WORLD

Release: 1925, First National Pictures
Description: Silent, 9700 feet
Classification: SF
References: No. 1, p. 24, 215, 442; No. 7, p. 92; No. 14, p. 286; No. 20, p. 32, 71, 75, 89, 145, 150, 155; No. 26, p. 68, 152, 153, 158, 170; No. 33, p. 10, 13-16, 21, 23, 44, 48, 86, 89, 92, 101, 235; No. 36, p. 85; No. 45, p. 33, 34, 48, 49, 95; No. 47, p. 220; No. 48, p. 208-211; No. 49, p. 277; No. 50, p. 267; No. 51, p. 13, 24, 29, 32, 54, 76; AFI, F2.3201, p. 453; FAM, Vol. 19, p. 30; FID, 2-15-25; MPH, Vol. 20, p. 74, 76; MPN, Vol. 30, p. 2764, 2765; NYR, 2-9-25; PHO, 2-1925; VAW, 2-11-25, p. 31

Credits

Producer.......................... Earl Hudson and Watterson R. Rothacker
Director.......................... Harry O. Hoyt
Screenplay.......................... Marion Fairfax
Special Effects.......................... Willis O'Brien
Camera.......................... Arthur Edeson and Fred Jackman
Editor.......................... George McGuire
Prop Models.......................... Marcel Delgado
Architecture.......................... Milton Menasco
Research.......................... Willis O'Brien

Cast

Professor Challenger.......................... Wallace Beery
Paula White.......................... Bessie Love
Sir John Roxton.......................... Lewis S. Stone
Edward Malone.......................... Lloyd Hughes
Professor Summerlee.......................... Arthur Hoyt
Gladys Hungerford.......................... Alma Bennett
Marquette.......................... Virginia Brown Faire
Ape Man.......................... Bull Montana
Austin.......................... Finch Smiles
Zambo.......................... Jules Cowles
Mrs. Challenger.......................... Margaret McWade
Major Hibbard.......................... Charles Wellesley
Colin McArdle.......................... George Bunny

The film begins with a scene of a large museum-like structure. Inside, standing next to the skeleton of a prehistoric animal, is Sir John Roxton, a famous hunter and explorer. He has come to the museum, along with a large number of students, to hear Professor Challenger's presentation concerning the existence of prehistoric animals in a remote section of the Amazon jungles. A young reporter, Edward Malone, is also present. He has been assigned by his newspaper to glean information on Professor Challenger's amazing disclosure. However, the professor's speech is closed to the press and Malone therefore appears unable to gain entrance. He soon spots Sir Roxton and seeks his aid in gaining access to

One of the amazing animated prehistoric creatures from Willis O'Brien in the film *The Lost World* (1925).

the auditorium where he can learn more of the professor's revelations regarding the prehistoric animals of the Amazon. Roxton immediately senses Malone's skeptism concerning Challenger's claims. He points out to the young man that the Amazon contains over 50,000 miles of unexplored waterways; therefore, there might indeed be all sorts of unusual and fantastic living creatures in the area. Roxton manages to secure admittance for the reporter, hoping that he will understand Challenger's theories and write a favorable report for his newspaper.

Professor Challenger is introduced to the audience by Professor Summerlee, an eminent coleopterist. His introduction is filled with acerbic comments designed to cast doubt on the visitor's credibility. The audience is likewise obviously there to heckle him as the general feeling is that his claims are totally unjustified, without scientific basis, and plain unbelievable. Professor Challenger, a rather short man with dark, bushy hair and beard, walks to the podium and demands silence. This stimulates the audience to vociferous outcries of, "Bring on your mastadon; bring on your dinosaur."

The professor next challenges the group by stating that he will indeed furnish the evidence if any of the audience members has the spine to accompany him back to the Amazon and aid in the capture of such beasts. Silence befalls as Challenger emphasizes that he is not there to defend his statements, but to plan and organize a second venture back to the jungle. The audience remains still, apparently unwilling to lift the gauntlet of their speaker's challenge.

Finally, Sir John Roxton rises from his seat and volunteers to accompany him to the deep regions of the Amazon. Timidly, Malone follows Roxton by indicating his desire to become a part of the expedition. The professor doesn't recognize this young man and asks his name. In response to the next question, "What is your occupation?" Malone ponders for several moments, realizing the professor's antagonism toward newspapers, but then he resolutely answers, "A reporter for the London *Record Journal,* Sir." At this, Challenger flies into a violent rage and chases Malone down the aisle and out the building. After being unable to apprehend Malone, the professor returns home for the evening.

The scene now changes as we see the professor, Malone (obviously forgiven by Challenger), and Roxton in the professor's den. They are pondering the contents of a diary the professor possesses. Soon he orders his servant to summon Miss White. As she enters the room, she is warmly greeted by Sir John, but her eyes are almost immediately transfixed to those of Edward Malone. It seems he is equally entranced by Miss White until he is jerked back to reality as the professor introduces her as Miss Paula White, daughter of Maple White. Mr. White is the author of the diary that they are so cautiously examining, and which the professor carefully guards. It seems Maple White and his daughter were exploring the deep regions of the Amazon when they accidentally discovered a high plateau inhabited by prehistoric animals, sketches of which White included in the pages of his diary. Miss White believes her father is marooned on the high plateau among these terrible beasts, but since the way up the plateau was unknown to her, she could not rescue him. This is the reason she has sought Professor Challenger's assistance, and she again urges the group to return to the Amazon in the hope of saving her poor father's life. At this, the three men each vow that they will do everything in their power to save Maple White.

Edward Malone, realizing that this may be a fantastic human interest story, suggests that his newspaper might be interested in printing sections from the diary. Roxton and Malone visit the managing editor of the paper with the hope of convincing him to help finance the expedition. The editor does indeed agree to help support their venture.

Meanwhile, Roxton makes his intentions known to Paula, that the reason he is going on the trip is for her benefit since he has a strong interest in her–much more than a mere fatherly affection. However, at the moment her only ambition and goal is to save her father's life. Therefore, she cannot be interested in any amorous adventure with either Malone or Roxton.

The party makes their way to the South American coast, then up the Amazon via a small steamboat, finally reaching a narrow tributary which can only be navigated by canoe. The scenes along the banks of the cruel jungle are filled with vicious animals and huge snakes slithering along the overhanging branches of the trees. The only friendly animal appears to be Joco, Paula's small pet monkey, and he stays very close to the group in this strange land.

The group finally reaches an area where they must travel by foot. After several days of moving slowly through the thick jungle underbrush, the expedition reaches the edge of the plateau. Several members attempt to locate a means of scaling the stone ediface while the rest establish a base camp. From the top of the plateau an ape-like creature (played by Bull Montana) can be spotted peering over the edge,

The ape creature from *The Lost World* (1925).

apparently examining the campsite hundreds of feet below him. The professor and several others examine the immense outcropping above them and soon discover a protrusion that seems to have splintered from the main section. This leads them to wonder if perhaps a bridge of some sort could be fashioned between the two pieces.

That evening, from the edge of the plateau they see a large prehistoric bird devouring its prey. The sight of a pterodactyl provides definite proof that Maple White's diary and the pictures he drew are indeed based on fact. The members of the expedition spend a sleepless night with the expectation of scaling the heights of the rock the next day. Even Professor Summerlee has now removed all his suspicions and doubt concerning Challenger's story and joins in the anticipation of the ascent. (At this point in the picture, the audience is treated to a large segment of film that evidences the unusual talents of O'Brien in depicting the extinct animals as though they were real. The animation of this sequence is by far the best done up to this point in the film industry, and many believed that it would be 20-30 years before this work would be paralleled.) The group succeeds in chopping down a large tree that then falls to the other side of the plateau, thus providing a natural bridge to allow them to cross from one side of the narrow rock ledge to the immense plateau. No sooner do they all safely cross to the other side than a Brontosaurus appears at the edge uprooting trees as he nears the group. Professor Challenger warns the group to stay out of its way. The Brontosaurus, he explains, is a completely harmless animal as he feeds on vegetation and would have little or no interest in humans as a source of food. The animal, however, is obviously ignorant of the professor's comments and continues to advance. As he reaches the tree across the gorge between the two rocks, the tree that had provided safe passage to the plateau, he grasps it in his powerful jaws and hurls the bridge over the edge. The explorers are now trapped at the top, just as Maple White had been.

They attempt to move inland hoping to find some safe shelter for the night. Throughout this ordeal they are constantly being observed by an ape-like creature that follows them to their night camp. It climbs a nearby tree where it pays close attention to Paula (obviously the creature has a profound interest in the female of the human species).

Scenes of this part of the movie are littered with a plethora of prehistoric animals. Some are seen engaging in battle, some just foraging for food among the treetops and surrounding vegetation. At one point in this sequence, a mother Stegosaurus engages a Tyranosaurus in a ferocious battle as she attempts to protect her young. This unique film footage is so well done that it is hard to remember that it isn't real.

At night, the sounds of the animals send chills through the explorers' camp. As the night wears on, the camp is attacked by a Tyranosaurus, but they manage to scare it away with a lighted torch. The torch also reveals the ape-like creature staring at them from the top of the tree. Roxton shoots at the animal wounding it in the arm, but it manages to escape through the dark thick foliage. The members of the base camp have meanwhile been exploring the perimeter of the plateau in an effort to find a way of rescuing the stranded group.

Sir Roxton continues exploring the nearby caves where he finally discovers a skeleton and a watch which appears to have Maple White's initials engraved on it. As he opens the tarnished lid he finds a picture of Paula--the final proof that her father had indeed died on the lonely plateau. On his way back to the others he discovers a cave opening that is right above the base camp. He fires his gun to signal the group and immediately sends little Joco, the monkey, up the rocky surface with a cord tied to his waist. Using the cord, Roxton pulls a rope ladder up to the cave's entrance. After securing it, he dashes out of the cavern to announce to the other explorers that they are rescued.

Meanwhile, in another small cave Malone is making his amorous feelings known to Paula. As they embrace, Roxton appears. He realizes his chances for capturing Paula's affection and love are over. But being the gentleman that he is, he quickly congratulates them on their decision to marry. He must then, unfortunately, break the news to Paula about her father's death. Even though she has suspected the worst from the beginning, the sudden realization that her father is really dead comes as a great shock.

Elsewhere, Professors Challenger and Summerlee are stalking a Brontosaurus which is soon attacked by a Tyranosaurus. During the battle the Brontosaurus is hurled over the edge of the plateau, falling into a shallow stream that runs far below their rocky ledge.

As night falls, Roxton, Paula, and Malone seek refuge in their small cave. The professors have not returned yet from their exploring. As dawn breaks, Malone begins to search for the men; he must inform them of their escape. Suddenly, the whole sky begins to glow a pale red (the film was actually tinted red) as a small volcano on the northern side of the plateau erupts. It sends lava and molten rock high into the air

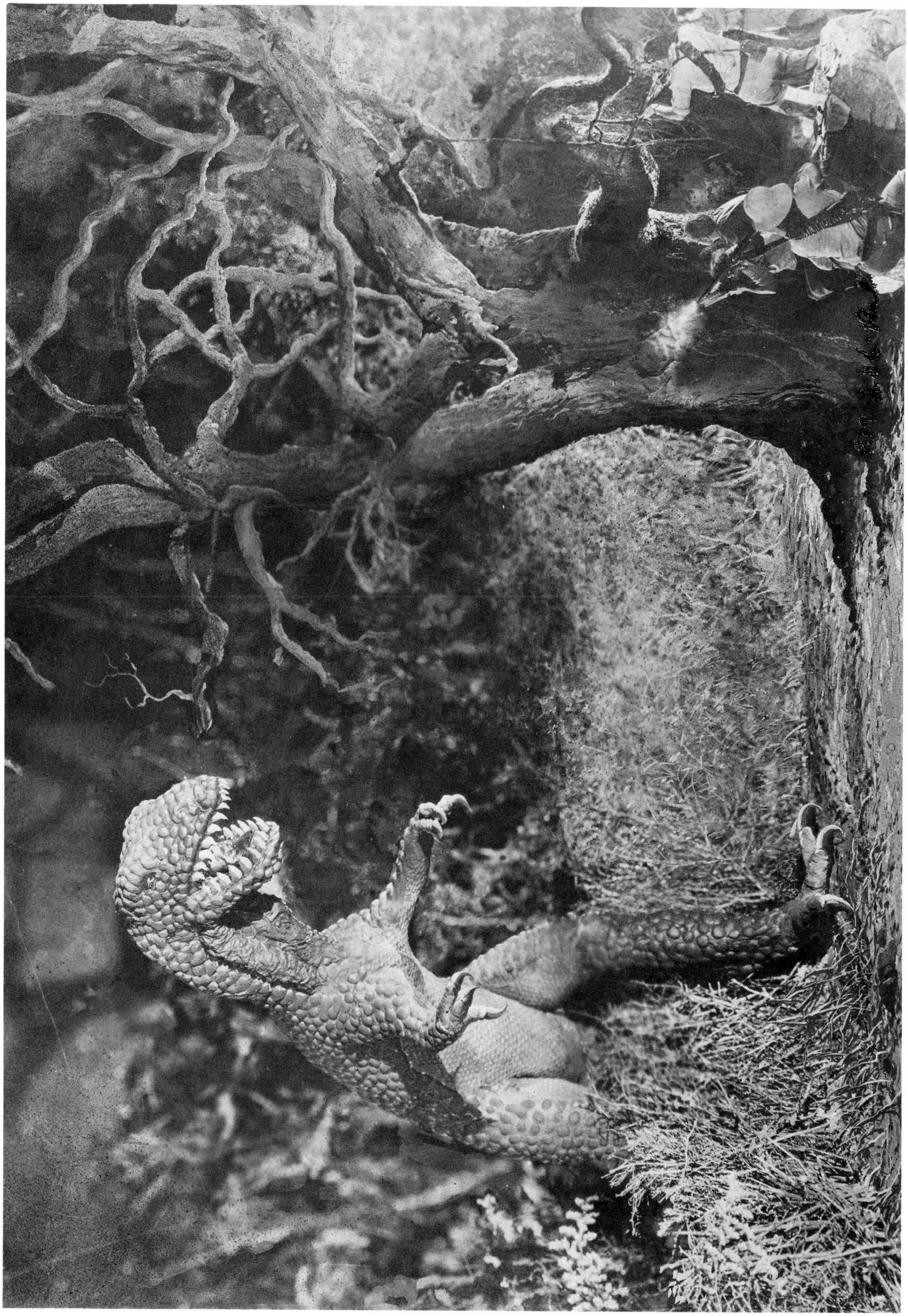

The search party is confronted by one of the prehistoric monsters in *The Lost World.*

A Brontosaurus munches on a nearby tree while Professor Challenger and Paula seek safety behind a rock.

Near the end of the feature, Professor Challenger is trapped by an enormous dinosaur. Only the timely eruption of a volcano saves him from becoming the entree.

and the vegetation begins to blaze, sending animals scurrying away. As the morning grows late, the area has been ravaged by fire and many animals have become victims of the ordeal. Miraculously, Professors Summerlee and Challenger have been guided by Malone to a small cave out of danger from the fires and destruction. Later they are able to continue on to the cave where Roxton and Paula were waiting.

The group begins the perilous descent down the rope ladder, all the while carefully observed by the same ape-like creature they had encountered before. As they continue their escape they keep watch on the dinosaur that had fallen earlier to the muddy waters below. The last to descend is Malone. Midway down the ladder, the ape begins to pull and shake the rope in an effort to dislodge him, but somehow he manages to reach the safety of his comrades on the ground.

Sufficiently recovered from their ordeal, they later investigate the huge animal still lodged in the quagmire. They decide that such a unique prehistoric specimen must be captured and returned to England. Moments later they are surprised by Major Hibbard of the Brazilian geodetic survey who just happened to be in the region. (Remember, however, that this particular region had not been previously explored.) The major is horrified at the sight of the dinosaur, but is eventually persuaded by Roxton and Challenger to have his natives aid in the task of building a cage and raft to carry the beast back to London.

Later in London, at the same natural history lecture hall where Challenger had been jeered and heckled, he is about to reveal not only his observations and notes from their adventure, but the dinosaur as well. However, the beast has yet to arrive. Malone calls the harbor to see what is causing the delay. Terrified he informs the professor that the cables restraining the cage failed and the dinosaur has escaped. The beast is moving through the streets of London ravaging the population. (This is probably the first scene in SF movie history in which a prehistoric animal terrified an entire city's population.) The lecture audience now believes they have been subjected to yet another Challenger hoax. They disregard his urging for them to stay off the streets until the animal is recaptured. Instead they angrily stomp out of the hall. To their surprise, however, they are greeted by a ferocious dinosaur--an animal they thought was simply a figment of Challenger's imagination.

The beast continues to run rampant through the city, destroying statues, buildings, cars, and maiming helpless victims. Finally, it makes its way to the famous London Bridge. Half-way across, the bridge collapses and sends the dinosaur plunging into the Thames. (Obviously, this was the film maker's attempt to give credibility to the Loch Ness monster, a theory which was quite popular in the late 1920's and has remained so today.)

Malone and Paula are extremely happy that peace has been restored and they rush off to make wedding plans while Challenger is seen peering over the edge of the bridge obviously contemplating the poor monster's fate and wondering: will he ever again see his evidence that *The Lost World* does indeed exist, or will it lie forever somewhere in the deep regions of the Thames?

The Lost World was a major contribution to the SF film genre, but even more importantly, it showcased the brilliant animation achievements of Willis O'Brien. His first science fiction film was *The Dinosaur and the Missing Link* (1917), a short animated film financially supported by Herman Wobber. It took Wobber nearly a year to sell the film, finally closing a deal with the Edison Film Company (a deal which started a relationship that lasted for eight years). O'Brien produced a second SF film, *10,000 B. C.* which was released in mid-1917. These and other animation achievements led O'Brien to his first feature length film, *The Lost World.* Watterson Rothacker was so enchanted with O'Brien's genius that he spent over one million dollars on the film--an enormous amount for this era. *The Lost World* took over two years to complete and used more than 45 separate models of prehistoric creatures.

The story was based on Sir Arthur Conan Doyle's 1912 novel by the same name and provided a fitting vehicle for O'Brien's genius. While the feature attempts to follow the original story, the celluloid version has some significant changes. The character of Paula White, portrayed by Bessie Love, was obviously added to provide a romantic interest. Additionally, Professor Challenger never returned to London with any creatures, but the film provided the first SF depiction of a monster ravaging a major city.

Doyle's novel became the basis for other significant science fiction films, such as *King Kong, Mighty Joe Young,* and of course, the many remakes of *The Lost World* and *King Kong.*

The Lost World ascended to a new height in SF film quality, easily making it one of the most important science fiction films of the period 1897-1929.

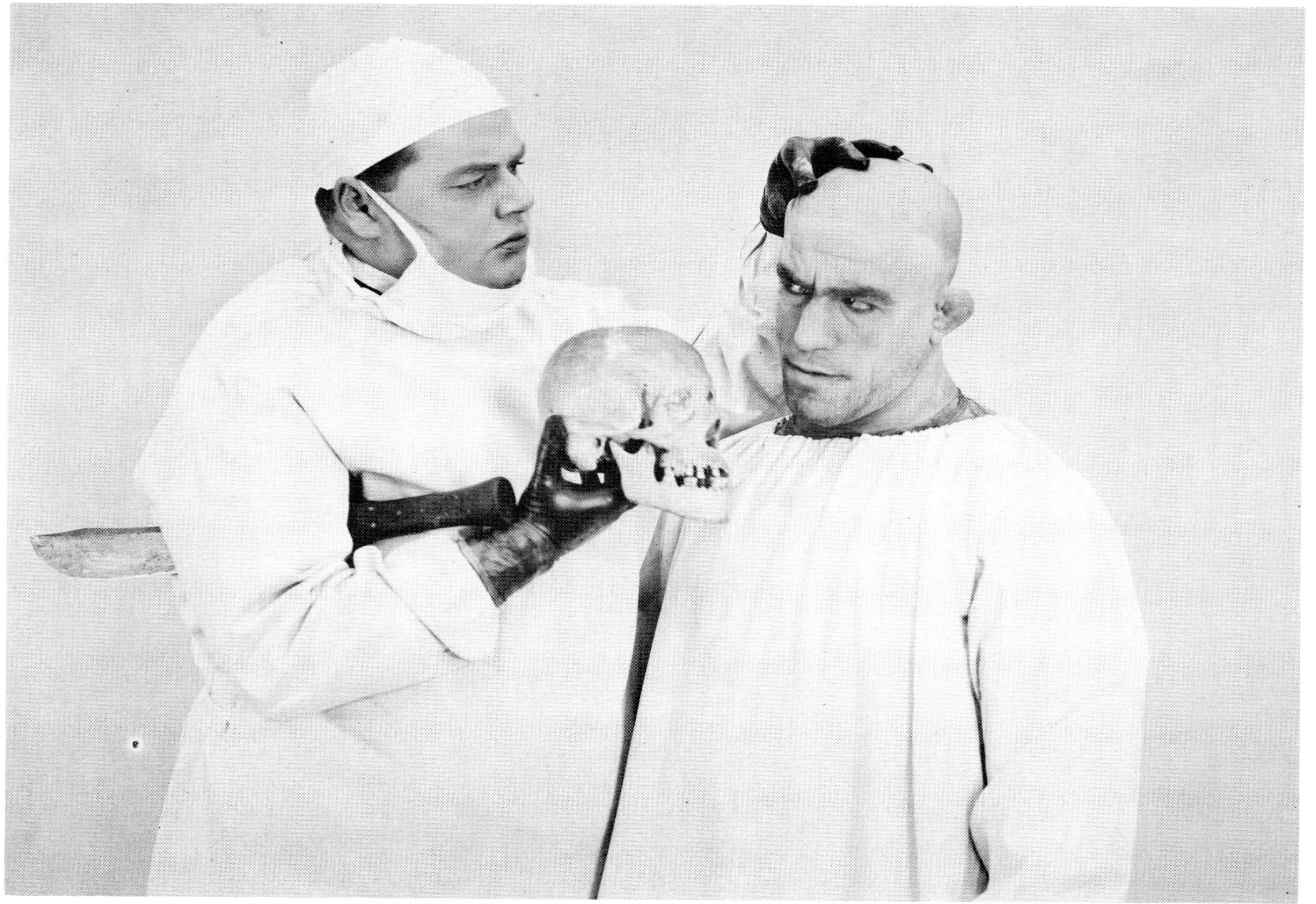

With or without the ape costume, Bull Montana presents a gruesome portrait. Montana played ape men in a number of silent films.

The final sequence of the feature provides unique footage of a Brontosaurus ravaging metropolitan London.

"Without doubt an unusual and interesting picture. A picture that will get a load of money at the boxoffice, create a tremendous amount of discussion and achieve about as much word of mouth advertising as anything has ever had in motion picture history."

Variety, 2-11-25, p. 31

"I'm anxious to see 'The Lost World'. In the first place, it's more or less something new in pictures. Secondly, ten Boston newspaper critics agree that it's great and when ten newspaper critics agree on anything, it must be different, whether or not the critics agree on the right or wrong side of the fence."

Motion Picture Herald, Vol. 20, p. 74

"Through wonderful photographic skill and infinite patience in the camera work, Sir Arthur Conan Doyle's fantastic story, 'The Lost World', makes a memorable motion picture, weakened by some subtitles and the unnecessary inclusion of countless protestations of affection by both the hero and the heroine at inopportune moments. This photoplay, which was presented last night at the Astor Theatre before a gathering in which there were a number of the heads of the film industry and screen celebrities, is a unique production which will create a lot of talk, as some of the scenes are as awesome as anything that has ever been shown in shadow form. It has also been fashioned with a keen sense for comedy relief and, for the most part, the continuity has been worked out so as to create excellent suspence."

New York Times, 2-9-25, p. 235

ONE WAY STREET

Release: 1925, First National Pictures
Description: Silent, 5596 feet
Classification: SF
References: No. 14, p. 367; No. 50, p. 350; AFI, F2.4020, p. 571, 572; LC, LP21251; MPH, Vol. 21, p. 45; MPN, Vol. 31, p. 646

Credits

Producer .... First National Productions
Associate Producer .... Earl Hudson
Director.................... John Francis Dillon
Screenplay.................... Arthur Statter, Mary Alice Seully, and Earl Hudson

Cast

Bobby Austin .... Ben Lyon
Lady Sylvia Hutton .... Anna Q. Nilsson
Kathleen Lawrence .... Mona Kingsley
Sir Edward Hutton.................... Lumsden Hare
Elizabeth Stuart .... Marjorie Daw
Lady Frances .... Dorothy Cumming
John Stuart.................... Thomas Holding
Fat Man .... Jed Prouty
Don Jose.................... M. Gonzales

One Way Street is based on the novel of the same title and written by Beale Davis. It presents another in a series of films which illustrated the attention that rejuvenation and gland transplantation received during the mid-1920's. This feature followed closely on the heels of *Vanity's Price* (1924) and *Sinners in Silk* (1924). Additionally, First National made a rejuvenation film in 1924 entitled *Black Oxen.* In that particular feature the rejuvenation of an Austrian countess who had returned to New York after being treated by a mysterious surgeon was the focus. *One Way Street* is, therefore, not very dissimilar to *Black Oxen* or the other two mentioned pictures.

As the story begins, we find young Bobby Austin is being sent to Madrid on a diplomatic mission. Lady Sylvia Hutton, who has become infatuated with Bobby and is also a leading member of British society, follows him to Madrid where she continues to shower him with gifts and lavish parties.

Sometime after arriving in Madrid, Lady Sylvia invites Bobby on a yachting trip to Monte Carlo. On this voyage he meets Kathleen Lawrence, a notorious kept woman. She tries to tell Bobby about how Lady Sylvia is using him, warning that she will discard him as soon as a more attractive and exciting male comes on the scene. At first, Bobby pays little attention to her warnings, but soon he begins to see Sylvia's attentions being diverted to a young Italian. It is then that Bobby begins to become involved with Kathleen. Unfortunately, her notoriety causes him so many problems with his diplomatic mission that he loses his post and must return to London.

Now out of diplomatic service, he resorts to gambling as a profession. He is quite successful and happy as well since Kathleen introduced him to Elizabeth Stuart, a sweet young girl. However, one evening he runs into Lady Sylvia who again desires his attentions. Bobby refuses to become part of this vicious circle again and tells her he wants no part of her ruse. She becomes furious at being refused and manages to discredit him claiming he is a card cheat. As a result he is thrown out of his gambling club.

After Bobby is discredited, Kathleen goes to Lady Sylvia and confronts her with the deception she perpetrated about Bobby's card playing. She then forces Lady Sylvia to admit she is the culprit who had wrongly maligned his character.

Evidently, Lady Sylvia's anger and forced apology is so grotesque an ordeal for her that she suddenly begins to lose her beauty and within minutes becomes an old weathered woman.

Subsequently, she reveals that she had once been an operatic favorite and when her voice failed she went to Europe to recuperate. While there she met a young doctor who performed miraculous surgery on her and said that she would remain beautiful for some time. However, he warned that she should not become involved in drastic arguments or excited events which would cause the aging process to accelerate to its original true state. Evidently, the aging process in now irreversible and she must remain elderly.

In the end, Bobby tells Elizabeth of his love for her and they are wed. Additionally, he resumes his rightful place in society and is given another post in the diplomatic service. Meanwhile, Lady Sylvia finds solace in the arms of her husband and decides that the youth she once sought is not as comforting as his warm sincere love.

Obviously, during this era plastic surgery and the possibility of being rejuvenated by monkey gland or goat gland treatments was so real that crowds of viewers believed the fictional representations presented in the movies were realities. Many people were bilked out of money by so-called surgeons and others who claimed to be able to successfully recapture a patient's youth.

One Way Street was not as well produced as the First National *Black Oxen.* Nevertheless, it does appear to be a successful entry into the 1925 film market and is certainly a noteworthy science fiction film.

Anna Q. Nilsson (Lady Sylvia), interestingly enough, had played in the film *Vanity's Price* in 1924 and had been rejuvenated in that effort as well. Anna began her career in 1910 and had played in nearly 150 films prior to her role in *Vanity's Price.* Her performance in *One Way Street* was well received by the 1925 critics. She then went on to star in another 40 films before ending her career in 1954 with the memorable *Seven Brides for Seven Brothers.*

THE POWER GOD

Release: 1925, Vital Exchanges, Inc.
Description: Silent, 15 episode serial, each episode approximately 2000 feet
Classification: SF-A
References: No. 8, p. 122, 248, 249; No. 14, p. 384; No. 32, p. 43; No. 50, p. 379; BIO, Vol. 67, 6-3-26, p. 32

Credits

Producer .... Davis Distributing Co.
Director .... Ben Wilson
Story .... Rex Taylor and Harry Haven

Cast

Jim Thorpe .... Ben Wilson
Aileen Sturgess .... Neva Gerber
Aileen's Mother .... Mary Brooklyn
Maid .... Mary Crane
John Sturgess .... John Bahaglia

Chapters 1-15 of *The Power God*

Chapter 1: The Ring of Fate
References: LC, LP22187
Chapter 2: Trapped
References: LC, LP22188
Chapter 3: The Living Dead
References: LC, LP22189
Chapter 4: Black Shadows
References: LC, LP22251
Chapter 5: The Death Chamber
Chapter 6: House of Peril
Chapter 7: Hands of the Dark
Chapter 8: 59th Second
Chapter 9: Perilous Waters
Chapter 10: The Bridge of Doom
Chapter 11: Treachery
Chapter 12: The Storm's Lash
Chapter 13: The Purloined Papers
Chapter 14: The Flaming Menace
Chapter 15: The Wages of Sin

Apparently Vital Exchanges, Inc. only had chapters 1 through 4 of *The Power God* copyrighted, thus the reason for only four references from the Library of Congress records.

The Power God is another Wilson/Gerber serial. Between 1919 and 1921 this pair of performers had completed *The Trail of the Octupus, The Screaming Shadow, The Branded Four,* and *The Mysterious Pearl.* They returned to the serial circuit in 1925 and 1926 with three more: *The Power God, Mystery Box,* and *Officer 444.* The latter three appearances, however, do not seem to have been of comparable quality to their earlier features. Nevertheless, this duo were favorites of the audiences and their names brought crowds to the theaters each week to see yet another exciting chapter.

The Power God begins with an elderly scientist named John Sturgess developing an atomic energy engine. Realizing that the engine's secret might be in jeopardy due to the presence of some unscrupulous capitalists, he carefully commits the assembly of the device to memory. As an added precaution, he shares the secret with his daughter Aileen.

After a large financial syndicate attempts to make several offers to Professor Sturgess--all of which he refuses--they develop a more diabolical plan to secure the treasured engine. But in their clumsy attempt to secure the invention, it is destroyed and Professor Sturgess is killed during its explosion. Further complicating matters, Aileen, who had gone for help, loses her memory in an automobile accident on the way to the authorities.

The syndicate then uses one of their men to pose as her husband in an effort to gain the secret. Jim Thorpe, her lover, realizes this is a trick, but uses the time to plan her rescue. Since she has no memory, she cannot divulge the secret of the engine and will therefore remain safe for a while. Somehow Aileen, though her memory is gone, cannot conceive being married to this strange man. These strong suspicions finally lead her to provide false information concerning the invention.

Shortly after this Jim manages to rescue Aileen and the pair make an attempt to find sanctuary from their ruthless pursuers. During their getaway, Aileen receives another bump on the head and she awakens having recovered her memory. Realizing that they must quickly get to the patent office in Washington and register the atomic engine, they begin to make their perilous journey.

Each step of the way, the powerful syndicate sends its thugs to prevent the completion of their trip, and the final chapter ends in a fierce battle outside Washington with Jim and Aileen managing to make one last escape. They successfully patent the priceless engine.

This particular serial displays a valiant attempt to describe atomic energy with its unlimited power and ability to regenerate fuel. It is probably the first SF glimpse of atomic energy. Even though Jules Verne hinted at atomic power in *20,000 Leagues Under the Sea* and *Mysterious Island,* only a brief prefunctionary description was given.

The Power God seemed to lack the intensity and continuity of earlier attempts and gave the appearance of being put together hastily and with a very limited budget. The idea was a very good one, but unfortunately the actualization was less than adequately carried out on the screen.

SUPER-HOOPER-DYNE LIZZIES

Release: 1925, Pathe
Description: Silent, 1850 feet
Classification: SF-C
References: No. 14, p. 462; No. 50, p. 468; LC, LU6748; MPN, Vol. 31, p. 2968; MPW, Vol. 74, p. 765

Credits

Producer .... Mack Bennett
Director .... Del Lord
Screenplay .... Jefferson Moffitt and Frank Capra

Cast

Billy .... Billy Bevan
Andy .... Andy Clyde
Lil .... Lillian Knight
Negro .... J.J. Richardson

This feature, *Super-Hooper-Dyne Lizzies,* is a short Pathe comedy which attempted to provide humor during an election year when so many orators were coming across the radio waves making resounding promises, none of which they intended to keep. The film's three main characters, Billy, Andy, and Lil, provided typical slapstick humor that placed them in various situations which provided extremely funny scenes for the audiences.

The title, *Super-Hooper-Dyne Lizzies,* is easily explained when one understands the terminology of this period. The "super-hooper" referred to the person on the radio who boomed across the air waves, giving great gusto to his voice without any added amplification on the station's behalf. It seems Billy invented a device that could transfer the vociferiousness of the announcer into energy that would propel his modified automobile. The term "dyne-lizzies" referred to his automobile. Dyne is a unit of work in the metric system which meant (in this movie's interpretation) that the vocal energy coming over the radio waves was being transformed into mechanical energy which propelled the auto down the road.

The film provided an interesting theory, which, if it were indeed a reality, could have helped us gather sufficient energy over the years from the countless public speeches and campaign promises--all delivered in those booming, falsely cheerful voices--echoing across the radio waves of the United States to solve everyone's transportation problems.

UP THE LADDER

Release: 1925, Universal Pictures Corp.
Description: Silent, 5922 feet
Classification: SF
References: No. 14, p. 505; No. 50, p. 515; AFI, F2.5998, p. 851, 852

Credits

Producer .... Universal-Jewel
Director .... Edward Sloman
Screenplay .... Tom McNamara
Camera .... Jackson Rose
Adaptation .... Grant Carpenter

Cast

Jane Cornwall .... Virginia Valli
James Van Clinton .... Forrest Stanley
Helen Newhall .... Margaret Livingston
Robert Newhall .... Holmes Herbert
Judge Seymore .... George Fawcett
Peggy .... Priscilla Moran
Dancer .... Olive Ann Alcorn
Housekeeper .... Lydia Yeamans Titus

Up the Ladder is a weak science fiction melodrama which focuses on the development of a device called a "tele-vision-scope," created by the genius James Van Clinton. The device operates much like a telephone except you are allowed to see the person you are talking with. While Jim's model works perfectly, he needs large capital investments in order to put the invention into production and market it nationwide.

One afternoon he is introduced to Jane Cornwall, a young heiress. Immediately, they fall in love and within only a few short weeks are wed. Jane is so enthusiastic about Jim's marvelous telecommunication device that she invests her entire fortune into the production and marketing of it. Within five years the company has grown enormously and its distribution of the tele-vision-scope has been unbelievably successful.

But, alas, Jim becomes bored with his station in life and soon his attentions begin to be directed toward Helen Newhall, Jane's best friend. Jim's infidelity is discovered by Jane, but she elects not to reveal that she is aware of the affair. Instead, she leaves him. Jim is soon forced into a financial plight such that he must work in a subordinate position in his own company.

Gradually, Jim finds himself and evaluates what is really worthwhile in his life. He is soon promoted to the head of the firm again as he and Jane reconcile their differences and resume their once happy marriage.

1926

THE BLOCK SIGNAL

Release: 1926, Lumas Film Corp.
Description: Silent, 5900 feet
Classification: SF-A
References: No. 14, p. 55; No. 50, p. p-7; AFI, F2.0471, p. 68; BIO, Vol. 70, 2-3-27, p. 54; LC, LP23154; MPW, Vol. 82, p. 371; VAW, Vol. 84, p. 14, 18; Vol. 85, p. 68

Credits

Producer .... Gothan
Director .... Frank O'Connor
Screenplay .... Edward J. Meagher
Camera .... Ray June

Cast

"Jovial Joe" Ryan .... Ralph Lewis
Grace Ryan .... Jean Arthur
Jack Milford .... Hugh Allan
Bert Steele .... George Cheeseboro
"Roadhouse" Rosen .... Sidney Franklin
"Unhandy"Andy .... Leon Holmes
Jim Brennan .... "Missouri" Royer

The Block Signal is a weak science fiction adventure film which focuses on the development of an automatic signaling device and an unusual braking system for locomotives. The acting of Ralph Lewis and Jean Arthur is extremely well performed. Lewis, as the old locomotive engineer, gives one of those unusual impersonations that stands out as a remarkable achievement, and Jean Arthur as Grace Ryan gives an unusually strong supporting performance.

As the story begins, we find Joe Ryan--Jovial Joe to his friends--suddenly realizing that after 20 years of being an engineer on the train his eyes have gone through a transformation which results in color blindness. While he attempts to conceal this abnormality from his fellow workers, his fireman Burt Steele is still able to discern that Joe's eyes aren't what they once were. Believing that Joe is color blind (and wishing to take advantage of Joe's dilemma), Burt creates a situation which will expose Joe's malady to all. It seems that for some time Burt has been in love with Joe's daughter Grace. He has been anxious to marry her, but has been awaiting a promotion so that he can financially support her and a future family.

The wreck Burt creates involves the engine and several parked cars when Joe is unable to identify the properly colored track signals. The resultant damage is severe enough to cause investigation, and when they discover that Joe is color blind he is immediately demoted.

Obviously, Joe is despondent over this turn of events, but decides to continue to work for the railroad and the betterment of train travel in general. In his laboratory he invents an automatic braking device that can be installed on freight cars and passenger trains to help them stop, thus preventing future accidents. Additionally, Joe perfects an automatic signaling device so that the signal is transmitted directly into the cab of the locomotive without having to be viewed out the cab window. Joe is assisted in the development of these devices by a young civil engineer, Jack Medford.

As their association becomes more involved, Jack begins to pay particular attention to Grace, and eventually a bond between the two of them develops as they begin to fall in love. Naturally, this does not make Burt happy. While he has his promotion, he has lost Grace in the process.

Finally, Burt's sense of evil gets the better of him and when Jack and Grace board a train for a nearby city to get some parts for Joe's inventions, Burt sees his opportunity for revenge. He arranges for the train to have an accident half way through the journey resulting in a runaway train. Unfortunately, his plan does not operate as well as he would have liked. Instead of the accident occuring on the way to town, it happens on the way back.

As the train goes speeding by the station, Joe realizes that it is a runaway. He quickly grabs his device, and using a second locomotive, overtakes the train. Going car to car, he carefully installs his device in each of the cars. Then as he reaches the locomotive he pushes the switch which releases it and at the same time engages his automatic braking system. It is a huge success as the cars slowly come to a stop just before they are in danger of plummeting over the edge of a trestle.

Joe, once again, is a hero in the railroad's eyes as they realize that he was framed in the earlier accident. They decide that, even though he is color blind and can no longer be an engineer, he certainly should have a position of high esteem in the company.

As for Burt, he has slunk into the shadows to escape the railroad detectives who have vowed they will bring him to justice. And as the movie ends, Grace and Jack finally reach the point where they ask for Joe's permission to marry. He gladly gives them his blessing.

> "O'Connor, directing, has thrown in a wreck, a fist fight while a train runs wild and various 'shots' from other railroad films. He evidently thought enough of some of these lifted views to repeat 'em. They're unquestionable on tap twice and could advantageously be cut to once apiece, inasmuch as the film uses up six minutes over an hour, and that's unnecessary."
>
> *Variety Weekly,* 10-27-26

> "Though there is nothing out of the ordinary in this picture, the vicissitudes of humble folk, pleasing character studies, and swiftly moving trains, keep the interest alive and provides satisfactory entertainment. The plot is simple and the continuity excellent."
>
> *Bioscope,* 2-3-27, p. 54

OFFICER 444

Release: 1926, Davis Distributing Division
Description: Silent, 10 episode serial, each episode approximately 2000 feet
Classification: SF-A
References: No. 8, p. 130, 253; No. 14, p. 362; No. 32, p. 43; No. 50, p. 344; BIO, Vol. 68, 12-23-26, p. 31

Credits

Director .... Ben Wilson and Francis Ford

Cast

Officer 444 .... Ben Wilson
Gloria Grey .... Neva Gerber
The Frog .... Al Ferguson
Gang Member .... Phil Ford
Gang Member .... August Vollmer
Officer 444's Partner .... Jack Mower

Chapter 1-10 of *Officer 444*

Chapter 1: Flying Squadron
Chapter 2: Human Rats
Chapter 3: Trapped
Chapter 4: Gassed
Chapter 5: Missing
Chapter 6: The Radio Ray
Chapter 7: Death's Shadow
Chapter 8: Jaws fo Doom
Chapter 9: Underground Trap
Chapter 10: Justice

The ten episode serial, *Officer 444,* is the last in the series of Wilson/Gerber productions. Their teamwork began in 1919 with a string of four serials followed by a group of three between 1925 and 1926. In 1919 *The Trail of the Octupus* prompted exciting reviews and overwhelming response from the public. Wilson and Gerber were the darlings of the serial world. This epic adventure was followed by *The Screaming Shadow* (1920) and *The Branded Four* (1920), both classified in this reference guide as science fiction-adventure. A year later these were followed by *The Mysterious Pearl,* an exciting mystery. For some unexplainable reason there was a four year period in which the two performers were unable to be teamed as serial attractions. In 1925, Wilson, an aging, but still powerful box office attraction, directed and starred in *The Power God, The Mystery Box,* and finally *Officer 444* in 1926. This last serial was the last picture in which Wilson appeared. Ironically, he had also starred in the very first serial ever made, *What Happened to Mary?,* produced by the Edison Film company in 1912.

The plot of *Officer 444* focuses on Professor Haverly's invention of an unusual chemical gas which could be of immense benefit to mankind in the elimination of many diseases. It could also be a serious threat since it has the capability of destroying much of the population of the world if controlled by evil forces.

Before Professor Haverly can devulge the secret to the public, an accidental fire takes place in his laboratory. He is seriously injured and is immediately carried to the emergency room of the nearest hospital where little hope is given for his recovery. The professor, realizing that he is dying, decides he must dictate the secret formula and selects an attractive, young nurse, Gloria Grey to perform this task. He warns her to guard the secret with her life since it holds such immense power for mankind. He beseeches Gloria to communicate his formula to his son, a New York police officer with the badge number of 444. Gloria reluctantly agrees while she comforts the poor man in his dying moments.

Unfortunately for Gloria (but fortunate for the serial audience, as there would not have been a continuing story otherwise), the plot is overheard by a master criminal who disguises himself as "the Frog," proprietor of a disreputable Chinese restaurant. This notorious crook (admirably played by Al Ferguson) is a master of disguise. He not only dons the facade of the notorious restaurteur, but that of the eminent Dr. Blakely, respected and renowned surgeon on the hosital staff where nurse Grey is employed, and also that of a Professor Kalium, president of the International society of Scientists.

Disguised as Professor Kalium, he has the perfect opportunity since his sole purpose as this character is to acquire the formula to Professor Haverly's gas supposedly for the benefit of mankind.

Much of the action and excitement takes place in underground sewers where an assortment of trap doors and hidden panels enable the crooks to make their escapes. Officer 444 and Gloria Grey constantly search for the crooks' lair in these underground passages which are littered with snares and traps into which this fearless duo seem to find themselves entangled during each thrilling chapter, only to miraculously escape in the beginning moments of the next week's episode.

Even though Wilson's performance at the age of 52 doesn't provide the sharpness and forcefulness of his earlier years, the audience was still enthralled with his and Neva's performances.

Officer 444, while not the huge success of earlier productions, was nevertheless a popular one during 1926. The supporting role of Officer 444's relentless sidekick, acted by Jack Mower, showed the experience he had gained in his 60 or more film roles. Additionally, Al Ferguson's portrayal of the villain displayed his skills as a seasoned performer. All these factors assured the serial's success.

Wilson had been such a marvelous serial performer during the 1912 to 1926 period that the producers of this film, his last, must have felt a great loss when Ben Wilson passed away four years later, leaving a permanent void in the film industry.

> "The interiors of buildings specially designed for the convenience of crime, factories, slums, Chinese restaurants, and all the usual paraphernalia of sensational drama are reproduced with more realism and artistic effect than is usual in films of this class. The photography is most effective."
>
> *Bioscope,* Vol. 68, 12-23-26, p. 31

THE RADIO DETECTIVE

Release: 1926, Universal Pictures Corp.
Description: Silent, 10 episode serial, each episode approxiamtely 2000 feet
Classification: SF-A
References: No. 5, p. 16; No. 8, p. 127-188, 253, 254; No. 14, p. 395; No. 50, p. 390; PHO, 6-1926

Credits

Director .... William Craft and William A Crinley
Screenplay .... Carl Krusada
Camera .... E.U. Ulman

Cast

Eastern Evans .... Jack Daugherty
Mrs. Evans .... Margaret Quimby
Craig Kennedy .... Jack Mower
Flo .... Florence Allen
Syndicate Boss .... John T. Prince
Crooks .... Sammy Gervon
Crooks .... Wallace Balwin
Policeman .... Howard Enstedt
Boy Scouts .... Boy Scout Troop

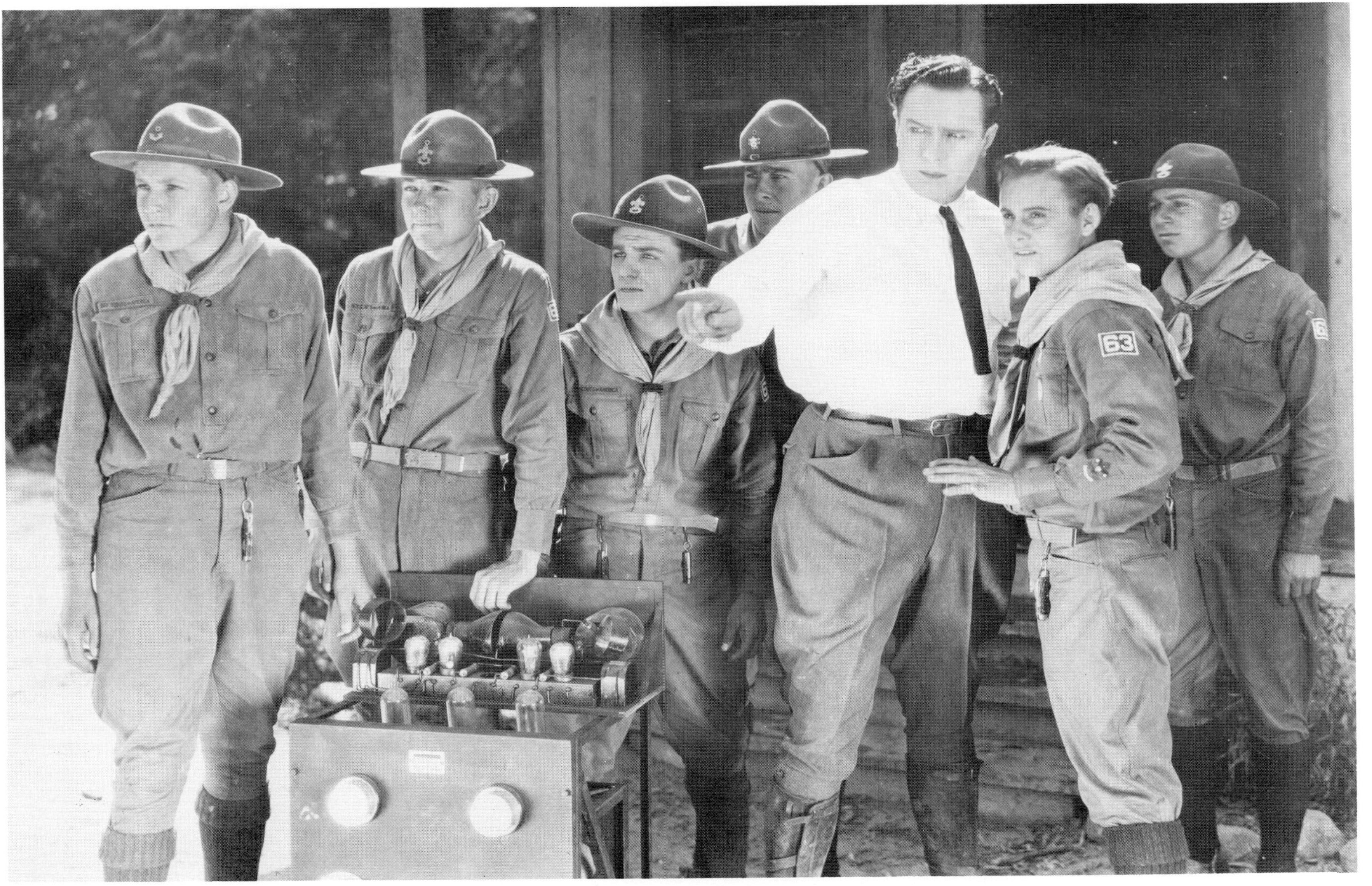

Scout leader Eastern Evans (Jack Daughtery) and his scouts with his "Edisight" invention.

Chapters 1-10 of *The Radio Detective*

Chapter 1: The Kick-off
References: LC, LP22525
Chapter 2: The Radio Riddle
References: LC, LP22526
Chapter 3: The Radio Wizard
References: LC, LP22527
Chapter 4: Boy Scout Loyalty
References: LC, LP22620
Chapter 5: The Radio Secret
References: LC, LP22638
Chapter 6: Fighting for Love
References: LC, LP22685
Chapter 7: The Tenderfoot Scout
References: LC, LP22691
Chapter 8: The Truth Teller
References: LC, LP22740
Chapter 9: The Fire Fiend
References: LC, LP22781
Chapter 10: Radio Romance
References: LC, LP22787

This was an attempt to revitalize the Craig Kennedy serials of the past. These features had excited the audiences of 1914 in *The Exploits of Elaine,* then again in 1915 with *The New Exploits of Elaine* and *The Romance of Elaine.* In all, from 1914 to 1921, the Craig Kennedy stories had utilized more than 246,000 feet of film.

Probably one of the most exciting aspects of any Craig Kennedy story or serial was the marvelous characterizations of villains. In earlier films, they were played by outstanding actors such as Maurice Costello and Lionel Barrymore in the roles of such evil men as "the Clutching Hand," Marcus Delmar, and Wu Fang. These portrayals certainly gave strength to the element of surprise and mystery that drove the viewers to the edges of their seats each and every week.

The Radio Detective, based on a story by Arthur Reeve as printed in *Boy's Life* magazine, fell far short of this excellence. The syndicate boss, played by John Prince, never really develops into a seriously threatening role. And while the syndicate searches for a marvelous invention known as "Evansite" (created by the Boy Scout leader, Eastern Evans), the plot never seems to achieve the drama audiences had become accustomed to seeing from Kennedy productions.

While Jack Mower attempted to carry out his duties as Craig Kennedy with admirable precision he lacks the flavor and flare, as well as the support of the other actors, to create the desired role.

The band of Boy Scouts who go to the aid of Kennedy and Eastern Evans almost sends the serial out of the classification of science fiction and into straight comedy. This certainly weakened the effect attempted by Arthur Reeve. Nevertheless, there are some exciting episodes within its ten parts, and the radio devices utilized by the hero live up to the Craig Kennedy reputation. They are not only ingenious but they are scientifically sound and marvelous in their effects.

Universal had to be less than encouraged by the lack of enthusiasm this serial received in their theater markets. Viewers, while interested in the first two or three episodes, suddenly began to disappear as the chapters continued. The weakness of this particular production had to cause them some serious second thoughts about other serial productions.

THE SAVAGE

Release: 1926, First National Pictures
Description: Silent, 6275 feet
Classification: SF-C
References: No. 14, p. 414; No. 50, p. 418; AFI, F2.4811, p. 682; BIO, Vol. 69, p. 53; COF, No. 6, p. 38; LC, LP22889; PHO, 10-26; VAW, Vol. 84, p. 13

Credits

Producer .... First National
Director .... Fred Newmeyer
Screenplay .... Jane Murfin and Charles E. Whittaker
Art Director .... Milton Mensaco
Camera .... George Folsey
Editor .... Arthur Tavares
Titles .... Ralph Spence
Supervisor .... Earl Hudson

Cast

Danny Terry .... Ben Lyon
Ysabel Atwater .... May McAvoy
Professor Atwater .... Tom Maguire
Howard Kipp .... Philo McCullough
Managing Editor .... Sam Hardy
Mrs. Atwater .... Charlotte Walker

The Savage, a feature film based on a story by Ernest Pascal, is a delightful science fiction comedy entry and appears to have been patterned after Arthur Conan Doyle's *The Lost World.* Earl Hudson, who worked as a crew member of *The Lost World* (1925), was the supervisor for the film and most likely added a great deal to the detail of the prehistoric creatures seen in *The Savage.*

As the story begins, the editor of a scientific publication becomes involved with Professor Atwater in the controversy surrounding the subject of evolution. After a very heated debate, it is decided that the dispute will only be solved by an expedition to the Mariposa Islands. A young journalist on the staff of the scientific publication, Danny Terry, is dispatched to accompany them to report all the events of the adventure.

In addition to Danny Terry, Professor Atwater, and his fellow scientists, the professor's daughter, Ysabel, accompanies the expeditionary force. Her presence seems to provide the film with its necessary entanglements needed for appropriate rescues and dilemmas. In fact, the trip has hardly begun when love is seen in young Danny's eyes. His romantic longing is thwarted, however, by Professor Atwater, who wishes his beloved daughter to have nothing to do with a lowly reporter.

As it turns out, when the party reaches the islands and investigates its environment, they are unable to come up with any "missing links" or any unusual findings that would support the theory of evolution. Therefore, one of the scientists, in order to gain recognition among his colleagues, decides to produce a counterfeit missing link. He produces this fake evidence to convince the world that the theory is based on sound evidence. What the expeditionary members don't know, however, is that there is indeed a prehistoric animal (friendly, of course) that seems to have developed an affection toward Danny Terry.

This affable dinosaur pursues him back to New York where Danny is indeed amazed that his prehistoric friend made such a journey.

Danny Terry (Ben Lyon) talks to his friend the dinosaur in a humorous science fiction comedy, *The Savage* (1926).

As the comedy draws to a close, Terry is made a hero for having discovered the true missing link, and the charleton scientist is exposed as a fraud. Naturally, Ysabel Atwater falls madly in love with the young hero, and, as the curtain falls, the three of them, Ysabel, Danny, and the dinosaur, are destined to live happily ever after.

> "The basic idea of this story is decidedly funny and if it had been maintained on the lines of pure comedy, would have made an excellent picture. Unfortunately, it is allowed to degenerate into a rough and tumble farce. Nevertheless, the rapid action sustains the interest, and there is a first-class thrill in the shape of a huge brontosaurus."
>
> *Bioscope,* Vol. 69, 11-4-26, p. 53

> "A two-reel knock-about comedy, spread out very thin to make a five-reel feature. Quality of its humor is childish and appeal is guaged to four-year-old intelligence instead of the 12-year level at which the average film fan is supposed to be--supposed to be, that is, by those who make a business of that kind of films."
>
> *Variety,* Vol. 84, 8-4-26, p. 13

THE SCARLET STREAK

Release: 1926, Universal Pictures Corp.
Description: Silent, 10 episode serial, each episode approximately 2000 feet
Classification: SF
References: No. 8, p. 126, 127, 254; No. 14, p. 416; No. 50, p. 420; BIO, Vol. 66, 3-11-26, p. 601

Credits

Producer .... Pathe Freres
Director .... Henry McRae

Cast

Bob Evans .... Jack Daugherty
Mary Crawford .... Lola Todd
Richard Crawford .... Albert J. Smith
Monk .... Albert Prisco
Monk's Accomplice .... Virginia Ainsworth

Chapters 1-10 of *The Scarlet Streak*

Chapter 1: The Face in the Crowd
References: LC, LP22002
Chapter 2: Masks and Men
References: LC, LP22020
Chapter 3: The Rope of Hazard
References: LC, LP22026
Chapter 4: The Death Ray
References: LC, LP22177

Chapter 5: The Lost Story
References: LC, LP22178
Chapter 6: The Plunge of Peril
References: LC, LP22179
Chapter 7: The Race of Terror
References: LC, LP22280
Chapter 8: The Cable of Courage
References: LC, LP22312
Chapter 9: The Dive of Death
References: LC, LP22360
Chapter 10: Universal Peace
References: LC, LP22391

By 1925 Pathe had emerged as an obvious serial powerhouse. The production facilities at their studio had become so efficient at making serials that the estimated cost was about $125,000 each, considerably lower than that of five years earlier. Additionally, their serials seemed to be popular enough to reach a majority (rumored at the time to be almost 80%) of the 20,000 theaters across the United States.

Universal made a major decision in 1926 to purchase six to eight of Pathe's serials to accompany their full-length features shown in movie houses throughout the nation. The first of these purchases was *The Scarlet Streak,* based on the story *Dangers of the Deep* by Leigh Jacobson. It appears to be of a better quality than others in the group and surely provided interesting entertainment for the audiences.

As the feature begins, we find that Bob Evans, a star reporter for the *Times,* has been assigned a story which the paper believes may have serious implications toward the world's balance of military power.

It seems that Professor Richard Crawford has invented a new device known as the "scarlet streak" which directs a red ray for several thousand yards, destroying whatever intercepts its path. Professor Crawford and his daughter Mary have been perfecting the machine and are in the final stages of its development. They are therefore glad to welcome Bob Evans as he will hopefully provide the necessary publicity for their device needed to insure a higher price when marketed.

The Professor and Mary have also become concerned the past few months as a house near the laboratory has the curtains drawn and the shutters consistently closed, yet people enter and exit at very strange hours of the day and night.

Unknown to the three of them this is the headquarters of the notorious foreign agent known as Monk. He has been observing the professor's work for some time and has waited until the invention is near completion before planning his dastardly move.

Late one evening, the professor, his device and its blueprints are kidnapped. Mary secures Bob Evans' aid in tracking down the agents responsible.

As the serial progresses we find Bob attempting to rescue the professor. He engages the villainous Monk in a careening ride which results in both of them narrowly escaping death as their car collides with a train. As Monk hastily departs during this catastrophe, Bob manages to secure the scarlet streak's plans.

In the next episode, there is a costume ball at the Crawford home, and Monk and his accomplice enter in disguise. They manage to rifle the safe, but don't find the plans for the invention. They are discovered during their attempted theft by Mary. Immediately, they take her captive as ransom for acquiring the needed plans.

Through the next episodes, the conflict between Bob and the gang continues. Always looming in the background is the terrible scarlet ray which can at any moment be perfected and provide the most awesome military weapon mankind has known.

As the serial draws to a close, Bob manages to overcome the agents and not only secures Mary's release, but her father and his device as well. In the end, Bob and Mary are seen affectionately embracing as they make plans for their wedding.

While this particular serial lacks a great deal of depth, the movie does provide numerous action scenes and a variety of technological weapons that are designed to thrill the audience. *The Scarlet Streak* is an exciting SF entry for 1926 and deserves attention for the special effects and stunts performed. It is probably one of the most ambitious efforts since 1920.

> "Jack Daugherty, who plays the agile young reporter, has a pleasant personality and great athletic powers and makes an ideal hero for this class of play. Lola Tod is a charming heroine, and all the other parts are capable played.
>
> In invention, excitement and qualities of mounting and acting, this serial, from its opening chapters, promises to be well up to the high standard of the Pathe Studios."
>
> *Bioscope,* Vol. 66, 3-11-26, p. 60

1927

BLAKE OF SCOTLAND YARD

Release: 1927, Universal Pictures Corp.
Description: Silent, 12 episode serial, each episode approximately 2000 feet
Classification: SF-A
References: No. 8, p. 136, 150, 257; No. 14, p. 54; No. 31, p. 184-186; No. 50, p. 39

Credits

Producer .... Universal Pictures Corp.
Director .... Robert F. Hill
Screenplay .... Robert F. Hill and William Lord Wright
Special Effects .... William Lord Wright

Cast

Angus Blake .... Hayden Stevenson
Lady Diane Blanton .... Gloria Gray
The Spider .... Monty Montague
Lady in White .... Grace Cunard

Chapters 1-12 of *Blake of Scotland Yard*

Chapter 1: The Castle of Fear
References: LC, LP24139
Chapter 2: The Spider's Web
References: LC, LP24167
Chapter 3: The Vanishing Heiress
References: LC, LP24176

Chapter 4: The Room Without a Door
References: LC, LP24263
Chapter 5: Shots in the Dark
References: LC, LP24271
Chapter 6: Ambushed
References: LC, LP24300
Chapter 7: The Secret of the Cabin
References: LC, LP24323
Chapter 8: Into the Web
References: LC, LP24352
Chapter 9: The Baited Trap
References: LC, LP24353
Chapter 10: The Lady in White
References: LC, LP24423
Chapter 11: The Closing Web
References: LC, LP24424
Chapter 12: The Final Reckoning
References: LC, LP24445

The serial *Blake of Scotland Yard* created some spine tingling adventures in its twelve episodes and provided the audience with a sense of suspence that had been lacking in many of the serials from 1925 through 1927.

As the first chapter, *The Castle of Fear,* begins we are introduced to Angus Blake, a world renowned criminologist who retired from Scotland Yard several years ago. He is being visited by his good friend, Lady Diana Blanton, who begins to relate the bizarre events which have plagued the Blanton castle for the past fortnight.

Her father, Lord Blanton, recently discovered a process by which base metals could be converted into gold. Since discovering this process and recording its secret formula, the Blantons have been terrorized by a nefarious sinister criminal, "the Spider." In fact, there have been two recent attempts on Lord Blanton's life, both thwarted only by a servant's timely interruption. Lady Blanton is, therefore, seeking help from Angus, who reluctantly agrees to return to the Blanton estate with Diana.

The pair no sooner arrive than the Spider makes another vicious attack on their household. This event convinces Angus that he must come out of retirement and stop this rogue of the underworld.

Each week the audience is treated to another adventure in which Blake and the Spider battle each other in the isolated and remote Blanton castle. The audience soon learns that Blake's resourcefulness and deductive reasoning even rival that of the infamous Sherlock Holmes. Moreover, Blake seems to have a secret weapon. Each time he is in complete peril with no seemingly possible means of escape, a mysterious "woman in white" (portrayed by Grace Cunard) appears to aid in his spectacular rescue.

In chapter 11, we find that Blake is closing the gap on the Spider and will soon have him in control. In the final chapter, entitled *The Final Reckoning,* Angus and his mysterious accomplice manage to confront the Spider at last. During the struggle the Spider accidentally falls on a sharply pointed instrument, thus ending his reign of terror.

Angus Blake has once again mastered the powers of evil with the aid of his deductive reasoning and superior intellect which allowed him to solve a case that from the outset seemed to be virtually unsolvable.

Needless to say the audience was enthralled by Angus Blake and the excitement created by this Sherlock Holmes-type character, as well as the mystery surrounding him. They didn't have to wait long before a sequel was forthcoming. In 1929, Universal returned to the screen with an adventure entitled *The Ace of Scotland Yard.* Though not considered science fiction, this new serial still provided a lot of action and suspence for the Blake fans.

THE MISSING LINK

Release: 1927, Warner Brothers
Description: Silent, 6485 feet
Classification: SF-C
References: No. 14, p. 322; No. 50, p. 306; AFI, F2.3646, p. 517, 518; BIO, 3-17-27, p. 56; LC, LP23882; MPW, 5-14-27, p. 133, 156, 157; NYR, 5-7-24

Credits

Producer	Warner Brothers
Director	Charles F. Reisner
Assistant Director	Sandy Roth
Screenplay	Darryl Francis Zanuck
Camera	Dev Jennings and Fred West

Cast

Arthur Wells	Syd Chaplin
Beatrice Braden	Ruth Hiatt
Col. Braden	Tom McGuire
Lord Dryden	Crauford Kent
Captain	Nick Cogley
Missing Link	Sam Baker
Chimpanzee	Akka

The Missing Link is another in a long line of films designed to provide a plausible explanation for Darwin's theory of evolution--the link between man and his ancestoral primates.

As the film begins, Arthur Wells, a young struggling poet, is forced to leave London before being captured by his creditors. He makes good his escape by stowing away on an oceanliner just moments before it sails. Once aboard, Arthur becomes friends with Lord Dryden, a famous game hunter, who is on his way to Africa in search of the missing Darwinian link.

After several weeks aboard the ship, Arthur and Dryden become the best of friends. Dryden, constantly plagued by reporters and autograph seekers, persuades Arthur to switch identities with him. Thus, Wells now becomes the famous game hunter as far as anyone is concerned.

As the boat docks in a remote African port, Dryden and Wells, still in their reversed roles, begin their overland journey to Colonel Braden's mansion. Braden is to be their host for the "missing link" safari.

Suddenly, Arthur, whose misogynous behavior was frequently displayed during the ocean voyage, finds himself confronted by the beautiful Beatrice Braden (the Colonel's daughter) as they arrive at the palatial estate. During the next few days, he makes every effort to avoid her, but somehow the two seem to be constantly bumping into each other.

Arthur's severe timidity is revealed when Colonel Braden's pet chimpanzee, Akka, is suddenly found in his room. This causes Arthur to go into an hysterical fit and at this point Dryden and Wells confess their ruse of disguise to their hosts. The colonel takes it all in good stride and assures them that Arthur is welcome to remain and accompany them on the safari.

As time passes, Arthur has a series of hilarious misadventures with the various animals around the estate. A leopard wanders into the compound, sending Arthur scurrying for refuge in a tree only to discover that the tree is the leopard's lair. Another of Arthur's blunders occurs when he is exploring outside the compound and stumbles upon a group of lion cubs and believes they are young innocent kittens, until, that is, the cubs' mother appears and terrifies the poor man. The film contains much of

Beatrice held captive by "The Missing Link" (1926).

this sort of slapstick comedy, but in the waning moments of the feature, there are some more serious scenes.

Arthur finally realizes that his long developed hatred of women has been overcome by the kindness and beauty of Beatrice. When the two acknowledge their love, however, it is almost too late. Beatrice has been carried away by the mysterious "missing link." Arthur's love for her is strong enough to help him overcome his timid nature and fear of the unknown jungle. He courageously tracks the creature to its rocky cave where he heroically rescues Beatrice. They flee the gloomy cave and beat their way through the thick jungle brush. Their pace quickens as they hear the creature rapidly closing the distance between them. As the pair reaches a clearing, they are relieved to see Colonel Braden and Lord Dryden. Dryden shoots in an attempt to scare the animal off, but instead fatally wounds it. The evidence they had hoped would complete the bridge between the primates and man lay dead at their feet.

While *The Missing Link* is a weak science fiction-comedy, it certainly is an entertaining film. Syd Chaplin's hilarious antics and brand of slapstick comedy make the movie a definite box office hit. Additionally, the well trained chimpanzee, Akka, provided a convenient focus for much of Chaplin's humor.

> "Between Syd Chaplin, the chimpanzee, and a rapid-fire collection of genuinely humorous situations and gags most of which are new, 'The Missing Link' is a wow when it comes to getting the laughs."
>
> *Moving Picture World,* 5-14-27, p. 133

> "The plot of this production is of small importance, the film being simply a succession of farcical misadventures, chases and thrills. Interest is sustained not only by the brilliant performance of the star, but the remarkable proceedings of the intelligent ape."
>
> *Bioscope,* 3-17-27, p. 56

THE WIZARD

Release: 1927, Fox Film Corp.
Description: Silent, 5629 feet
Classification: SF-H
References: No. 3, p. 23, 25; No. 14, p. 533; No. 50, p. 545; AFI, F2.6445, p. 913; FID, 12-11-27; LC, LP24711; MPW, Vol. 90, p. 26, 43; VAW, 11-30-27, p. 19

Credits

Producer.................................... Fox Film Corp.
Director .... Richard Rosson
Screenplay.................... Harry O. Hoyte and Andrew Bennison
Camera.. Frank Good
Titles .... Malcolm Stuart Boylan

Cast

Stanley Gordon.............................. Edmund Lowe
Anne Webster .... Leila Hyams
Dr. Paul Coriolos..................... Gustav Von Seyffertitz
Edwin Palmer................................. E. H. Calvert
Reginald Van Lear .... Barry Norton
Sam.. Oscar Smith

Detective Murphy.. Perle Marshall
Judge Webster... Norman Trevor
The Ape... George Kotsonaros
Mrs. Van Lear .... Maude Turner Gordon

The film *The Wizard* is a classic science fiction-horror movie based on a story, *Balaoo*, by Gaston Leroux, the author of *The Phantom of the Opera*, among other works.

The Wizard focuses on Dr. Paul Coriolos' motive of revenge for his son's death. To achieve this, Dr. Coriolos trains an ape to do his bidding--as well as his morbid deeds. He grafts a human face onto the ape's skull, making it extremely gruesome. He then dispatches the poor creature to extract the vengeance he demands on a myriad of people, all of whom the doctor feels were instrumental in his son's execution.

It seems that Coriolos' son had been convicted of murder and was sentenced to die in the electric chair. The obvious conclusion is that the old man feels his son was unjustly tried and sentenced. He blames the judge and district attorney as well as the members of the jury who handed down the ill-fated verdict.

The strange mystery surrounding the sudden deaths of many who were connected with young Coriolos' trial does not go unnoticed. A young, aggressive newspaper reporter, Stanley Gordon, seeks to investigate a new angle on these mysterious murders. In doing so, he accidently discovers the key is the father's crazed revenge. This new information enables him to predict the next doomed victims and thus save them from death at the hands of the ape-like monster–Judge Webster and his daughter Anne. Quite naturally, Anne and Stanley become amorously involved as they seek to discover the whereabouts of the mysterious Dr. Coriolos and his ape.

As the film draws to a close, we see Dr. Coriolos, the sinister mentor of the ape creature, in the process of beating the poor animal once too often. The horrible, tortured beast turns on his master and crushes his body with his huge hands. Anne, who was being held prisoner by the doctor, then manages to pick up a rifle and shoot the beast, finally putting it out of its misery. Stanley arrives moments later and immediately relays the entire story of Dr. Coriolos' evil plot of revenge to his newspaper.

While the reviews of the film indicated there was some humor involved in the production, the script certainly does not indicate that any degree of levity was intended. On the contrary, the script seems to dictate that the production be treated as a serious SF-H work. It is also apparent from these many reviews that the film was extremely well made, and that the characterization by Gustav von Seyffertitz as Dr. Coriolos was very impressive to both audiences and critics. Obviously, the story had a great deal of success as Twentieth Century Fox (Fox Film Corporation in 1927) remade the movie in 1942, renaming it *Dr. Renault's Secret*.

1928

THE CHINATOWN MYSTERY

Release: 1928, Syndicated Pictures
Description: Silent, 10 episode serial, each episode approximately 2000 feet
Classification: SF-A
References: No. 8, p. 141, 263, 264; No. 14, p. 85; No. 50, p. 64; BIO, Vol 77, No. 1154; FDY, 1928; STI, Vol. 1, p. 14

Credits

Director .... J.P. McGowan

Cast

Joe Masters .... Joe Bonomo
Chemist .... Ruth Hiatt
The Sphinx .... Francis Ford
Crook .... Al Baffert

Chapters 1-10 of *The Chinatown Mystery*

Chapter 1: The Chinatown Mystery
Chapter 2: The Clutching Claw
Chapter 3: The Devil's Dice
Chapter 4: The Mysterious 13
Chapter 5: Galloping Fury
Chapter 6: The Depth of Danger
Chapter 7: The Invisible Hand
Chapter 8: The Wreck
Chapter 9: Broken Jade
Chapter 10: The Thirteenth Hour

The Chinatown Mystery is a ten episode science fiction-adventure serial featuring Joe Bonomo, a Hollywood "he man" noted for his immense size and unusual strength. Bonomo plays the part of Joe Masters, a secret service agent who is trying to protect a young chemist. It seems she has discovered a formula for producing artificial diamonds. Masters battles a powerful and resourceful villain known in the adventure as "the Sphinx" (admirably played by Francis Ford).

As in the case of so many serials of the past, a young girl, the chemist, is kidnapped. Before being abducted, however, she cleverly hid the formula for the process in a safe place. The Sphinx attempts to make the girl reveal the formula, but she is rescued just in time (in fact, she continues to be rescued "just in the nick of time" throughout the serial) by the powerful Joe Masters.

In one part of the series, our hero's great physical strength is demonstrated when he picks up one of the crooks (portrayed by 6′ tall, 210 lb. Al Baffert) and hurls him across the room like a sack of potatoes. The intent of the serial was obviously to display the star's physique since the script lacked both the finesse and depth that serials usually maintained during this great era.

Even the chapter titles show a lack of imagination. Chapter 1, *The Chinatown Mystery,* is expected since it reiterates the epic's main title, but Chapter 2, *The Clutching Claw,* is obviously borrowed from the Craig Kennedy mystery title, *The Clutching Hand,* and shows lack of forethought used.

In the final episode, *The Thirteenth Hour,* Joe finally comes face to face with the Sphinx. The two battle with the result being the Sphinx' ultimate capitulation.

The serial's only claim to being classified science fiction is the development of the artificial diamonds through the use of a secret formula. Obviously, this is not a new plot, as it was first introduced in SF films in the period from 1897-1909, and it is doubtful that this work did much to improve on those earlier plots.

The Chinatown Mystery, though a weak science fiction-adventure serial, does deserve attention. Not, however, for its plot or the use of science in converting materials into artificial diamonds, but rather for the portrayal of a unique villain--the Sphinx--artfully created by Francis Ford.

This was the last serial in which Ford appeared in a villainous role. He had played countless "bad guys" during his 15 years on the screen, giving each characterization his all and his great success could be measured by the many "boos" and hisses emitted by audiences whenever he (as a dastardly, evil villain) appeared in a scene.

Ford's career began with Thomas Edison in the early 1900's and spanned the period of silent films into the sound era. Not only was Ford an outstanding actor, but he also became an eminently respected director and producer. Certainly his immense talent and noteworthy achievements should not go unnoticed even in a weak SF film such as *The Chinatown Mystery*.

> "A good cast is headed by Joe Bonomo as a Hercules, who literally throws his opponents at one another. Ruth Hiatt is excellent as the girl who has everything to lose, and sound support is provided by the rest."
>
> *Bioscope*, 11-14-28, Vol. 77, p. 40

CODE OF THE AIR

Release: 1928, Bischoff Productions
Description: Silent, 5700 feet
Classification: SF
References: No. 14, p. 89; No. 50, p. 70; AFI, F2.0994, p. 135; FID, 12-16-28; VAW, 12-19-28, Vol. 93, p. 23

Credits

Producer..Bischoff
Director...James P. Hogan
Screenplay ....Barry Barringer
Camera..William Miller
Editor ....De Leon Anthony
Titles..De Leon Anthony

Cast

Blair Thompson ....Kenneth Harlan
Helen Carson ....June Marlowe
Alfred Clark...Arthur Rankin
Professor Ross ....William V. Mong
Doc Carson ....Paul Weigel
Stuttering Slim.................................James Bradbury, Jr.
Silverstreak ....Silverstreak
Mrs. Carson ....Edna Mae Cooper

Code of the Air is a weak science fiction film whose only redeeming features seem to be the outstanding performance by a dog named Silverstreak and the introduction of a weapon that fires mysterious "kappa rays".

As the feature begins, we find Professor Ross, a power hungry genius, consummating a plan that is sure to gain him immense wealth and power. The professor recently perfected an awesome weapon which emits deadly kappa rays. In an experiment with these rays the professor discovers that when directed at an aircraft, the plane loses its power and, engulfed in flames, plummets to the earth. The weapon's effect on aircraft is soon the basis for the inventor's diabolical plan.

Professor Ross and his gang move to a western base that lies in the flight path of a fleet of commercial aircraft. These planes regularly carry cargoes of stocks and bonds. The valuable securities are stored in large fire proof metal boxes. Thus, the impact of a plane's crash and the intense flames which would surely engulf the craft would not affect the paper cargo.

Blair Thompson, a secret agent, and his wonder dog, Silverstreak (obviously an attempt to parallel the great success of Rin Tin Tin), are dispatched to investigate these bizarre crashes and the disappearance of large quantities of stocks and bonds. In his quest to discover the villains behind these hideous crimes,

Blair receives the aid of Helen Carson and her father, Doc Carson. The search forces Helen and Blair to spend a great deal of time together, resulting (naturally) in a romantic entanglement.

The feature draws to a close when Blair discovers the villains' hideout and destroys their weapon. As the final scene fades, the audience is left with Helen and Blair clasped in a tender embrace as Silverstreak happily tries to gain their attention.

From the reviews of this film, it appears that the acting and direction were only fair at best. The plot, while based on a sound premise, never delivers sufficient excitement or mystery to equal the audience's anticipation. The kindest thing said seems to be centered on the clever tricks performed by Silverstreak, the dog.

The unfavorable criticism would not have been predicted if one looks at the cast. Kenneth Harlan, William V. Mong, and Arthur Rankin were all experienced actors. In fact, Harlan and Mong had appeared in more than 100 films, and eventually their careers spanned nearly 50 years in the film industry. This must lead one to infer that the blame for lack of success lies with the director rather than the performers or the script.

> "Picture, and audience, suffers from extremely bad direction which has, among many other oversights, allowed enough superfluous footage to intervene between actual sequences to make another states righter."
>
> *Variety*, 12-19-28, p. 23

THE EAGLE OF THE NIGHT

Release: 1928, Pathe
Description: Silent, 10 episode serial, each episode approximately 2000 feet
Classification: SF-A
References: No. 8, p. 142, 143, 264; No. 14, p. 127; No. 50, p. 118; MPN, Vol. 38, No. 14, p. 1098

Credits

Producer .... Pathe
Director .... Jimmie Fulton

Cast

Brad Russell .... Frank Clarke
Nancy Lemont .... Shirley Palmer
Professor Carl Lemont .... Joseph Swickard
Gus .... Max Hawley
Boss .... Earl Metcalfe
Crooks .... Roy Wilson
.... Jack Richardson
Old Mechanic .... Maurice Costello

Chapters 1-10 of *The Eagle of the Night*

Chapter 1: The Death Plunge
References: LC, LP25686
Chapter 2: Snatched into Space
References: LC, LP25687
Chapter 3: Trapped in the Flames
References: LC,LP25670

Chapter 4: Dead Wings
References: LC, LP25688
Chapter 5: The Brink of Eternity
References: LC, LP25701
Chapter 6: The Fangs of the Wolf
References: LC, LP25724
Chapter 7: The Sky Hitcher
References: LC, LP25779
Chapter 8: The March of Death
References: LC, LP25821
Chapter 9: Headlong to Earth
References: LC, LP25822
Chapter 10: No Man's Land
References: LC, LP25823

The Eagle of The Night is a weak science fiction-adventure serial in which the hero of the epic (played by Frank Clarke) attempts to recover an ingenius device known as the "magic muffler." This invention has the capability of reducing the noise created by an airplane engine to only a faint sound. Obviously, this would be of great advantage to the military, but the film's story centers on the opportunities provided to smugglers since their planes would be nearly silent as they crossed the border. This would make them undetectible by the border patrols.

The gang of smugglers attempts to capture the inventor, Professor Lemont, and his daughter, Nancy, in an effort to gain the magic muffler. Fortunately for the captives, Frank Clarke shows up and wards off the kidnappers.

The film offers many aviation stunts as well as excellent flying scenes, but lacks the depth of character development that is so critical in a good serial. Moreover, the episodes don't seem to have any continuity. The result is a product that is not only poorly written, but also very badly directed. The plot's intensity wanes as it approaches chapter 10. In fact, it would seem appropriate to give any film viewer who lasted through all ten chapters, a prize for endurance above the call of duty of an average film patron.

Maurice Costello had a somewhat minor role in this serial, but in an earlier (1916) SF adventure entitled *The Crimson Stain* he was one of the stars and was heralded as one of the finest actors of the silent period. Joseph Swickard was also a veteran actor, but even his talents, combined with those of Costello, did not turn the tide of this ill conceived and badly written serial.

THE KID'S CLEVER

Release: 1928, Universal Pictures Corp.
Description: Silent, 5792 feet
Classification: SF-C
References: No. 14, p. 268; No. 50, p. 241; AFI, F2.2867, p. 404; BIO, Vol. 77, No. 1150, p. 34; LC, MP5946; MPN, Vol. 41, No. 11, p. 88; VAW, 5-15-29, Vol. 95, p. 49

Credits

Producer .... William James Craft
Director .... William James Craft
*Screenplay .... Jack Foley

Art Director .... Charles D. Hall
Camera .... Al Jones
Editor .... Charles Craft
Titles .... Albert Demond
Production Supervision .... Harry L. Decker

*According to some sources, Earnest S Pagano was responsible for the Screenplay. I was unable to substantiate this.

Cast

Bugs Raymond .... Glenn Tryon
Ruth Decker .... Kathryn Crawford
John Decker .... Russell Simpson
Ashton Steele .... Lloyd Whitlock
Hank .... George Chandler
A Girl .... Joan Standing
Magician .... Max Asher
Matron .... Florence Turner
Secretary .... Virginia Sale
Negro Man .... Stepin Fetchit

Bugs Raymond, a young mechanic, has invented an amphibious vehicle that runs without a conventional fuelled motor. This unique, creative device looks like it was resurrected from a junk yard, but Bugs claims it can travel on land or water, and doesn't need the fuel that other automobiles must rely on. At this point, however, he has been unable to generate any interest in his invention. But fate turns a smiling face in his direction when he is invited to a dance at the local seminary. He meets the charming and beautiful Ruth Decker (portrayed by Kathryn Crawford), daughter of the famous automobile manufacturer, John Decker.

After Ruth takes a ride in Bugs' machine, she is convinced that her father should pay attention to his invention. She believes it is worthwhile, but her main motive is because she has developed a strong attraction for this young inventor. After much pleading, Ruth finally arranges for her father to take a ride in Bugs' car.

Bugs' assistant, Ashton Steele, upon hearing the plan to have Decker take a test ride in the invention, panics. He has arranged with another manufacturer to receive the contract with Decker's company for the invention. Thus, he is forced to prevent any deal between Bugs and Decker. His attempt at sabbotage is more than successful as the ride Decker takes with Bugs nearly kills him. Needless to say, he becomes quite irrate and vows to have nothing to do with Bugs or his invention.

Bugs is quite naturally depressed and Ruth tries to comfort and encourage him. Suddenly the two of them get the idea that the car might have been tampered with. As they examine it, Bugs finds the source of the malfunction and realizes that the only person capable of doing such a thing is his once trusted assistant. Both Bugs and Ruth corner Ashton, who breaks down and confesses that he was paid to sabbotage it.

Ruth quickly informs her father of these turn of events, but he states that he has just a few minutes before signed a contract with another motor manufacturer. Bugs pleads with him to get in the car so they can pursue this unscrupulous industrialist. They soon overtake the schemer and troy the contract.

The picture draws to a close with Bugs and Ruth warmly embracing as John Decker presents a contract to Bugs which will make him the successful manufacturer of his amphibious invention.

The Kid's Clever is a very entertaining science fiction-comedy feature. The device created by the film's leading character is prophetic of the actual efforts of automobile manufacturers some 20 years later.

Bugs Raymond (Glen Tryon) shows Ruth Decker (Kathryn Crawford) a new speedboat design in *The Kid's Clever* (1928).

The players all had experienced backgrounds. Glen Tyron had a modest number of films to his credit with most of them being comedic in nature. Two other performers, Russell Simpson and Lloyd Whitlock, were very experienced actors, each having participated in more than 50 films before this venture.

> "Played at express speed with great spirit and dash, this film should be a bright attraction for any house. Of course, the story is only a vehicle for the exhibition of Glen Tyron's hectic activities. . ."
>
> *Bioscope,* 10-17-28, Vol. 77, p. 34

RANSOM

Release: 1928, Columbia Pictures
Description: Silent, 5484 feet
Classification: SF
References: No. 50, p. 392; AFI, F2.4464, p. 634; BIO, Vol. 78, No. 1164, p. 38; LC, LP25516; VAW, 8-15-28, Vol. 92, p. 17

Credits

Producer .... Harry Cohn
Director .... George B. Seitz
Assistant Director .... Joe Nadel
Screenplay .... Elmer Harris
Art Director .... Joseph Wright
Camera .... Joseph Walker
Continuity .... Dorothy Howell
Titles .... Mort Blumenstock

Cast

Lois Brewster .... Lois Wilson
Burton Meredith .... Edmund Burns
Wu Fang .... William V. Mong
Oliver .... Blue Washington
Scarface .... James B. Leong
Bobby .... Jackie Coombs

Burton Meredith, a young chemical genius, discovers a formula for a highly deadly gas while working in a government laboratory. This gas is colorless, odorless, and attacks the nervous system of its victims. As in most film stories, the knowledge of this secret discovery does not stay within the confines of the laboratory. Soon a nefarious Chinese warlord named Wu Fang (expertly played by William B. Mong) makes an attempt to steal the formula for the volatile new gas. Unable to breech the security of the laboratory, however, Wu Fang and his band of mercenaries, attack Burton Meredith through a different avenue.

Burton's fiancee, Lois Brewster, has a young teenage son, Bobby, and Wu Fang and his henchmen successfully capture the boy on his way home from school. Wu Fang then personally delivers the ultimatum to Lois: he will promise to return the boy unharmed if Lois obtains the nerve gas formula for him by midnight the next night.

Lois is obviously torn between the love she has for her son and that of Burton Meredith. She goes to the laboratory and reveals Wu Fang's sinister plot to Burton. But he feels that he cannot compromise his position with the government and endanger the national security by giving this awesome weapon to the Chinese warlord. He asks Lois for some time to consider a plan, but Lois, in a high state of anxiety, steals a vial of the gas and rushes out before Burton can stop her.

Believing that she has secured the poison gas, Lois immediately delivers the material to Wu Fang. However, after carefully testing the vial, he discovers that it is not the nerve gas, but a container of carbon dioxide. Furious, Wu Fang ties up Lois and vows to torture her unless Burton delivers the real formula.

Meanwhile, Burton has received aid from several government agents who then help track Lois to Wu Fang's hideout. In a spectacular confrontation the agents and Burton overpower Wu Fang and his gang, rescuing Bobby and Lois in the process. During the battle, the cannister of carbon dioxide accidentally ruptures and the crooks, trapped in the tight confines of their hideout, die of suffocation.

Burton is acclaimed a hero by the government and his new spectacular nerve gas is hailed by the army experts as a major breakthrough in weaponry.

This feature is a well done SF film. William B. Mong, who portrayed the villainous Wu Fang (the name of a dastardly villain in an earlier Craig Kennedy serial) also played the part of a villain in the 1928 *Code of the Air.* Both of these performances are outstanding characterizations of the typical SF villain during this time.

> "Though not free from the melodramatic exaggerations generally associated with the conventional serial, this picture contains much to interest and amuse. The production is excellent, the mother-love interest strong, and the acting quite good. The film should please workingclass audiences."
>
> *Bioscope,* 1-23-29, Vol. 78, p. 38

1929

THE DIAMOND MASTER

Release: 1929, Universal Pictures Corp.
Description: Silent, 10 episode serial, each episode approximately 2000 feet
Classification: SF-A
References: No. 8, p. 149, 271; No. 14, p. 127; No. 50, p. 101; BIO, Vol. 77, No. 1159, p. 50

Credits

Producer .... Universal
Director .... Jack Nelson

Cast

Mark Allen .... Hayden Stevenson
Doris Harvey .... Louise Lorraine
Prof. Jason Ramsey .... Al Hart
Frank Wilson .... Monty Montague
Mr. Harvey .... Louis Stern
Drake .... Walter Maly

Chapters 1-10 of *The Diamond Master*

Chapter 1: The Secret of the Night
References: LC, LP25838
Chapter 2: The Diamond of Death
References: LC, LP25839
Chapter 3: The Tunnel of Terror
References: LC, LP25872
Chapter 4: Trapped
References: LC, LP54
Chapter 5: The Diamond Machine
References: LC, LP94
Chapter 6: The Wolf Pack
References: LC, LP123
Chapter 7: The Death Trap
References: LC, LP124
Chapter 8: Into the Flames
References: LC, LP140
Chapter 9: The Last Stand
References: LC, LP141
Chapter 10: The Reckoning
References: LC, LP142

After a brief absence from the serial market, Universal decided to reenter during 1929 with several offerings. One of these, *The Diamond Master,* based on the novel by Jacques Futrelle, is a remake of the 1921 Universal serial, *The Diamond Queen*. Only a few of the characters were changed, and all of these were minor roles. The most significant difference between *The Diamond Queen,* and *The Diamond Master* was its length. *The Diamond Queen* was an 18 episode serial, while *The Diamond Master* was a 10 chapter feature.

As the first chapter begins, *The Secret of the Night,* Doris Harvey tells her story to Mark Allen, a famous detective. It seems that Doris' father has invented a process by which dust can be turned into diamonds through the use of mechanical and chemical devices. Unfortunately for Doris and her father, he lets this new revelation slip out during cocktails one evening and his financial contemporaries immediately determine that he can no longer be allowed to create these artificial diamonds. Thus, she and her father were forced to flee to the United States in hopes of avoiding these vicious financiers.

They are still relentlessly pursued, however, by Mr. Harvey's enemies. One evening they are accosted in their hotel room and a vicious struggle follows. Mr. Harvey is killed but Doris manages to escape by seeking refuge in another room. As fate would have it, the room belongs to Mark Allen.

After hearing Doris' story, he agrees to take the case and help her find Mr. Harvey's murderers and perfect his artificial diamond technique.

As the serial progresses through its various episodes, the intensity of the drama increases. Mark and Doris are constantly placed in jeopardy by villains hired by the powerful diamond merchants. But each time they manage to escape and leave the audience on the edges of their seats as they anticipate the next week's chapter.

The Diamond Master, while not an outstanding SF serial, certainly attracted audiences and was considerably more successful than *The Diamond Queen.* Perhaps the basic reason for this was due to the acting. The cast of *The Diamond Master* was more experienced and had a wider array of talents than its predecessor. In addition, the length of the second serial was probably a drawback. It seems to have been better written as a 10 episode serial than the 1921 original's 18 chapters, resulting in the action of each week's feature being increased through this condensation. In any case, the audience was very pleased with the serial, and Universal's entry back into the serial market was considered a moderate success.

> "The serial is well produced and beautifully photographed, and is quite up to the recognized standard."
>
> *Bioscope,* Vol. 77, No. 1159, p. 50

THE FIRE DETECTIVE

Release: 1929, Pathe
Description: Silent, 10 episode serial, each episode approximately 2000 feet
Classification: SF-A
References: No, 8, p. 272; No. 14, p. 162; No. 50, p. p-23; BIO, Vol. 80, No. 1193, p. 37; Vol. 80, No. 1196, p. 49

Credits

Producer .... Pathe
Director .... Spencer Gordon Bennet and Thomas L. Storey

Cast

Gladys Samuels .... Gladys McConnell
Captain Jeff Tarrant .... Hugh Allan
Chief Carson .... Leo Maloney
Dist. Attorney Samuels .... John Cossar
Mr. Tarrant .... Frank Lacksteen
Charles Lewis .... Lawrence W. Steers

Chapters 1-10 of *The Fire Detective*

Chapter 1: The Arson Trail
References: LC, LP179
Chapter 2: The Pit of Darkness
References: LC, LP180
Chapter 3: The Hidden Hand
References: LC, LP205
Chapter 4: The Convict Strikes
References: LC, LP210
Chapter 5: On Flaming Waters
References: LC, LP214
Chapter 6: The Man of Mystery
References: LC, LP217
Chapter 7: The Ape Man
References: LC, LP235
Chapter 8: Back from Death
References: LC,LP236

Chapter 9: Menace of the Past
References:LC, LP277
Chapter 10: The Flame of Love
References: LC, LP297

The Fire Detective is a weak science fiction-adventure serial. The action centers on the quest of Captain Jeff Tarrant, a young fire detective, and a reporter, Gladys Samuels, to track down a well organized gang of arsonists. Captain Tarrant employs a number of scientific devices to help him locate the headquarters of these notorious criminals. Charles Lewis, the head of this gang of crooks who make their living collecting the insurance money from fires, turns out to also be Gladys' fiance. The gang's scientific ingenuity and scheming result in the corruption of several scientists who produce weapons and other devices to aid in their power hungry drive.

In chapter 7, *The Ape Man,* a creature that is a cross between a large primate and a man is hired by the gang to scale tall buildings and set them afire. The "ape man" was a product of a diabolical scientific experiment. The creature is soon killed while fleeing Jeff Tarrant's undaunting·pursuit.

As time passes, Gladys and Jeff become emotionally involved as their work brings them closer together. This only adds fuel to Charles Lewis' infuriation and finally leads to his weakness.

In the final chapter, Lewis gives himself away and Jeff and Gladys now realize that he is behind the arson gang. Additionally, Gladys learns that Jeff is not just an arson investigator, but is also the son of an extremely wealthy man. They have little time for discussing these things, though, as they find themselves trapped in a large building that is being engulfed in flames. A fierce battle between Jeff and the gang produces a great deal of excitement for the culmination of the serial. When Jeff finally reaches Charles, the two engage in a duel in which neither seems to gain any ground. However, when Charles lunges for Jeff and misses, he crashes through a window and falls to his death ten floors below. Somehow, Jeff and Gladys then manage to escape the fire and reach the safety of the Manhattan street.

> "The rush of engines and the magnificent fire spectacles are the chief assets of this chapter play, the plot being of the stock pattern type. A certain amount of mystery is introduced by the problem of the arson gang and its elusive chief, but to the discerning picturegoer this presents few difficulties."
>
> *Bioscope,* Vol. 80, No. 1193, p. 37

THE ISLE OF LOST SHIPS

Release: 1929, First National Pictures
Description: Silent-Sound, 7576 feet (approximately 75 minutes)
Classification: SF-A
References: No. 50, p. 22; AFI, F2.2758, p. 388; LC, LP785, MP626; MPN, Vol. 41, No. 11, p. 88; NYR, 10-26-29, p. 565; VAW, 10-30-29, p. 25, 26

Credits

Producer .... Richard A. Rowland and First National
Director .... Irvin Willat
Screenplay .... Fred Myton
Camera .... Sol Polito
Editor .... John Rawlings
Titles (Dialogue) .... Paul Perez and Fred Myton

Cast

Frank Howard .... Jason Robards, Sr.
Dorothy Renwick .... Virginia Valli
Aunt Emma .... Clarissa Selwynne
Captain Peter Forbes .... Noah Beery
Detective Jackson .... Robert O'Connor
Gallagher .... Harry Cording
Mrs. Gallagher .... Margaret Fielding
Mother Joyce Burke .... Katherine Ward
Mr. Burke .... Robert Homans
Harry .... Jack Acroyd
Sam Baker .... Sam Baker

The Isle of Lost Ships is a melodrama based on the book *The Isle of Dead Ships* (1909) by Crittendon Marriott. First National originally made the film in 1923, and it was well received by the public. The 1929 version was produced with sound as well as in a silent version. While the silent copy received mediocre acceptance by the audiences, the sound version enjoyed overwhelming success as lauded by audiences and critics alike. This response was probably due to the seasoned actors who appeared in the film, some in their very first talking roles.

As the story begins, we find passengers boarding the steamship "The Queen" at a Puerto Rican port. The camera focuses on those who will become the main characters in the film: a young society girl, Dorothy Renwick, accompanied by her Aunt Emma; boarding just behind is Frank Howard who is handcuffed to Detective Jackson, a New York policeman. These four people become the nucleus for the film as their trip from Puerto Rico to New York soon proves to be a memorable ocean journey.

Not long at sea, the ship is caught in a storm center with hurricane force winds. As they near the remote islands of the Bahamas, the ship begins to take on water as the high rolling waves toss it like a ping pong ball. The large waves start to sweep Dorothy overboard, but Frank Howard's quick thinking saves her from certain peril. Obviously, this act helps bind the two together as their mutual affection strengthens.

The storm's fury rages through the night and by morning the ship is nearly half-submerged. Jackson, Frank, Dorothy, and her Aunt board a small lifeboat as they flee the sinking vessel. Soon, Dorothy learns that Frank, a former naval officer, has been charged with misappropriation of naval funds, a charge which Frank claims is unfounded. Detective Jackson realizes that Frank has no means of escape and removes the handcuffs that had bound him thus far. The four of them must work together if they are to survive the ordeal that confronts them.

Detective Jackson is a burly man in his mid thirties who talks with a gruff New York accent. The viewer can easily sense his worry over the peril in which they are placed.

By mid-day the small life raft has approached an area that is thick with seaweed. The two men begin to pull the boat across the seaweed. By the early afternoon they are suddenly surrounded by a dense layer of fog, and a strange eerie silence falls over the waters. The passengers have heard tales of people who were caught up in the Sargasso Sea, and the strange events which now are upon them send chills down their spines as they realize they have been swept into this dreaded area. As they pull their way further across the thick entanglements they encounter the wooden and steel hulls of wreckages. Darkness begins to fall and the party pulls their way to a vessel that appears to be a half-submerged steamer. Making fast the lifeboat, they board this freighter hoping to find safety for the night. No sooner are they reasonably comfortable in the damp ship than strange screams fill the air.

As Frank peers out the porthole, a long procession of torches seem to be approaching from the starboard side. The lights move across the marsh as though gliding across the thick seaweed. It isn't long before the lights reveal men, and their low gruff voices confirm Frank's feeling of impending danger. The men soon board the steamer and confront the four newcomers to the "Island of Lost

Ships." The leader, Captain Peter Forbes (exquisitely portrayed by Noah Beery), is a large man who half-heartedly welcomes the group to their imprisonment in the Sargasso Sea. He quickly informs them of the rules which will govern their lives as long as they live--carefully emphasizing the word "live."

Frank and Jackson realize their plight is more perilous than the two women since females seem to be in scarce supply. But Frank, who has developed strong feelings for Dorothy, must protect her from Forbes' demands. The captain tells them that the young woman is to be married immediately to prevent quarrels among his men. She has 24 hours after arriving within the confines of the Isle of Lost Ships to find a mate. If she is unable to do so, Forbes will find one (obviously meaning himself) for her, Dorothy quickly says that if she must choose, she will pick Frank Howard.

Thus the physical struggle between the two men which will eventually come to a final collision is set. Forbes and Howard begin to battle immediately with the victor having the right to claim Dorothy as his bride. Howard decks Forbes with his first blow, much to the chagrin of the captain's motley crew. Frank and Dorothy are quickly married, but Forbes is obviously not one to easily forget a beating.

Time, which has lost all meaning in the constantly hazy fog laden environment, passės without the inhabitants even realizing. The battles of Jackson and Frank against the other inhabitants of the Sargasso Sea continue (fight scenes which naturally provide much action and excitement for the viewer). At every turn, Captain Forbes tries to kill or injure Frank. Luckily, he avoids each of the captain's ploys.

Before long, Frank and Jackson encounter a strange old engineer named Harry, who has kept a German U-boat in semi-working order since his capture in the Sea. Frank and Jackson devise a plan by which they can use the submarine to escape. As they gather the women and board the vessel, a last battle must be fought. At last they manage to secure the hatch and Harry sends the boat under the surface.

Many of the instruments are malfunctioning, but it still manages to inch forward beneath the deep roots of seaweed lying near the surface of the water. The growth, however, soon becomes entangled in the propellers, and the ship finally lies motionless eight fathoms below. They are clear of the Sargasso Sea, but unable to get enough power to surface.

Frank decides the only way to get the ship to the top is for someone to go outside and cut the seaweed away. He is shot through one of the torpedo tubes and swims along the ocean bottom at the rear of the submarine where he manages to cut through the weeds and ascend to the surface. In moments, the stranded vessel joins him above the water where he is greeted by his fellow passengers as they all rejoice.

After traveling for several miles, they come upon a United States Naval cruiser. The ship picks them up, and as the scene fades, the safe adventurers arc telling their strange tale to the crew.

The 1929 version of *The Isle of Lost Ships* is obviously improved over the 1923 version. The addition of sound made the characterizations of Captain Peter Forbes and Frank Howard more forceful than in the silent production. Additionally, Jason Robard's portrayal of Frank Howard and Noah Beery's portrayal of Captain Forbes were extremely strong and provided the continuity that the feature needed to carry off the intensity of the action. The movie could have suffered considerably had their performances not been superbly effective in focusing the audience's attention on the .conflict of these two men.

> "The talker version of *The Isle of Lost Ships* will clean up in any type of house. A little more attention to dialog, which occasionally slumps into the bromidic, and a more careful directorial eye on the knitting of some of the situations would have unquestionably rounded this into a Broadway topper set for an enviable long term.
>
> In its present release as a program feature it is without a competitor in the current market of thrillers. The originality of the story this time shares honors with the weird effect established by sets and the camera angles at which they are focused."
>
> *Variety*, 10-30-29, p. 25

THE KING OF THE KONGO

Release: 1929, Mascot Pictures Corp.
Description: Silent-Sound, 10 episode serial, each episode approximately 2000 feet
Classification: SF-A
References: No. 8, p. 147, 148, 272, 273; No. 14, p. 270; No. 50, p. 243; FID 8-25-29

Credits

Producer .... Mascot Pictures
Director .... Richard Thorpe
Music .... Lee Zahler

Cast

Nancy Wilson .... Jacqueline Logan
Mike Warren .... Walter Miller
R.L. Wilson .... Richard Tucker
Murdoc .... Boris Karloff

Chapters 1-10 of *The King of the Kongo*

Chapter 1: Into the Unknown
Chapter 2: Terrors of the Jungle
Chapter 3: The Temple of Beasts
Chapter 4: Gorilla Warfare
Chapter 5: Danger in the Dark
Chapter 6: The Fight at the Lion's Pit
Chapter 7: The Fatal Moment
Chapter 8: Sentenced to Death
Chapter 9: Desperate Chances
Chapter 10: Jungle Justice

King of the Kongo, released August 20, 1929, is the first silent-sound serial. Moreover, it is the first *science fiction* silent-sound serial, and also marks the first SF appearance of Boris Karloff, an actor whose portrayal of various villains and monsters in films became legendary.

Mascot Pictures, noted for their thrilling serials, added special synchronized sound created by Victor Sound Systems to their venture. These sound effects, a special synchronized musical score, and a theme song, "Love Thoughts of You," were all parts of this innovative serial production.

Mike Warren (portrayed by Walter Miller) is a secret service agent who has been dispatched to the far off jungles of Africa to search for an agent who disappeared while trying to track down the mysterious Arnold Jackson, a millionaire and financial tycoon. The only clue that Miller has is a small golden dagger on a gold chain. He believes this is some sort of symbol of an ancient culture whose temple must lie in the deep jungle. However, after several months of scouring the countryside he has been unable to locate the temple or any sign of the missing agent.

Returning for a rest and replenishment of supplies at the local trading post, Warren encounters Nancy Wilson, daughter of the mysterious millionaire whom the agent was tracking. She has also been scouring the countryside for some three months trying to uncover any clue to her father's strange disappearance. In her hand she holds her only clue--a gold chain with a small golden dagger attached. When Mike realizes that they both have the same clue, he immediately takes her aside. Together they plot a strategy for locating the mysterious temple.

After sufficient rest, they begin their safari to a new region of the jungle that may offer some promise of the temple. After several weeks of tracking they finally locate an overgrown structure which looks like a temple. As they wander about the foliage, attempting to find an entry to the building, they discover a large stone carving with a golden necklace similar to theirs. With great excitement they realize this must be the temple that has been the focus of their search these many months. As they move closer they discover a brightly colored stone door. There is a tiny slot about the size of their golden daggers. Mike inserts his into the slot, and the door begins to rumble open.

Inside they find a chamber that looks more new than old, the center of which opens to the sky through a large hole that has been worn away by the many years of erosion. They are suddenly startled as the door rumbles shut and slams before they can escape to the outside. No sooner has the door closed, than they are treated to an array of beasts that evidently have been housed within the temple's walls. One of these resembles a medium sized dinosaur and another a very large burley ape, (obviously this was a King Kong-type creature.) Mike and Nancy believe their end is near as they slink back into the shadows of one of the compartments. They watch as the ape begins to struggle with one of the other beasts, causing the animals' attention to be diverted from them. They quickly insert the dagger into the door's slot and escape to the outside.

That night, the horrors of the day's events take their toll as they question the value of continuing their search, but they are suddenly visited by a strange man named Murdock. He seems to have wandered through the jungle without any supplies or proper equipment, and yet, he is in an area that as far as they know has been void of all exploration. He offers no explanation for his presence and instead begins to question them as to their business in this uncharted area. It isn't long before they discover that Murdock has a sinister nature about him as he threatens their lives if they don't leave immediately. This leads Nancy and Mike to wonder if perhaps this is the area in which Nancy's father is captive.

As the serial draws to a close, Mike and Nancy discover her father and design an elaborate escape route through the temple of beasts. Unfortunately, Murdock and his henchmen are not so fortunate and are trapped behind the door of the temple. The shrill cries of their agony carry through the dense jungle as Mike, Nancy and her father escape.

Although *King of the Kongo* is a weak SF-A serial, it does provide a vehicle for Boris Karloff to demonstrate his variety of talents in a sinister role. The characterization of the ape more closely resembles that of King Kong (which appeared four years after this one) than any other feature we have seen to date.

While *King of the Kongo* is not an epic adventure, it is noteworthy in the sense that it was the first sound serial to be presented to the American public.

> "From the above it will be seen that this chapter play contains everything that admirers of these melodramatic serials love to contemplate. It is only necessary to add that each episode is a complete and rousing adventure, that interest is cleverly carried from one to another, and that production and photography are of a high standard."
>
> *Bioscope,* Vol. 82, No. 1218, p. 29

THE LOST ZEPPELIN

Release: 1929, Tiffany Productions
Description: Sound, 6882 feet
Classification: SF-A
References: No. 50, O. 267; AFI, F2.3202, p. 453; BIO, Vol. 82, No. 1200, p. 28; LC, LP909; MPH, Vol. 97, p. 72; NYR, 2-3-29, p. 600; VAW, Vol. 98, 2-5-30, p. 19, 24

Credits

Producer .... Tiffany-Gaumont Productions
Director .... Edward Sloman
Screenplay .... Frances Hyland
Dialog .... Charles Kenyon
Recording Engineer .... Jerry Eisenberg
Sound Technology .... John Buddy Myers
Camera .... Jackson Rose
Editor .... Martin G. Cohn and Donn Hayes

Cast

Commander Hall .... Conway Tearle
Miriam Hall .... Virginia Valli
Tom Armstrong .... Ricardo Cortez
Lieutenant Wallace .... Duke Martin
Nancy .... Kathryn McGuire
Mr. Wilson .... Winter Hall

The Lost Zeppelin is a very weak SF adventure film. This is mainly due to an unimaginative screenplay. The story focuses on a zeppelin's attempt to travel over the South Pole and return. From a science fiction perspective, one should remember that in this period of time such an adventure was still considered mild science fiction, even though there had been several prior explorations to the South Pole. In fact, at the very time this feature was released (December 20, 1929), Admiral Bird was on an expedition to the South Pole. Such a historic dirigible flight as portrayed in the film certainly would have been praiseworthy and extremely risky.

As the movie opens we find the crew and their guests at a large pre-flight banquet. Commander Hall, the zeppelin's captain, has just learned that his wife, Miriam, has become enamoured with Lieutenant Tom Armstrong, who is also Commander Hall's second in command and his best friend. At the evening's end, Miriam asks her husband for a divorce. Though quite upset by these events, Hall still wishes to provide his wife with as much happiness as possible, and so tells her he will grant her the divorce upon his return from his voyage. He then departs for the air station where the blimp is moored.

An hour or so later Tom arrives accompanied by the other crew members. The men begin their meticulous count down as the enormous airship slowly ascends into the still night air above its moorings. (The interior and exterior scenes depicting the activity within the dirigible are exquisitely done, and the special effects which provide the illusion of ascent is flawless. This was achieved through the use of several animated models of the zeppelin, developed by Willis O'Brien who first developed these same techniques in *The Lost World* [1925].)

After several weeks in the air, the explorers finally reached Antarctica and began preparation for their trek across the South Pole. A severe wind storm is raging as they approach the polar area. These gale force winds have more velocity than had been expected by the ship's designer or the Commander as they inflict severe damage to the zeppelin's superstructure. Soon they have an unexpected loss of gasoline caused by the storm's force which sends the proud vessel and its fearless crew plummeting to the ground below.

Even though the airship is destroyed, most of the men escape unscathed. After recovering from the disaster which has befallen them, Commander Hall gathers his men together and expresses his grave concern for their safety if they remain at the crash site with the approaching winter storms. The men decide that their only hope is to divide into small parties and attempt to locate a rescue team.

Tom and Commander Hall make their way in one direction while the rest of the crew proceeds in the opposite direction. Within an hour they stumble upon a small plane which had been originally moored to the zeppelin's fuselage. The plane had apparently been dislodged during the gale and had fallen to the icy terrain below. After carefully inspecting it, Commander Hall and Tom agree that it is fliable. Unfortunately it will hold only one person. Hall insists that Tom be the one to go. After a lengthy debate, Tom finally agrees to fly the plane out of the area. He takes off and eventually is rescued by a naval vessel.

Upon his return to Washington, Tom is greeted as a hero. Everyone assumes he is the only survivor of the ill fated arctic expedition. Tom has also anticipated that Miriam will be ready to fall into his open arms and that they will get married immediately. However, she has had definite second thoughts. The sudden loss of her husband has brought her to the reality that she deeply cared for the commander and doesn't wish to be involved with anyone else.

Within a month news reaches Washington that Hall has made a miraculous trek across the frigid terrain of Antarctica to a remote weather station manned by the Norwegians. Hall's rescue and his subsequent recovery from frostbite and exposure sends Washington into a frenzy over his anticipated arrival. Once there he is greeted with a stupendous hero's welcome. Much to his surprise Miriam comes to him with the eager anticipation of fulfilling her wifely obligations for the rest of their lives.

Virginia Valli who plays Miriam Hall also appeared in the 1929 version of *The Isle of Lost Ships.* Miss Valli's performance in this film was in a considerably weaker role and does not measure up to that of her previous film. The rest of the actors, Conway Tearle who had recently returned from the stage to appear on the screen, and Richard Cortez, provide satisfactory performances. Perhaps one of the problems with this particular film is that the dialogue was extremely strained and even seemed at times unappropriate. A plausible explanation for the inadequacy of this film could have been the recent application of sound to films, resulting in a lack of experience by producers and directors to provide sufficient dialogue for the players to establish their characters. Nevertheless, the feature was a unique adventure film in which the special effects created for the zeppelin's movement across the ice were well done and deserve the attention of the film critics.

> "Conway Tearle, whose return to screen activity is still of recent date, gives one of his best performances within memory. Given a dramatic part of the more restrained sort, Tearle's stage training comes out. Virginia Valli does nicely as also Ricardo Cortez. Upon these three players rests the name appeal of the picture. Kathryn McGuire is billed although limited to one speech but getting a laugh on it.
>
> In sets, productions values and unhurried direction, 'Lost Zeppelin' represents distinction. And that should convert into rentals."
>
> *Variety,* Vol. 988, 2-5-30, p. 19, 24
>
> "Magnificent production, skillful direction and clever acting by three well-known performers make this film one of considerable interest. If the story is conventional it is presented in a manner which convinces. But it is the extraordinary realism of the Antarctic pictures, with blinding snowstorms, howling winds, vast snowfields, jagged icebergs, and avalanches which hold the spectator spellbound, while the Zeppelin's interior, with stern-faced men and a faithful canine, arouse commiseration. Well dovetailed with these are scenes at the home of the Commander, broadcasting stations, and newspaper activities. So well are these alternated that there is no sense of disjointedness."
>
> *Bioscope,* Vol. 82, No. 1220, p. 28

MIDSTREAM

Release: 1929, Tiffany Pictures
Description: Silent, 7472 feet; sound, 6337 feet
Classification: SF-A
References: No. 14, p. 318; No. 50, p. 300; AFI, F2.3610, p. 512; LC, LP687; VAW, 9-18-29

Rejuvenation is the central theme of the science fiction adventure film *Midstream* (1929).

Credits

Producer	Tiffany-Stahl Production
Director	James Flood
Screenplay	Frances Guihan
Music	Hugo Riesenfeld
Camera	Jackson Rose
Editor	Desmond O'Brien
Dialogue	Frederick and Fanny Hatton
Titles	Frederick and Fanny Hatton

Cast

James Stanwood	Ricardo Cortez
Helen Craig	Claire Windsor
Dr. Nelson	Montagu Love
Martin Baker	Larry Kent
Mary Mason	Helen Jerome Eddy
Mephistopheles	Leslie Brigham
Faust	Louis Alvarez
Marguerite	Genevieve Schrader
Marthe	Florence Foyer

Midstream is a weak science fiction adventure film in which the process of rejuvenation is the central focus. Some aspect of rejuvenation has been contained in SF films since the early 1900's, with the peak occurring in the early 1920's.

As the story opens, we find Jim Stanwood, who is about to turn 50 years of age, in his plush Wall Street office. Stanwood is a successful financier and he has forced himself into a dilemma. He has fallen in love with a young and beautiful girl named Helen Craig. It seems Helen is the "girl-next-door" type, and Stanwood is convinced she would repell any romantic advances on his part because of his age. He has, therefore, resigned himself to admiring her from afar.

He soon discovers an article describing a miraculous rejuvenation process which is being offered in some of the remote European health centers. Wishing to recapture his lost youth and then possibly having a chance with Helen, he decides to take a trip to Europe and see for himself this marvelous age reversal process.

He arrives at one of the spas and is convinced that the treatment is all it is claimed to be. Afterwards he creates a fictious nephew thereby providing a new identity for himself. He sends his secretary back in the States a wire telling her that he has found his long lost nephew. After sufficient passage of time, Stanwood, as the nephew, sends a telegram telling of his uncle's sudden accidental death.

Jim Stanwood returns to the United States a young man, hoping that this time around excitement and romance will be his. It isn't long after his arrival that he receives the inheritance from his dead uncle's estate and begins to court the lovely Helen Craig. Within only a few short weeks, Helen agrees to marry Jim.

On the eve of their wedding they attend an operatic performance of *Faust*. Somehow the young girl's dislike for the performance results in a heated argument which precipitates a biological process in Stanwood that causes an immediate reversal of the rejuvenation. Within moments, the figure that stands before Helen is no longer the young man to whom she was to be wed, but that of her old acquaintance, Jim Stanwood. Needless to say, she is not pleased with the ruse Stanwood has created as she runs from the opera house vowing never to speak to him or see him again.

Stanwood finally sees the folly of the rejuvenation process as he realizes that youth is only in one's state of mind and that true happiness can be found at any age. With this thought in mind, he returns to his office and then suddenly realizes that his faithful secretary, Mary, has had a deep affection for him these many years. As the movie draws to a conclusion, we see Jim and Mary embraced as they vow to marry and live the rest of their lives together in bliss.

This sound version of *Midstream* was infinitely better than its silent counterpart. In fact, the silent version was only shown in a few movie houses and the critics gave it little notice as they concentrated on the noteworthy dialogue of the "sound" production.

> "Good feature for the daily changers. With a little editing it would make the grade in the split-week neighborhood houses.
>
> Cortez, Miss Windsor and Montagu Love handled the dialog sequence at the finish in neat style, with Miss Eddy also worthy of favorable mention for the manner in which she plays a minor role."
>
> *Variety*, 9-18-29

THE MYSTERIOUS ISLAND

Release: 1929, MGM Pictures
Description: Sound, Technicolor, 8569 feet
Classification: SF
References: No. 1, p. 225; No. 5, p. 39, 41; No. 14, p. 342; No. 20, p. 36, 37; No. 45, p. 22, 36, 27; No. 50, p. 323; No. 53, p. 56; AFI, F2.3762, p. 534; BIO, Vol. 88, No. 1235, p. 43; FAM, No. 10, p. 26; FDY, 1930; LC, LP799; MPH, Vol. 97, p. 58; MPN, Vol. 41, No. 11, p. 94; NYR, 12-12-29, p. 583; SIS, Vol. 5, p. 43, 44; VAW, Vol. 97, No. 11, p. 30

Credits

Producer .... MGM
Associate Producer .... J. Ernest Williamson
Director .... Jucien Hubbard
*Additional Directors .... Maurice Tourneur and Benjamin Christiansen
Special Effects .... J. Ernest Williamson
Art Director .... Cedric Gibbons
Music .... Martin Broones and Arthur Lange
Camera .... Percy Hilburn
Editor .... Carl L. Pierson
Technical Effects .... James Basevi, Louis H. Tolhurst, Irving Ries
Recording Engineer .... Douglas Shearer

*Footage shot by Maurice Tourneur and Benjamin Christiansen during 1926 and 1927 was eventually incorporated into the final production.

Cast

Dakkar .... Lionel Barrymore
Sonia .... Jane Daly
Nikolai .... Lloyd Hughes

A unique scene of the submersible craft used in *The Mysterious Island* (1929).

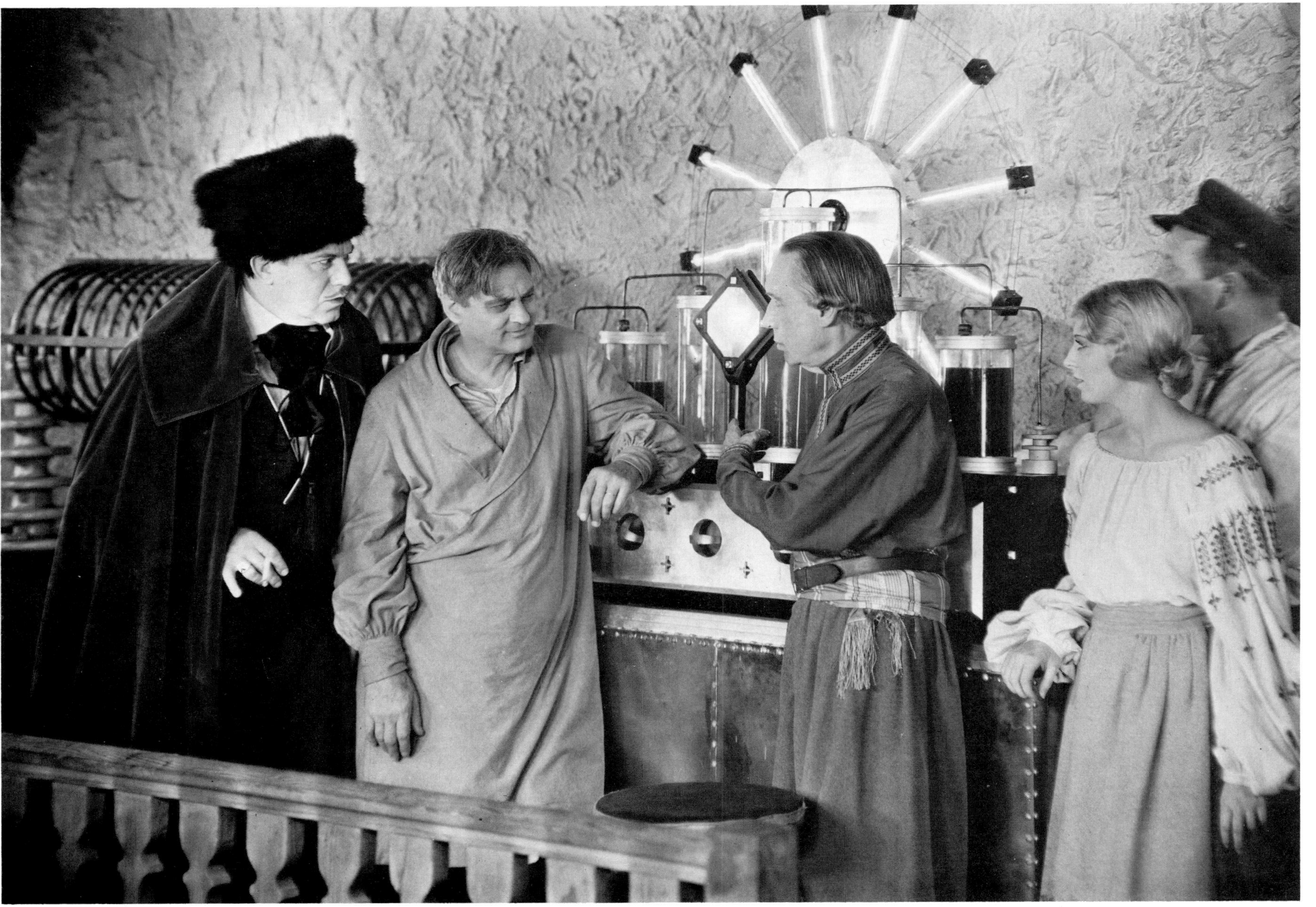

Count Dakkar explains the vast potential of his experiments, which eventually leads to Falon's corrupt actions.

Falon .... Montagu Love
Mikbail .... Harry Gribbon
Anton .... Snitz Edwards
Dmitry .... Gibson Gowland
Teresa .... Dolores Brinkman

In 1915 James Ernest Williamson became infatuated with the works of Jules Verne and began to develop a screenplay for his classic novel, *20,000 Leagues Under the Sea.* After many months of laboring on the screenplay and developing cameras that could be used in special underwater photography to provide a sense of realism for the production, Williamson finally interested Universal in the project and *20,000 Leagues Under the Sea,* became the first American version of this great novel.

Looking back at the 1916 feature film, one can only do so with a sense of amazement and appreciation for the technology and artistry that Williamson displayed in creating such a careful masterpiece of a fine literary work. The film's success at the box office was overwhelming. Williamson had established a brand of cinematography that was to endow him for the remainder of his life with the prestige of being the expert in underwater photography.

No sooner had the project been completed and released than Williamson began to work on a sequel to the epic film. He felt this should be a simple process since Jules Verne had already created the perfect sequel when he wrote *L'Isle Mysterieuse* (Paris, 1874). It was upon this novel that he based his next Verne feature film. Unfortunately, the underwater film laboratory that he created in the Bahamas and several other projects seemed to get in the way during the next ten years. But finally in 1925 he created a screenplay based on this novel. His work was presented to a variety of studios in the Hollywood film community, but none seemed interested in *The Mysterious Island.* MGM saw promise in Williamson's work but they were unhappy with what they considered the low-key nature of the story. They didn't feel that the setting of the Civil War and the subsequent journey by balloon to the infamous mysterious island were sufficiently somber for the superb sequel they had envisioned. So they beseiged Williamson to rewrite the story and offered a plethora of suggestions, many of which seemed to border on absurdity. Nevertheless, he bent under the pressure of these mighty film moguls and Captain Nemo was transformed from the viril character that Verne had created into the sinister maniacal Count Dakkar (The film heads had also decided to make Captain Nemo of Russian descent). The scenes were supposed to be set in Russia but as time went on even Russia became an unsatisfactory setting for the movie titans. Instead they created a whole new world for Captain Nemo and called it the Kingdom of Hetvia. The film's action did take place during the era in which Verne intended, around the 1850's to 1860's, but the story took on a whole new meaning and one must search to find any resemblance to the original work. Sonia, Count Dakkar's daughter, was an additional character insisted on by the studio and added very little to the feature except to create a female presence.

As the picture opens, Count Dakkar, who had devoted his life to the pursuit of science, is seen in his laboratory obviously intensely involved in some serious reflections about his life and the value of his work to humankind. Over the years he had constantly invested his great wealth into exploring the ocean's depths; explorations which led to the successful development of a submersible craft. During most of his research efforts he had remained cloistered in his laboratory, a virtual stranger to the inhabitants of the island.

Meanwhile, a power hungry nobleman, Falon, had been devising a master plan by which he could overthrow the throne of Hetvia and seize control of the kingdom. In order to accomplish this task he needs Dakkar's genius and inventions. He also realizes that Dakkar would not willingly overthrow the rulers of Hetvia. To set his plan in motion, Falon and a few loyal followers assemble near Dakkar's remote, but well fortified, laboratory.

Using a secret passage they gain entrance into his experimental chambers and capture the scientific genius and his entire laboratory crew. Falon's plan calls for the use of Dakkar's submersible craft to gain entrance into the port guarding the imperial residence. Falon is incognizant of the fact that Dakkar had

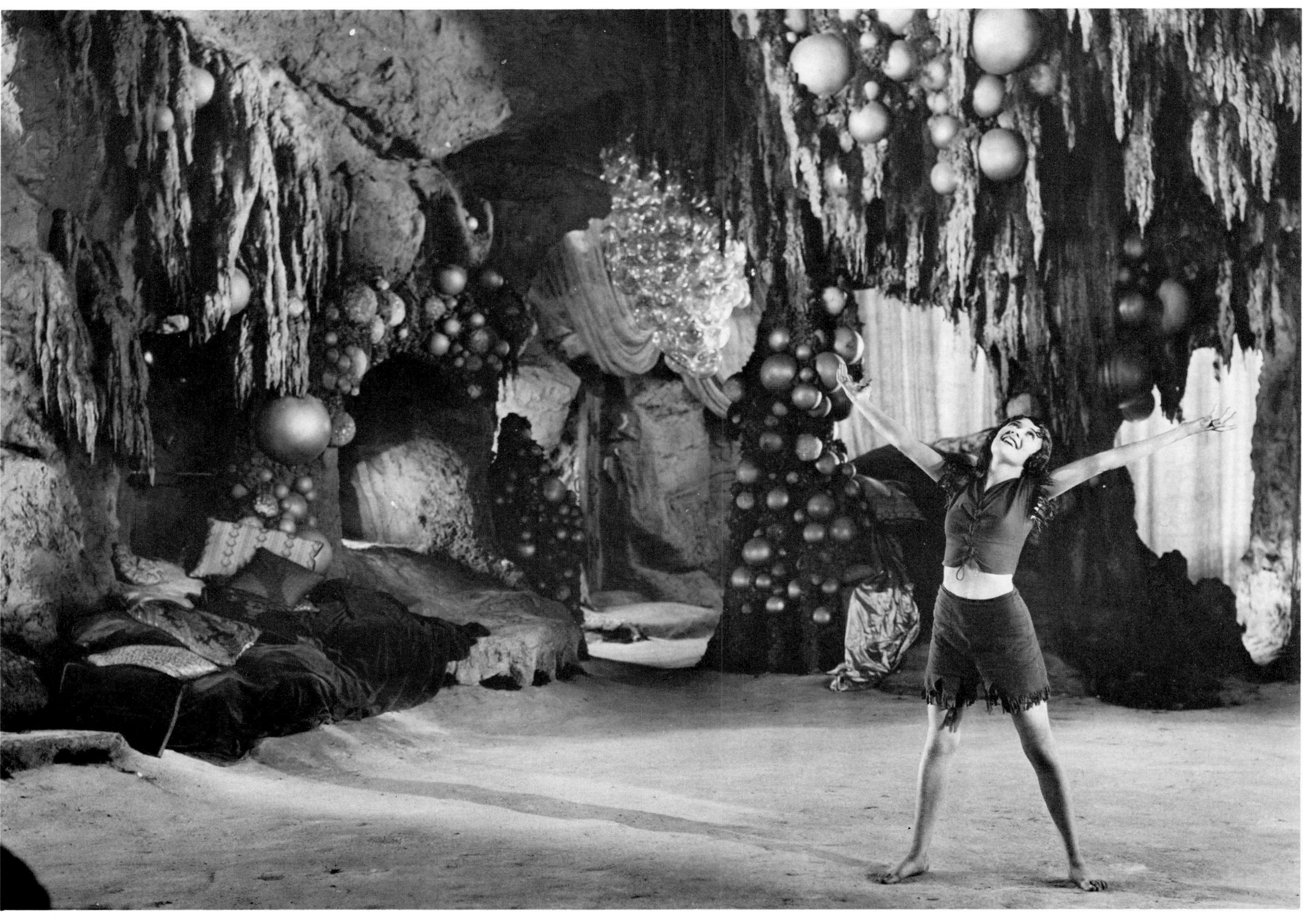

Sonia locates the rich treasure room of the tiny creatures who dwell on the ocean bottom.

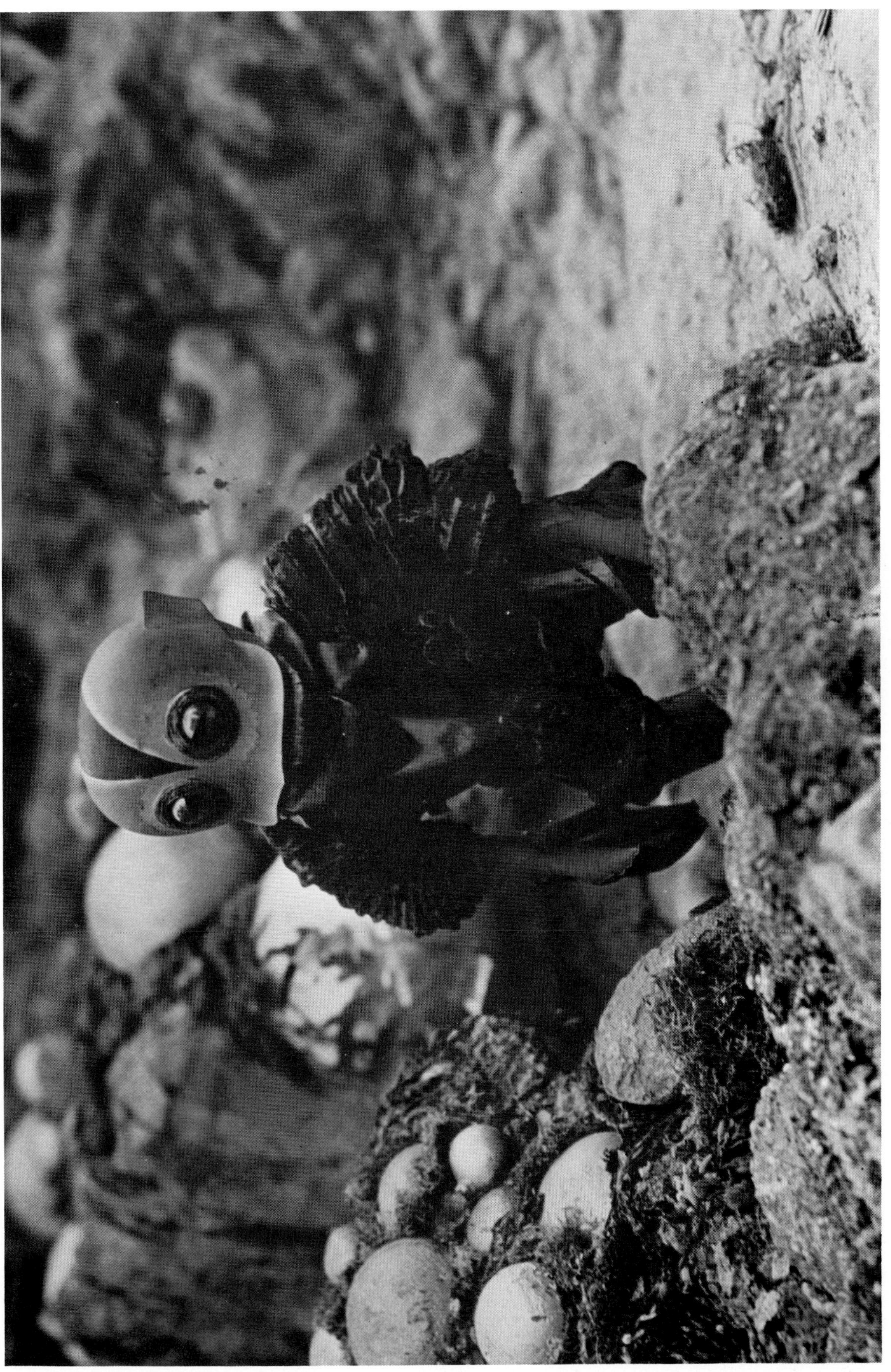

A mutation of sorts in this world beneath the sea.

created two submersible boats, the second of which his trusted assistant, Nikolai, is testing only several fathoms from the secret harbor. Falon's oversight allows Nikolai to return undetected.

After successfully mooring the submarine, Nikolai and his crew sense some misfortune has befallen Dakkar and their comrades as no one is there to greet them. Their wireless transmission signaling their re-entry also went unanswered. He soon discovers that Dakkar and the others have been imprisoned by Falon and will soon undergo torture, forcing their submission to Falon's will.

Nikolai manages to free the prisoners, all of whom hurry aboard the submarine. As they are submerging, Falon's henchmen hurl explosives at the disappearing craft. One of these damages the rudder system of the ship forcing it to the bottom of the bay. As the ship rests there, Dakkar notices from one of the portholes that the lost city he had been searching for so long has been right beneath the Isle of Hetvia the whole time. Much to their surprise they learn that this underwater city is actually inhabited by small dwarf-like creatures. These small beings, about one-tenth the size of an average man, have funny-shaped heads with bulging eyes. Both their hands and feet have webbing between the digits to aid in their swimming. Obviously they are able to gather oxygen through the water with some gill-like device.

It seems this underwater city and its dwarf-like inhabitants are plagued by a giant sea serpent (which is characterized in the film as a dragon). As the serpent approaches the city, Dakkar reacts almost instantaneously by firing a torpedo into the serpent's jowls. The torpedo explodes, leaving the creature lifeless on the ocean floor. The small residents regard Dakkar as their hero for slaying the dragon, offering the hospitality of their kingdom to their guests.

Meanwhile, Falon has discovered how to operate the other submarine and, using Sonia (Dakkar's daughter) as his hostage, descends to the ocean's depths where a fierce underwater battle between the two submarine crews ensues. The ferocity of their battle causes the water about the two vessels to turn almost opaque as dirt and seaweed are churned up by the fighting. Sonia is able to escape from her captors and sabotage Falon's submarine. When Falon's submarine explodes, his body is literally ripped apart, as are many who are fighting near the submarine. The sea is suddenly filled with the rich redness of fresh blood. The sudden appearance of this human blood intensifies some primevil instinct among the dwarf creatures and they respond by releasing a giant octopus which then attacks Dakkar's ship.

In the effort to free the submarine from the octopus' enormous tentacles most of the crew is annihilated, and Dakkar is mortally wounded. Only the valor and perseverence of the remaining crew members finally overcome the octopus and bring the vessel to the surface.

Once back in port, Dakkar releases his crew to return to the safety of Hetvia. Realizing that Sonia and Nikolai have developed a mutual affection, Dakkar urges Nikolai to take care of her, beseiging them to continue his experimental work. Sensing he has but moments to live, he opens all the ballasts of his submarine thus sending it to the bottom and encasing its occupant in a watery steel tomb for eternity.

Mysterious Island received a great deal of notoriety and public acclaim for an exquisite feature film. It is unfortunate that the picture took so long to make that it was plagued with problems even after completing the script and getting the final okay in mid-1926. Enormous obstacles still lay in the way of its completion. The film crew's journey from California to Florida was a fatiguing ordeal with many becoming ill along the way. Their final leg of the trip led them to the Bahamas to Williamson's underwater film laboratory. As fate would have it, within weeks after the crew's arrival a hurricane (September, 1926) descended upon the small island chain, totally destroying their boats and much of their precious film equipment. All of this required nearly ten months to eventually overcome and finally begin filming the epic.

Within two months of the first shooting, one of the executives decided he would like to see some drastic changes in some of the film's structure. Obviously this required a great deal of additional shooting and several more rewrites, all totally unexpected.

Several directors had been employed at various times, the first being Maurice Tourneur who gave up after being beset by many of these frustrating events. In late 1927 Benjamin Christiansen spent a great deal of money and wasted vast quantities of film in an effort that was well below the expectations of the producers. But it was Lucien Hubbard who somehow managed to bring the film to its fruition in early 1929.

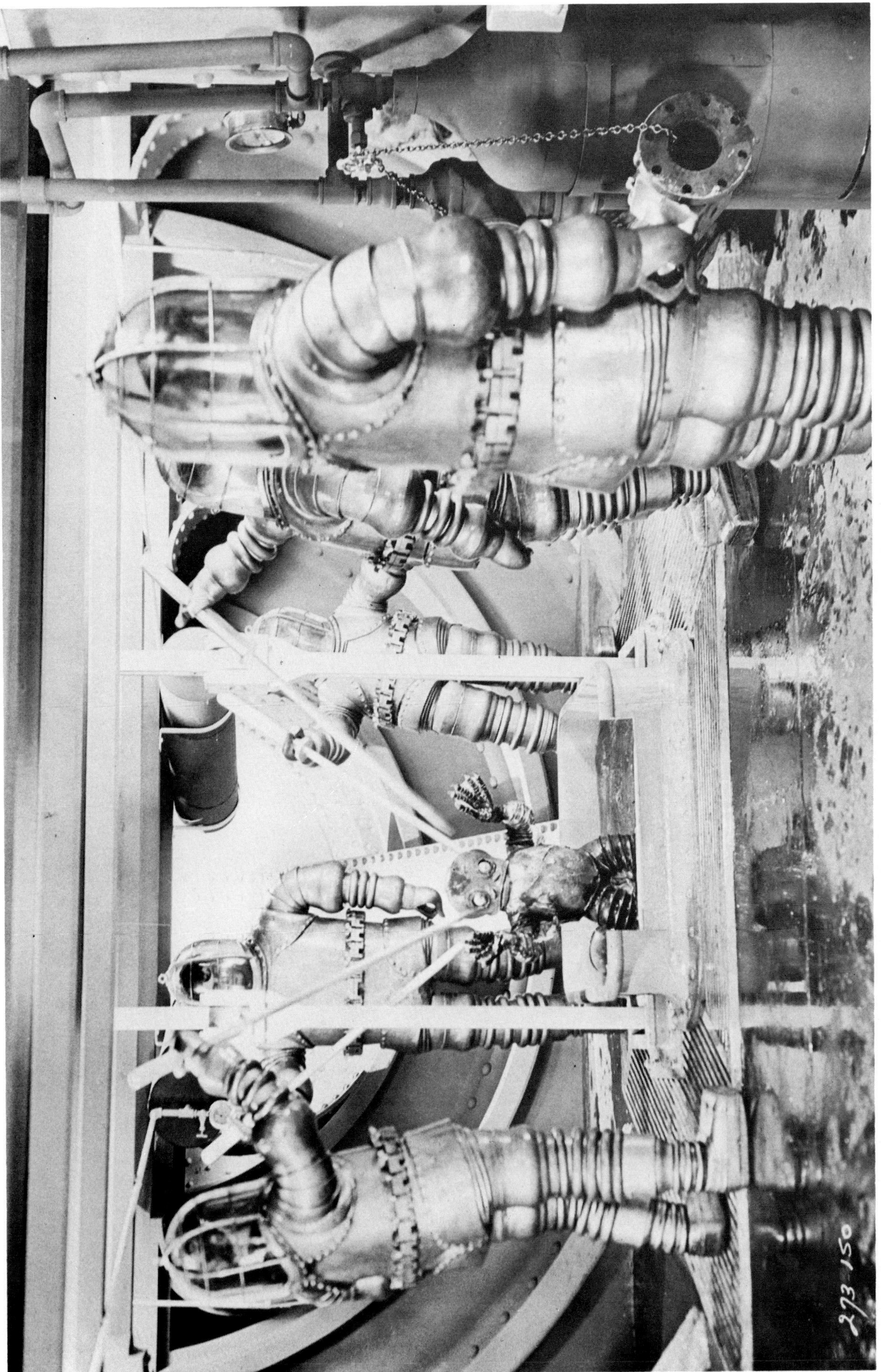

One of the little creatures is captured by Falon's henchmen.

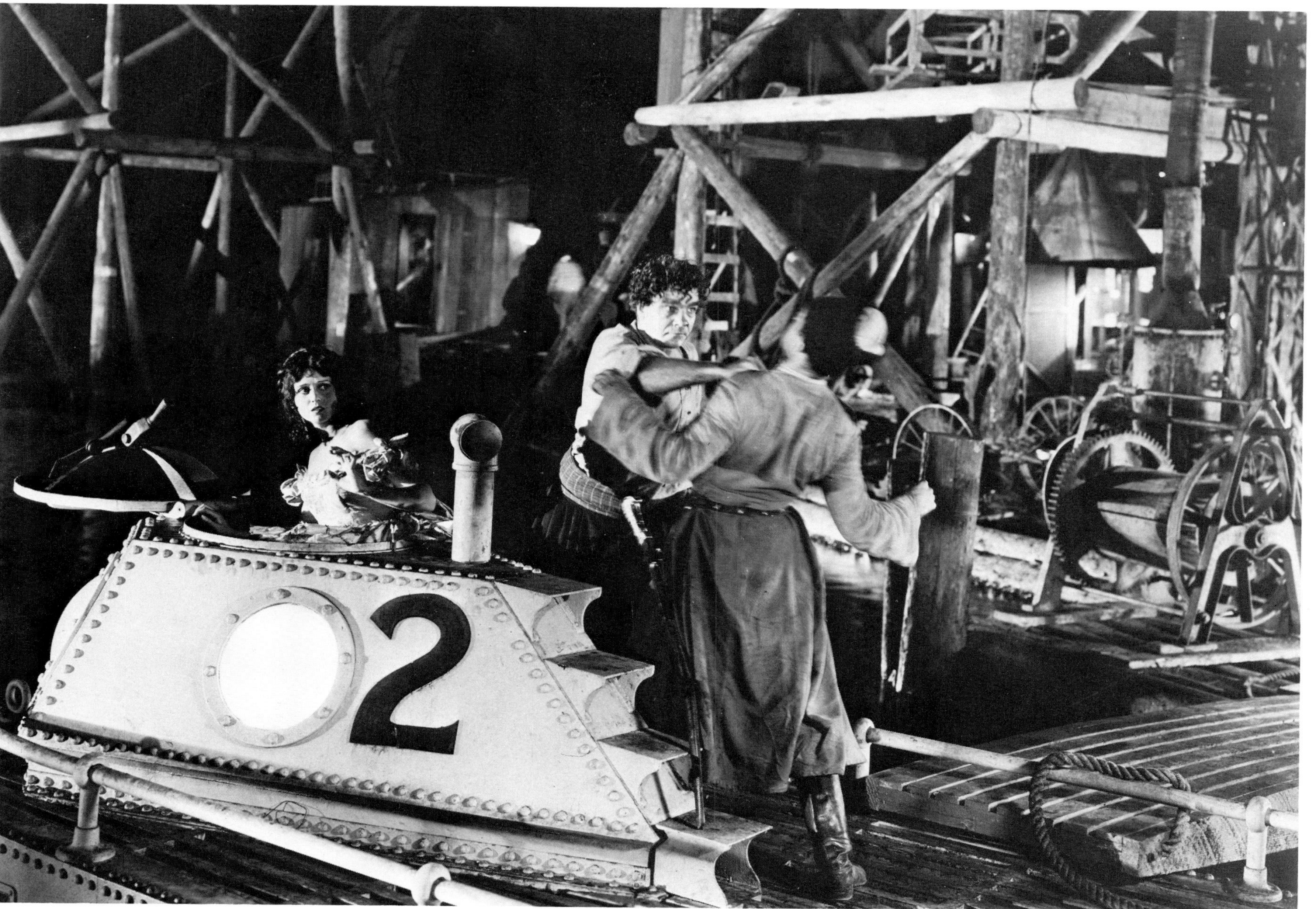

Sonia (Jane Daly) is captured by Falon (Montagu Love), but escapes using the duplicate submarine.

Tiny creatures from the depths of the ocean welcome Dakkar (Lionel Barrymore).

Originally *The Mysterious Island* was intended to be the first completely technicolor feature ever released, but due to the length of the filming it did not become heralded as the first. It was still among the few films during that era that was 90% technicolor.

Totally unexpected to the film producers and Williamson was the advent of sound in feature films. Only as a hasty last minute jesture was a sound track added to it, and even then it only constituted 5% of the film footage.

The Mysterious Island still has a great deal of appeal for any film buff, but Jules Verne would have a hard time finding enough of his original story to recognize.

> "Aside from the continual novelty of scenes, performance of Lionel Barrymore as the inventive genius is predominant. He never fails to hold tense interest, from the moment he explains his mechanical creations to the time he demands to be buried alive in his one remaining submarine. It is a powerful yet perfectly toned role. Lloyd Hughes and Jane Daly as the love interest supply an attractive background."
>
> *Variety,* 12-25-29, p. 30
>
> "A fantastic undersea melodrama, known as 'The Mysterious Island,' which was inspired by the Jules Verne story of the same name, is now on view at the Capitol. It is a craftily contrived film, most of which is photographed in technicolor, and just the sort of thing that will fill children with mingled feelings of awe and delight. There are a few dialogue sequences, but the greater part is silent except for the so-called sound effects.
>
> It is a long film, perhaps a trifle too long, but it is strikingly ingenious and effectively directed by Lucien Hubbard. It is also well served by J. E. Williamson's undersea photographic work, which was filmed off the Bahamas. This production has had a hectic career, for work was started on it more than two years ago, but after a few months it was temporarily abandoned."
>
> *New York Times,* 12-12-29, p. 583
>
> "The story value of this film is negligible and at times obscure in development, particularly in the antagonism between the scientist and his people of the island and those of the mainland. To stimulate interest the producer has given us a triangular love affair between the scientist's daughter, his right hand man, and his arch enemy. Naturally, the main features of the film are the undersea shots, and these are really remarkably conceived and extraordinarily well photographed. The idea of hordes of little imps sucking the blood of real live Europeans in the depths of the ocean, and releasing various monsters to do battle in their cause, may appear absurd, though nothing was too weird for the imaginative brain of Verne, and the producer is to be complimented on his work. No idea of period is given, and as wireless telegraphy, torpedoes and many other inventions known to science today are introduced, it might easily pass as a twentieth century adventure. As already stated, considerable cutting is necessary to knit the story together and strengthen interest."
>
> *Bioscope,* Vol. 88, No. 1235, p. 43

THE SKY SKIDDER

Release: 1929, Universal Pictures
Description: Silent, 4364 feet
Classification: SF-A
References: No. 14, p. 438; No. 50, p. 444; AFI, F2.5145, p. 731; BIO, Vol. 74, No. 1117, p. 48; LC, LP24915; PHO, 3-29; VAW, Vol. 94, 2-20-29, p. 17

Credits

Producer .... Universal
Director .... Bruce Mitchell
Screenplay .... Val Cleveland
Camera .... William Adams
Editor .... Harry Marker
Titles .... Gardner Bradford

Cast

Al Simpkins .... Al Wilson
Stella Hearns .... Helen Foster
Silas Smythe .... Wilbur McGaugh
Bert Beatle .... Pee Wee Holmes

Universal's *The Sky Skidder* is filled with daring airplane feats, providing an ample quantity of excitement. Unfortunately, the story is centered around a poorly written and weak plot resulting in a weak science fiction adventure presentation.

The focus of the film is on the development of a new formula as a fuel substitute for gasoline. This new substance is called "economo." The remarkable claim by its inventor, Al Simpkins, is that this fuel will get 1,000 miles to the pint. Stella Hearns, a wealthy debutante, has helped finance Simpkins' formula development and the two of them have become sweethearts in the process. A rather well-to-do and unscrupulous businessman, Silas Smythe, has learned of this formula through Stella who accidently let the information slip out. His greed and lust for power eventually lead him to develop a scheme by which he can acquire the secret formula.

His diabolical plan includes kidnapping Stella. He carefully lures her over to his automobile and then shoves her into the backseat, speeding away with her screaming. Simpkins hears her screams and quickly boards his aircraft and gives pursuit. As the plane approaches the automobile, Simpkins lowers a rope ladder which Stella then manages to climb up, escaping Smythe's clutches and ruining his plot to gain control of the secret fuel.

The next day at the special demonstration of "economo" for several industrialists, Al's airplane engine suddenly goes dead while he is several thousand feet above the airfield. Unable to restart the engine, he makes a periolous parachute jump while the plane goes into a tail spin (a very tricky and unique stunt). Later, while examining the wreckage, he discovers that the secret fuel had been replaced with ordinary gasoline, thus the reason for the plane's sudden loss of power. Al, quite discouraged by his dismal performance before the group of potential buyers, is buoyed by Stella's encouragement and her vow of continued financial assistance, as she decides to back him for another demonstration before a different group of industrialists. This time the airplane's fuel tanks are filled with "economo" and sealed to prevent tampering. Just prior to demonstration, Smythe manages to break into the small laboratory used by Simpkins to create his invention, and after searching the desk discovers the secret formula written on the underside of a drawer. He also steals a barrel of "economo" and empties its contents into the tanks of his own aircraft, thus assuring his escape. (At this point in the film, an exciting air duel between Smythe and Simpkins takes place and offers the viewer some spectacular aviation stunts.) Eventually Simpkins overtakes Smythe's airplane, using a rope ladder to descend onto the crook's craft (leading the audience to believe that Simpkins must surely have some sort of automatic steering device on his craft) where the two men begin to battle with their fists. Gradually, Simpkins overcomes the weaker Smythe and manages to steal back his formula. As he ascends the rope ladder back to his own plane, Smythe's plane goes into a steep dive and plunges into the ocean.

Al returns to the airfield where the industrialists are ecstatic about his new fuel. They offer him production contracts and enormous sums of money. Both he and Stella are pleased with the outcome as they reaffirm their commitment to each other to remain together, partners for life.

The Sky Skidders was orginally released in January of 1929 and therefore missed the advent of sound films. Although, after reviewing the script and examining the critics' comments concerning the film, the addition of dialogue probably would have only resulted in an even poorer film than the one the audience suffered through.

> "Though the film contains practically no story value, sufficient opportunities have been afforded for Wilson to display his daring. His rescue of the girl from a runaway car by descending a rope ladder from his machine, and the spectacular transfer from one plane to another and back again while flying at a great height certainly provides thrills which will appeal to the majority of audiences."
>
> *Bioscope*, Vol. 74, No. 1117, p. 48

> "Couple of minutes of thrilling air stuff and long sequences of straight flying stand out. Otherwise particularly flagrant example of bad writing, worse acting and indifferent direction. Half double bill in daily change neighborhood about fixes its status."
>
> *Variety*, 2-20-29, p. 17

CLASSIFICATION OF SCIENCE FICTION FILMS FROM 1920 TO 1929

Science Fiction

Dr. Jekyll and Mr. Hyde 1920
Dr. Jekyll and Mr. Hyde 1920
Flaming Disk, The 1920
Sky Ranger, The 1921
Witching Hour, The 1921
Evolution 1921
Story Without a Name, The 1923
Lost World, The 1924
One Way Street 1925
Up The Ladder 1925
Scarlet Streak, The 1925
Code of the Air 1926
Ransom 1928
Mysterious Island 1929

Science Fiction - Comedy

Dr. Jekyll and Mr. Hyde 1920
Electric House, The 1922
Minnie 1922
Sky Splitter, The 1922
Back to Earth 1923
Last Man on Earth, The 1924
Sinners in Silk 1924
Dr. Pyckle and Mr. Pride 1925
From Mars to Munich 1925
Super-Hooper-Dyne Lizzies 1925
Missing Link, The 1927
Kids Clever, The 1928

Science Fiction - Adventure

Branded Four, The 1920
Empire of Diamonds, The 1920
Invisible Ray, The 1920
Mystery Mind, The 1920
Screaming Shadow, The 1920
Terror Island 1920
Diamond Queen, The 1921
Hell Diggers, The 1921
Nan of the North 1921
Radio King, The 1922

Around the World in Eighteen Days 1923
Blow Your Own Horn 1923
Eleventh Hour, The 1923
Isle of Lost Ships, The 1923
Legally Dead 1923
Red Lights 1923
Wasted Lives 1923
Black Oxen 1923
Laughing at Danger 1924
Perils of Paris, The 1924
Vanity's Price 1924
Power God, The 1925
Block Signal, The 1926
Officer 444 1926
Radio Detective, The 1926
Blake of Scotland Yard 1927
Chinatown Mystery, The..1928
Eagle of the Night, The 1928
Diamond Master, The 1929
Fire Detective, The..1929
Isle of Lost Ships, The 1929
King of the Kongo 1929
Lost Zeppelin, The 1929
Midstream 1929
Sky Skidder, The 1929

Science Fiction - Horror

Devil to Pay 1920
A Blind Bargain 1922
Unknown Purple, The 1923
On Time 1924
Wizard, the 1927

Science Fiction - Fantasy

Hidden Code, The 1920
Gambling with the Gulf Stream......................................1920
Young Diana, The 1922
Radio-Mania 1923
All Aboard for the Moon 1924

COMPANIES RELEASING FILMS FROM 1920 TO 1929

Arrow

Dr. Jekyll and Mr. Hyde 1920
Nan of the North 1921

Bischoff Productions

Code of the Air 1928

Bray

All Aboard for the Moon 1924

Columbia Pictures

Ransom 1928

Davis Distributing

Officer 444 1926

F.B.O.

Blow Your Own Horn 1923
Laughing at Danger 1924
Perils of Paris, The 1924
Vanity's Price 1924
Dr. Pyckle and Mr. Pride 1925

First National Pictures

Electric House, The 1922
Minnie 1922
Isle of Lost Ships, The 1923
Black Oxen 1924
Lost World, The 1925
One Way Street 1925
Isle of Lost Ships, The 1929

Fox Film Corporation

Eleventh Hour, The 1923
Last Man on Earth, The 1924
From Mars to Munich 1925
Wizard, The 1927

Frohman Amusement Corporation

Invisible Ray, The 1920

Goldwyn Pictures Corporation

A Blind Bargain 1922
Red Lights 1923

Hallmark Pictures Corporation

Screaming Shadow, The 1920

Hodkinson

Gambling with the Gulf Stream 1922
Sky Splitter, The 1922
Radio-Mania 1923

Lumns Film Corporation

Block Signal, The 1926

MGM

Sinners in Silk 1924
Mysterious Island 1929

Moscot Pictures

King of the Kongo 1929

Paramount Pictures Corporation

Dr. Jekyll and Mr. Hyde 1920
Terror Island 1920
Hell Diggers, The 1921
Witching Hour, The 1921
Young Diana, The 1922
Story Without a Name, The 1924

Pathe

Devil to Pay 1920
Empire of Diamonds, The 1920
Sky Ranger, The 1921
Super-Hooper-Dyne Lizzies 1925
Eagle of the Night, The 1928
Fire Detective, The 1929

Second National Film Corporation

Wasted Lives 1923

Select Films

Branded Four, The 1920

Syndicated Pictures

Chinatown Mystery, The 1928

Tiffany Productions

Lost Zeppelin, The 1929
Midstream 1929

Truart Film Company

Unknown Purple, The 1923
On Time 1924

Universal Film Manufacturing Company

Flaming Disk, The 1920
Diamond Queen, The 1921
Radio King, The 1922
Around the World in Eighteen Days 1923
Back to Earth 1923
Legally Dead 1923
Up the Ladder 1925
Radio Detective, The 1926
Scarlet Streak, The 1926
Blake of Scotland Yard 1927
Kids Clever, The 1928
Diamond Master, The 1929
Sky Skidder, The 1929

FILMOGRAPHY

Sausage Machine, The 1897
Fun In The Butcher Shop 1901
Dog Factory 1904
Dr. Skinum 1907
Hair Restorer 1907
Liquid Electricity 1907
Love Microbe, The 1907
Mechanical Statue And The Ingenious Servant, The 1907
Nature Fakirs 1907
Work Made Easy 1907
Airship, The 1908
An Animated Doll 1908
Doctor's Experiment, The 1908
Dr. Jekyll And Mr. Hyde 1908
Electric Hotel, The 1908
Energizer 1908
Galvanic Fluid 1908
Heating Power 1908
Invisible Fluid, The 1908
Love Germs 1908
Oh What An Appetite 1908
Professors Anti-Gravitation Fluid, The 1908
Brain-Serum 1909
Diamond Maker, The 1909
Earthquake Alarm, The 1909
Hair Restorer, The 1909
Inventions Of An Idiot 1909
Measure For Measure 1909
Professor's Love Tonic, The 1909
Rubber Man, The 1909
Talkative Lady 1909
Wonderful Electro-Magnet, The 1909
A Trip To Mars 1910
Betty's Electric Battery 1910
Comet, The 1910
Electric Insoles, The 1910
Frankenstein 1910
Inventor, The 1910
Looking Forward 1910
Mechanical Husband, The 1910
Dr. Growenquick's Feeding Power 1911
Electrified Pig, The 1911
House Of Mystery, The 1911
Inventor's Secret, The 1911
Caveman, The 1912

Jack Spratt And The Scales Of Love 1915
Jungle Lovers, The 1915
Kite, The 1915
Lady Baffles And Detective Duck, The 1915
Let There Be Light 1915
Life Without Soul 1915
Mechanical Man, The 1915
Mr. Jarr's Magnetic Friend 1915
Monopolist, The 1915
Mysterious Contragrav, The 1915
New Exploits Of Elaine, The 1915
Pawns Of Mars 1915
Plague Spot, The 1915
Return Of Maurice Donnelly, The 1915
Romance Of Elaine, The 1915
Secret Room, The 1915
Ventures Of Marguerite, The 1915
War O' Dreams, The 1915
When The Mind Sleeps 1915
Beggar King, The 1916
Comet's Come-Back, The 1916
Crimson Stain Mystery, The 1916
Dare Devils In Danger 1916
Five Franc Piece, The 1916
Flying Torpedo, The 1916
Half Wit, The 1916
Hand Of Peril, The 1916
Her Father's Gold 1916
Insurance Swindlers, The 1916
Intrigue, The 1916
Lion's Breath, The 1916
One Thousand Miles An Hour 1916
Secret Of The Submarine, The 1916
Through Solid Walls 1916
Twenty Thousand Leagues Under The Sea 1916
Without A Soul 1916
Dinosaur And The Missing Link, The 1917
Hidden Hand, The 1917
Inspirations Of Harry Larrabee, The 1917
Love Dope, The 1917
Lust Of The Ages, The 1917
Magic Jazz Bo, The 1917
Speed 1917
10,000 Years B. C. 1917
Water On The Brain 1917
Zeppelin Attack On New York 1917
Craving, The 1918
House Of Hate 1918

On Time ... 1924
Perils Of Paris, The ... 1924
Sinners In Silk ... 1924
Story Without A Name, The ... 1924
Vanity's Price ... 1924
Dr. Pyckle And Mr. Pride ... 1925
From Mars To Munich ... 1925
Lost World, The ... 1925
One Way Street ... 1925
Power God, The ... 1925
Super-Hooper-Dyne Lizzies ... 1925
Up The Ladder ... 1925
Block Signal, The ... 1926
Officer 444 ... 1926
Radio Detective, The ... 1926
Savage, The ... 1926
Scarlet Streak, The ... 1926
Blake Of Scotland Yard ... 1927
Missing Link, The ... 1927
Wizard, The ... 1927
Chinatown Mystery, The ... 1928
Code Of The Air ... 1928
Eagle Of The Night, The ... 1928
Kids Clever, The ... 1928
Ransom ... 1928
Diamond Master, The ... 1929
Fire Detective, The ... 1929
Isle Of Lost Ships, The ... 1929
King Of The Kongo ... 1929
Lost Zeppelin, The ... 1929
Midstream ... 1929
Mysterious Island ... 1929
Sky Skidder, The ... 1929

CLASSIFICATION OF SCIENCE FICTION FILMS FROM 1897 TO 1929

Science Fiction

Airship, The 1908
Dr. Jekyll and Mr. Hyde 1908
Galvanic Fluid 1908
Invisible Fluid, The 1908
Brain-Serum 1909
Diamond Maker, The 1909
Rubber Man, The 1909
Comet, The 1910
Frankenstein 1910
Inventor, The 1910
Dr. Growenquick's Feeding Power 1911
Cave Man, The 1912
Dr. Jekyll and Mr. Hyde 1912
Man's Genesis 1912
Navigation by Wireless 1912
Serpents, The 1912
Bolt from the Sky, A 1913
Cave Man's War, The 1913
Cursed Be War 1913
Demonyte 1913
Diamond Makers, The 1913
Doctor Maxwell's Experiment 1913
Dr. Jekyll and Mr. Hyde 1913
Primitive Man 1913
Whirl of Destiny, The 1913
Birth of Emotion, The 1914
Bomb, The 1914
Bully's Doom, The 1914
By Radium Rays 1914
Naidra, The Dream Woman 1914
Surgeon's Experiment, The 1914
Foster Brother, The 1915
Let There Be Light 1915
Mysterious Contragrav, The 1915
Pawns of Mars 1915
Plague Spot, The 1915
Return of Maurice Donnelly, The 1915
Secret Room, The 1915
War of Dreams, The 1915
Comet's Come-Back, The 1916
Flying Torpedo, The 1916

Intrigue, The 1916
Twenty Thousand Leagues Under the Sea 1916
Without A Soul 1916
Dr. Jekyll and Mr. Hyde 1920
Dr. Jekyll and Mr. Hyde 1920
Flaming Disk, The 1920
Sky Ranger, The 1921
Witching Hour, The 1921
Evolution 1923
Story without a Name, The 1924
Lost World, The 1925
One Way Street 1925
Up the Ladder 1925
Scarlet Streak, The 1926
Code of the Air 1928
Ransom 1928
Mysterious Island 1929

Science Fiction - Comedy

Sausage Machine, The 1897
Fun in the Butcher Shop 1901
Dog Factory 1904
Dr. Skinum 1907
Hair Restorer 1907
Liquid Electricity 1907
Love Microbe, The 1907
Mechanical Statue and the Ingenious Servant, The 1907
Nature Fakirs 1907
Work Made Easy 1907
An Animated Doll 1908
Doctor's Experiment, The 1908
Electric Hotel, The 1908
Energizer 1908
Heating Power 1908
Love Germs 1908
Oh What an Appetite 1908
Professors Anti-Gravitation Fluid, The 1908
Earthquake Alarm, The 1909
Hair Restorer, The 1909
Inventions of an Idiot 1909
Professor's Love Tonic, The 1909
Talkative Lady 1909
Wonderful Electro-Magnet, The 1909
A Trip to Mars 1910
Betty's Electric Battery 1910

Science Fiction - Adventure

Measure for Measure 1909
Theft of the Secret Code 1912
Diamond Maker, The 1914
Exploits of Elaine, The 1914
Reader of Minds, The 1914
Silent Peril, The 1914
Won in the Clouds 1914
Beneath the Sea 1915
Black Box, The 1915
Diamond from the Sky, The 1915
Electric Alarm, The 1915
Inventor's Peril, The 1915
Jungle Lovers, The 1915
Kite, The 1915
Lady Baffles and Detective Duck, The 1915
Monopolist, The 1915
New Exploits of Elaine, The 1915
Romance of Elaine, The 1915
Ventures of Marguerite, The 1915
When the Mind Sleeps 1915
Beggar King, The 1916
Five Franc Piece, The 1916
Half Wit, The 1916
Hand of Peril, The 1916
Her Father's Gold 1916
Insurance Swindlers, The 1916
Secret of the Submarine, The 1916
Through Solid Walls 1916
Hidden Hand, The 1917
Inspirations of Harry Larrabee, The 1917
Lust of the Ages, The 1917
Zeppelin Attack on New York 1917
Craving, The 1918
House of Hate 1918
Mystery Ship, The 1918
A Scream in the Night 1919
Carter Case, The 1919
Poison Pen, The 1919
Branded Four, The 1920
Empire of Diamonds, The 1920
Invisible Ray, The 1920
Mystery Mind, The 1920
Screaming Shadow, The 1920
Terror Island 1920

Diamond Queen, The 1921
Hell Diggers, The 1921
Nan of the North 1921
Radio King, The 1922
Around the World in Eighteen Days 1923
Blow Your Own Horn 1923
Eleventh Hour, The 1923
Isle of Lost Ships, The 1923
Legally Dead 1923
Red Lights 1923
Wasted Lives 1923
Black Oxen 1924
Laughing at Danger 1924
Perils of Paris, The 1924
Vanity's Price 1924
Power God, The 1925
Block Signal, The 1926
Officer 444 1926
Radio Detective, The 1926
Blake of Scotland Yard 1927
Chinatown Mystery, The 1928
Eagle of the Night, The 1928
Diamond Master, The 1929
Fire Detective, The 1929
Isle of Lost Ships, The 1929
King of the Kongo 1929
Lost Zeppelin, The 1929
Midstream 1929
Sky Skidder, The 1929

Science Fiction - Horror

Life Without Soul 1915
Crimson Stain Mystery, The 1916
Devil to Pay 1920
A Blind Bargain 1922
Unknown Purple, The 1923
On Time 1924
Wizard, The 1927

Science Fiction - Fantasy

Dances of the Ages 1913
10,000 Years B.C. 1917
Hidden Code, The 1920
Gambling with the Gulf Stream 1922
Young Diana, The 1922
Radio-Mania 1923
All Aboard for the Moon 1924

COMPANIES RELEASING FILMS FROM 1897 TO 1929

Alhambra - Kiterion

Birth of Emotion, The 1914

American Film Manufacturing Company

Let There Be Light 1915
Comet's Come-Back, The 1916
Dare Devils in Danger 1916
Secret of the Submarine, The 1916

American Mutoscope & Biograph Company/Biograph Company

Sausage Machine, The 1897
Dr. Skinum 1907
Love Microbe, The 1907
Energizer 1908
Invisible Fluid, The 1908
Inventor's Secret, The 1911
Man's Genesis 1912
Primitive Man 1913

Arrow

Dr. Jekyll and Mr. Hyde 1920
Nan of the North 1921

Bischoff Productions

Code of the Air 1928

Bison

Silent Peril, The 1914

Bluebird

Craving, The 1918

Bray

All Aboard the Moon 1924

Columbia Pictures

Ransom 1928

Conquest Films

10,000 Years B.C. 1917

Consolidated Film Corporation

Crimson Stain Mystery, The 1916

Cosmopolitan

Electrified Pig, The 1911

Crystal

Sure Cure 1914

Danube

Navigation by Wireless 1912

Eclair

Diamond Maker, The 1914

Edison Film Company

Fun in the Butcher Shop 1901
Dog Factory 1904
Wonderful Electro-Magnet, The 1909
A Trip to Mars 1910
Frankenstein 1910
Dr. Brompton-Watt's Adjuster 1912
Dances of the Ages 1913
Absent Minded Mother 1914
Dinosaur and the Missing Link, The 1917

Elite Film Company

Bumke Discovers the Turning Microbe 1913

Empress Film Company

Automatic House, The 1915

Essanay Film Manufacturing Company

An Animated Doll 1908
Oh What An Appetite 1908
Professor's Love Tonic, The 1909
Electric Insoles, The 1910
Jack Spratt and the Scales of Love 1915

Falstaff

Hattie, The Hair Heiress 1915

F.B.O.

Blow Your Own Horn 1923
Laughing at Danger 1924
Perils of Paris, The 1924
Vanity's Price 1924
Dr. Pyckle and Mr. Pride 1925

Film Releases of America

Demonyte 1913

Fine Arts

Flying Torpedo, The 1916

First National Pictures

Electric House, The 1922
Minnie 1922
Isle of Lost Ships, The 1923
Black Oxen 1924
Lost World, The 1925
One Way Street 1925

Isle of Lost Ships, The 1929

Fox Film Corporation

Eleventh Hour, The 1923
Last Man On Earth, The 1924
From Mars to Munich 1925
Wizard, The 1927

Frohman Amusement Corporation

Invisible Ray, The 1920

Gaumont Company

Doctor's Experiment, The 1908
Talkative Lady 1909

General Film Company

Inspirations of Harry Larrabee, The 1917

Gold Seal

By Radium Rays 1914

Goldwyn Pictures Corporation

A Blind Bargain 1922
Red Lights 1923

Hallmark Pictures Corporation

Screaming Shadow, The 1920

Hepworth

Professors Anti-Gravitation Fluid, The 1908

Hodkinson

Gambling with the Gulf Stream 1922
Sky Splitter, The 1922
Radio-Mania 1923

Independent Moving Picture Company

Dr. Jekyll and Mr. Hyde 1913

Kalem Company

Nature Fakirs 1907
Comet, The 1910
Bolt From the Sky, A 1913
Cave Man's War, The 1913
Indestructible Mr. Jenks, The 1913
Professor Oldboy's Rejuvenator 1914
Ventures of Marguerite, The 1915
When the Mind Sleeps 1915

Kay - Bee

Kite, The 1915

Keystone

His Prehistoric Past 1914

Kriterion

Blown Upon 1914

LCC

Mechanical Husband, The 1910

Lubin

Heating Power 1908
Love Germs 1908
Brain-Serum 1909
Inventions of An Idiot 1909
Measure for Measure 1909
Rubber Man, The 1909
Kissing Pills 1912
Doctor Maxwell's Experiment 1913
Bomb, The 1914
Bully's Doom, The 1914
Beneath the Sea 1915
Inventor's Peril, The 1915
Beggar King, The 1916
Half Wit, The 1916

Lumas Film Corporation

Block Signal, The 1926

Majestic

Hypnotic Chair, The 1912
Surgeon's Experiment, The 1914
Electric Alarm, The 1915

Mascot Pictures

King of the Kongo 1929

MGM

Love Dope, The 1917
Sinners in Silk 1924
Mysterious Island 1929

Mica Film Corporation

Foster Brother, The 1915

Mundstuk Features

Whirl of Destiny, The 1913

North American Film Company

Diamond from the Sky, The 1915

Ocean

Life Without Soul 1915

Ogden Independent Productions

Lust of the Ages, The 1917

Oliver Films

Carter Case, The 1919

Pallas

Intrigue, The 1916

Paramount Pictures Corporation

Dr. Jekyll and Mr. Hyde 1920
Terror Island 1920
Hell Diggers, The 1921
Witching Hour, The 1921
Young Diana, The 1922
Story Without a Name, The 1924

Passing Show Comedies

Rejuvenators, The 1918

Pathe

Hair Restorer, The 1909
Betty's Electric Battery 1910
Inventor, The 1910
House of Mystery, The 1911
Exploits of Elaine, The 1914
Monopolist, The 1915
New Exploits of Elaine, The 1915
Romance of Elaine, The 1915
Secret Room, The 1915
Hidden Hand, The 1917
House of Hate 1918
Devil to Pay 1920
Empire of Diamonds, The 1920
Sky Ranger, The 1921
Super-Hooper-Dyne Lizzies 1925
Eagle of the Night, The 1928
Fire Detective, The 1929

Pioneer Film Corporation

Dr. Jekyll and Mr. Hyde 1920
Hidden Code, The 1920
Mystery Mind, The 1920

Red Seal Pictures Corporation

Evolution ... 1923

Rex Motion Picture Company

Diamond Makers, The ... 1913

Rothacker

Zeppelin Attack on New York ... 1917

Schultze

Earthquake Alarm, The ... 1909

Second National Film Corporation

Wasted Lives ... 1923

Select Films

A Scream in the Night ... 1919
Branded Four, The ... 1920

Selig Polyscope Company

Dr. Jekyll and Mr. Hyde ... 1908
Jungle Lovers, The ... 1915
War of Dreams, The ... 1915
Five Franc Piece, The ... 1916

Solax

The Year 2000 ... 1912

Starlight

Dr. Jekyll and Mr. Hyde ... 1914

Syndicated Pictures

Chinatown Mystery, The ... 1928

Thanhouser

Looking Forward ... 1910
Dr. Jekyll and Mr. Hyde ... 1912
Miser's Reversion, The ... 1914
Naidra, The Dream Woman ... 1914
Reader of Minds, The ... 1914
Her Father's Gold ... 1916

Tiffany Productions

Lost Zeppelin, The 1929
Midstream 1929

Truart Film Company

Unknown Purple, The 1923
On Time 1924

Universal Film Manufacturing Company

Bumbles Diminisher 1913
Won in the Clouds 1914
Black Box, The 1915
Lady Baffles and Detective Duck, The 1915
Mechanical Man, The 1915
Mysterious Contragrav, The 1915
Insurance Swindlers, The 1916
Lion's Breath, The 1916
One Thousand Miles an Hour 1916
Through Solid Walls 1916
Twenty Thousand Leagues Under the Sea 1916
Magic Jazz Bo, The 1917
Water on the Brain 1917
Mystery Ship, The 1918
Flaming Disk, The 1920
Diamond Queen, The 1921
Radio King, The 1922
Around the World in Eighteen Days 1923
Back to Earth 1923
Legally Dead 1923
Up the Ladder 1925
Radio Detective, The 1926
Scarlet Streak, The 1926
Blake of Scotland Yard 1927
Kids Clever, The 1928
Diamond Master, The 1929
Sky Skidder, The 1929

U.S. Motion Picture Corporation

Speed 1917

Vitagraph Company of America

Liquid Electricity 1907
Mechanical Statue and the Ingenious Servant, The 1907
Work Made Easy 1907

Airship, The 1908
Electric Hotel, The 1908
Galvanic Fluid 1908
Diamond Maker, The 1909
Cave Man, The 1912
Serpents, The 1912
Mr. Jarr's Magnetic Friend 1915
Pawns of Mars 1915
Plague Spot, The 1915
Return of Maurice Donnelly, The 1915

Vital Exchanges, Inc.

Power God, The 1925

Vitascope Company

Theft of the Secret Code 1912

Walter Daw

Dr. Growenquick's Feeding Power 1911

Warner Brothers

Missing Link, The 1927

Williams, Brown and Earle

Hair Restorer 1907

World Film Corporation

Hand of Peril, The 1916
Without A Soul 1916
Poison Pen, The 1919

Releasing Company Unknown

Cursed Be War 1913

REFERENCES

Reference Number

1 *The film index VI: Film as art.* The Museum of Modern Art Film Library, Inc., 1966.

2 *Motion pictures from the Library of Congress paper print collection 1894-1912.* University of California Press, 1967.

3 Everson, W. K. *Classics of the horror film.* The Citadel Press, 1974.

4 Fitzgerald, M. G. *Universal pictures.* Arlington House, 1977.

5 Gifford, D. *Science fiction film.* New York: E. P. Dutton, 1971.

6 Gifford, D. *Movie monsters.* New York: E. P. Dutton, 1969.

7 Cowie, P. (Ed.) *Hollywood.* New York: A. S. Barnes & Co., 1977.

8 Lahue, K. C. *Continued next week: A history of the moving picture serial.* Norman, OK: University of Oklahoma Press, 1964.

9 Capra, F. *Frank Capra, the name above the title.* New York: MacMillan & Co., 1971.

10 Blum, D. *A pictorial history of the talkies.* New York: Grosset & Dunlap, 1958.

11 Halliwell, L. *Halliwell's film guide.* New York: Charles Scribner's Sons, 1979.

12 Maltin, L. *The great movie shorts.* New York: Crown Publishing Co., Inc., 1972.

13 O'Leary, L. *The silent cinema.* New York: E. P. Dutton & Co., 1965.

14 Willis, D. *Horror and science fiction films: A checklist.* Metuchen, NJ: Scarecrow Press, 1972.

15 Weiss, K., & Goodgold, E. *To be continued. . .* New York: Crown Publishing, Inc., 1972.

16 Niver, K. R. *Biograph bulletins 1896-1908.* Los Angeles: Artisan Press, 1971.

17 Barbour, A. G. *Days of thrills and adventures.* New York: The Macmillan Co., 1970.

18 Maltin, L. *Movie comedy teams.* New York: Signet, New American Library, 1970.

19 Barbour, A. G. *The serials of Republic.* Kew Gardens, NY: Screen Facts Press, 1965.

20 Menville, D. *An historical and critical survey of the science fiction film.* Unpublished masters thesis, University of Southern California, 1959.

21 James, J. R. *Fantasy films and their fiends.* Oklahoma City, OK: Jones, 1964.

22 Clarens, C. *An illustrated history of horror films.* New York: G. P. Putnam & Sons, 1967.

23 Jacobs, L. *The rise of the American film, a critical history.* New York: Harcourt, Brace Co., 1939.

24 *National film archive catalog, Part III: Silent fiction film 1895-1930.* London: British Film Institute, 1966.

25 Kitson, C. *A history of American animation (program notes).* Los Angeles: Los Angeles County Museum of Art, 1972.

26 Brosnan, J. *Movie magic: The story of special effects in the cinema.* New York: New American Library, 1976.

27 Quigley, M., & Gertner, R. *Films in America 1929-1969.* New York: Golden Press, 1970.

28 Nicholls, P. (Ed.) *The science fiction encyclopedia.* Garden City, NY: Doubleday & Company, 1979.

29 Barbour, A. G. (Ed.) *Screen facts.* Kew Gardens, NY: Screen Facts Press, 1963.

30 Barbour, A. G. *The serials of Columbia.* Kew Gardens, NY: Screen Facts Press, 1965.

31 Harmon, J., & Glut, D. F. *The great movie serials.* Garden City, NY: Doubleday & Company, 1972.

32 Stedman, R. W. *The serials: Suspense and drama by installment.* Norman, OK: University of Oklahoma Press, 1977.

33 Rovin, J. *From the land beyond beyond: The making of the movie monsters you've known and loved.* New York: Berkley Windhover Books, 1977.

34 Gifford, D. *British film catalog 1895-1970: A reference guide.* New York: McGraw Hill Book Co., 1973.

35 Limbacher, J. L. *Four aspects of the film.* New York: Brussell & Brussell, 1969.

36 Baxter, J. *Science fiction in the cinema.* New York: A. S. Barnes & Co., 1970.

37 Miller, D. *B movies: An informal survey of the American low budget film 1933-1945.* New York: Curtis Books, 1973.

38 Rotha, P., & Griffith, R. *Film till now, a survey of world cinema.* London: Vision Press and Mayflower Co., Ltd., 1960.

39 Steinbrunner, C., & Goldblatt, B. *Cinema of the fantastic.* New York: Saturday Review Press, 1972.

40 Nealon, J. *An historical and critical survey of the American horror film since 1930.* Unpublished masters thesis, University of Southern California, 1953.

41 Glut, D. F. *The frankenstein legend: A tribute to Mary Shelley and Boris Karloff.* Metuchen, NJ: Scarecrow Press, 1973.

42 Agee, J. *Agee on films: Reviews and comments.* New York: McDowell Obolensky, 1958.

43 Barbour, A. G. *The serial, volume 1.* Los Angeles: Barbour, 1967.

44 Barbour, A. G. *The serial, volume 2.* Los Angeles: Barbour, 1968.

45 Brosman, J. *Future tense: The cinema of science fiction.* New York: St. Martin's Press, 1978.

46 Lauritzen, E., & Lundquist, G. *American films: Index 1908-1915.* Stockholm, Sweden: University of Stockholm, 1976.

47 Everson, W. K. *American silent film.* New York: Oxford University Press, 1978.

48 Parish, J. R., & Pitts, M. R. *The great science fiction pictures.* Metuchen, NJ: Scarecrow Press, 1977.

49 Blum, D. *A pictorial history of the silent screen.* New York: Grosset and Dunlap, 1953.

50 Lee, W. *Reference guide to fantastic films: Science fiction, fantasy, and horror, Volume 1, 2, and 3.* Los Angeles: Chelsea-Lee Books, 1976.

51 Menville, D., & Reginald, R. *Things to come.* New York: Times Books, 1977.

52 Glut, D. F. *Classic movie monsters.* Metuchen, NJ: Scarecrow Press, 1978.

53 Eames, J. D. *The MGM story.* New York: Crown Publishers, 1979.

Bibliography

FILM PERIODICALS

Abbreviation	Periodical Source
AFI	THE AMERICAN FILM INSTITUTE CATALOG OF MOTION PICTURES PRODUCED IN THE UNITED STATES. New York: R.R. Bowker Company, 1971.
BFI	BRITISH FILM INSTITUTE DISTRIBUTION CATALOGUE. London: British Film Institute, 1962.
BGB	BIOGRAPH BULLETINS 1896-1908. Los Angeles: Locare Research Group, 1971. Compiled by Kemp R. Niver.
BIO	THE BIOSCOPE. British motion picture trade magazine. London, 1909-1914.
BOX	BOXOFFICE. Kansas City: Associated Publications. Weekly motion picture trade publication begun in 1934.
CNF	CINEFANTASTIQUE. Elmwood Park, IL. Frederick S. Clarke, Editor. Periodical devoted to fantastic films.
COF	CASTLE OF FRANKENSTEIN. North Bergen, NJ. Calvin T. Beck, Editor. 1959-?
EDK	EDISON KINETOGRAM. Orange, NJ: Thomas A. Edison, Inc., 1909-1914.
FAM	FAMOUS MONSTERS OF FILMLAND. New York: Warren Publishing Company. Bi-monthly publication.
FAN	FANGORA. O'Quinn Studios, Inc., 475 Park Avenue S., New York, NY.
FDY	FILM DAILY YEARBOOK OF MOTION PICTURES. 1920-1970.
FID	FILM DAILY. Film Trade Publications, 1915-1970.
FIR	FILMS IN REVIEW. New York: National Board of Review, 1950-?
HRP	HOLLYWOOD REPORTER. James Powers, Editor. Hollywood, CA.
LAD	LOS ANGELES DAILY NEWS. Defunct newspaper. Many film clippings are in the Motion Picture Academy Library files in Los Angeles.

LAE LOS ANGELES HERALD-EXAMINER. Los Angeles, CA. Daily newspaper.

LAT LOS ANGELES TIMES. Los Angeles: Times-Mirror Square. Daily newspaper. Many of their clippings are on file in the Motion Picture Academy Library.

LC LIBRARY OF CONGRESS CATALOG OF COPYRIGHT ENTRIES. Superintendent of Documents, U.S. Government Printing Office, 1894-1912 (Vol. I), 1912-1939 (Vol. II), 1940-49 (Vol. III), 1950-59 (Vol. IV), 1960-69 (Vol. V)

MFB MONTHLY FILM BULLETIN. Jan Dawson, Editor. London: British Film Institute.

MGY MOTOGRAPHY. Chicago, 1911-15. Motion picture trade periodical.

MOM MODERN MONSTERS. Los Angeles: Prestige Publications, 1965-67? Bi-monthly horror film magazine.

MPA INTERNATIONAL MOTION PICTURE ALMANAC. Quigley Publishing Company.

MPH MOTION PICTURE HERALD. Martin Quigley, Jr., Editor. New York: Quigley Publishing Company. Trade periodical.

MPN MOTION PICTURE NEWS. New York: Motion Picture News, Inc., 1914-1930.

MPW MOVING PICTURE WORLD. New York: Chalmers Publishing, Co., 1907-1928. Trade periodical.

NYR NEW YORK TIMES. New York: New York Times Company, 1913-?

NYT NEW YORK TIMES. New York: The New York Times Company, 1913-? Daily newspaper.

PHO PHOTOPLAY. Chicago: Photoplay Publishing Company, 1924-?

SCL STUDIO CAST LIST. Furnished by each studio for their respective films. Listing of complete casts and credits.

SEP SATURDAY EVENING POST.

SFD SCIENCE FICTION DIGEST.

S/S	SIGHT AND SOUND. Penelope Houston, Editor. London: British Film Institute, 1932-? Quarterly periodical devoted to films.
STI	SCREEN THRILLS ILLUSTRATED. Samuel M. Sherman, Editorial Director. New York: Warren Publishing Company, 1962-1965.
VAW	VARIETY WEEKLY. Syd Silverman, Publisher and Executive Editor. New York: Variety, Inc., 1905-? Weekly show-business newspaper.
VFI	VIEWS AND FILM INDEX. New York: Film Publishing Company, 1906-10. Motion picture trade publication.
WID	WID'S WEEKLY. Hollywood, CA, 1915-?

INDEX

Film Title **Page #**